"While valuable to give international inspectors tips about where to go or what to examine, national intelligence presented or peddled is often problematic as evidence. In the case of Iraq, defective intelligence contributed to a war against weapons of mass destruction that did not exist. Could unreliable or cooked intelligence one day lead to an attack on Iranian intentions that may not exist? I feel grateful to Gareth Porter for his intrusive and critical examination of intelligence material passed to the IAEA. When security organizations do not shy away from assassinating nuclear scientists we can take it for certain that they do not for a moment hesitate to circulate false evidence."

— **HANS BLIX**
Former Director General of the IAEA

"Gareth Porter is among the last of that rare breed—the independent investigative journalist who brings to bear long experience in foreign policy reporting with a keen and critical eye for K Street propaganda. He is essential."

—**JUAN COLE**
Richard P. Mitchell Collegiate Professor of History,
University of Michigan

"Want to understand why a peaceful U.S. modus vivendi with Iran has been so elusive? Read this exceptionally timely, gripping account of the Iranian nuclear program and the diplomacy surrounding it! Porter meticulously documents both Iranian misjudgments and American and Israeli diplomatic overreach based on willful self-deception and political, bureaucratic, and budget-motivated cherry-picking of intelligence to support unfounded preconceptions. He shows how these have combined to produce a steady escalation of both Iranian enrichment activities and Western sanctions. *Manufactured Crisis* is essential reading for anyone interested in the resolution by diplomacy of a confrontation that otherwise threatens a reprise of the delusional decision-making that led to the Iraq War of 2003–11 but with even more catastrophic consequences."

—Hon. **CHAS W. FREEMAN, JR.**
Former U.S. Ambassador to Saudi Arabia,
author, *America's Misadventures in the Middle East*

D0465814

"At a time of irrational hype and often irresponsible western journalism on the subject of a 'nuclear Iran'—promoting heightened confrontation and even the possibility of war—this book provides disturbing and detailed insight into the manipulation—even invention—of 'facts' marshaled to achieve dubious US and Israeli policy objectives. Gareth Porter, one of our most distinguished and dogged investigative journalists and historians, provides a striking and vital corrective on the geopolitically damaging course of our last decades of manufactured confrontations with an already prickly Iran."

—GRAHAM E. FULLER
Former vice-chair of the
National Intelligence Council at CIA,
author of *A World Without Islam* and
*Three Truths and a Lie* (a memoir)

"Gareth Porter has become a one-man truth squad for the American government and its acolytes in the mainstream press corps... His probing and digging is a reminder that those in power, and those who report on that power, must be held to the highest possible standard."

—SEYMOUR M. HERSH
Pulitzer Prize-winning investigative journalist

"Those who regularly follow Iranian affairs and Iran's relations with the United States, always knew that Iran's nuclear dossier was closely linked with the broader problems of how to deal with Iran and what strategies to adopt towards the Islamic Republic. Now, Gareth Porter through extensive and meticulous research demonstrates these elaborate linkages. In understanding these linkages Iran watchers would be better able to predict the future trajectory of the Iran nuclear dossier."

—SHIREEN T. HUNTER
Visiting Professor, Georgetown University

"Porter has been investigating the Iranian nuclear case for the best part of a decade. The result of his researches is both a fascinating addition to a growing corpus, unlike any previous work on the issue, and a disturbing indictment of US and Israeli policies."

**—HON. PETER JENKINS, CMG**
UK Ambassador to the IAEA 2001–6

"*Manufactured Crisis* is untold history at its finest! Gareth Porter systematically and masterfully debunks three decades of U.S. and allied lies and distortions about an Iranian nuclear weapons program that never really existed."

**—OLIVER STONE and PETER KUZNICK**
Co-authors, *The Untold History of the United States*

## ABOUT

# JUST WORLD BOOKS

### "TIMELY BOOKS FOR CHANGING TIMES"

Just World Books produces excellent books on key international issues—and does so in a very timely fashion. All of our titles are published first as quality paperbacks. Most are later also released as e-books and some in hardcover. Because of the agility of our process, we cannot give detailed advance notice of fixed, seasonal "lists."

To learn about our existing and upcoming titles, to download author podcasts and videos, to find our terms for bookstores or other bulk purchasers, or to buy our books, visit our website:

 www.justworldbooks.com

Also, follow us on Facebook and Twitter!

**Our recent titles include:**

- *Gaza Writes Back: Short Stories from Young Writers in Gaza, Palestine,* edited by Refaat Alareer
- *1973: The Road to War* by Yigal Kipnis
- *The Gaza Kitchen: A Palestinian Culinary Journey,* by Laila El-Haddad and Maggie Schmitt
- *Interesting Times: China, America, and the Shifting Balance of Prestige,* by Chas W. Freeman, Jr.
- *The General's Son: Journey of an Israeli in Palestine,* by Miko Peled

# MANUFACTURED CRISIS

# Other works by
# Gareth Porter

*A Peace Denied: the United States, Vietnam and the Paris Agreement*
(Indiana University Press, 1976)

*Global Environmental Politics*—with Janet Welsh Brown
(Westview Press, 1990)

*Vietnam: The Politics of Bureaucratic Socialism*
(Cornell University Press, 1993)

*Perils of Dominance: Imbalance of Power
and the Road to War in Vietnam*
(University of California Press, 2005)

# MANUFACTURED CRISIS

## THE UNTOLD STORY OF
## THE IRAN NUCLEAR SCARE

### GARETH PORTER

JUST WORLD
BOOKS

CHARLOTTESVILLE, VIRGINIA

Just World Books is an imprint of Just World Publishing, LLC.

All text in this work © 2014 Gareth Porter.

All rights reserved. No part of this book may be reproduced or transmitted in any form or by any means, electronic or mechanical, including photocopy, recording, or any information storage retrieval system, without permission in writing from the publisher, except brief passages for review purposes. Visit our website, www.justworldbooks.com.

Typesetting and cover design by Jane T. Sickon for Just World Publishing, LLC. Cartography and diagram by Lewis Rector for Just World Publishing, LLC. Front cover photo © Jason Szenes/epa/Corbis and reproduced by permission. Author photo by William B. Quandt for Just World Publishing, LLC.

**Publisher's Cataloging-in-Publication**
**(Provided by Quality Books, Inc.)**


Porter, Gareth, 1942-
    Manufactured crisis : the untold story of the Iran
nuclear scare / Gareth Porter.
    pages cm
    Includes bibliographical references.
    LCCN 2013954363
    ISBN (pb.): 978-1-935982-33-3
    ISBN (e.):  978-1-935982-45-6

    1. Nuclear weapons—Iran. 2. Nuclear arms control—
Iran. 3. National security—Middle East. 4. Iran—
Strategic aspects. 5. Iran—Politics and government—
1997– 6. Iran—Military policy. 7. United States—
Military policy. 8. United States—Foreign relations—
Iran. 9. Iran—Foreign relations—United States.
    I. Title.

UA853.I7P67 2013          355.02'17'0955
                    QBI13-600196

# Contents

Map of Iran . . . . . . . . . . . . . . . . . . . . . . . . . . . . . . . . . . . . . . . . . . . . . . 11

Diagram: Nuclear Power Cycle in Iran. . . . . . . . . . . . . . . . . . . . . . . . . . 12

Abbreviations and Acronyms . . . . . . . . . . . . . . . . . . . . . . . . . . . . . . . . 13

Introduction . . . . . . . . . . . . . . . . . . . . . . . . . . . . . . . . . . . . . . . . . . . . . 15

1.  The US Denial Policy and Its Consequences . . . . . . . . . . . . . . . . . 23

2.  The Politics of Iran's Nuclear Secrecy. . . . . . . . . . . . . . . . . . . . . . . 39

3.  Iran's Unknown Nuclear Politics. . . . . . . . . . . . . . . . . . . . . . . . . . . 59

4.  US Political Origins of the Nuclear Scare. . . . . . . . . . . . . . . . . . . . 87

5.  Israeli Political Origins of the Nuclear Scare. . . . . . . . . . . . . . . . . 113

6.  Choosing Regime Change Over Diplomacy. . . . . . . . . . . . . . . . . . 135

7.  The IAEA Comes Up Empty. . . . . . . . . . . . . . . . . . . . . . . . . . . . . . 161

8.  The Mystery of the Laptop Documents . . . . . . . . . . . . . . . . . . . . 191

9.  Intelligence Failure . . . . . . . . . . . . . . . . . . . . . . . . . . . . . . . . . . . . . 217

10. The Phantom Bomb Test Chamber of Parchin . . . . . . . . . . . . . . 243

11. Phony War Crises. . . . . . . . . . . . . . . . . . . . . . . . . . . . . . . . . . . . . . . 269

Epilogue . . . . . . . . . . . . . . . . . . . . . . . . . . . . . . . . . . . . . . . . . . . . . . . . . 299

Dramatis Personae . . . . . . . . . . . . . . . . . . . . . . . . . . . . . . . . . . . . . . . . 305

Acknowledgments. . . . . . . . . . . . . . . . . . . . . . . . . . . . . . . . . . . . . . . . . 309

This book is dedicated to
Huda, who understood.

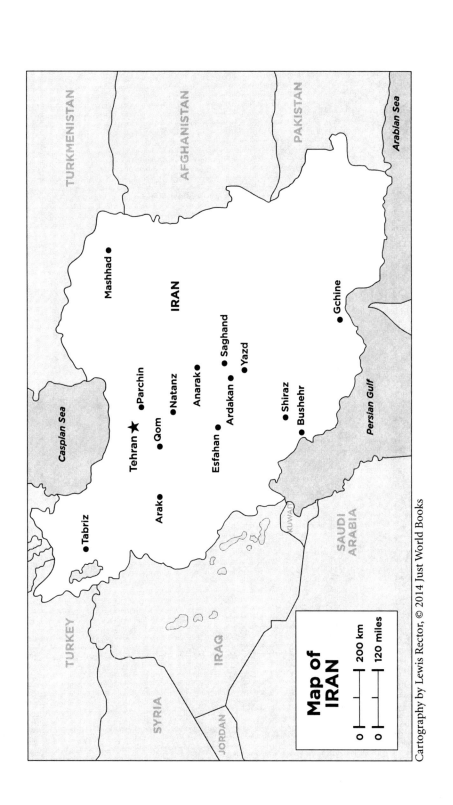

Cartography by Lewis Rector, © 2014 Just World Books

# Nuclear Power Cycle in Iran

1. Uranium oxide $U_3O_8$ (yellowcake) is milled at Ardakan from ore mined at Saghand and Gchine

2. The uranium is converted to $UF_6$ gas at Esfahan

3. It is enriched in centrifuges to 3.5% U-235 at Natanz

4. Fuel rods of $UO_2$ are fabricated at Esfahan

5. Fuel is used in a light water reactor to generate electricity at Bushehr

6. Spent fuel can be stored or reprocessed (not occurring)

7. Waste is disposed at Arak

Diagram by Lewis Rector, © 2014 Just World Books

# Abbreviations and Acronyms

| | |
|---|---|
| **AEOI** | Atomic Energy Organization of Iran |
| **AIPAC** | American Israel Public Affairs Committee |
| **AP** | Associated Press |
| **BND** | Bundesnachrichtendienst (German Federal Intelligence Service) |
| **CIA** | Central Intelligence Agency (US) |
| **CPD** | Counter-Proliferation Division of the CIA |
| **CWC** | Chemical Weapons Convention |
| **DIA** | Defense Intelligence Agency (US) |
| **EBW** | exploding bridge wire |
| **ENTEC** | Esfahan Nuclear Technology Center |
| **EU-3** | European three (France, Germany, United Kingdom) |
| **IAEA** | International Atomic Energy Agency |
| **IDF** | Israel Defense Forces |
| **IRGC** | Islamic Revolutionary Guard Corps (Iran) |
| **ISIS** | Institute for Science and International Security |
| **JHL** | Jabr Ibn Hayan Multipurpose Laboratories |
| **MEK** | Mujahedeen-e-Khalq (People's Mujahedeen of Iran) |
| **NCA** | US-China Nuclear Cooperation Agreement |
| **NCRI** | National Council of Resistance of Iran |
| **NIE** | National Intelligence Estimate (US) |

| | |
|---|---|
| **NPC** | Nonproliferation Center of the CIA |
| **NPT** | Nuclear Non-Proliferation Treaty |
| **NSA** | National Security Agency (US) |
| **NSC** | National Security Council (US) |
| **NSG** | Nuclear Suppliers Group |
| **PHRC** | Physics Research Center |
| **PLO** | Palestine Liberation Organization |
| **SNSC** | Supreme National Security Council (Iran) |
| **TRR** | Tehran Research Reactor |
| **TNRC** | Tehran Nuclear Research Center |
| **UCF** | uranium conversion facility |
| **WINPAC** | Weapons Intelligence, Nonproliferation, and Arms Control Center of the CIA |
| **WMD** | weapons of mass destruction |

# Introduction

In November 2013, the United States and five other states concluded a preliminary agreement with Iran on its nuclear program that was to be followed by a longer-term comprehensive deal. The agreement offered a way out of a crisis that had already lasted more than a decade and had involved both threats of war against Iran by the US and Israeli governments and efforts to cripple the Iranian economy by interfering with its international trade.

But the secret at the heart of the crisis is that the central assertions underlying the American, Israeli, and European pressure on Iran were not based on historical reality. This book documents the way in which US and Israeli officials "manufactured" the crisis quite deliberately, in order to maximize pressure on Iran to give up its nuclear program. They did this by creating a narrative portraying Iranian behavior as evidence that the Islamic Republic had long been hiding a nuclear weapons program. That narrative was then conveyed to the public through uncritical news media coverage of the official line.

This book shows that virtually nothing about the nuclear scare over Iran that was reported in the Western news media was what it seemed. It aims to unravel the false narrative that sustained the decade of crisis and to recover the real history of the Iranian nuclear program and the interactions between that program and the governments of the United States and Israel.

*Manufactured Crisis* shows that US-Israeli strategy was aimed at using the International Atomic Energy Agency (IAEA) to build a case that Iran's nuclear program had been merely a cover for a nuclear weapons program. That case would serve as the basis for United Nations Security Council actions that would punish Iran, or even for unilateral US military action against Iran. As a result the IAEA, which had previously been a relatively nonpolitical actor performing technical analysis of nuclear programs, was transformed over the 2003–8 period into an adjunct of the anti-Iran strategy.

The book tells the story of a "manufactured crisis" that unfolded in the years from 2002 through 2013 in three identifiable stages, corresponding to the major shifts in the US-Israeli strategy. It does not view every move by the United States and Israel as part of a master plan that was thought through from the start. On the contrary, it shows how each stage of the strategy developed in response to new political opportunities and problems that arose in regard to the broader aim of weakening and coercing Iran on the nuclear issue.

The first stage was triggered by the announcement of Iran's Natanz enrichment facility in an August 2002 press conference by the Iranian armed opposition group Mujahedeen-e-Khalq (MEK). That dramatic event, which the book shows was the result of a strategic decision by Israel, opened the way for the United States and Israel to put Iran on trial for allegedly deceiving the IAEA for many years and secretly seeking to become a nuclear weapons state. The main thrust of the strategy for the next few years was to have the IAEA intensively investigate a series of issues that the IAEA's Safeguards Department had identified, with the help of US and Israeli intelligence, as indications of a secret Iranian nuclear weapons program. These IAEA investigations generated one round of news stories after another that portrayed each activity under investigation as suggesting that Iran's nuclear program was a cover for nuclear weapons. To the chagrin of the United States and Israel, however, these investigations ended in early 2008 without having found any evidence to support that charge.

But Israel and the United States had a more potent weapon for consolidating the nuclear scare over Iran. In 2008, they quickly shifted the focus of the IAEA inquiry to a collection of documents, purportedly stolen from a secret Iranian nuclear weapons program, which had been given to the United States by an unknown party. Thus began the second stage of the crisis, from 2008 to late 2011, ostensibly aimed at holding Iran "accountable" for what the IAEA called the "alleged studies" documents. But the actual aim at that stage was to maneuver Iran into a position where it could be accused of noncompliance with the resolutions of the US-dominated IAEA Board of Governors.

In late 2011, the third stage of the strategy began, aimed explicitly at imposing much more aggressive sanctions and increasing diplomatic pressure on Iran to give up its nuclear program. The first move in the new stage was the IAEA's release of a report in November 2011, based largely on Israeli intelligence information, that accused Iran not only of having done nuclear weapons-related testing in 2003 but also of continuing that work as recently as 2007. That accusation was the lead-in to US and European decisions to target Iran's oil export and banking sectors. The United States negotiated with European and Asian states that had been buying Iranian crude oil to get them to cut back dramatically on their purchases and to curtail their dealings with Iran's central bank. Against that background,

Israeli prime minister Benjamin Netanyahu dramatically heightened the threat of war against Iran's nuclear sites. That threat was accompanied by apparent signs of growing tensions between Washington and Tel Aviv over the issue. But as *Manufactured Crisis* documents, both Netanyahu and Obama were engaging in an intricate political charade.

Netanyahu never intended to use military force against Iran, and the Obama administration was well aware of that but was hoping to exploit the threat to gain diplomatic leverage on Iran. In late 2012, Netanyahu's aggressive posture toward Iran fizzled out, after his government revealed that the threat of war had been in part a device to pressure Obama to give Iran an ultimatum over its nuclear program, and Obama made it clear that he had no intention of doing so. But it did not bring an end to the two decades of dissimulation by both governments about Iran's nuclear program.

*Manufactured Crisis* shows how each of these new stages of the crisis added yet another layer of blatant misinformation and disinformation about the Iranian nuclear program on top of previous such layers. The falsification process proceeded on multiple levels, from deceptive US statements about what it knew about Iran's supposed nuclear intentions to misleading innuendoes planted in IAEA reports to documents and intelligence reports fabricated by the Israelis. Blatantly false stories were leaked to the news media, reflecting the media's disinterest in investigating or even fact-checking official claims about Iran's nuclear program.

By 2012, this long history of false information was dramatically symbolized by the story, embraced by the IAEA on the basis of information from Israel, of a bomb test chamber designed by a former Soviet nuclear weapons specialist and installed at the Iranian military facility at Parchin. That story was given general credence in the Western news media, but like the rest of the narrative created over the years, it fell apart upon careful investigation.

The usual form in writing history involves blending official sources and other sources in a single narrative flow. But in the case of the Iran nuclear crisis and the nuclear scare that has gone with it, the heart of the story is in fact the deception propagated by official sources. Thus, the narrative of this book is organized primarily around the contrast between what the United States, Israel, and the IAEA were conveying to the public and the reality that can be reconstructed from a deeper inquiry into the facts.

Chapter 1 of *Manufactured Crisis* begins with a reconstruction of the real origins of the issue of Iran's nuclear program in a US-enforced embargo on nuclear cooperation with Iran's nascent nuclear program that began in 1984. That naked use of US power to try to strangle what was an extremely modest Iranian nuclear program forced Iran to choose between giving up its right to nuclear technology and obtaining its own enrichment technology. That pivotal historical episode has unfortunately been excluded from the public discourse on Iran and replaced by an official narrative suggesting that Iran was already secretly pursuing nuclear weapons development during the 1980s.

Chapter 2 reexamines the discovery of the Iranian enrichment facility at Natanz in 2002 and the subsequent IAEA finding that Iran had been carrying out a "clandestine enrichment program" for nearly two decades. This chapter does what the IAEA failed to do: it explains that there were other reasons why Iran did not report to the IAEA a series of experiments and tests with nuclear material or its decision to begin construction of Natanz. It also shows that contrary to the media coverage of the IAEA report, Iran's alleged "18-year enrichment program" actually consisted of obtaining the basic enrichment technology and testing it for only a few months in 2002–3.

Chapter 3 digs deeper into the development of Iranian policy toward nuclear and chemical weapons. It describes two episodes in which Islamic fatwas by the supreme leader of the Islamic Republic were crucial in determining Iranian policies toward such weapons. In the first episode, opposition to weapons of mass destruction by Ayatollah Ruhollah Khomeini, based on Shi'a Islamic jurisprudence, forced the Iranian government to forego the use of chemical weapons during the entire Iran-Iraq War, despite continuing Iraqi chemical attacks. In the second episode, Khomeini's successor as supreme leader, Ayatollah Ali Khamenei, invoked Islamic principles in 2003 in order to reinforce a ban on any work relating to nuclear weapons.

The chapter further explores the political-strategic considerations shaping Iranian nuclear policy that have been systematically ignored in official and media discourse in the West. Like other states with uranium enrichment capabilities, Iran expected such capabilities to add a "latent deterrent" to its overt conventional deterrence of foreign aggression. The chapter documents the fact that US officials and some intelligence analysts were well aware of that motive and recognized that it did not mean that Iran intended to obtain nuclear weapons. But one administration after another deliberately confused the two issues in public pronouncements. Similarly, those administrations ignored the Iranian interest in accumulating enriched uranium as an asset to be given up in future negotiations with the United States. Instead, US officials cited the enriched uranium as evidence of Iran's interest in nuclear weapons.

The United States began in the early 1990s to portray Iran's civilian nuclear program as a cover for its alleged ambitions to obtain nuclear weapons. Chapter 4 shows how that accusation was a function of the desperate need of the Central Intelligence Agency (CIA) and the Pentagon in particular for a substitute for the threat from the Soviet Union and its allies that had evaporated by 1990–91. The supposed threat of nuclear weapons proliferation from Iran provided the most advantageous answer to that bureaucratic-political problem for senior CIA and Pentagon officials. This chapter also shows how the administration of President Bill Clinton added a second major motive for the newly heightened hostility and suspicion toward Iran and its nuclear program: the political decision to align US policy toward Iran with that of Israel.

The other half of the story of the origins of the manufactured crisis, recounted in chapter 5, is how Israeli Labor and Likud governments from 1992 to 1999 used the alleged threat from Iran's nuclear and missile programs to achieve a set of political-strategic aims that had little or nothing to do with Iran. The chapter shows how Prime Ministers Yitzhak Rabin and Benjamin Netanyahu professed alarm about an Iranian threat that Israel's top intelligence officials did not accept and that served multiple political-diplomatic ends for their respective governments. The account of those episodes also highlights the price Israel paid for its aggressive posture toward Iran, which was that Iran came to regard Israel as a military threat for the first time.

Chapter 6 shows how the administration of President George W. Bush first turned Iran's nuclear program into a "crisis" in 2003. It explains how the main interest of the administration, focused on the occupation of Iraq as the fulcrum of policy toward the rest of the region, was to keep open a path to regime change in Iran. That entailed explicitly refusing to countenance an agreement between the European three (the United Kingdom, France, and Germany) with Iran in 2004–5 that would have committed Iran to a minimal nuclear program that would not have constituted a proliferation threat.

Chapter 7 recounts the story of the IAEA's investigation of a series of Iranian nuclear activities from 2003 through 2007 in anticipation that it would find evidence that Iran had carried out a secret nuclear weapons program. Virtually every new quarterly report from the IAEA on its investigation in 2004 and 2005 generated a new round of media stories of suspected Iranian covert enrichment or weapons work. As this chapter shows, however, none of those suspicions turned out to be correct, and the IAEA had to acknowledge in the end that it had found no evidence of Iranian weapons-related activity in any of the cases it investigated.

Beginning in 2008, the focus of the strategy of the United States and Israel shifted to a collection of documents supposedly coming from a covert Iranian nuclear weapons program. Chapter 8 reveals the real story behind those documents—who brought them out of Iran, where they came from, and why they could not be genuine Iranian documents. The chapter also reveals new evidence from WikiLeaks cables that in 2008, the IAEA Safeguards Department was working closely with the United States and its allies to create a new political strategy for convincing the rest of the world falsely that Iran was unwilling to cooperate with the IAEA investigation.

The US government's own intelligence assessments of the Iranian nuclear program should have put a brake on the continued development of the manufactured crisis over the program. But chapter 9 shows how a systemic failure of US intelligence on the Iranian nuclear issue parallels the well-known 2002 intelligence debacle on weapons of mass destruction (WMD) in Iraq. This chapter explains how intelligence assessments on WMD in Iran were distorted by the same set of incentives to find evidence of a WMD program that had produced the discredited national intelligence estimate on Iraq. And even the November 2007 National Intelligence Estimate (NIE), which concluded Iran had stopped work on nuclear weapons in 2003, was still affected by the institutional dynamics that had distorted the Iraq estimate.

Chapter 10 dissects the climactic episode in the run-up to the enactment of harsh sanctions against Iran's crude oil export and banking sectors: the publication by the IAEA of a dossier of "intelligence" it had collected since 2007 making new claims about secret Iranian nuclear weapons work. But this account reveals that most of the information in that dossier came from Israel and explains in detail how and why the most sensational allegations in the dossier—the tale of an ex-Soviet nuclear weapons specialist helping Iran build a bomb-test cylinder—failed to withstand expert scrutiny.

That IAEA report was the signal for a new stage of the manufactured crisis, marked by what was sold to the public around the world as a heightened threat of Israeli attack on Iran's nuclear sites. Chapter 11 tells the full story behind Prime Minister Netanyahu's supposed readiness to use military force against Iran, showing it was merely a ploy to influence international policy toward Iran. The chapter shows the degree to which Obama's policy was focused on attempting to coerce Iran diplomatically rather than seeking to reach a solution that would respect Iran's nuclear rights.

The narrative and analysis close before the election of Hassan Rouhani as Iran's president in June 2013. A brief Epilogue describes the diplomatic opening created by that election and the preliminary agreement on the nuclear issue that followed.

*Manufactured Crisis* offers the first systematic alternative to the official and media account of the background to and unfolding of the Iran nuclear crisis. It documents the fact that the real origins of the Iran nuclear issue in international politics lay not in an Iranian urge to obtain nuclear weapons but in two aspects of US national security policy during and after the Cold War: first, an effort by the United States as the dominant power in the Middle East to deny Iran its right—as guaranteed in the Nuclear Non-Proliferation Treaty (NPT)—to have any nuclear program at all in the 1980s, and second, the adjustment by US national security institutions to the end of the Cold War by portraying Iran as posing a WMD threat. *Manufactured Crisis* also reveals just how long a shadow the US-Israeli alliance, rooted in American domestic politics, has cast on US policy toward Iran.

The web of falsehoods that accompanied the manufacture of the Iran nuclear crisis came at a heavy price. It made it impossible to conduct an objective political discussion of the issue in the United States. The inability or unwillingness of most members of the US political elite to confront the truth about the origins and development of the crisis postponed for many years the adoption of a rational policy toward Iran. It thus contributed to the distortion of global and regional politics by aligning the United States with Iran's foes and encouraging the deepening of the sectarian strife that came to threaten much of the Middle East. Even as the Rouhani opening provided an opportunity for US-Iran rapprochement, the false nuclear narrative represented a serious political obstacle to such a fundamental shift in US policy.

**Gareth Porter**
November 30, 2013

# 1

# The US Denial Policy and Its Consequences

What consumers of news coverage of foreign affairs have learned over more than a decade about Iran's nuclear policy is that in the 1980s, Iran began a secret enrichment program, in violation of its safeguards agreement with the International Atomic Energy Agency (IAEA), and maintained that program for 18 years with the intention of producing nuclear weapons, or at least keeping that option open. Fortunately, according to this account, a secret Iranian enrichment facility was revealed by Iranian opponents of the regime in 2002, and the full investigation by the IAEA that followed uncovered the illicit nuclear activities that Iran had been pursuing in secret for many years.

That thumbnail sketch represents a nuclear scare that has surrounded the Iranian program since 2002 and has been the rationale for the long international crisis over the issue. But that version of the history of the Iranian nuclear program is a fundamental falsification achieved by eliminating the single most important historical fact about Iran's nuclear program: Iran's decision to enrich uranium was a direct response to a US policy that had challenged Iran's right to have any peaceful nuclear power program at all.

The US policy that later became a determination not to allow Iran to have "a single centrifuge spinning"[1]—meaning that no uranium enrichment would be countenanced—began in the early to mid-1980s with an effort to deny Iran even the Bushehr nuclear reactor in which the country

---

1. Robert B. Joseph reportedly told Mohamed ElBaradei, director general of the IAEA, "We cannot have a single centrifuge spinning in Iran." Seymour Hersh, "The Iran Plans," *New Yorker*, April 17, 2006.

had already invested billions of dollars and which was 80 percent completed when the shah was overthrown. It was only because of that US policy that Iran decided to get into enriching its own uranium to fuel Bushehr. The story of that action-reaction dynamic between a US policy of denial of Iran's right to obtain technology for the peaceful uses of nuclear power, as guaranteed by the Nuclear Non-Proliferation Treaty (NPT), and the Islamic Republic's ultimate decision to acquire its own capabilities for uranium enrichment is the pivotal chapter in the untold history of the manufactured crisis over the Iranian nuclear program.

## Iran's Original Nuclear Program

A deeply ironic fact about the nuclear program that has provoked such an intense and prolonged crisis is that the Islamic revolution to overthrow the shah was initially accompanied by the mullahs' strong reaction against nuclear power as a manifestation of the shah's penchant for expensive toys—and the US sponsorship of the original nuclear program. Former ambassador Seyed Hossein Mousavian, who worked for Ali Akbar Hashemi Rafsanjani, the powerful head of the Iranian legislature, or Majlis, beginning in 1984, recalled that in 1979, the revolutionaries considered the shah's ambitious plan for 23 nuclear power plants to be one of the "imperialistic projects" associated with the imperial regime and its American sponsors.[2]

In July 1979, the revolutionary government halted construction at Bushehr, the flagship facility of the shah's extensive nuclear program, along with nearly all the other projects that had launched by the Atomic Energy Organization of Iran (AEOI). It also stripped the AEOI of most of its budget and staff. Some thought was even given to using the 80 percent completed Bushehr reactor for something else entirely, but after officials from Tehran made an inspection trip there, they decided it could serve no other use. Two years later, the government reversed the decision to strip the AEOI of its budget and staff, largely because the severe electricity shortages that marked the first two years of the revolutionary era persuaded policymakers that there might be a role for nuclear power reactors after all.[3]

Even after the decision to resume the nuclear program in 1981, however, the Islamic Republic's nuclear ambitions remained extremely modest compared with those of the shah. "We didn't want to have 20 nuclear power plants or to have enrichment," Mousavian recalled. "The only things remaining [in the program] were to complete Bushehr and to continue the

---

2. Author's interview with Seyed Hossein Mousavian, Washington, DC, July 5, 2013.

3. David Patrikarakos, *Nuclear Iran: The Birth of an Atomic State* (London: I. B. Taurus, 2012), 96–97; Akbar Etemad, "Iran," in Harald Muller, ed., *A European Non–Proliferation Policy: Prospects and Problems* (Oxford: Clarendon, 1987), 214.

Tehran Research Reactor for medical purposes. We would have one nuclear power plant, with fuel from France."[4]

Iran still hoped to obtain enriched uranium for fuel plates for Bushehr from the Iranian stake in the French-owned uranium enrichment consortium Eurodif. The shah had invested a total of $1.18 billion toward the construction of Eurodif's enrichment facility, which entitled Iran to 10 percent of the production of enriched uranium it produced. Soon after the overthrow of the shah, Tehran canceled his contract with Eurodif. In February 1980, the French government refused to refund the sum Iran had invested in Eurodif, or to provide the uranium that Iran was due under the shah's contract. Then, in the early 1980s, Iran sought to work out a deal under which it could reclaim its share of the production of the facility. But after the Socialist Party's François Mitterrand came to power in May 1981, he reiterated France's refusal to provide the enriched uranium from Eurodif that Iran was requesting. Nevertheless, according to Mousavian, Iran continued to negotiate with France over access to the nuclear fuel it would need once Bushehr could be restored, even as the question of the disposition of the money Iran had invested in Eurodif was being contested in French courts.[5]

Meanwhile, the Islamic Republic was also hoping to get help from the IAEA for its scaled-down nuclear program. In 1983, the AEOI approached IAEA Director Hans Blix to request the IAEA's help in building the Iranian nuclear organization's technical capacity. The AEOI asked Blix to send a team to do surveys of its Esfahan Nuclear Technology Center (ENTEC) and the Tehran Nuclear Research Center (TNRC) as the basis for further cooperation. Blix sent the Iranian request to Deputy Director Maurizio Zifferero, who in turn directed IAEA official Herman Vera Ruiz to conduct the survey in October 1983.[6]

By then, AEOI was only a shadow of the organization that existed at the end of the shah's regime, when its staff had consisted of 862 scientists and it had commanded an annual budget of more than $3 billion.[7] But ENTEC still had considerable expertise and equipment, and it had already decided to focus primarily on fuel fabrication and uranium conversion rather than on uranium enrichment. ENTEC's largest department, with 23 scientists and what the IAEA judged to be "impressive" laboratory equipment, was

---

4.  Interview with Mousavian.

5.  Ibid.; Patrikarakos, *Nuclear Iran*, 105.

6.  This account of the IAEA's mission to Iran in 1983 and subsequent decisions is based on Mark Hibbs, "U.S. in 1983 Stopped IAEA from Helping Iran Make UF6," *Nuclear Fuel* 28 (August 4, 2003): 12.

7.  Ali Vaez and Karim Sadjadpour, *Iran's Nuclear Odyssey* (Washington, DC: Carnegie Endowment for International Peace, 2013), 5.

the fuel-fabrication department, which was responsible for carrying out experiments on the fabrication of uranium oxide pellets. It also had a chemistry department with 20 scientists, which had responsibility for conducting experiments on the conversion of yellowcake ($U_3O_8$) into uranium dioxide ($UO_2$) for fuel rods for nuclear reactors like Bushehr.

After his visit, Ruiz reported to Blix and Zifferero that ENTEC officials had informed him about plans to build a uranium conversion pilot plant to produce uranium hexafluoride ($UF_6$), the form of uranium that is ready for enrichment. Ruiz's memo made no mention of any AEOI request for assistance in uranium enrichment, reflecting the fact that Iran was still hoping to get enriched uranium from the French company Eurodif.

The memo from Ruiz recommended that the IAEA provide "expert services" in eight different fields to assist all of ENTEC's departments, including designing a "pilot plant for fuel conversion," which was a primary goal of the Iranian nuclear program. The IAEA Technical Cooperation Department was also prepared to assist ENTEC and TNRC on several of the items on the list of recommendations that Ruiz compiled in late 1983.[8]

Iran was thus poised to take advantage of its rights under the NPT to international cooperation for the pursuit of peaceful nuclear power. But that was before US officials saw the Ruiz report. Apparently, neither Iran nor the IAEA had anticipated that the Reagan administration would intervene to stop the proposed cooperation. That decision, unannounced at the time, began a process that would lead eventually to a crisis over what the world would be told was the threat of an Iranian nuclear weapon.

## US Nuclear Embargo and the Iranian Response

The overthrow of the shah's regime in 1979 was a traumatic shock to the US national security system. The Department of Defense and the CIA had built deep ties with the shah's regime (as had Israel). Under the shah, Iran had served as the keystone of policy in the region for a quarter century. Preserving his regime had been seen as so important by some top officials that, as the State Department's desk officer on Iran later recalled, when the popular uprising took place, national security adviser Zbigniew Brzezinski recommended that the United States urge the shah to have his troops "shoot down as many people as necessary and bring an end to the rebellion once and for all."[9]

---

8. Hibbs, "U.S. in 1983," 12.
9. "The Iranian Revolution 25 Years Later: An Oral History with Henry Precht, Then State Department Desk Officer," *Middle East Journal* 58, no. 1 (Winter 2004): 17.

Once the shah had been toppled, the major thrust of US policy was, in effect, to watch for an opportunity to replace the Islamic regime so the United States could resume its former position of power in Tehran. When President Jimmy Carter's administration got word in September 1980 that Iraqi president Saddam Hussein was planning to attack Iran to overthrow the regime, the United States did nothing to oppose the scheme, despite the enormous risk of regional instability inherent in such a war. Vice President Walter Mondale would later explain, "We believed that this war would put further pressure on the Iranian regime."[10]

When Ronald Reagan entered the White House in 1981, internal discussions on Iran revolved around the expressions by senior officials of the desirability of removing the founder and leader of the Islamic revolution, Ayatollah Ruhollah Khomeini. CIA Director William Casey was tasked with exploring the possibility of a covert plan to oust Khomeini and replace him with the shah's son, Reza Pahlavi.[11] And when Iran was preparing to mount a massive counteroffensive against Iraq in spring 1982, the United States became an active supporter of the Iraqi war effort. Reagan agreed to a secret national security decision directive that the United States would do everything "necessary and legal" to prevent Iran from defeating Iraq. The staff of Reagan's National Security Council worked closely with CIA Director Casey and his deputy, Robert M. Gates, to persuade third-country suppliers to ship to Iraq a variety of forms of weapons, including cluster bombs and anti-armor penetrators (most of them of Soviet origin). The United States also provided strategic advice to Saddam's military on how best to use its troops.[12] That initiative was followed in late 1983 by Operation Staunch, a diplomatic campaign to convince US allies and friends to stop selling arms to Iran in the interests of "achieving a negotiated end to the Iran-Iraq war."[13]

The decision to do whatever could be done to support Iraq against Iran in the war was followed by a series of interventions by the Reagan administration to prevent international assistance of any kind to the Iranian nuclear program. The earliest documented US intervention to try to obstruct any progress by Iran toward completion of its nuclear reactor

---

10. Flynt Leverett and Hillary Mann Leverett, *Going to Tehran* (New York: Metropolitan Books, 2013), 49.

11. Bob Woodward, *Veil: The Secret Wars of the CIA 1981–1987* (New York: Pocket Books, 1987), 109–110.

12. The secret Reagan administration policy is documented in a legal affidavit by former National Security Council official Howard Teicher dated January 31, 1995, http://www.gwu.edu/~nsarchiv/NSAEBB/NSAEBB82/iraq61.pdf.

13. Lee H. Hamilton and Daniel K. Inouye, *Report of the Congressional Committees Investigating the Iran-Contra Affair* (Collingdale, PA: Diane Publishing, 1995), 159.

at Bushehr was the objection the United States registered to the IAEA's late 1983 proposal to provide Iran with technical assistance for fuel production and uranium conversion. After the United States "directly intervened" to block any such IAEA assistance, those two major elements of the proposed assistance to the Iranian program were dropped by the IAEA. "We stopped that in its tracks," a former US official recalled many years later.[14]

The US decision to prevent the IAEA from helping Iran in the same way it helped other states in good standing with the agency was simply an adjunct of the Reagan administration's policy toward Iran and Iraq. "It was the war," recalled Geoffrey Kemp, who was senior director for the Near East and South Asia on Reagan's National Security Council staff. "We had made a decision to tilt toward Iraq across the board. It was part of the Iran-Iraq War syndrome."[15]

The IAEA intervention was only the beginning of a much broader US policy of denial of international cooperation with the Iranian nuclear program. In April 1984, the State Department confirmed that the United States' goal was to block all technology transfers to Iran's nuclear program by external suppliers. In a written reply to a reporter's question, the department spokesman said, "Previous actions by the Government of Iran do not provide us with great assurance that it will always abide by its international commitments." Therefore, the State Department declared that the United States would not allow any US nuclear technology to be shared with Iran. "In addition," the statement said, "we have asked other nuclear suppliers not to engage in nuclear cooperation with Iran, especially while the Iran-Iraq war continues."[16] That wording left open the possibility that the United States might continue its effort to deny all nuclear technology to Iran even after the Iran-Iraq War was over.

One might expect such a virtual declaration of war on a country's nuclear program to be accompanied by some claim of evidence of covert nuclear weapons work or at least of Iran having committed serious violations of its NPT-derived safeguards agreement with the IAEA. But the State Department made clear that it had no evidence of bad faith on the part of Iran in regard to its commitments under the NPT. It admitted that it had "no evidence" that Iran had violated its pledge under the NPT to place its nuclear activities under international safeguards. Its spokesman even suggested that he did not see the Iranian nuclear reactor at Bushehr as a proliferation risk, saying there was "no evidence" of any construction of facilities

---

14. Hibbs, "U.S. in 1983," 12.
15. Author's interview with Geoffrey Kemp, July 18, 2013.
16. Reuters dispatch, "Possibility of Treaty Violation Cited as US Seeks Nuclear Boycott of Iran," *Globe and Mail* (Toronto), April 26, 1984.

there that could separate plutonium from spent reactor fuel. Instead, State Department officials justified the policy of denying all nuclear technology to Iran by telling reporters off the record that Iran was about to launch an all-out offensive against Iraq that could threaten Saddam's regime, implying that Iran could emerge as the dominant power in the region.[17] The Reagan administration was justifying its intervention to prevent Iran from having a nuclear power program purely on the basis of its assertion of geopolitical interests in the Middle East.

That policy was soon impinging on Iran's relations with France and Germany, whose cooperation was crucial to the plan to complete the Bushehr reactor. Mousavian began following the nuclear issue in 1984, when he went to work as chief of staff for Rafsanjani, then the speaker of the Iranian parliament. He recalled later, "The French came to us saying we cannot give fuel for Bushehr. They were telling us, 'This is an international decision.'" The French government was clearly implying to Iran that the United States was not willing to allow France to participate in its nuclear program. Meanwhile, Iran also had a serious problem with Germany. When Mousavian became head of the Iranian Foreign Ministry's West Europe division in 1986, he recalled, it immediately became apparent that the German government was refusing to allow the German contractor Kraftwerk GmbH to complete the work on the Bushehr plant for which Iran had paid 8.7 billion deutschmarks ($4.78 billion at 1979 exchange rates) before the overthrow of the shah. In 1986, Foreign Minister Hans-Dietrich Genscher told Rafsanjani that completion of the Bushehr contract would not be permitted.[18]

Seldom in the modern era has a major power interfered in the affairs of a lesser state on the basis of such a blatant expression of power interests as the Reagan administration's policy of denying all nuclear technology to Iran's fledgling nuclear program. Notably absent from the policy enunciated by the State Department was any recognition of Iran's legitimate right to such technology under the NPT or of US obligations under that treaty. In putting pressure on its allies to not cooperate with the Iranian nuclear program—even if that cooperation had already been agreed to previously—the United States was openly violating a central provision of the international agreement it would later cite as the basis for condemning Iran for failing to live up to its international obligations: the Non-Proliferation Treaty. That treaty, opened for signature in 1968, had been an explicit bargain between the existing nuclear weapons states and all those who

---

17. Bernard Gwertzman, "US Urges Ban on Atom Sales to Iran," *New York Times*, April 26, 1984.
18. Interview with Mousavian.

did not have nuclear weapons. The nonnuclear weapon states agreed that they would not acquire nuclear weapons, on the condition that the nuclear weapon states agreed to share the benefits of peaceful nuclear technology and to negotiate nuclear disarmament with the ultimate aim of eliminating all nuclear weapons.

Article IV of the treaty had been absolutely central to that bargain. It provides, "Nothing in this Treaty shall be interpreted as affecting the inalienable right of all the Parties to the Treaty to develop research, production and use of nuclear energy for peaceful purposes without discrimination and in conformity with Articles I and II of this Treaty." The same article also says, "All the Parties to the Treaty undertake to facilitate, and have the right to participate in, the fullest possible exchange of equipment, materials and scientific and technological information for the peaceful uses of nuclear energy."[19]

This was the provision of the NPT that the United States was blatantly violating in pressuring other states with nuclear technology and the IAEA itself not to cooperate with Iran in its extremely modest nuclear program. In violating the provision of the treaty that was central to the bargain underlying the NPT, moreover, the United States made no attempt whatever to argue that Iran had violated Article II, which enjoined parties to the treaty not to "manufacture or otherwise acquire nuclear weapons or other nuclear explosive devices; and not to seek or receive any assistance in the manufacture of nuclear weapons or other nuclear explosive devices." Instead, the US national security bureaucracy was simply substituting its own unilateral interests and policy on proliferation for its legal obligations.

Iran had intended to continue the plan adopted by the shah's regime of relying on Western European firms for the enrichment of uranium to fuel the Bushehr project. But the United States' public declaration of its intent to deny Iran any nuclear technology, along with clear indications that US pressure had persuaded France not to provide enriched uranium for reactor fuel for Bushehr, and prevented Germany from agreeing to complete its construction work there, made it clear to Iranian policymakers that the US technology-denial policy had rendered that plan infeasible. "They were saying we had no right to even one power plant or to have access to the international fuel market," Mousavian said. "We began to think, either we will have to withdraw from the NPT or we will have to be self-sufficient."[20]

19. Treaty on the Non-Proliferation of Nuclear Weapons, INFCIRC/140, International Atomic Energy Agency Information Circular, April 22, 1970, http://www.iaea.org/Publications/Documents/Infcircs/Others/infcirc140.pdf.
20. Interview with Mousavian.

In a talk given at IAEA headquarters in 2003, the director of the AEOI, Reza Aghazadeh, recalled how Iranian leaders had concluded after their experience with Eurodif that Iran could not count on Western governments in regard to the supply of enriched uranium. "Having despaired of Western cooperation," he said, "we turned to the policy of self-sufficiency."[21]

Aghazadeh was referring to the decision to acquire the means to carry out uranium enrichment on Iranian soil. The first step was for Iran to begin shopping for the gas centrifuge technology it would need to produce its own supply of enriched uranium. The man in charge of the AEOI's new centrifuge program was Dr. Masud Naraghi, a PhD in plasma science from Case Western Reserve University in Cleveland who had previously worked at the National Aeronautics and Space Administration. He began contacting commercial technology suppliers and middlemen. During a 1985 visit to the office of Leybold-Heraeus in Cologne, Germany, he met Gottwald Lerch, a member of the nuclear procurement network associated with the Pakistani nuclear scientist A. Q. Khan that was selling nuclear secrets surreptitiously.[22]

Iran's dealing with the Khan network is often viewed as evidence of its interest in nuclear weapons, because in the early 1990s, the same network sold a complete package to Libya that included a turnkey uranium enrichment plant complete with 10,000 centrifuges, 20 tons (over 18,000 kilograms) of uranium—and a Chinese design for a nuclear weapon.[23] If Iran had planned to produce a nuclear weapon with the enrichment capabilities it was seeking, this was the perfect opportunity to do so. A one-page offer that Lerch gave to Iran (and that was later turned over to the IAEA) included drawings and specifications for centrifuges, plans for a complete enrichment plant, and "uranium re-conversion and casting capabilities"— technology that would be indispensable if Iran were thinking of eventually making nuclear weapons.[24]

But when Naraghi met with Lerch and other members of the Khan network in Dubai in 1987, to purchase what was essentially a starter kit

21. Reza Aghazadeh, "Iran's Nuclear Policy," Vienna, May 6, 2003, http://www.iranwatch.org/IAEAgovdocs/iran-iaeastatement-aghazadeh-050603.pdf.

22. David Albright, *Peddling Peril: How the Secret Nuclear Trade Arms America's Enemies* (New York: Simon and Schuster, 2010), 72–75.

23. David Albright and Corey Hinderstein, "Uncovering the Nuclear Black Market," report for the Institute for Nuclear Materials Management 45th Annual Meeting, Orlando FL, July 7, 2004, http://www.isis-online.org/publications/southasia/nuclear_black_market.html.

24. "Developments in the Implementation of the NPT Safeguards Agreement in the Islamic Republic of Iran and Agency Verification of Iran's Suspension of Enrichment-related Reprocessing Activities," update brief by the deputy director general for safeguards, January 31, 2006, 1; GOV/2006/15, February 27, 2006, 3. Hereafter, all IAEA "GOV" reports are identified by the document number and date.

for centrifuges, there is no indication that he exhibited any interest in the technology for making a bomb. Later, the IAEA's Safeguards Department official responsible for Iran, Olli Heinonen, intensively interviewed the Khan network intermediaries who dealt with Naraghi in 1987 as part of the IAEA's investigation of Iran's interactions with the Khan network. Those interviews did not produce any indication that Iran had expressed an interest in the inputs or precursors for a nuclear bomb program. And the United States had access to Naraghi himself: he lost his job at AEOI in 1992, apparently over the dubious quality of the centrifuge parts he had obtained, and left Iran for the United States, where he reportedly fully debriefed the CIA on everything he knew about the Iranian nuclear program.[25]

The Khan network operatives indicated that when Naraghi and a colleague picked up the centrifuge components and plans in Dubai in early 1987, Lerch and another network member threw in for free a 15-page document that included a one-and-a-half-page outline of the steps for casting uranium metal to be used for a nuclear weapon, evidently as an inducement to try to get Iran to purchase all of that technology too.[26] No US, Israeli, European, or IAEA official has ever tried to explain why, if Iran was interested in a nuclear weapon, it did not take advantage of the opportunity to buy that technology when it was offered by the Khan network in 1987.

## Using the Nuclear Suppliers Group

Despite its desire to deny all nuclear technology to Iran, the United States lacked any legal basis in the NPT for such a campaign. That fact explains why the United States began in 1991 to go outside the existing global institutions governing nuclear proliferation—the NPT and the IAEA—in order to impose new restrictions on the supply of nuclear technology to Iran. It turned to a group of nuclear technology supplier nations to establish such restrictions and openly targeted Iran as a state to be particularly shunned by the supplier states.

---

25. Douglas Frantz and Catherine Collins, *The Nuclear Jihadist* (New York: Twelve, 2007), 202.

26. Frantz and Collins, *Nuclear Jihadist*, 160–61. The Frantz-Collins account of the 1987 deal is based on interviews with two "senior diplomats" (presumably meaning IAEA officials) who met with Iranian officials about the transaction and the notes from the IAEA interview with Bukhary Sayed Abu Tahir, one of the members of the Khan network who was present in Dubai (p. 381). Although their account of those sources' testimony appears to be reasonably accurate, the authors add their own references (p. 156) to Iran's "growing appetite for nuclear weapons" and "shopping in earnest for a nuclear weapon," which are not based on any documentary evidence.

The Nuclear Suppliers Group (NSG) had begun in 1974 as an informal group of seven states with extensive nuclear capabilities: the United States, the Soviet Union, the United Kingdom, France, the Federal Republic of Germany, Japan, and Canada. (The group is sometimes also called "The London Club" because it originally met in London.) By late 1977, it had acquired eight new member states, all of them European, and its 15 members had agreed on guidelines for the export of nuclear technology to states that did not already have nuclear capabilities.

Those guidelines, published by the IAEA in February 1978, were based on the norms of the NPT and the rules of the IAEA.[27] NSG member states agreed not to authorize transfers to nonnuclear weapon states of any of the items on a so-called trigger list unless it had "formal government assurances from recipients explicitly excluding uses which would result in any nuclear explosive device." Transfers of items on the trigger list were only to take place when "covered by IAEA safeguards."

Nothing in these 1978 guidelines prevented supplier states from selling or otherwise transferring nuclear technology to Iran. But in the mid-1980s, the United States began using its clout with key allies who were members of the NSG to adopt restrictions that went well beyond what the IAEA required. The policy that US officials were pushing on other nuclear supplier states was so restrictive that a number of NSG members resisted Washington's suggestion.[28]

In late 1990, after 13 years in which the NSG had not met once, the George H. W. Bush administration initiated a new round of NSG meetings to discuss what it hoped would be a new set of much tougher guidelines, in light of what Washington called "problem NPT states"—a clear reference to those NPT member states that the United States suspected of aspiring to acquire nuclear weapons capabilities.[29] Iran was the "problem NPT state" on which the United States was primarily focused. During a series of NSG meetings held over the year that followed, US officials called for the members to agree on a separate regime for Iran consisting of a complete ban on all trade in nuclear technology and material.

The new US campaign was accompanied by leaks to the US news media breathlessly warning of Iranian schemes to acquire the technology needed

27. INFCIRC/254, IAEA Information Circular, Communication Received from Certain Member States Regarding Guidelines for the Export of Nuclear Material, Equipment or Technology, February 1978, at http://www.iaea.org/Publications/Documents/Infcircs/Others/infcirc254.shtml.

28. Tadeusz Strulak, "The Nuclear Suppliers Group," *Non-Proliferation Review* (Fall 1993): 3.

29. Strulak, "Nuclear Suppliers Group," 3; US Congress, Office of Technology Assessment, *Nuclear Safeguards and the International Atomic Energy Agency*, OTA ISS-615 (Washington, DC: Government Printing Office, 1995), 19.

for nuclear weapons. In one such leak, published in the *Los Angeles Times* in late January 1991, reporter Jim Mann wrote that Bush administration officials had "grown increasingly worried about new signs that Iran was starting down the same path as Iraq . . . with secret efforts to buy nuclear technology and build nuclear weapons." He quoted an unnamed State Department official as saying, "It's fair to say that Iran's scientists are conducting research on enrichment and reprocessing for nuclear weapons programs."[30]

In November 1991, Assistant Secretary of State Edward P. Djerejian told a House subcommittee, "The United States engages in no nuclear cooperation with Iran, and we have urged other nuclear suppliers, including China, to adopt a similar policy." In an indirect allusion to the US campaign within the NSG, Djerejian said, "We have been in touch with a number of potential nuclear suppliers [to warn] that engaging in any form of nuclear cooperation, whether under safeguards or not, is highly imprudent."[31]

But there was still little international support for the US proposal from other delegations, mainly because it was widely viewed as an explicit violation of Article IV of the NPT.[32] The French government was particularly incensed at what it regarded as Washington trying to impose its own vendetta against Iran on the supplier community. "This is not only an export control policy," a French official scoffed. "This is politics. Full stop." The Americans disliked the regime in Iran, he said, "and they want us to buy into their hatred of the moment."[33] Antipathy toward the aggressiveness of the US denial policy among Europeans was not confined to the specialists on high-tech trade. In late 1993, French nuclear weapons specialist Pierre Villaros, a member of the IAEA delegation visiting Iran, was quoted as "deploring" the fact that Iran was subject to a "de facto embargo on nuclear equipments [sic]."[34]

What the NSG finally adopted after four rounds of negotiations was the addition of further items to the main trigger list and the creation of an additional set of guidelines to regulate the export of dual-use items—in this case, those that could be used for either nuclear or nonnuclear purposes.

---

30. Jim Mann, "Iran's Nuclear Plans Worry U.S. Officials," *Los Angeles Times*, January 27, 1991.

31. Norman Kempster, "US Calls for Nuclear Embargo against Iran," *Los Angeles Times*, November 21, 1991.

32. Office of Technology Assessment, Nuclear Safeguards and the International Atomic Energy Agency, 97, 19.

33. *Financial Times* (London), November 21, 1991, cited in Mark D. Skootsky, "U.S. Nuclear Policy toward Iran," January 1, 1995, at http://people.csail.mit.edu/boris/iran-nuke.text.

34. Claude van England, "Iran Defends Its Pursuit of Nuclear Technology, Despite U.S. Concerns over Plans for Weapons," *Christian Science Monitor*, February 18, 1993.

At the end of a meeting in Warsaw in March–April 1992, the 26 participating supplier states agreed that they would not export dual-use items on the list to nonnuclear countries under any of three conditions: first, if the items would be used in nuclear explosive activities or in an unsafeguarded nuclear fuel cycle; second, if there was "unacceptable risk of their diversion to such activities"; or third, if the "transfer would be contrary to the objective of averting the proliferation of nuclear weapons."[35]

Each of these conditions was defined in such broad terms as to allow decisions based on political interests rather than evidence.[36] Notably, they avoided any requirement for an official IAEA conclusion about diversion of nuclear material to military purposes, or even noncompliance with safeguards agreements. The NSG document then called for export licensing procedures for the technologies listed in the annex and included a checklist of "relevant factors" to be taken into account. Most of the factors on the list were reasonably related to the objective of avoiding proliferation, such as NPT membership and an IAEA safeguards agreement in force for the recipient country. But the list also required supplier states to consider "whether the recipients have been engaged in clandestine or illegal procurement activities." That language had obviously been pushed by the United States to put pressure on other suppliers to reject any export license requests from Iran.

US and allied intelligence services had been collecting and selectively sharing intelligence on the methods that the Iranians were using to get around restrictions aimed at denying Iran nuclear technology, in order to build pressure on otherwise reluctant supplier states. They knew that AEOI had been using a number of private companies to purchase dual-use items from suppliers all over the world, often routing the purchases through Dubai, where the government had a laissez-faire policy toward such transactions. In the early 1990s, US intelligence began intercepting telexes from Iran to nuclear suppliers around the world and sharing them with friendly intelligence agencies and the IAEA. The telexes showed that Iran's Sharif University was often the listed purchaser of dual-use equipment, which intelligence officials quickly decided was being used for a covert enrichment program they suspected involved the Iranian military. In many cases, Sharif University itself sent the request to the supplier, as in the case of an

35. INFCIRC/254/Rev.1/Part2, IAEA Information Circular, Communication Received from Certain Member States Regarding Guidelines for the Export of Nuclear Material, Equipment and Technology, "Nuclear-related Dual-Use Transfers," July 1992.

36. Mark Hibbs, *The Future of the Nuclear Suppliers Group* (Washington, DC: Carnegie Endowment for International Peace, 2011), 6.

order from the German company Thyssen in 1991 for ring magnets that analysts believed could be used in centrifuges.[37]

The US and allied intelligence agencies would cite just such Iranian procurement practices as evidence that Iran was guilty of violating the "clandestine or illegal" standard in order to justify rejection of an export license for a technology sought by Iran.

Using front companies or a university as the ostensible purchaser may have been "clandestine" in the sense that the AEOI was using subterfuges to get around restrictions on technology exports to Iran, but was not a violation of either the NPT or of Iran's safeguards agreement with the IAEA. The charge of clandestineness implied that Iran was using deception to hide a nuclear weapons program rather than because the United States and some other suppliers had already made it clear that they would deny any nuclear or dual-use technology that Iran requested in a normal, straightforward manner.

Throughout the years that followed, Iran continued to complain that the United States' overt and covert campaign to prevent it from obtaining basic nuclear infrastructure, such as had already been acquired by more than two-dozen other countries, was a blatant violation of the NPT. In 1994, a senior Iranian diplomat threatened to reconsider the country's membership in the NPT, on the ground that the United States and its allies were violating Article IV by preventing Iran from having access to technology for a nuclear power program, despite Iran's having honored its NPT obligation.[38] In 2000, Iran threatened to halt inspections by the IAEA if the United States continued to deny basic nuclear technology to Iran.[39] But Tehran took no action to carry out either of these threats, and the United States ignored them. Meanwhile, Washington continued to work to deprive Iran of even the single nuclear reactor that it had inherited from the shah.

In a rare moment of candor, Robert Gates, then CIA director, noted in congressional testimony in 1992 that one of the main reasons that "proliferation" of missiles and weapons of mass destruction (WMD) seemed to be increasing was that the technologies used to make WMD were "relatively old technologies . . . and more easily absorbed by Third World countries than ever before. Nuclear weapons and missile technologies date back to

---

37. Joby Warrick, "Formerly Secret Telexes Reveal Iran's Early Use of Deceit in Nuclear Program," *Washington Post*, February 11, 2012; Andrew Koch and Jeanette Wolf, "Iran's Nuclear Procurement Program: How Close to the Bomb?" *Non-Proliferation Review* (Fall 1997): 124; David Albright, "What the United States Knew," *Bulletin of Atomic Scientists* 60 (March–April 2004): 63.

38. Mark Hibbs, "Iran May Withdraw from NPT over Trade Barriers," *Nucleonics Week*, September 22, 1994.

39. Mark Hibbs, "Iran Won't Accept More Inspections Unless U.S. Stops Nuclear Blockade," *Nucleonics Week*, June 1, 2000.

the 1940s." He also noted that most of these technologies were "dual use," having "legitimate civilian applications." Restricting trade in those items in order to prevent proliferation, he acknowledged, "would be limiting the ability of developing nations to modernize."[40] It was an extraordinary acknowledgment by a senior US official that US policymakers understood that the US technology-denial campaign was an effort to impede Iran's scientific and technological development.

## Consequences of the Denial Policy

It has been a fundamental characteristic of the United States as the dominant state in world politics that it tends to use its coercive power in ways that impinge on the legitimate and even vital interests of weaker states. That overreach inevitably provokes reactions that were not anticipated. And US policymakers then view the unanticipated consequences as hostile, aggressive, or otherwise unacceptable responses caused by something other than the overly aggressive US policy.

The policy of nuclear denial toward Iran is a perfect example of that pattern. It was adopted without considering how unrealistic it was to expect that Iran would passively submit to such an intervention in its development policy and whether such a policy would generate an Iranian policy response that would be much worse than allowing Iran to continue with its existing plans for a nuclear program. As the head of the Iranian parliamentary committee on foreign affairs, Mohammad Larijani, observed in an interview with the BBC, Iran is a "huge nation, with a huge human resource. It is very impossible and impractical . . . in the modern world, to keep a nation from advancement. I think it is very naïve if they think it is possible."[41] The US pressures on France, Germany, and other allied nations merely pushed Iran into a decision to seek its own independent enrichment capability, despite the fact that in the first few years of its nuclear program, the Islamic Republic had planned to depend on Western sources of enriched uranium for its nuclear reactor fuel. And the US campaign to deny Iran's right to peaceful nuclear power established a structure of conflict that was bound to last as long as the United States insisted on its policy.

---

40. Non-Proliferation of Weapons of Mass Destruction and Regulatory Improvement Act of 1992: Hearings on H.R. 4803, May 8, 1992, before the House Comm. on Banking, Finance and Urban Affairs, 102nd Cong., 2nd sess., statement by CIA Director Robert M. Gates, 36–37.

41. Quoted in Herbert Krosney, *Deadly Business: Legal Deals and Outlaw Weapons* (New York: Four Walls Eight Windows, 1993), 248.

Despite multiple US diplomatic efforts to prevent it, Iran did eventually find a way to construct and equip its own uranium enrichment facility. The construction of such a facility at Natanz began in secret in 2001, and was well along but not yet near completion when its existence was revealed by the armed opposition group Mujahedeen-e-Khalq (MEK), or People's Mujahedeen of Iran, in mid-2002. That disclosure was the first move in a deliberate strategy, originating in Israel but led by the United States, to create a political-military crisis over Iran's nuclear program that still has not ended.

# 2

# The Politics of Iran's Nuclear Secrecy

## Keeping Natanz Secret

On August 14, 2002, Alireza Jafarzadeh, the US representative of the National Council of Resistance of Iran (NCRI), appeared before the Washington press corps. NCRI was merely a front for the Mujahedeen-e-Khalq (MEK), an organization with an unsavory history of carrying out terrorist bombings in Iran against US and Iranian officials as well as Saddam's domestic opponents on behalf of his regime. The US State Department had listed the MEK as a terrorist organization during the Clinton administration.

But the Washington press corps didn't care about that fact. The story offered by Jafarzadeh was too sensational: he identified two previously unknown Iranian nuclear sites that he said were supporting a covert nuclear weapons program. He gave reporters the precise location of the two facilities in Natanz and Arak, which he identified as a nuclear fuel production plant and heavy water production plant, respectively. Jafarzadeh even gave the precise dimensions of the two production halls of the Natanz facility buried 25 feet underground beneath eight feet of concrete.

But the MEK press conference was a carefully constructed bit of political theater. The MEK claim of sources within the regime leaking secret information on a covert nuclear weapons program was purely propaganda. The terrorist group had been given the intelligence about Natanz and Arak by Israel's foreign intelligence agency, Mossad, which had gotten it from its own satellite photography and intelligence shared by the Bush administration. Investigative journalist Seymour Hersh later reported that a "senior IAEA official" had told him that Israeli intelligence had passed their satellite intelligence on to the MEK.[1] That report was confirmed, in effect, by two Israeli authors, who wrote, "A way to 'launder' information from Western intelligence to IAEA was found so that agencies and the sources could be protected. Information is 'filtered' to the IAEA via Iranian opposition groups, especially the National Council of Resistance of Iran."[2] Another Iranian opposition figure, an adviser to Reza Pahlavi, the heir to the shah, also confirmed the substance of Hersh's report, telling Connie Bruck of *New Yorker* magazine, "That information came not from the M.E.K. but from a friendly government, and it had come to more than one opposition group, not only the mujahideen," he said. When asked if the "friendly government" was Israel, the opposition figure smiled and said, "The friendly government did not want to be the source of it, publicly. If the friendly government gives it to the U.S. publicly, then it would be received differently. Better to come from an opposition group."[3]

The MEK revelation nevertheless appeared to confirm the suspicions of Iranian deception that had been voiced by successive US administrations for more than a decade. And it contributed to the credibility of a media narrative that Iran had been developing its nuclear program in secret because it was seeking to acquire nuclear weapons. A similar political dynamic occurred with regard to the nuclear experiments and tests that Iran had carried out over the years without informing the IAEA. But the real story of the secrecy surrounding the Iranian nuclear program was dramatically different from what was declared by US officials and reported in the commercial news media.

Iran was not obligated by its safeguards agreement to notify the IAEA about the existence of the Natanz facility until 180 days before the introduction of nuclear material into it, which was still far from happening in August 2002. But Iran's secrecy about the construction at Natanz was portrayed as evidence of the intention to hide its development of nuclear weapons. The actual calculations underlying that secrecy, however, remain a crucial unknown chapter in the history of Iran's nuclear program.

The secrecy about the existence of the enrichment facility at Natanz was very different from the way Iran dealt with the construction of a uranium conversion facility (UCF) in Esfahan. The AEOI had notified the IAEA about the plan to build the UCF in 1999, and in July 2000, it provided "preliminary design information" for the UCF to the IAEA. But the wording of that declaration appears to have been aimed at keeping the agency in the

1. Seymour M. Hersh, *Chain of Command: The Road from 9/11 to Abu Ghraib* (New York: HarperCollins, 2004), 349.

2. Yossi Melman and Meir Javadanfar, *The Nuclear Sphinx of Tehran* (New York: Carroll and Graf, 2007), 163–64.

3. Connie Bruck, "Exiles," *New Yorker*, March 6, 2006, 56.

dark about Iran's plans to build an enrichment facility. The AEOI described the UCF as intended for the conversion of uranium ore concentrate into a form of uranium, uranium hexafluoride (UF[6]), which would be enriched outside Iran.[4] Thus Iran was avoiding any implication that it intended to enrich uranium on Iranian soil.

Why, then, did Iran choose to keep Natanz secret, if not to hide its intention to use it for clandestine production for a nuclear weapon? Iran's secrecy about Natanz was linked to both the continued US political-diplomatic interventions to prevent Iran from having an independent enrichment capability and the initial threats Israel had made, in the late 1990s, to use military force against the Iranian nuclear program. Iran's decision-makers were clearly calculating that notifying the IAEA about the Natanz facility would trigger hostile responses by the United States and/or Israel that would put the successful opening and operation of the facility at risk.

One of the reasons for Iran's refusing to telegraph plans for an enrichment facility when the AEOI provided the design information on the UCF in 2000, and again when it began construction on Natanz, was certainly the anticipation that such a notification could lead to the discovery of Iran's commercial sources for key parts for the enrichment equipment. Iranian engineers working on the P-1 centrifuges still needed to acquire thousands of steel ball bearings, for which they were still dependent on the A. Q. Khan network intermediaries in Europe. Customs data that Western intelligence agencies obtained later indicated that large numbers of ball-bearing "preforms" were shipped to Pakistan and then forwarded to Iran in 2000 and 2001.[5] If the Natanz facility had been declared before those preforms had been secured, and the Western intelligence learned about Iran's intermediaries, it would risk losing supplies that were vital to making the centrifuges work.

When the construction on the Natanz facility began in 2001, the AEOI had not yet finished testing its centrifuges to see if they would actually work. It was not until 1999 that a single P-1 centrifuge was actually tested with the introduction of UF[6]. And only in 2002 was nuclear material first fed into a number of machines, according to the later Iranian account.[6] Iran did not want the IAEA to know about testing, because it would lead immediately to the discovery of a supply of uranium it had kept from the IAEA—and the likely loss of the supplier, which was China (see details later in this chapter).

4. Mark Hibbs, "Iran Told IAEA It Will Build Chinese UF6 Plan at Isfahan," *Nuclear Fuel*, December 16, 1996; GOV/2003/75, November 11, 2003, 5.

5. Mark Hibbs, "Iranians Claimed Bearing Impasse Halted Work on P-2 Centrifuge," *Nuclear Fuel*, February 27, 2006, 3.

6. GOV/2003/83, November 15, 2004, 6.

But Iran's decision to keep the Natanz facility secret also reflected a genuine fear of a possible attack on the facility. In a 2004 talk to the Supreme Cultural Revolution Council, Hassan Rouhani, the secretary of Iran's Supreme National Security Council (who in August 2013 became president of the country), alluded to a serious challenge central to any decision about Natanz. Iranian strategists, he said, were certain that the United States would not allow an independent country to have a capability for uranium enrichment, which would also give the country a potential nuclear weapons option. A country that was "nowhere near this capability," said Rouhani, "is not put under pressure." But countries that are "standing on the threshold of having this technology," he said, "are put under a tremendous amount of pressure to force them to stop their activities and to not move toward achieving this capability. It is at this point that the pressures are redoubled."[7]

Rouhani and his colleagues at the Supreme National Security Council believed that once the United States knew that Iran was constructing an enrichment facility at Natanz, the threat of a US-Israeli attack would be substantially increased. Iranian leaders had to decide both when and how Iran would be prepared to deal with the consequences of US-Israeli knowledge of an Iranian enrichment facility. At two conferences held in Tehran in March 2005, Iranian officials and scholars told a Turkish scholar that Iran had built the Natanz facility secretly because if the IAEA had been notified, "the United States definitely would have prevented the completion of the construction of the project."[8]

That was hardly an unreasonable fear. Beginning in late 1997, Israel's then prime minister Benjamin Netanyahu had begun citing the 1981 Israeli attack on Iraq's Osirak nuclear reactor as the model for what might need to be done if Iran continued its nuclear program. Israeli officials circulated rumors through diplomatic channels and planted stories in the news media of plans for a strike against Iranian nuclear targets.[9] The beginning of Israeli threats of an air attack against Iran's nuclear sites in 1997 and 1998 came just as Tehran was deciding to accelerate its enrichment program and begin planning for a full-scale enrichment plant.[10]

---

7. Text of speech by Supreme National Security Council Secretary Hassan Rouhani to the Supreme Cultural Revolution Council, place and date not given: "Beyond the Challenges Facing Iran and the IAEA Concerning the Nuclear Dossier," *Rahbord* (in Persian), September 30, 2005, Foreign Broadcast Information Service, FBIS-IAP200601113336001. Hereafter cited as "Rouhani speech."

8. Mustafa Kiraboglu, "Good for the Shah, Banned for the Mullahs: The West and Iran's Quest for Nuclear Power," *Middle East Journal* 60 (2006): 209.

9. Joseph Fitchett, "Israeli Reaction to Iran's Buildup Is Heightening Nuclear Fears in Mideast," *International Herald Tribune*, December 19, 1997, 6; Christopher Walker, "Israel Steps Up Plans for Air Attacks on Iran," *Times* (London), December 9, 1997, 14.

10. Patrikarakos, *Nuclear Iran*, 167.

The Iranian perception of threat was certainly heightened further in January 2002, when President George W. Bush identified Iran as a "hostile regime" and part of the "axis of evil." The implication was that Iran could be targeted for attack in the future. Soon thereafter, the Bush administration's nuclear policy review ordered the Pentagon to draft contingency plans for the use of nuclear weapons against a set of countries that included Iran. The list of states targeted in the nuclear policy review was leaked to the *Los Angeles Times*, which published the story in early March 2002.[11] Iran's leaders were well aware of all those developments.

The Iranian decision-makers knew, however, that keeping a completed or nearly completed enrichment facility secret was not a realistic option. The Natanz facility was too big, and located too close to a main highway, to remain covert. As a Western diplomat asked after the MEK revelation, if Natanz was meant to be a covert facility, why would it have been put in a location where "anybody can see it"?[12] In his 2004 talk, Rouhani stated explicitly that it had been understood in advance that the facility could not be kept secret. "We wanted to keep it secret for a while," he said. But, he added, "Of course we all knew at some point this would become public knowledge."[13] Iranian officials were quite aware that the United States had been keeping suspected nuclear sites under satellite surveillance since at least the early 1990s, when this had first been reported in the US press.[14]

The central problem for Iranian strategists, therefore, was how to deter an Israeli or US attack on Natanz once those states learned about the Natanz facility. That was a serious worry, because Iran's main deterrent weapon system in the late 1990s—the Shahab-3 intermediate range ballistic missile, which was based on North Korea's Nodong design—had proved unreliable in flight tests. The Shahab-3's first flight test, on July 22, 1998, was a dramatic failure. The missile exploded in less than 100 seconds. The second flight test did not take place until two years later, and the missile traveled only about 850 kilometers—roughly 500 to 700 miles—which was less than the Nodong's maximum range. In a third test in September 2000, the missile failed immediately after ignition.[15]

11. William M. Arkin, "Secret Plan Outlines the Unthinkable," *Los Angeles Times*, March 9, 2002.

12. Scott Peterson, "A Push for Candor on Iran Nukes," *Christian Science Monitor*, September 19, 2003.

13. Rouhani speech.

14. Steve Coll, "U.S. Intervention Blocks Nuclear Transfer to Iran," *Washington Post*, November 17, 1992, A1.

15. Michael Elleman, *Iran's Ballistic Missile Capabilities: A Net Assessment* (London: International Institute for Strategic Studies, 2010), 21–22.

Iran had another problem with the Shahab-3 that was even more trou-bling to its strategists: It could not reach Israel, the one state that had been threatening to attack Iran. After the July 1998 test, Israeli defense minister Yitzhak Mordechai said he didn't believe Iran had a missile that could reach Israel.[16] That observation was confirmed years later when an analysis by London's International Institute for Strategic Studies concluded that the Shahab-3 had a range of only about 1,000 kilometers (620 miles) when carrying a 1,650-pound payload—not the 1,300-kilometer (800-mile) range officially claimed—and therefore could reach only a very limited area of Israel.[17] Besides, the missile was still only in an early phase of its development. In 1997, Israeli analyst Yiftah Shapir had estimated that it could take Iran as long as six or seven more years of tests to complete the development stage.[18]

Nevertheless, in early 2001, the Iranian military announced that the Shahab-3 would soon go into "serial production." The most authoritative Western analysis of the Iranian missile program suggests, however, that the announcement was a ploy to convince the Israelis and the Americans that Iran would soon have a viable deterrent at a time when it was actually still far from possessing such a capability.[19] That Iranian ploy came just as Iran was secretly planning the construction of the Natanz enrichment facil-ity. Thus, the construction of Natanz was taking place while the Iranian military was still working frantically to develop a new ballistic missile with a conventional warhead that would meet its deterrent requirements. The Bush administration's overt identification of Iran as a state to be targeted in early 2002 must have confirmed for Iranian strategists the wisdom of a strategy of accelerating its missile-development program.

But Iran's urgent quest for a deterrent would take time. The first test of the follow-on to the Shahab-3, a missile that Iran called the Ghadr-1, was not conducted until August 2004.[20] Meanwhile, Iran's elite Islamic Revolutionary Guard Corps (IRGC) was creating another element in the country's deterrence strategy that also appeared to have been decided in 2001—an extensive "passive defense" system of tunnel facilities dug into mountainsides. Years later, satellite photographs acquired by the IAEA showed that in 2002, the IRGC's Passive Defense Organization began dig-ging tunnel facilities into mountainsides all across Iran, which could be

16. Robin Wright, "Missile Has No Impact on U.S. Hope for Iran," *Los Angeles Times,* July 24, 1998, 12.

17. Elleman, *Iran's Ballistic Missile Capabilities,* 23.

18. Steve Rodan, "Israel in Iranian Missile Range by 1999," *Jerusalem Post,* October 1, 1997.

19. Elleman, *Iran's Ballistic Missile Capabilities,* 23.

20. Ibid., 20, 23.

used to protect some of Iran's most sensitive assets, including elements of its enrichment program, in case of attack. They would also complicate US and Israeli targeting and thus enhance deterrence.[21]

In 2001 and early 2002 Iran was still working on putting its deterrence strategy and its passive defense system into place and knew that US satellites would be watching for signs of construction of any enrichment program. The pace of construction of Natanz, therefore, would have been carefully planned. The Iranian calculus was presumably based on the belief that US intelligence analysts would not be able to identify Natanz as an enrichment facility until certain types of equipment going into the site signaled its purpose clearly.

By early 2002, US intelligence had already begun to suspect from the size and configuration of the big hole at Natanz that it was for an enrichment facility. Those suspicions were not sufficient, however, for the United States to publicly accuse Iran of building an enrichment plant, or even to ask the IAEA to demand access to Natanz. The AEOI had not moved any equipment to the site that would allow intelligence analysts to identify it as an enrichment facility. It may have even paused the construction deliberately. Only in October 2002, two months *after* the MEK had identified the site, did US officials feel enough confidence in their evidence to brief the IAEA on the site's purpose.[22] That identification evidently reflected an Iranian move to accelerate the construction schedule and to begin moving enrichment-related equipment to the site, on the assumption that the IAEA would ask to visit it. By February 2003, when the IAEA visited Natanz, it found more than 100 of the planned 1,000 centrifuges already installed in the "pilot enrichment facility." The rest would be delivered by the end of the year.[23]

But Israel was the wild card in the unfolding of the Natanz drama. The Israelis had their own satellite imagery, and they had a way of making an accusation public without having to take responsibility for it themselves. They simply gave the information to the MEK to make a dramatic revelation in August 2002.

21. GOV/2009/74, November 16, 2009, 3–4; Paul Brannan, "Qom Gas Centrifuge Enrichment Site in Iran May Have Been Re-purposed Tunnel Facility," ISIS Imagery Brief, Institute for Science and International Security, September 29, 2009.

22. Mark Hibbs, "U.S. Briefed Suppliers Group in October on Suspected Iranian Enrichment Plant," *Nuclear Fuel*, December 23, 2002, 1.

23. GOV/2003/40, June 6, 2003, 5–6.

## Eighteen Years of Covert Enrichment?

IAEA director general Mohamed ElBaradei arrived in Tehran on February 21, 2003, along with Pierre Goldschmidt, deputy director for safeguards, and Olli Heinonen, director of safeguards operations (B), the office responsible for Iran. It was the first IAEA visit to Iran since the MEK had drawn public attention to the existence of two new nuclear facilities six months earlier. ElBaradei knew that the IAEA was embarking on a long and politically consequential investigation of Iran's nuclear program. The reason was that, shortly before leaving the IAEA's Vienna headquarters, Goldschmidt and Heinonen had learned two of Iran's most sensitive nuclear secrets.

During the IAEA team's first meeting in Tehran, Iranian vice president and AEOI director Reza Aghazadeh formally declared that Iran was constructing two facilities at Natanz: a smaller pilot fuel enrichment plant and a larger, commercial-scale fuel enrichment plant. But ElBaradei and his staff had an unpleasant surprise for Aghazadeh. They informed him that they also knew that Iran had purchased three batches of uranium from China in 1991 that had never been reported to the IAEA.

When the IAEA officials confronted Aghazadeh with this information, he had no choice but to admit that Iran had indeed imported the uranium, and that it had been stored at the Jabr Ibn Hayan Multipurpose Laboratories at the Tehran Nuclear Research Center, which had never been declared to the IAEA. He said that most of the uranium tetrafluoride ($UF_4$) from China had been converted to uranium metal in 2000 at the Jabr Ibn Hayan labs, and that the AEOI had used some of the uranium dioxide ($UO_2$) from China for the testing of processes to be undertaken by a uranium conversion facility.[24] The AEOI chief nevertheless denied that any uranium had been used for either conversion or enrichment experiments or for testing centrifuges, and he repeated this denial on other occasions between February and July.[25]

But the IAEA officials were also armed with a second piece of information: they had been tipped off by Israeli intelligence that Iran had been constructing centrifuges at a workshop in Tehran called Kala Electric Company. The IAEA generally preferred to cite open source information wherever possible in its contacts with Iran, and the NCRI, which had been used by Israeli intelligence to announce the discovery of the two previously secret nuclear facilities in August 2002, had revealed the company's role in "testing" centrifuges in a press conference the day before the IAEA

---

24. Ibid., 4–5.
25. GOV/2003/63, August 26, 2003, 4.

delegation arrived in Tehran.[26] When the IAEA delegation asked Aghazadeh about a centrifuge workshop at Kala Electric Company, he admitted that the workshop, which was actually called Kalaye Electric Company, had indeed been used to construct centrifuges.[27]

The Iranians initially refused the request from Goldschmidt and Heinonen to inspect the workshop and take environmental samples there. When the two IAEA officials finally were allowed to visit in March, they were denied access to a warehouse with the specious explanation that no key was available. Meanwhile, the AEOI had been removing all evidence of the introduction of uranium hexafluoride ($UF_6$) into centrifuges by putting in a new floor and repainting the walls of the workshop—or so it thought.[28] What it didn't know was that the IAEA's laboratory could detect the presence of plutonium or uranium down to a picogram, one-trillionth of a gram.[29] When the environmental swipes finally carried out in August 2003 came back from the lab, the IAEA inspectors could confirm what they had suspected all along—that the centrifuges had been tested with $UF_6$, the gaseous form of uranium used for enrichment. In an October 21, 2003, letter to the IAEA, Iran admitted for the first time that it had carried out "a limited number of tests, using small amounts of $UF_6$," on centrifuges at the Kalaye Electric Company in 1999 and again in 2002.[30] Even worse for the Iranians, however, the baseline environmental samples taken at the pilot fuel enrichment plant at Natanz between March and June 2003—*before* Iran had publicly introduced $UF_6$ into one of the centrifuges there—indicated the presence of high-enriched uranium (HEU). The IAEA reported that finding, which suggested that Iran might have been covering up enrichment as part of a nuclear weapons program, in August 2003.[31]

The Bush administration leapt to that conclusion, even though the IAEA was only beginning to investigate the matter. Only years later would the IAEA officially confirm that there was an innocent explanation for the finding. Meanwhile, the finding was another major building block in the

---

26. National Council of Resistance of Iran, press conference on Iran's clandestine nuclear projects, February 20, 2003, http://www.iranwatch.org/privateviews/NCRI/perspex-ncri-nuclear-022003.htm.

27. Scott Ritter, *Target Iran* (New York: Nation Books, 2006), 63–65.

28. The story of the effort to clean up Kalaye is told in a number of sources. See, for example, Carla Anne Robbins, "As Evidence Grows of Iran's Program, U.S. Hits Quandary," *Wall Street Journal*, March 18, 2005; Felicity Barringer, "Inspectors in Iran Find Highly Enriched Uranium in an Electrical Plant," *New York Times*, September 26, 2003.

29. *The International Atomic Energy Agency's Laboratories: Seibersdorf and Vienna* (Vienna: IAEA, no date), 47, http://www.iaea.org/Publications/Booklets/Seibersdorf/seibersdorf.pdf.

30. GOV/2003/75, November 10, 2003, 3, 5–6.

31. GOV/2003/63, August 26, 2003, 4.

construction of the Iran nuclear scare. The November 2003 IAEA report did state clearly, "To date, there is no evidence that the previously undeclared nuclear material and activities referred to above were related to a nuclear weapons programme." But the Bush administration ridiculed that conclusion, and news media coverage tended to support its skepticism.

The news media picked up and amplified the statement in the IAEA report that Iran had "acknowledged that it has been developing, for 18 years, a uranium centrifuge enrichment programme, and, for 12 years, a laser enrichment programme."[32] That language suggested that Iran had actually been secretly enriching uranium by two different methods for a combined total of 30 years.

The detailed chronology in the annex to the IAEA's November 2003 report showed something quite different, however. It revealed that no enrichment by gas centrifuges took place until a few centrifuges were tested with $UF_6$ briefly in 1999 and then again in 2002. It revealed that only milligram amounts of uranium were produced by laser enrichment, but gave no details about precisely when that took place.[33]

This was not what readers of American newspapers and viewers of American television news were told about the IAEA reporting. Not a single news story on the report covered the fact that Iran carried out centrifuge enrichment tests only for brief periods in 1999 and again in 2002. Instead of referring to the brief few months of experiments testing centrifuges, news coverage of the report suggested that Iran had been continuing to enrich for nearly two decades. As the Los Angeles Times summarized the November 2003 report, "Over 18 years, the regime concealed from the United Nations both a centrifuge uranium enrichment program and a laser enrichment program."[34] The Times of London reported that Iran had used its civilian nuclear program to "covertly produce plutonium and enriched uranium, which could be used in nuclear bombs."[35] And the Christian Science Monitor reported three months later that the IAEA had found that Iran "had been hiding a vast clandestine nuclear effort for 18 years."[36] The Minneapolis Star-Tribune editorialized that, since Iran had admitted hiding a "quite sophisticated effort to enrich uranium," and the IAEA had been

32. GOV/2003/75, November 10, 2003, 8–9.

33. Ibid., 8–11.

34. Paul Richter, "U.S. Questions UN Findings on Iran's Bid for Nuclear Arms," Los Angeles Times, November 13, 2003.

35. Roland Watson, "Allies Tough Stance against Iran over Nuclear Breaches," Times (London), November 21, 2003, 24.

36. Scott Peterson, "Evidence of Possible Work on Nukes Tests Iran's Credibility," Christian Science Monitor, February 26, 2004, 7.

fooled for so long, the IAEA might also have been deceived in concluding there was no evidence of a nuclear weapons program.[37]

National Public Radio's *All Things Considered* program provided what may have been the most seriously distorted coverage of that pivotal story. On November 13, 2003, co-host Melissa Block introduced a segment on the IAEA report by declaring that the IAEA was about to meet to "decide what to do about Iran's nuclear weapons program" and that the IAEA report contained "more damning evidence of an extensive nuclear weapons infrastructure," even though neither the IAEA nor the US government had made such an extreme claim. Reporter Mike Schuster then summarized the report as describing enrichment of both uranium and plutonium that had "taken place over the past 18 years—all in secret." Schuster went on to suggest that the agency's conclusion that there was no evidence that Iran had been covering up a nuclear weapons program could not have been truthful and must have been merely a political tactic to manage leaders in Tehran who might otherwise refuse to cooperate further with the agency.[38]

In November 2004, the IAEA reported that further investigation had shown that no laser enrichment took place until 2002, and that from October 2002 through May 2003, when the equipment was dismantled, Iran's laser enrichment experiments were able to enrich only up to 0.8 percent—less than 25 percent of the minimum required.[39] But the news media ignored the information in the report indicating that the earlier media coverage had vastly exaggerated the actual Iranian enrichment program. The *Washington Post*'s Dafna Linzer simply repeated the original narrative: "Over 18 years," she wrote, "Iran secretly assembled uranium enrichment and conversion facilities that could be used for a nuclear energy program or to construct an atomic bomb."[40] Other news outlets had no coverage of the new information, even though the Associated Press, the *New York Times*, and the *Financial Times* all devoted entire stories to the charge by NCRI that Iran had obtained the design for a nuclear weapon from the Khan network.[41]

---

37. "Iranian Nukes: Why Should World Believe U.S.?" *Minneapolis Star-Tribune*, November 19, 2003.

38. "UN Report Reveals Scope of Nuclear Program," National Public Radio, November 14, 2003; Richter, "U.S. Questions UN Findings."

39. GOV/2004/83, November 15, 2004, 13–14.

40. Dafna Linzer, "UN Finds No Nuclear Bomb Program in Iran," *Washington Post*, November 16, 2004.

41. Associated Press, "Group Says Tehran Has Bomb Plans, Is Violating Deal," *Charleston Daily Mail* (Charleston, WV), November 17, 2004, 11B; Douglas Jehl, "Group Says Iran Has Secret Nuclear Arms Program," *New York Times*, November 17, 2004, A4; Daniel Dombey, "Iran Alleged to Have Obtained Plans for a Nuclear Bomb," *Financial Times*, November 17, 2004, A1.

The false narrative that Iran had carried out uranium enrichment continuously for 18 years, and its implication that that effort could only have been related to a nuclear weapons program, would continue to color media coverage of Iran's nuclear program for years to come. In late 2007, the US national intelligence estimate's conclusion that Iran had halted nuclear weapons work in 2003 was made public. But even then, the *New York Times* reminded readers that the IAEA had earlier "found that Iran, working in secrecy for 18 years from 1985 to 2003, pursued many techniques to enrich uranium."[42]

The confusion sown by the heavily slanted media coverage of the issue made it easy for the George W. Bush administration to charge that Iran had been hiding a nuclear weapons program. In November 2003, the administration's lead policymaker on nuclear proliferation, John Bolton, the undersecretary of state for arms control, proliferation, and international security, referred to "the massive and covert Iranian efforts to acquire sensitive nuclear capabilities," which he said, "makes sense only as part of a nuclear weapons program."[43] But that statement only expressed what most newspaper readers would have already concluded from reading the coverage of the IAEA report.

On August 17, 2004, in a speech at the Hudson Institute, Bolton said that Iran had "concealed a large-scale, covert nuclear weapons program for over 18 years."[44] That was a blatant falsehood, unsupported by any evidence. Strangely, not a single news outlet saw fit to cover the Bolton claim. The one story on the Bolton speech, published in the *Washington Post*, simply ignored that statement.[45] That lack of interest in Bolton's charge evidently reflected the feeling that there was nothing particularly new in the statement. The news media had apparently interpreted the language of the November 2003 report as implying the Iranian concealment of such a weapons program.

Despite the unanimity with which commercial news media reported this crucial episode in the construction of a nuclear scare over Iran in alarming terms as evidence of nefarious intent, at least one journalist who covered the issue for the next decade later acknowledged that the reality of Iranian nuclear secrecy during those 18 years was a good deal more complicated. David Sanger, whose own coverage of the Iranian nuclear program for the *New York Times* was consistently and markedly alarmist, nevertheless

---

42. William J. Broad and David E. Sanger, "US Showed the World Exhibit A, Iran as Nuclear Threat, Now Exhibit B Upends That," *New York Times*, December 4, 2007, A20.
43. Richter, "U.S. Questions UN Findings."
44. John R. Bolton, "Preventing Iran from Acquiring Nuclear Weapons," remarks to the Hudson Institute, August 17, 2004, http://2001-2009.state.gov/t/us/rm/35281.htm.
45. Dafna Linzer, "Iran a Nuclear Threat, U.S. Says," *Washington Post*, August 18, 2004.

commented in his book *The Inheritance* that there was "no dispute" about the fact that Iran "had no choice but to operate in great secrecy, because the Americans were doing everything they could to choke the country off."[46]

## How "Secret" Was the Enrichment Program?

The 18-year-covert-nuclear-program theme in official and media commentary suggested that the 2002 and 2003 revelations about Iran's conversion and enrichment programs had somehow come as a surprise to the IAEA, Western governments, and Western media. But that impression, too, was highly misleading. The IAEA and the coalition of states led by the United States, along with some leading writers in the Western media, had been well aware of the broad outlines and many of the details of the Iranian conversion and enrichment programs at each stage of their development.

US and allied intelligence services had already begun to acquire considerable information on Iran's acquisition of centrifuge technology by the early 1990s. A large part of its knowledge came from Masud Naraghi, the former head of Iran's centrifuge program, who had lost his job with the AEOI because of the shoddiness of the centrifuges he had obtained from the Khan network under a 1987 deal. Naraghi fled to the United States in 1992 and had provided the CIA with the entire history of Iran's effort to obtain centrifuge technology and components. That information included not only the AEOI's deal with the Khan network intermediaries but his own work in obtaining other equipment for centrifuge enrichment from suppliers in Europe from 1988 through 1990.[47]

Based on the detailed information that it obtained from Naraghi, the CIA could have acted to shut down the Khan network as early as 1992. "We could have stopped the Khan network, as we knew it, at any time," recalled Robert Einhorn, US assistant secretary of state for nonproliferation in the Clinton administration. "The debate was do you stop it now, or do you watch it and understand it better so that you are in a stronger position to pull it up by its roots later?"[48] The US decision to keep its own knowledge of Iran's centrifuge acquisition program secret from the IAEA was part of a broader cat-and-mouse game involving the CIA and the Khan network.

In 1994 and 1995, the US and technical news media published stories about Iran's acquisition of enrichment technology on the international market. Germany's foreign intelligence agency, the *Bundesnachrichtendienst* (BND), leaked to journalist Mark Hibbs some details about Iran's procure-

46. David E. Sanger, *The Inheritance* (New York: Harmony, 2009), 37.

47. Frantz and Collins, *Nuclear Jihadist*, 202; Albright, *Peddling Peril*, 74–75.

48. Douglas Frantz, "A High Risk Nuclear Stakeout," *Los Angeles Times*, February 27, 2005.

ment of "dual-use" technology that could have been used for uranium enrichment.[49] The *Washington Post* reported that Israeli intelligence and the CIA had "confirmed that Iran was shopping in Germany and Switzerland for a facility to enrich uranium using gas centrifuges." And the *Christian Science Monitor* reported Iran was using "front companies" in Europe and other regions to buy such technologies.[50]

Meanwhile, Iran's negotiations with Argentina, Russia, and China for conversion and enrichment technology were all well known to both the United States and the IAEA. Negotiations with governments on matters of high politics that touch on the political interests of the United States seldom remain completely secret, and those negotiations were no exception. In fact, Iran's negotiations with Argentina, Russia, and China on conversion and enrichment were not only reported in the news media but were also the subject of public comment and diplomatic actions by US government officials from 1992 through 1997.

After Iran had negotiated with Argentina in 1987–88 for the purchase of equipment for the conversion of natural uranium into a form that could then be enriched, the US ambassador to the IAEA, Richard T. Kennedy, intervened to head off the supply of that equipment by Argentina. Kennedy was able to get Argentina to cancel the agreement in 1992 only by promising alternative markets for the Argentine company involved in the deal, Investigaciones Aplicadas, as reported by the *Washington Post*.[51]

Iran's efforts to obtain fuel-cycle technology from Russia and China in the 1990s were similarly played out in full view of the world's media. Iran's tentative agreement with Russia in early 1995 to negotiate an agreement for the provision of an enrichment facility was soon revealed by an unsympathetic Russian official, and then was covered by the US news media (see details in chapter 3). And in April 1996, a State Department spokesman said Secretary Warren Christopher might discuss the issue of the Chinese agreement to sell Iran a complete uranium conversion facility with China's foreign minister, Qian Qichen, at an upcoming conference in The Hague.[52] If the Clinton administration was quiet thereafter about the issue, it was only because it was also involved in delicate negotiations with China over

49. Mark Hibbs, "German-U.S. Nerves Frayed over Nuclear Ties to Iran," *Nuclear Fuel*, March 14, 1994, 10; Mark Hibbs, "Sharif University Activity Continues Despite IAEA Visit, Bonn Agency Says," *Nuclear Fuel*, March 28, 1994, 10.

50. Thomas W. Lippman, "Stepped-up Nuclear Effort Renews Alarm about Iran," *Washington Post*, April 17, 1995, A12; Jonathan Landay, "Why US Thinks Iran Is Building Nuclear Weapons," *Christian Science Monitor*, June 1, 1995, 1.

51. Steve Coll, "U.S. Halted Nuclear Bid by Iran," *Washington Post*, November 11, 1992.

52. Bill Gertz, "U.S. Fears Iran's Use of Chinese Know-How," *Washington Times*, April 18, 1996, A7.

the US demand for the cancellation of the deal in return for winning Washington's certification of China as "qualified" for bilateral US-China nuclear cooperation. US policymakers evidently believed it would be easier to get China to cancel the deal by keeping this effort out of the news.[53]

In early 1996, the United States reportedly raised the issue of the scope of Iran's enrichment program with the IAEA. Unnamed "Western sources" revealed to Mark Hibbs, who wrote for specialized nuclear-industry publications, that both the CIA and Department of Energy had obtained intelligence on "an experimental program by Iran to develop and bench-test gas centrifuges for uranium enrichment." Hibbs wrote that US officials shared the information they had with the IAEA, expecting that the IAEA would raise with Iran the allegation that Iran was engaged in a "clandestine pilot program to enrich uranium using gas centrifuges."[54]

Hibbs's sources acknowledged, however, that US intelligence did not know whether Iran's program had "reached the threshold for reporting to the IAEA," which was that uranium had been used in the experiments. He quoted one Western official as saying that the US intelligence "should not be interpreted as evidence that Iran is violating the NPT" or that it had failed to report to the IAEA as required. We now know that at that time, Iran had not yet introduced uranium into a single centrifuge. That would not happen for another four years.[55]

Thus, not only the fact that Iran had a centrifuge enrichment program but many of the details of its origins and much of the information about purchases connected with it were well-known to the IAEA, and US officials had been referring publicly to it several years before the IAEA's November 2003 report made splashy headlines about an "18-year clandestine enrichment program." The IAEA had known for years that Iran had acquired the basic enrichment technology, that Iran had begun testing the centrifuges, and that it had sought technical assistance for a full fuel cycle. It also knew that the United States was tracking in great detail the nuclear-related technology that Iran was purchasing. What the agency did not know was how far the Iranian program had progressed.

The IAEA's public posture in the November 2003 report of declaring that Iran had operated a clandestine enrichment program as though it were a major revelation of a secret was thus more than a little disingenuous. And

53. "Foreign Ministry Holds Regular News Conferences on Nuclear Cooperation with Iran," IRNA (Tehran), January 9, 1996, FBIS Document FTS19960109000041, January 9, 1996; "China Says Deals to Sell Iran Nuclear Reactors Scrapped," Associated Press, January 9, 1996.

54. Mark Hibbs, "IAEA Will Explore New Charges Iran Has Enrichment Program," Nucleonics Week, February 22, 1996, 4.

55. GOV/2003/75, November 11, 2003, annex 1, p. 2.

the agency soon knew, even if it did not already know at the time of the report, that Iran had sound reasons for its secrecy on enrichment activities over the years. In early 2004, shortly after the Iranians had admitted and formally "declared" to the IAEA the nuclear materials and activities that they had not previously reported, Iranian officials explained to the agency why the United States' longstanding campaign of technology denial had left them with no choice but to keep the details of these acquisitions and activities connected with them from the IAEA. In his 2011 memoir, ElBaradei recalled that the Iranians recounted to him the story of how the French and other fuel suppliers had been prevented by the Americans from providing enriched uranium for Bushehr, forcing the AEOI to obtain the capability to enrich uranium in Iran without informing the IAEA. He acknowledged, moreover, that the Iranians had a legitimate complaint. "The Americans did not want to consider the Iranian arguments," he wrote, "despite having themselves been in the driver's seat of the effort to isolate Iran for more than two decades." The United States preferred to view the Iranian secrecy as "proof positive that Tehran intended to produce nuclear weapons," he wrote. "Many representatives of developing countries were, by contrast, more sympathetic to Iran's need to go underground to evade the sanctions."[56]

## The Chinese Dimension

Iran's failure to report to the IAEA a number of nuclear experiments and tests undertaken between 1981 and 2003 has been cited as prima facie evidence of a military intent behind the entire nuclear program. However, so long as Iran believed the IAEA was going to assist the Iranian program, it fully declared its intention to work on both fuel fabrication and uranium conversion— including plans for a uranium conversion pilot plant.[57] Those experiments were then carried out with uranium that had been imported in 1977 and exempted from safeguards at Iran's request in 1978.[58] In 1998, Iran informed the IAEA about those experiments in uranium conversion,

---

56. Mohamed ElBaradei, *Age of Deception: Nuclear Diplomacy in Treacherous Times* (New York: Metropolitan Books, 2011), 119.

57. Mark Hibbs, "U.S. in 1983 Stopped IAEA from Helping Iran Make UF6," *Nuclear Fuel* 28 (August 4, 2003): 12.

58. Iran's safeguards agreement allowed for the exemption of small quantities of uranium from safeguards. See Article 37, "Text of the Agreement between Iran and the Agency for the Application of Safeguards in Connection with the Treaty on Non-Proliferation of Nuclear Weapons," INFCIRC/214, December 13, 1974. That provision was a common feature of all agreements signed by member states in the 1970s and 1980s, before the agency tightened up the safeguards agreements considerably. See the basic IAEA safeguards text in INFCIRC/153, June 1972.

along with experiments using yellowcake concentrate imported from South Africa in 1982.[59]

Iran thus had no problem informing the IAEA about experiments using uranium that had come from South Africa, which was not a significant potential source of nuclear technology. However, when it came to nuclear activities using uranium coming from China, the Iranian attitude was much more secretive. None of those tests and experiments was reported to the IAEA until late 2003, after it had become impossible to deny those activities. The reason for treating the latter set of experiments with such secrecy was that China had become Iran's most important partner in nuclear cooperation but was also subject to heavy political pressure from the United States to end that cooperation.

The pivotal Iranian agreement with China was its 1991 purchase of a total of 1,800 kilograms (almost two tons) of natural uranium. The uranium was purchased in three separate batches: 1,000 kilograms of uranium hexafluoride ($UF_6$), 400 kilograms of uranium tetrafluoride ($UF_4$), and 400 kilograms of uranium dioxide ($UO_2$). Over the 12 years that followed, neither China nor Iran informed the IAEA of the sale. Iran later argued that the .13 kilograms of enriched uranium that could be produced from the 1.8 tons of natural uranium was too small an amount to be covered by the safeguards agreement. The IAEA asserted that the 1-kilogram minimum to which Iran was referring was the amount above which advance notification was required.[60]

The real reason that neither Iran nor China reported the sale to the IAEA, however, was China's need for secrecy in order to avoid retaliation by the United States. Under a 1985 agreement, China had agreed to supply Iran with four small nuclear reactors for teaching and research, as well as fuel for the reactors. It also provided training for Iranian nuclear engineers, including in the design of large plutonium reactors. But the agreement was not made public at the time, because the US-China Nuclear Cooperation Agreement (NCA), initialed in 1984, was to be signed and submitted to the US Congress in July 1985. Despite the fact that Iran was in full compliance with its safeguards agreement with the IAEA, China had good reason to fear that US opponents of the NCA would use any Chinese nuclear cooperation with Iran to argue that China could not be trusted to implement its nonproliferation commitments.[61]

---

59. GOV/2003/75, November 10, 2003, annex 1, p. 2.

60. GOV/2003/40, June 6, 2003, 4.

61. John Garver, *China and Iran: Ancient Partners in a Post-Imperial World* (Seattle: University of Washington Press, 2006), 143–44; Evan S. Madeiros, *Reluctant Restraint: The Evolution of China's Nonproliferation Policies and Practices, 1989–2004* (Singapore: National University of Singapore Press, 2009), 59–60.

From the beginning of the negotiations over the NCA, the Reagan administration had demanded that China put all its nuclear activities and materials under IAEA safeguards, in order to provide assurances against exports that would support a nuclear weapons program. But China had steadfastly resisted any such move. So Ambassador Kennedy resorted to the device of drafting a classified State Department "non-paper" to which Chinese officials "nodded their assent," according to the testimony of Rep. Ed Markey, chairman of a House subcommittee dealing with energy matters, who had been briefed on the issue. Deputy Assistant Secretary of State James Devine confirmed in congressional testimony that the Chinese had assured the United States orally that they would require safeguards on all their nuclear exports.[62] But since it had not signed off on any written commitment, China evidently felt it had maintained leeway to cooperate with Iran without informing the IAEA and incurring US sanctions.

US intelligence did not know the details of the June 1985 Chinese-Iranian nuclear cooperation agreement, but shortly before the signing of the NCA in October 1985, rumors started circulating that China had agreed to sell sensitive nuclear technology to Iran. In February 1986, China explicitly denied any nuclear cooperation with Iran. But Chinese-Iranian nuclear cooperation continued to develop secretly. In 1989, China agreed to supply Iran with a calutron—a rudimentary device for isotope separation that was created in the 1940s—for research purposes. In 1991, it promised to supply a 27-kilowatt reactor for the same purpose.[63] The Chinese Foreign Ministry acknowledged those two agreements publicly for the first time only in November 1991, after the US State Department made both sales public and expressed "concern" about any Chinese nuclear assistance to Iran.[64] US officials reacted to the Chinese announcement by accusing China of having supplied technology that would enable Iran to build a nuclear weapon.[65] But in February 1992, the IAEA inspected the calutron in Esfahan and confirmed that it did not have any enrichment capability or facilities for handling radioactive material and therefore could be used only for production of isotopes for medical purposes, as China and Iran had asserted.[66]

62. Shirley Kan and Mark Holt, "U.S.-China Nuclear Cooperation Agreement," Congressional Research Service, December 13, 2005, 9–11.

63. Associated Press, "U.S.-Chinese Nuclear Agreement Endangered by Peking-Iran Deal," *Houston Chronicle*, October 24, 1985, 6; Garver, *China and Iran*, 144–45.

64. Garver, *China and Iran*, 147.

65. Uli Schmetzer, "James Baker Trip to China—U.S. Weighs Trade with China against Jailed Dissidents," *Chicago Tribune*, November 5, 1991, 11.

66. Michael Z. Wise, "Atomic Team Reports on Iran Probe," *Washington Post*, February 15, 1992, A29–30.

Meanwhile, the most important Chinese-Iranian nuclear agreement of all, China's sale of nearly two tons of natural uranium to Iran, was carried out secretly in 1991. Neither country wanted to announce that sale. Had it been admitted at the time, the sale would have cost Beijing dearly in terms of relations with the United States. The administration of George H. W. Bush was under intense domestic pressures to force China to halt all nuclear cooperation with Iran as the congressional vote approached on most favored nation (MFN) status for China. Several pieces of legislation had already been passed conditioning MFN status on various issues, including nonproliferation. The Bush administration began pressing China to reverse the decision it had announced to provide Iran with the 27-kilowatt research reactor. In March 1992, US Ambassador Stapleton Roy emphasized to the Chinese government the determination of the United States to prevent Iran from acquiring any nuclear technology, on the grounds it could ultimately be used for nuclear weapons development. The pressure continued when Washington learned that China had also agreed to supply Iran with a 20-megawatt reactor. But in October 1992, China canceled the agreement for that reactor, ostensibly for "technical reasons," but almost certainly in response to US pressure.[67]

The lesson for Iran from the experiences of the period from 1985 to 1992 was that it could not report the uranium to the IAEA without jeopardizing its nuclear cooperation with China. From 1990 through 1997, Iran was negotiating with China more or less continuously on the provision of a uranium conversion facility (UCF), which was a primary objective of the Iranian nuclear program at the time. During that period, Iran continued to keep from the IAEA the fact that it was carrying out some small-scale experiments using the uranium it had purchased from China. Had it reported those experiments, it would also have had to disclose the uranium imports from China that were used in them. That would have unleashed new diplomatic pressures from the United States for a termination of all nuclear cooperation with Iran.

Most of the $UF_4$ imported from China under the 1991 purchase agreement was used in a series of experiments between 1995 and 2000 at the Jabr Ibn Hayan lab to convert $UF_6$ into uranium metal, intended for later use in its laser enrichment program.[68] In 1997, China, under heavy US pressure, canceled the UCF purchase agreement. But even after that, Iran still had a powerful incentive to avoid informing the IAEA about the uses of uranium

67. Madeiros, *Reluctant Restraint*, 62–63; Steve Coll, "US Halted Nuclear Bid by Iran; China, Argentina Agreed to Cancel Technology Transfers," *Washington Post*, November 17, 1992.
68. GOV/2003/75, November 10, 2003, annex 1, p. 5.

from China: some of the Chinese uranium was used for testing centrifuges between 1999 and 2002.[69]

The same logic applied as well to Iran's laser enrichment program, which was heavily dependent on imported technology from China and another state that was never identified by the IAEA but was probably Russia.[70] Each of the previously unreported nuclear experiments that Iran finally declared to the IAEA in 2003 involved suppliers of nuclear technology or material, or both, that Iran knew would come under heavy US political-diplomatic pressure if the supplier's role were to be discovered by the United States. Iran's motive for keeping hidden from the IAEA the various experiments and tests using uranium can thus be explained without assuming that these activities were related to a clandestine nuclear weapons program, as the official US narrative asserted.

The United States and its allies had nevertheless exploited Iran's nuclear secrecy effectively to create a pervasive suspicion that Iran was using its civilian nuclear program to hide a covert ambition for nuclear weapons. That climate of suspicion helped ensure the discourse on Iran's nuclear program would lack any real understanding of the political and religious factors that shaped the Islamic Republic's approach to the nuclear issue. It is to that part of the untold story of the nuclear scare that we now turn.

69. Ibid.
70. Ibid., annex 1, 10; Garver, *China and Iran*, 150–51.

# 3

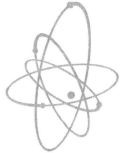

# Iran's Unknown Nuclear Politics

## Iran and Chemical Weapons

Western analysts have systematically denied that Shi'a Islamic jurisprudence has played a significant role in Iran's policy toward nuclear weapons. The Islamic Republic's key institution of Velayat-e Faqih ("guardianship of the jurist"), which gives ultimate power over a range of issues to the supreme leader, has been viewed by critics as a theocratic institution incompatible with democracy. But, as has been clear since the beginning of the 1980–88 Iran-Iraq War, the supreme leader's Islamic jurisprudence has been a decisive barrier to the acquisition and use of weapons of mass destruction by Iran.

A crucial part of the untold story of the Iranian nuclear program is what *didn't* happen in regard to chemical weapons during that war. Iranians suffered the horrors of chemical weapons in a way that no other people have suffered since World War I. The official toll was 20,000 killed, 7,000 of whom died instantly, with at least 100,000 people "severely injured" by the nerve agents sarin and soman as well as the blistering agent mustard gas. Even 20 years after the war's end, 55,000 people were still being treated for their illnesses from chemical weapons.[1] Most of the casualties were apparently from mustard gas, which has the distinctive characteristic that the symptoms of survivors increase in severity gradually over time, so that the victims die only after suffering agony that can last decades. In 2002, one such victim, former Iranian soldier Morteza

---

1. Scott Peterson, *Let the Swords Encircle Me* (New York: Simon and Schuster, 2010), 63; Farnaz Fassihi, "In Iran, Grim Reminders of Saddam's Arsenal," *Newark Star-Ledger* (Newark, NJ), October 27, 2002.

Aminpour, was quoted as saying, "I sometimes wish I was killed with a bullet."[2]

Yet Iran never responded to Saddam's use of chemical weapons with its own campaign of chemical warfare against Iraqi forces. American officials and news media should have been asking why that was the case and what the implications were for the nuclear issue. That line of inquiry would have led to a re-evaluation of the role of fatwas against weapons of mass destruction in Islamic Iran.

A fatwa is a judgment on Islamic law issued by a qualified Islamic scholar. It is not a formal legal document and does not have to take published form, but when it is issued by the guardian jurist of the Islamic Republic of Iran, it has a particularly direct and powerful impact on policy. That impact was most dramatically demonstrated during the Iran-Iraq War, when a fatwa by the founding guardian jurist of the Islamic regime, Ayatollah Ruhollah Khomeini, against the possession or use of chemical weapons prevented Iran from deploying or using such weapons for the entire eight years of war.

That episode of the missing Iranian chemical weapons should have profoundly affected the debate on the subject of the Islamic Republic's attitudes toward weapons of mass destruction, including nuclear weapons. Unfortunately, the episode has been muddied by the general belief in the United States that Iran and Iraq were both guilty of using chemical weapons in the worst chemical attack of the war, against the Iraqi-Kurdish city of Halabja in March 1988. That attack killed at least 5,000 people and had serious long-term effects on 7,000, making it the largest chemical weapon attack against civilians in modern history.

The main cause of the confusion is a classified US Defense Intelligence Agency (DIA) report circulated within the intelligence community at the time that blamed Iran and Iraq equally for the attacks on Halabja. The primary evidence cited by the DIA was that Iran had charged that Iraq had used hydrogen cyanide, which US intelligence knew Iraq did not have in its arsenal. "We are sure that Iran uses cyanide," an author of the study told Patrick Tyler of the *Washington Post*. "That's a piece of evidence that condemns them."[3]

The DIA officials also collected photographic evidence of that alleged cyanide in the form of photographs showing bluish discoloration of the skin and fingertips of Halabja victims. But in fact, such discoloration is not only an indicator of cyanide poisoning; it is also consistent with nerve gas

2. Fassihi, "In Iran, Grim Reminders."

3. Knut Royce, "Pattern of Exaggeration on Iraq Seen by Sources," *Newsday*, October 10, 1988; Patrick Tyler, "Both Iraq and Iran Gassed Kurds in War, U.S. Analysis Finds," *Washington Post*, May 3, 1990, A37.

poisoning.[4] Nevertheless, some CIA analysts, including Kenneth Pollack, assumed that both sides had used chemical weapons in Halabja, based on the evidence that they understood to show signs of death from cyanide poisoning and the fact that Iraq was not known to have hydrogen cyanide gas at the time. But Pollack acknowledged that no other evidence of Iranian chemical use during the war had ever turned up and that the CIA analysts who had previously advanced that conclusion had finally discarded it.[5]

For his part, Patrick Tyler later learned that the DIA officers who had written the report claiming Iranian use of hydrogen cyanide had a very direct personal interest in the issue. It turned out that they had been engaged in a Defense Department program in 1987–88 to provide the Iraqi high command with detailed plans for an Iraqi air offensive against targets in the Iranian rear areas, including Tehran and other cities. In an operation called Druid Lancer, Col. Pat Lang and his deputy, Lt. Col. Rick Francona, gave the Iraqis lists of Iranian targets to bomb, along with detailed satellite photographs. Then they shuttled between Washington and Baghdad with bomb-damage assessments to help the Iraqis plan each new set of strikes. They knew, moreover, that Saddam's air force was adding chemical weapons to the ordnance being dropped on the targets they had provided.[6]

So the authors of the DIA report on Halabja had a personal and institutional interest in deflecting as much of the blame for the chemical warfare atrocities away from Iraq to Iran as they could. In an interview for this book, Tyler said neither the DIA account of the gassing in Halabja nor the suggestion that the Iranians had used chemical weapons on other occasions had any credibility. "We know now that it was being trafficked by people who had a conflict of interest," he said.[7]

Tyler's conclusion was confirmed in A Poisonous Affair, Joost R. Hiltermann's 2007 book about the Halabja chemical attack. Hiltermann concluded on the basis of many interviews with Iraqi officials and others familiar with the chemical attacks during the war that not only had Iran not used chemical weapons against the population of Halabja, but also that no real evidence had ever surfaced that Iran had used chemical weapons

4.   Joost R. Hiltermann, A Poisonous Affair: America, Iraq and the Gassing of Halabja (Cambridge, UK: Cambridge University Press, 2007), 193–200.

5.   Personal communication to the author from Kenneth Pollack, May 30, 2013. In his book on Iran and the nuclear issue, however, Pollack makes no mention of the fact that CIA analysts had ultimately concluded that Iran had not used chemical weapons during the war and instead asserts that Khomeini had reversed his initial fatwa against chemical weapons and had ordered the development of such weapons for use against Saddam Hussein. Kenneth Pollack, Unthinkable: Iran, the Bomb and American Strategy (New York: Simon and Schuster, 2013), 59.

6.   Patrick Tyler, A World of Trouble (New York: Farrar, Straus and Giroux), 336–38.

7.   Author's interview with Patrick Tyler, May 17, 2013.

during the entire war. He also interviewed Lang, who confirmed that he had "insisted" on Iran's use of chemical weapons on Halabja after the atrocity had been carried out, and was continuing to argue that case in 2000.[8]

The absence of any credible evidence of Iranian retaliation in response to the systematic chemical war waged against its population by the Iraqi armed forces thus appears to be a singular anomaly in the annals of modern warfare. Hiltermann, who explicitly embraced in his book the official US view that Iran had long been pursuing a covert nuclear weapons program, sought to explain the chemical weapons anomaly by suggesting that the shah's research programs aimed at developing chemical weapons had not gotten very far when the regime was overthrown, and that the Islamic Republic "had to scramble to start its own program." He argued that Iran "gained the capability to field chemical weapons toward war's end" but offered no reason for Iran's failure to master the relatively simple technology of chemical weapons for as long as six years and to use that capability before the war ended.[9]

The absence of any Iranian chemical weapons response to the systematic Iraqi chemical onslaught during the war cannot be explained, however, by the absence of an Iranian technical capability to produce chemical weapons. Iran's chemical sector was quite advanced and perfectly capable of producing the same range of chemical weapons that Iraq was using in the war. "Everybody knows that during the war, Iran's chemical industry was much more advanced than Iraq's," Ali Asghar Soltanieh, Iran's ambassador to the IAEA, observed in a 2009 interview.[10] The advanced status of Iran's chemical sector during that period is documented in a DIA study.[11]

Hiltermann sought to bolster his argument by asserting, "Iran itself admitted in the 1990s that it had developed chemical weapons." However, in the statement in question, which was delivered to the Conference of States Parties to the Chemical Weapons Convention (CWC) in 1998, Ambassador Mohammad R. Alborzi recalled a decision made at the height of Iraq's chemical war to "develop a chemical weapons *capability*." The distinction between WMD capability and actual WMD is one to which the US intelligence community had referred in its estimates on the issues of Iranian nuclear and alleged chemical weapons programs since the early

---

8.   Hiltermann, *Poisonous Affair*, 157–82, 203–4.

9.   Ibid., 231–32.

10.   Author's interview with Ali Asghar Soltanieh, Vienna, September 7, 2009.

11.   Deborah L. Miller, Ben A. Farmer, and Sharon H. Scholl, *Industrial Chemical Capabilities in Selected Middle East Countries: A Defense S & T Study*, U.S. Defense Intelligence Agency and U.S. Army Intelligence Agency, DST-1820S-363-91-SI, September 3, 1991. Cited in J. P. Perry Robinson, "Dual Technology and Perceptions of Iranian Chemical and Biological Weapons," Harvard Sussex Program, July 26, 2005, 5.

1990s. Alborzi noted that after the ceasefire of August 1988, that decision had been reversed and "the process was terminated."[12] In 2003, Iran's delegate to the CWC confirmed that Iran had indeed "dismantled the facilities" under the supervision of the CWC secretariat.[13]

The real reason for Iran's failure to use chemical weapons was not the inability to formulate the necessary mix of chemicals but the fact that Ayatollah Khomeini had forbidden it on the grounds of Islamic jurisprudence. After the Iraqi forces began using chemical weapons against Iranian troops, Iranian military officials raised the issue of retaliating against Iraqi forces with chemical weapons, but Khomeini refused to allow it on the ground that it was forbidden by Islam, according to Seyed Hossein Mousavian, who was then a senior official in the Foreign Ministry and close to Rafsanjani, who was named commander of Iranian armed forces in mid-1988.[14] Khomeini's fatwa against chemical weapons also reflected the consensus of Shi'a clerical authorities in the holy city of Qom during the war that such weapons were proscribed by Islam, according to a senior Shi'a cleric interviewed by an American journalist in 2003.[15]

Khomeini's ruling created an obvious tension between Iran's adherence to Islamic principles and the need to deter further chemical and city attacks by Iraq. The chemical attacks were demoralizing to Iran's troops, as well as to the general population, especially in combination with the Iraqi attacks on cities. Iran sent dozens of victims of Iraqi chemical attacks to various European countries for treatment and pressed the United Nations to investigate Iraq's chemical warfare and condemn Iraq's violation of the laws of war. But the United States, Britain, and France remained silent, and the UN Security Council never condemned Iraq by name as violating the Geneva Protocol against the use of chemical weapons.[16]

12. Statement by Director General of the Iranian Foreign Ministry Ambassador Mohammad R. Alborzi to the 3rd Session of the Conference of States Parties to the Chemical Weapons Convention, November 17, 1998, *CWC Conventions Bulletin* 42 (December 1998): 43.

13. Statement by Iranian delegation to the First Review Conference of the Chemical Weapons Convention, April 28, 2003.

14. Seyed Hossein Mousavian, "Globalising Iran's Fatwa against Nuclear Weapons," *Survival* 55, no. 2 (April–May 2013): 148. See also Dilip Hiro, *The Longest War: the Iran-Iraq Military Conflict* (New York: Routledge, 1991), 201–2. For contemporary reporting of the Khomeini fatwa, see Safa Haeri, "Iran and Libya in Chemical Arms for Missile Deal," *Independent* (London), December 30, 1987; "Iran Threatens to Use Chemical Weapons against Iraq," Xinhua General Overseas News Service, May 1, 1988.

15. Robert Collier, "Nuclear Weapons Unholy, Iran Says/Islam Forbids Use, Clerics Proclaim," *San Francisco Chronicle*, October 31, 2003.

16. Javed Ali, "Chemical Weapons and the Iran-Iraq War: A Case Study in Non-Compliance," *Non-Proliferation Review* (Spring 2001): 48, 51–52.

The Iranians' desire for some degree of deterrence against Iraq's use of chemical weapons explains why no Iranian official ever mentioned Khomeini's fatwa explicitly during the war. Instead, on numerous occasions, high-ranking Iranian officials issued warnings that Iran's restraint in regard to chemical weapons would not continue indefinitely, and that Iran would be forced to act unless action was taken soon to stop Iraq's chemical attacks. But the statements always fell short of a straightforward threat to carry out chemical attacks if Iraq did not halt its chemical warfare.

In the earliest of those statements in March 1984, Rafsanjani, then speaker of the Majlis, said during Friday prayers at Tehran University, "At present we are committed not to resort to chemical attacks. However, I don't know how long this will remain so. . . . Can one be patient forever if they continue this course of action?"[17] Iran's ambassador to the United Nations elaborated Iran's stance further. "We are capable of manufacturing chemical weapons if the Iraqis repeat the crime, [and] we may consider using them," he declared in 1984. "But we think that to resort to retaliation can only be justified when all other means of preventing Iraq are exhausted and still Iraq repeats its crime."[18]

In early 1986, Foreign Minister Ali Akbar Velayati warned UN secretary general Javier Perez de Cuellar that Iran was "left with no recourse but to resort to a new course of action" to force a halt to the chemical attacks, unless international action was taken within days. And in August 1986, Rafsanjani, asked in an interview why Iran hadn't retaliated with chemical weapons, said, "In those early days, we took certain measures, and we can retaliate in kind."[19]

In late 1987, Iraq began an offensive to bomb Iranian cities with planes and missiles, which was reported to have caused nearly half the population of Tehran to flee the capital.[20] Iranian officials again began warning that their country had the capability to retaliate with the same chemical weapons used by Iraq. But the statements avoided claiming that Iran had actually manufactured chemical weapons. In December 1987, Prime Minister Mir Hossein Mousavi was quoted as saying, "The Islamic Republic is capable of manufacturing chemical weapons and possesses the technology." In

17. Tehran Radio, March 23, 1984, *BBC Summary of World Broadcasts,* March 24, 1984, pt. 4, A1.

18. Quoted in Michael Eisenstadt, *The Deterrence Series: Chemical and Biological Weapons: Deterrence Case Study no. 4: Iran* (Alexandria, VA: Chemical and Biological Arms Control Institute, 1998), 9.

19. Tehran Radio, February 13, 1986, *BBC Summary of World Broadcasts,* February 14, 1986, pt. 4, A1; "Rafsanjani's Interview and Friday Sermon Comments on War," *BBC Summary of World Broadcasts,* September 1, 1986, pt. 4, A1.

20. Youssef M. Ibrahim, "Iran Reports New Gas Raids; And Says Cities May Be Hit Next," *New York Times,* April 2, 1988, A1.

a separate statement, Mousavi said that a "Special Section" had been set up for "offensive chemical weapons." But he also suggested that Iran's freedom to manufacture the weapons might be limited by religious constraints. "We will produce them only when Islam allows us and when we are compelled to do so," he said.[21]

In May 1988, Deputy Prime Minister Ali Reza Moayyeri said on a television program, "Of course we have had the capacity to produce chemical weapons and to use them for years, but we have not done so. We will endeavor to maintain our restraint in this regard, but restraint and patience have a time limit."[22]

Iranian strategists evidently hoped that their statements suggesting the possibility of using chemical weapons might have some effect on Iraq through its American patrons. And in fact, the State Department did comment publicly that Iran was "developing a chemical weapons capability."[23] But the United States never backed away from its covert direct intelligence assistance to the Iraqi air offensive.

The fact that Iran was constrained by Khomeini's interpretation of Islamic law during the duration of the war sheds light on the role of Khomeini's successor as supreme leader, Ali Khamenei, in declaring nuclear weapons also forbidden by Islam. The Iran-Iraq War episode shows that the Islamic legal judgment of the guardian jurist had the power to prevent Iran from using or possessing chemical weapons, even despite the strong desire of Iranian military leaders to use those weapons. Those were stringent circumstances for a fatwa to overcome, but the evidence indicates that Khomeini's fatwa was nevertheless effective in spite of them.

## Khamenei's Nuclear Fatwa

The role of the fatwa by Supreme Leader Ali Khamenei against nuclear weapons is more complicated than Khomeini's fatwa against chemical weapons during the war with Iraq. The leaders of the Islamic revolution against the shah were in general agreement that nuclear weapons were inconsistent with Islam. But they were also inclined against them on political grounds unrelated to Islamic jurisprudence.

Khomeini's aversion to nuclear weapons was based in large part on the association of such weapons with both superpowers, which Khomeini considered to be equally enemies of the Iranian revolution. Ali Asghar

---

21. "Iran Says It Has Chemical Weapons," *San Francisco Chronicle*, December 28, 1987; Associated Press, "Iran Denies It's Building Chemical Weapons," *Toronto Star*, December 31, 1987.

22. *BBC Summary of World Broadcasts*, May 9, 1988, pt. 4, A1.

23. "US Fears Iran May Use Chemical Arms," *New York Times*, April 25, 1985, A3.

Soltanieh, who was in the AEOI even before the Islamic revolution, recalled in an interview that Khomeini, "speaking to masses of people on different occasions, openly deplored the nuclear weapons of the United States and the Soviet Union and called for uprising against them."[24]

Khomeini went along with the partial reconstitution of the shah's nuclear program after the 1979 Islamic revolution, but one of his most caustic commentaries on nuclear weapons came in November 1982—after the Iranian nuclear program had restarted. Khomeini declared in a speech that the two superpowers were "busy with plans to make certain weapons which are dangerous to the future of humanity." If the two superpowers went to war, he warned, "they will destroy the world."[25]

Khomeini did not issue a fatwa against nuclear weapons, however, presumably because the political leadership already had such a clear aversion to nuclear weapons on more general policy grounds that there was no need for a fatwa. Khamenei made speeches opposing nuclear weapons in 1992 and 1997.[26] And in 1993, then president Rafsanjani offered the public articulation of a strategic rationale for a policy of foregoing nuclear weapons in an unprecedented interview that he gave to *Time* magazine. Rafsanjani said it would be "irrational" for Iran to use its limited resources to develop nuclear weapons. He said nuclear weapons could never be used in the region. And he suggested that they would not help redress Iran's imbalance of power with the United States. A Third World country like Iran that might try to acquire such weapons, he argued, "could never complete with the major powers."[27]

Those two points—the inutility of nuclear weapons, which implied their irrelevance to regional politics, and the fact that other powers would still have many times more such weapons—represented the core elements of a "realist" strategic argument against possession of nuclear weapons that would later be articulated in greater depth, especially by officials in the Iranian foreign ministry. Mohammad Javad Zarif was deputy foreign minister for 10 years and UN ambassador from 2002 to 2007, and in August 2013 he was appointed foreign minister. In 2007, he noted in an essay that nuclear weapons had played no role in

---

24. Author's interview with Ali Asghar Soltanieh, Vienna, September 6, 2009.

25. Ruhollah Khomeini, "Superpowers, the Root of World Problems," speech on November 4, 1982, tr. by Steven Ditto, in "'Go Learn About Atoms': Iranian Religious Discourse on Nuclear Weapons, 1962–Present," June 2013, 14, http://selfscholar.files. wordpress.com/2013/03/irandiscourse5.pdf. Ditto used the name "Self-Scholar" on the paper and on his blog.

26. Ditto, "'Go Learn About Atoms,'" 25n4.

27. James R. Grimes and Karsten Prager, "Iran: Yes to Revolution and to Moderation," *Time*, May 23, 1993: 46–49.

the various conflicts in the Middle East since the end of the Cold War. He also wrote that Iranian policymakers believed that having nuclear weapons would not increase Iran's regional influence but, rather, would have the opposite effect, making it more difficult to gain the confidence of neighboring states. And Iran could not compete with the nuclear arsenals of its adversaries, he wrote. Indeed, such a policy would merely make the country more vulnerable.[28]

Despite the evidence of a consistent posture by Khomeini, Khamenei, and Rafsanjani of opposing nuclear weapons, purveyors of the official line on Iranian intentions have cited statements attributed to Khamenei that appear to reflect an Iranian policy under Khomeini of seeking nuclear weapons. The first such statement, published in the *Washington Post* in April 1987, was from a speech by then president Khamenei to an audience of AEOI officials two months earlier, in which he was quoted as saying:

> Regarding atomic energy, we need it now. . . . Our nation has always been threatened from outside. The least we can do to face this danger is to let our enemies know that we can defend ourselves. Therefore, every step you take here is in defence of your country and your revolution. With this in mind you should work hard and at great speed.[29]

The quoted statement makes it appear that Khamenei clearly signaled to AEOI employees that Iran's civilian nuclear program was simply a cover to obtain a nuclear weapon. But the text of the key section of the speech in question is available in the original Farsi, and it shows that Khamenei was not linking the nuclear program to military defense against foreign threat, but arguing that the program was necessary on both economic grounds and as a way of stimulating Iran's science and technology sectors. Khamenei was very clear in the speech about his primary concern. "We feel that atomic energy is needed for the growth and development of science in our country," he said. And he elaborated:

> Our need for nuclear energy is important because our nation is trying to embark on the path to modern industries and such a move requires ceaseless effort of our brothers and experts, and a

---

28. Mohammad Javad Zarif, "Tackling the U.S.-Iran Crisis: The Need for a Paradigm Shift," *Columbia Journal of International Affairs* (Spring–Summer 2007, no. 2): 76–77.

29. David Segal, "Atomic Ayatollahs: Just What the Mideast Needs—an Iranian Bomb," *Washington Post*, April 12, 1987, D1. Another article by the same author that included the same alleged Khamenei quote is "Iran Speeds Up Nuclear Bomb Development," in *Journal of Defense and Diplomacy* 6, no. 6 (1988), 55.

large-scale investment in all areas. Your scientific work is like a very effective weapon, which is of the utmost importance for the political, scientific, and technological future of this nation. One of the important duties of every nation is to preserve its precious resources and to make the most of them.[30]

Those remarks were consistent with Khamenei's frequent references in speeches to the high priority he placed on overcoming Iran's scientific retardation.[31] The quote that has been viewed as evidence of a nuclear weapons program, on the other hand, doesn't sound like Khamenei's rhetoric and appears to contradict the points he made so forcefully about the rationale for the nuclear program. The reason for that dissonance is clear from the fact that the quote came not from an official or neutral source but from the newsletter of the Tudeh Communist Party of Iran published in Stockholm two months after the Khamenei speech.[32] The Tudeh Party, which had long been closely linked to the Soviet Union, had supported the Islamic Republic, but the regime suppressed and outlawed the party in 1983 after a Soviet diplomat revealed the party's role in a Soviet plan to penetrate the regime's institutions, in part through the Tudeh.[33] The Tudeh Party had an obvious motive for misrepresenting Khamenei's words on the nuclear program.[34]

Further giving away its political purpose, the article also included an account of an alleged incident in May 1979 in which an Iranian official under the shah, Fereidun Fesharaki, was summoned by a senior figure in the regime, Ayatollah Mohammad Hosseini Beheshti, and agreed under pressure to "assemble a nuclear weapons team for the regime" before fleeing to the United States. Fesharaki, who was an economist specializing in oil and knew nothing about nuclear power, much less nuclear weapons, is now a senior fellow at the East-West Center, a congressionally founded research institute in Honolulu. He said the author, David Segal, did contact him, but that Segal "made up what he wrote" and that at Fesharaki's

---

30. Ali Khamenei, speech to the Atomic Energy Organization of Iran, February 18, 1987, original Farsi language text at http://islamicdoc.org/Multimedia/fbook/1879/index.htm. English translation in Ditto, "'Go Learn About Atoms,'" 11.

31. Karim Sadjadpour, *Reading Khamenei: The World View of Iran's Most Powerful Leaders* (Washington, DC: Carnegie Endowment for International Peace, 2008), 22.

32. Segal, "Atomic Ayatollahs," D1.

33. Shireen T. Hunter, *Iran and the World: Continuity in a Revolutionary Decade* (Bloomington: Indiana University Press, 1990), 87.

34. As one analyst observed, the author of the *Post* article "relied on a usually unreliable source." Ahmed Hashim, "Iran's Military Intentions," in *Iran's Strategic Intentions and Capabilities,* Patrick Clawson, ed., National Defense University, McNair Papers, no. 29, April 1994, 203.

insistence, the *Washington Post* published a small notice that he denied the story.[35]

After the deliberately engineered crisis over Iran's nuclear program went into high gear, however, the phony Khamenei quote took on a new life as a piece of primary evidence showing Iran's intention to acquire nuclear weapons.[36]

Another statement attributed to Khamenei that has been used to buttress the notion of a long-term Iranian plan for nuclear weapons is a summary of a purported "intelligence report" by an unnamed intelligence service. The report, said to be from an internal draft IAEA document, was published in 2012 by the Institute for Science and International Security (ISIS). The summary, in its entirety, said:

> The Agency [IAEA] was informed that in April 1984 the then President of Iran, H.E. Ayatollah Khamenei declared, during a meeting of top-echelon political and security officials at the Presidential Palace in Tehran, that the spiritual leader Imam Khomeini had decided to reactivate the nuclear programme. According to Ayatollah Khamenei this was the only way to secure the very essence of the Islamic Revolution from the schemes of its enemies, especially the United States and Israel, and to prepare it for the emergence of Imam Mehdi. Ayatollah Khamenei further declared during the meeting, that a nuclear arsenal would serve Iran as a deterrent in the hands of God's soldiers.[37]

But that story should have been identified immediately as false. Khamenei could not possibly have declared to high officials of Iran in April 1984 that Khomeini had decided to reactivate the nuclear program, because the decision to reactivate the program had been made three years earlier, as recounted in chapter 1. And the detail about using nuclear weapons to "prepare . . . for the emergence of the Imam Mehdi" is an equally clear indication that the story was a fabrication. Ayatollah Khomeini was well known to have strongly opposed as dangerous nonsense the idea advocated by some fundamentalist Shi'a that they should take actions to accelerate the

35. Personal communication to the author from Fereidun Fesharaki, October 16, 2013.

36. See Albright, *Peddling Peril*, 71; Pollack, *Unthinkable*, 59; David Patrikarakos, *Nuclear Iran: The Birth of an Atomic State* (London and New York: I. B. Taurus, 2012), 121.

37. "Internal IAEA Information Links the Supreme Leader to 1984 Decision to Seek a Nuclear Arsenal," ISIS Reports, Institute for Science and International Security, April 20, 2012. The story was dropped from the compendium of intelligence collected by the IAEA on "possible military dimensions" of the Iranian nuclear program before it was published as an annex to the November 2011 IAEA report.

return of the Muslim messiah, the Mehdi.[38] Despite those obvious indicators of fraud, however, mainstream news media and centrist think tanks alike accepted that fraudulent report as evidence of the Islamic Republic having long harbored the intent to acquire nuclear weapons.[39]

It was not until early 2003, in the wake of the intensified IAEA inquiry into the background and evolution of Iran's nuclear program, that Khomeini's successor as supreme leader, Ayatollah Khamenei, began to couch his anti-nuclear weapons stance in terms of Islamic principles. In a March 2003 speech at the Imam Reza Shrine in Mashad, he said, "We are not interested in an atomic bomb. We are opposed to chemical weapons.... These things are against our principles."[40] By linking nuclear weapons with chemical weapons, an issue that was decided purely on the basis of Islamic jurisprudence, Khamenei was implicitly invoking that same basis for Iran's rejection of nuclear weapons. In August 2003, in a speech before President Mohammad Khatami and cabinet members, Khamenei made this same association between the principles on which he was opposed to nuclear weapons and those on which he was opposed to other WMDs. He declared, "By principle and fundamentals we are against weapons of mass destruction, just like we have considered biological and chemical weapons as prohibited weapons even at the time of the Imposed War."[41]

Khamenei's invocation of Islamic jurisprudence for the first time on nuclear weapons may have reflected the desire to give new emphasis to the anti-nuclear policy he had embraced consistently in the past. But there was also an internal political reason for the fatwa that appears to have been more important: the need to discourage and finally terminate the advocacy of research on nuclear weapons by some elements in the regime. And although some of those advocating the option argued that it meant only having the ability to produce enriched uranium for Iran's nuclear reactors, others said it should include having "all the necessary elements and capabilities for producing weapons."[42]

38. Yossi Melman and Meir Javadanfar, *The Nuclear Sphinx of Tehran* (New York: Carroll and Graf, 2007), 45; Babak Sarfaraz, "The Hidden Imam and His Cult," Tehran Bureau, July 25, 2010.

39. See James Risen, "Seeking Nuclear Insight in Fog of the Ayatollah's Utterances," *New York Times*, April 13, 2012; Joby Warrick, "Iran's Supreme Leader Embraced Concept of Nuclear Arms, Archival Document Suggests," *Washington Post*, April 20, 2012; Pollack, *Unthinkable*, 59.

40. Text of Khamenei speech, March 21, 2003, "Speeches and Messages 2003/1," Imam Khamenei website, http://islam-pure.de/imam/speeches/speech2003.htm.

41. Quoted in Bill Samii, "Dr. Strangelove in Iran," *Iran Report*, Radio Free Europe/Radio Liberty, November 23, 2004, vol. 7, no. 41.

42. Nasser Hadian, "Iran's Nuclear Program: Context and Debates," in Geoffrey Kemp, ed., *Iran's Bomb: American and Iranian Perspectives* (Washington, DC: Nixon Center, 2004), 61–62.

The latter argument was apparently coming from military research centers, especially those affiliated with the Islamic Revolutionary Guard Corps (IRGC), which was playing a key role in development of the Iranian ballistic missile program. Beginning in the late 1990s, some of those individuals and institutions initiated research projects related to nuclear weapons without the approval of either the Supreme National Security Council (SNSC)—the interagency group that coordinated policy on national security issues—or Khamenei. Although Khamenei and the secretary of the SNSC, Hassan Rouhani, were undoubtedly aware that some research was going on, François Nicoullaud, the French ambassador at the time, had the impression that they were not aware of the scope and the details of the research.[43]

In October 2003, Rouhani was named first coordinator for nuclear policy in Iran. He immediately moved to define Iran's anti-nuclear weapons policy more precisely and to tighten control over those entities that had gone ahead with projects related to nuclear weapons. It was all part of his effort to avert a crisis with the United States and Europe over Iran's nuclear program. It began with the new policy of full cooperation with the IAEA that was communicated to the agency on October 16, 2003. On October 21, Rouhani reached a preliminary agreement with the foreign ministers of the United Kingdom, France, and Germany in which Iran said it had decided on a voluntary suspension of enrichment and acceptance of the Additional Protocol, the IAEA safeguards agreement giving the agency much more intrusive powers of inspection.[44]

The next day, Khamenei gave a speech in which he said, "The Islamic Republic of Iran, based on its fundamental religious and legal beliefs, would never resort to the use of weapons of mass destruction. In contrast to the propaganda of our enemies, fundamentally we are against any production of weapons of mass destruction in any form." Three days later, Rouhani told students at Shahrood Industrial University that Khamenei considered nuclear weapons religiously illegal.[45]

---

43. Personal communication to the author by Ambassador François Nicoullaud, July 28, 2013.

44. "Statement by the Iranian Government and Visiting EU Foreign Ministers," October 21, 2003, http://www.iaea.org/newscenter/focus/iaeairan/statement_iran21102003.shtml.

45. Samii, "Dr. Strangelove in Iran." Robert Collier of the *San Francisco Chronicle*, who was in Iran during the week after Khamenei's fatwa, found that it reflected the views of the clerical elite of Iran. Grand Ayatollah Yusef Saanei, one of the highest-ranking clerical authorities in Qom, told Collier that the clerics had reached a "complete consensus" that weapons of mass destruction were prohibited by Islam, and had expressed that view for "many years." In Collier, "Nuclear Weapons Unholy."

The purpose of drawing attention to the first fatwa against nuclear weapons was not to impress foreign governments but to enforce the other key nuclear decision made at the same time. A high-ranking Iranian official told French ambassador François Nicoullaud that Rouhani had sent a circular to all Iranian departments and agencies, civilian and military, directing them to report in detail any past or present nuclear activities. In July 2013, Nicoullaud described the circular as further ordering any unauthorized projects to be terminated. A few weeks later, an associate of Rouhani's told Nicoullaud that Rouhani's team was having difficulty getting researchers to give up their pet projects.[46]

Khamenei's allies understood that his October 22 statement referring to the un-Islamic nature of nuclear weapons was linked to Rouhani's crackdown on the unauthorized weapons-related research projects that various researchers had initiated. Hossein Shariatmadari, the editor of the conservative newspaper *Kayhan* and an adviser to Khamenei, alluded in an interview to tensions between the Rouhani team, backed by Khamenei, and those researchers who were not responding to or were resisting the Rouhani circular. Shariatmadari suggested that some researchers were being stigmatized for working "clandestinely"—and that their projects were being characterized as being just as un-Islamic as actual nuclear weapons. Khamenei was forcing those working on such projects to "admit that it is forbidden under Islam," Shariatmadari said.[47] Four years later, a US intelligence official said that at least one senior Iranian military officer and perhaps others as well had expressed dismay in 2007 that some unidentified nuclear weapons-related work had been shut down in 2003.[48]

Khamenei thus introduced his anti-nuclear fatwa in 2003 to enforce the injunction on any work on nuclear weapons in order to put an end to arguments and activities that threatened Iran's stance against nuclear weapons. Khamenei reintroduced it for a different purpose, however, in a sermon after Friday prayers on November 5, 2004. Khamenei said, "No sir, we are not seeking to have nuclear weapons," and added that "manufacture, possess or use them, that all poses a problem. I have expressed my religious convictions about this, and everyone knows it."[49] Khamenei's reiteration

---

46. François Nicoullaud, "Rouhani and the Iranian Bomb," *New York Times*, July 26, 2013.

47. Collier, "Nuclear Weapons Unholy."

48. Greg Miller, "New Data Set Off a Series of Recalculations by the U.S. Intelligence Community," *Los Angeles Times*, December 5, 2007; Dafna Linzer, "Diving Deep, Unearthing a Surprise," *Washington Post*, December 8, 2007.

49. Agence France-Presse, "Khamenei Denies Iran Seeking Nuclear Weapons, Hits Out at Bush," November 5, 2004, http://www.spacewar.com/2004/041105162221.qhnu5b84.html.

of the fatwa came at a particularly sensitive moment in Iran's negotiations with Britain, France, and Germany on a possible longer-term agreement on the nuclear issue and broader relations. On that same day, an Iranian envoy was meeting with the Europeans in Paris for a negotiating session that would last 23 hours.[50]

When Rouhani negotiated with the British, French, and German foreign ministers in December, a key issue in the discussion of a longer-term agreement was what "commitments" Iran would make to foreswear nuclear weapons. Rouhani recalled in a 2012 interview, "I told the three European ministers that they should know about two explicit guarantees from our side, one of which is the fatwa of the Supreme Leader." Rouhani recalled describing the fatwa as "more important to us than the NPT" or "any other law."[51]

For years, Western media and anti-Iran interests simply ignored Khamenei's fatwa prohibiting nuclear weapons. But speaking in Istanbul in April 2012, Secretary of State Hillary Clinton appeared to take seriously the reports she had received from Turkey's prime minister and foreign minister about Iran's religious prohibition on nuclear weapons. She added, "We, of course, would welcome that. Yet, I think it's important that it be operationalized."[52] Immediately a chorus of Israeli and US right-wing commentators derided the idea of a Khamenei fatwa against nuclear weapons.[53] Many US news media questioned the significance, if not the existence, of the fatwa. The *New York Times* published a news analysis suggesting that Khamenei's statements were "contradictory" and subject to "wildly different interpretation"—but provided no evidence of such confusion except the clearly fraudulent intelligence report about an alleged 1984 meeting that the ISIS had published. The *Washington Post* reported the same phony intelligence in dismissing the fatwa. National Public Radio's Mike Schuster reported that no written evidence of such a fatwa existed, and referred to "concepts in Shiite Islam—lying to protect the life of Muslims or expediency to guard the interests of the state."[54] That was a reference to the argument that the Islamic concept of *taqiyya* allows Muslims in general and Shi'a in particular to lie to protect the interests of Islam against enemies. In

50. Mousavian, *Iranian Nuclear Crisis*, 148.

51. Interview with Hassan Rouhani by *Mehr Nameh* magazine, tr. by Muhammad Sahimi, Tehran Bureau, May 12, 2012.

52. Remarks to the news media by Secretary of State Hillary Rodham Clinton, Istanbul, Turkey, April 1, 2012, at http://www.state.gov/secretary/rm/2012/04/187254.htm.

53. A Google search on Clinton and the Khamenei fatwa produces page after page of attacks on the idea that there was ever a fatwa by Khamenei against nuclear weapons.

54. James Risen, "Seeking Nuclear Insight in the Fog of Ayatollah's Utterances," *New York Times*, April 13, 2012; Warrick, "Iran's Supreme Leader Embraced Concept"; Mike Schuster, "Iran's Nuclear Fatwa: A Policy or a Ploy?" National Public Radio, June 13, 2012.

fact, the doctrine of *taqiyya* allowed Shi'a minorities in Sunni Muslim societies to say they were Sunnis in order to save their lives or property. It had long been a propaganda theme used by the Israelis and their supporters to charge Iran with lying, but it had been discredited by scholars of Islam.[55]

Iranian-British historian Ali Ansari cast doubt on the significance of the fatwa, suggesting that Khamenei had not followed established procedures for such a fatwa and claiming (*contra* the on-the-ground reporting from Robert Collier) that there was essentially no support for such a position from clerics at Qom.[56] Ansari also argued that fatwas could be easily changed and therefore do not represent a reliable indicator of long-term policy.[57] But Sasan Aghlani, a scholar working on a doctoral dissertation on how the views of Iran's *ulama* (Islamic scholars) have contributed to Iran's policy on nuclear weapons, said the form of the fatwa is irrelevant. "The fact that Khamenei has said it in front of thousands of people," said Aghlani, "is regarded as sufficient." He wrote that the fact that the fatwa was known to have come from the "guardian jurist" (*veli-ye faqih*) ensured that it was "binding on the Iranian government and takes precedence over ordinary legislation."[58] Mousavian also emphasized that a fatwa by the supreme leader is the equivalent in the Iranian legal system of "a state decree issued by a religious leader also governing the nation."[59]

---

55. Juan Cole, "Iran's Forbidden Nukes and the Taqiya Lie," *Informed Comment* (blog), April 16, 2012, http://www.juancole.com/2012/04/irans-forbidden-nukes-and-the-taqiya-lie.html. Israeli defense minister Ehud Barak invoked that argument against the Khamenei fatwa. See his interview with Christiane Amanpour of CNN, April 19, 2012, at http://edition.cnn.com/TRANSCRIPTS/1204/19/ampr.01.html.

56. Ali Ansari, "Iran: A Nuclear 'Fatwa'?" Chatham House, September 28, 2012, http://www.chathamhouse.org/media/comment/view/186019. For Ansari's argument that the June 2009 Iranian presidential election had been stolen, see Ali Ansari et al., *Preliminary Analysis of the Voting Figures in Iran's 2009 Presidential Election*, Programme Paper, Chatham House and the Institute of Iranian Studies, University of St. Andrews, June 21, 2009, http://www.chathamhouse.org/sites/default/files/public/Research/Middle%20East/iranelection0609.pdf.

57. Ali Ansari, "To Be or Not to Be: Fact and Fiction on the Nuclear Fatwa Debate," Lichtenstein Institute on Self-Determination, Princeton University, February 2013, cited in Mousavian, "Globalising Iran's Fatwa," 150.

58. Author's interview with Sasan Aghlani, May 12, 2013; Sasan Aghlani, "Nuclear Assurances: When a Fatwa Isn't a Fatwa," *Open Security*, March 8, 2013.

59. Mousavian, "Globalising Iran's Fatwa," 154. Ali Ansari argues that a fatwa can be reversed, citing the case of the fatwa against author Salman Rushdie, who was the subject of a fatwa by Khomeini in February 1989, accusing Rushdie of blasphemy over his novel *The Satanic Verses* and condemning him to death. In 1998, Iranian Foreign Minister Kamal Kharrazi promised his British counterpart that the Iranian government would do nothing to implement the fatwa. But Khamenei himself said in 2005 that the fatwa was still in existence, and a "senior British official" agreed that, "It can only be rescinded by the man who issued it or a higher authority, so in practice it will hold indefinitely." See Philip Webster, Ben Hoyle, and Ramita Naval, "Ayatollah Revives the Death Fatwa on Salman Rushdie," *Times* (London), January 20, 2005. Mousavian

These two episodes—Khomeini's wartime fatwa prohibiting Iran from manufacturing or using chemical weapons and Khamenei's 2003 fatwa against the manufacture, possession, or use of nuclear weapons—provided concrete evidence that religious prohibitions on WMD by the supreme leader have not been mere propaganda but have played a decisive role in determining Iran's policy on both chemical and nuclear weapons issues.

## Latent Deterrence

Iran's national security strategists believed that its ability to enrich uranium would confer security benefits on Iran. That belief is consistent with what has been called a "nuclear hedging" or "latent deterrent strategy," which is based on the assumption that having the knowledge that would allow the state to become a nuclear power if it chose to do so would tend to deter adversaries from attacking.[60]

Former IAEA director general Mohamed ElBaradei said in a 2004 interview with the *New York Times*, "If you are really smart, you don't need to develop a weapon, you just develop a capability. And that is the best deterrence." He called states like Iran that could make a convincing case that they had such a capability, but that do not make nuclear weapons, "latent weapons states."[61]

A number of states have embraced such a nuclear hedging strategy over the last few decades, some of which were discovered secretly carrying out a nuclear weapons program and then decided under pressure to give it up (e.g., South Korea, Taiwan). Others, such as Japan and Egypt, have discussed publicly the circumstances under which they might become nuclear weapons states but are not known to have made such a decision.[62] (Japan's ability to produce nuclear weapons within a relatively short time frame if it should choose to—like that of many nonnuclear European countries—is much more evident than Egypt's.)

The head of the nuclear program under the shah, Akbar Etemad, later recalled that the shah had told him his nonnuclear weapons policy would be reconsidered if any other state in the region acquired such weapons or

---

confirms that a fatwa is "permanent" and that the Rushdie fatwa "was simply not carried out." Mousavian, "Globalising Iran's Fatwa," 150.

60. For a discussion of the concept and its practice, see Ariel E. Levite, "Never Say Never Again: Nuclear Reversal Revisited," *International Security* 27/3 (Winter 2002/03): 59–60.

61. David E. Sanger, "When a Virtual Bomb May Be Better Than the Real Thing," *New York Times*, December 5, 2004.

62. T. V. Paul, *Power vs. Prudence: Why Nations Forgo Nuclear Weapons* (Montreal: McGill-Queen's University Press, 2000), 54.

Iran's security was threatened.[63] For Islamic Iran, the existence of the anti-nuclear weapons fatwa would make it very difficult, if not impossible, for the Islamic regime to justify a decision for nuclear weapons, regardless of other states in the region acquiring them. But Iranian strategists have long calculated that the existence of Iran's civilian nuclear program itself could have a deterrent effect on its adversaries. At a dinner during a conference in Tehran in 2005, then nuclear policy coordinator Hassan Rouhani told George Perkovich of the Carnegie Endowment for Peace, "We don't need a bomb. . . . If we have the mastery of the fuel cycle, our neighbors in the region will draw the necessary inference."[64]

In 1991, Rouhani became head of the Center for Strategic Research, a think tank officially attached to the president's office, then in 1997 moved (with former president Rafsanjani) to the Expediency Council. In 2006, a senior fellow at the center, Nasser Saghafi-Ameri, wrote in an analysis of Iran's nuclear policy options that Iran's nuclear program was consciously emulating the "Japan model." Like Japan, he noted, Iran wished to remain in "full compliance with the NPT"; but it was also entitled to "acquire the technology needed for peaceful production of nuclear fuel for its power plants." In an obvious effort to increase the deterrent value of the enrichment program, he added, "In a very drastic situation such as military attack against Iran," Iran might be compelled to follow the "North Korea model"—that is, to leave the NPT and become a nuclear weapons state.[65]

In 2010, Iran's Majlis speaker and nuclear negotiator, Ali Larijani, stated on a trip to Japan that Iran would follow the Japanese model in its nuclear program.[66] In citing the "Japan model," Saghafi-Ameri and Larijani were invoking a state that has amassed the world's largest stockpile

---

63. Patrikarakos, *Nuclear Iran*, 67–68. News reports had revealed the Israeli nuclear weapons program years earlier, so the shah was apparently ready to accept an Israeli nuclear weapon without responding with an Iran nuclear weapon. On the press reports of the Israeli weapons program in 1969–70, see Avner Cohen, *Israel and the Bomb*: (New York: Columbia University Press, 1998), 327, 338.

64. Author's interview with George Perkovich, January 3, 2009. Perkovich said that the *Washington Post* garbled his account of the conversation by attributing the remark in question to former president Rafsanjani and reporting that both Rafsanjani and Rouhani had "flatly declared that the country's nuclear weapons research had been halted because Iran felt it did not need the actual bombs." In fact, neither Rafsanjani nor Rouhani had said anything about halting weapons research, according to Perkovich. See Peter Baker and Dafna Linzer, "Diving Deep, Unearthing a Surprise," *Washington Post*, December 8, 2007, A10.

65. Nasser Saghafi-Ameri, "The Future of the NPT in the Light of Iran's Nuclear Dossier," Center for Strategic Research, April 2006, http://www.csr.ir/departments.aspx?lng =en&abtid=07&depid=74&semid=509.

66. "Iran's Nuclear Program Will Follow Japanese Model: Larijani," Mehr News Agency, Payvand Iran News, February 25, 2010, http://www.payvand.com/news/10/ feb/1260.html.

of plutonium, which would be available for weaponization the moment Tokyo should decide to leave the NPT. Moreover, top Japanese political leaders have periodically discussed in public the possibility of becoming a nuclear weapons power under certain conditions.[67] The invocation of the Japanese model appears to be a bid to exploit the obvious tolerance by the United States of a close ally's open embrace of a nuclear hedging strategy, thus conferring legitimacy on a similar stance by Tehran.

Gary Samore, the senior director for nonproliferation on the US National Security Council staff from 1996 to 2000, and President Barack Obama's special assistant for proliferation issues until late 2012, confirmed in 2008 that Iranian officials had told him privately that they were aiming at such a hedging capability. "They need to have—for their own survival and security, they need to have the ability *in extremis* to build nuclear weapons." Samore added that the Iranians told him "they would never actually build nuclear weapons, because they know that would scare the neighbors and it could risk war." He quoted the unnamed Iranian officials as saying, "We'll be content with a latent capability, with a breakout option, but we'll never actually use it."[68]

Some US intelligence analysts had been saying for years that they believed Iran was pursuing a hedging strategy in its nuclear program. Flynt Leverett, a former CIA analyst on Iran, told me in May 2006, "What [Iranians] seek is a technical basis for nuclear weaponization. They want to be like Japan."[69] Paul Pillar, who was the national intelligence officer for the Near East and South Asia from 2000 to 2005, recalled in an interview in 2009 that his assessment had been that Iran was pursuing precisely such a "hedging strategy" rather than a decision to actually make nuclear weapons. He said that he and other analysts of Iranian national security policymaking believed that any decision to build a nuclear weapon would "depend on circumstances of the time, and that's a decision yet to be made."[70]

Evidence on the public record shows that Iran's latent deterrent has already been effective in discouraging the United States from attacking Iran. George W. Bush's CIA director, Michael Hayden, stated in 2012, "When we talked about this in the government, the consensus was that

---

67. Maria Rost Rublee, "The Nuclear Threshold States: Challenges and Opportunities Posed by Brazil and Japan," *Nonproliferation Review* 17/1 (March 2010): 62–63.

68. "Symposium on Iran and Policy Options for the Next Administration, Session Two: The Nuclear Dimension and Iranian Foreign Policy," Council on Foreign Relations, September 8, 2008, http://www.cfr.org/iran/symposium-iran-policy-options-next-administration-session-two-nuclear-dimension-iranian-foreign-policy/ p17129.

69. Author's interview with Flynt Leverett, May 2, 2006.

70. Author's interview with Paul Pillar, January 27, 2009.

[attacking Iran] would guarantee that which we are trying to prevent—an Iran that will spare nothing to build a nuclear weapon and that would build it in secret."[71] That was most likely a reference to discussions the Bush administration had held in 2007 about proposals that Bush and Vice President Richard Cheney had made to launch an attack on Iranian nuclear facilities or on Islamic Revolutionary Guard Corps bases on the pretext of Iranian involvement in attacks on US troops in Iraq. Both those proposals were opposed and effectively stymied by the combination of Secretary of Defense Robert M. Gates, chairman of the Joint Chiefs of Staff Gen. Peter Pace, and the new commander of the Central Command, Adm. William Fallon.[72]

## Bargaining Chips

Iranian national security officials and Khamenei himself have also viewed the accumulating stocks of low-enriched uranium as a source of diplomatic leverage on the United States. For the realists who have dominated Iranian foreign policy, led by former president Rafsanjani and including Hassan Rouhani, whom Rafsanjani promoted to the position of secretary of the Supreme National Security Council in 1988, breaking out of Iran's international isolation and gaining recognition of its legitimate interests in the region have been central objectives of foreign policy. These figures understood that Iran would ultimately have to reach an agreement with the United States. In 1989, when he was president of Iran, Rafsanjani proposed that Iran should initiate a diplomatic dialogue with the United States aimed at striking a "Grand Bargain" to resolve all outstanding issues. But as Rafsanjani revealed in a 2011 interview, Khamenei had vetoed the idea.[73]

One of the main differences between Khamenei and Rafsanjani, however, was over when and under what conditions Iran should be prepared to negotiate with the United States. Khamenei believed the United States would not negotiate in good faith until Iran was in a much stronger position. In the 1990s, Iran was still weakened by its exhausting war against Iraq, and it needed more time to strengthen both its economy and its military forces—especially its ability to deter any new attack from outside. In January 1998, President Khatami spoke in an interview with CNN about

---

71. Josh Rogin, "Bush's CIA Director: We Determined Attacking Iran Was a Bad Idea," *The Cable, Foreign Policy*, January 19, 2012.

72. Seymour M. Hersh, "Preparing the Battlefield," *New Yorker*, July 7, 2008; Gareth Porter, "Military Resistance Forced Shift on Iran Strike," Inter Press Service, October 19, 2007.

73. "Rafsanjani Blames Khamenehi [sic] for Years of Sour Relations with America", *Iran Times*, July 19, 2011, cited in Mousavian, *Iranian Nuclear Crisis*, 83.

opening a dialogue with the American people. But just one week later, Khamenei declared at Friday prayers that talks with the United States "have no benefit for us and are harmful to us."[74] According to historian Shaul Bakhash of George Mason University, Khamenei gave several reasons for not holding such talks, but, he recalled, "One of them was you don't negotiate until you are strong enough."[75]

One of the developments Khamenei presumably expected would strengthen Iran's bargaining position with the United States at some point was the development of a ballistic missile that could retaliate in the event of an attack by the United States or Israel. But another important factor in Khamenei's calculus would certainly have been that Iran's ability to demonstrate its mastery of the nuclear fuel cycle by beginning to enrich uranium would bolster Iran's bargaining position with the United States by creating a problem about which the United States would then have an incentive to negotiate. So Khamenei apparently reasoned that there was no point in entering into talks with the United States before Iran would be able to exploit that new source of leverage.

In the late 1990s, political scientist Jalil Roshandel was working on a study titled "Impact of Nuclearization on the Security of the Third World Countries" for the think tank affiliated with Iran's foreign ministry. Roshandel, who later took up a teaching job at East Carolina State University, recalled that in 1998–99, some well-connected figures with whom he spoke believed that having a latent weapons capability in the form of enriched uranium would constitute a set of bargaining chips that could be used in negotiations with the United States over the sanctions that had been imposed on Iran and recognition of Iran's legitimate role in the region.[76]

In April 2006, President Mahmoud Ahmadinejad announced that Iran had achieved a 3.6 percent level of enrichment of uranium at its Natanz facility.[77] Just one month later, Khamenei's top foreign-policy adviser, Ali Akbar Velayati, who had been Khamenei's foreign minister from 1981 to 1989 and Rafsanjani's foreign minister from 1989 to 1997, stated explicitly that it was time for Iran to engage the Americans in negotiations. Velayati told a seminar in Tehran that "We have at no time until now had such

---

74. "Iranian Assails U.S., Shuns Dialog," Associated Press, *Deseret News* (Salt Lake City, UT), January 16, 1998.

75. Author's interview with Shaul Bakhash, May 9, 2013.

76. Author's interview with Jalil Roshandel, May 13, 2013. The project on which he worked is mentioned by name in Farideh Farhi, "To Have or Not to Have: Iran's Domestic Debate on Nuclear Options," in Geoffrey Kemp, ed., *Iran's Nuclear Weapons Options: Issues and Analysis* (Washington, DC: Nixon Center, 2001), 50.

77. "Iran Declares Key Nuclear Advance," BBC, April 11, 2006.

powerful means for haggling." He concluded, "Now that we have the power to haggle, why don't we haggle?"[78]

The former foreign minister referred specifically to "the influence we have now in Iraq and Palestine" as increasing Iran's bargaining power. He and Khamenei doubtless hoped to take advantage of Iran's apparent influence in both countries to gain bargaining leverage with the United States. But they had remained silent on this point in 2004 and 2005, even as US troubles in Iraq became increasingly apparent. Velayati did not refer explicitly in his address to the seminar to the stocks of low-enriched uranium (LEU) that Iran was then accumulating. But senior Iranian national security officials had been saying in private conversations since 2003 that they viewed the accumulation of a stockpile of LEU as a bargaining asset that could give Iran leverage in future negotiations with the Europeans and the United States.[79]

Iranian negotiators had already tried in 2005 negotiations with the Europeans to draw on the bargaining chips they believed were accruing to them in anticipation of the enrichment program that Iran had declared. In March 2005, Iran offered to limit the number of centrifuges in operation at Natanz and even to immediately convert all enriched uranium to fuel rods for its nuclear reactors in return for political-security benefits.[80] The premise that even potential stockpiles of enriched uranium could be used as negotiating chips with the West proved faulty: the Bush administration was simply not interested in negotiations with Iran. But that Iranian effort to exploit anticipated future enrichment nevertheless provides a window on the Iranian strategic calculus.

In September 2009, the Obama administration proposed a deal that would require Iran to ship three-fourths of its LEU out of the country and then wait for more than a year for 20 percent enriched uranium fuel rods to be returned to it. The Iranians understood that Iran's right to enrich would be implicitly recognized under the deal. But the US proposal for a swap of three-quarters of all the LEU Iran had accumulated to fuel Iran's Tehran Research Reactor (TRR) seemed aimed at stripping Iran of most of its LEU. All of Iran's political factions united in objecting to the US demand on the grounds that it would deprive Iran of the leverage it had gained from its LEU stockpile. It should not have been a surprise that Iran agreed only to a straight swap of LEU for fuel rods, batch by batch, which

78. Gareth Porter, "Khamenei in Control and Ready to 'Haggle,'" *Asia Times*, May 31, 2006.

79. Author's interview with an Iranian who had private conversations with senior Iranian officials over several years and who asked not to be identified, February 7, 2006.

80. Gareth Porter, "U.S. Rejected 2005 Iranian Offer Ensuring No Nuclear Weapons," *Inter Press Service*, June 7, 2012.

meant that it would retain all its bargaining chips for negotiations with the United States.[81]

Meanwhile, Iran was working on another technical advance that it hoped would translate into diplomatic leverage on the United States. Iran's inability to produce the fuel rods from abroad for its TRR had given the United States the opening to try to pry away the bulk of Iran's LEU stockpile. But on the eve of the second round of talks in Vienna in October 2009 with the United States, Russia, and France on an agreement on the external supply of fuel to the TRR, a spokesman for the AEOI said that if no deal was reached on the matter, Iran would begin enriching uranium to 20 percent itself, and then turn it into fuel rods for the TRR.[82] Enriching uranium to 20 percent would also bring Iran closer to the capability to enrich to weapons grade (90 percent), which the Iranians knew the United States would use to accuse Iran of moving closer to the ability to make a bomb. But they also calculated that it would give the United States a new incentive to agree to the compromise offer from Iran.

Iran began enriching uranium to 20 percent in February 2010, but made it clear it was ready to stop that enrichment if the United States and Russia agreed to supply the fuel without attaching additional conditions on Iran. In an interview with Al Jazeera, AEOI chief Ali Akbar Salehi said, "If they are ready to supply the fuel plates, we will stop the [20 percent] enrichment." He indicated that he had told the Russian ambassador the same thing.[83]

The belief that Iran's enrich capabilities and actual stockpile of enriched uranium were significant sources of diplomatic leverage on the United States has been a central thread in Iran's diplomatic behavior for the past decade. Although they also sought to exploit Iran's influence in various trouble spots from Iraq to Israel-Palestine, Iranian strategists have depended on Western concern about Iran's enrichment capabilities to make the United States more willing, eventually, to accommodate Iran's interests. The refusal of the United States to recognize that fact and its insistence that the accumulation of enriched uranium was evidence of the military aim of the program was part of the construction and maintenance of a political crisis over the nuclear program.

---

81. Gareth Porter, "Iran's Fuel for Conflict," *Le Monde Diplomatique*, December 2009. For a longer account of the "fuel swap" negotiations, see Trita Parsi, *A Single Roll of the Dice: Obama's Diplomacy with Iran* (New Haven, CT: Yale University Press, 2012), 114–142.

82. "Iran Issues Atom Fuel Warning Ahead of Talks," Reuters, October 11, 2009.

83. Al Jazeera interview with Ali Akbar Salehi, February 12, 2010, http://www.unz.org/Pub/AlJazeeraEnglish-2010-00675.

## The Role of Iranian Nationalism

Before 2003, the nuclear program had been a high-profile political issue in Iran that was widely discussed by the Iranian public. But the high-visibility campaign that Western nations launched in 2003 to pressure Tehran to give up enrichment and make far-reaching concessions regarding the monitoring of its nuclear program touched a raw nerve of Iranian nationalism.

Two moves that the United States and its allies launched via the influence they exercised in the IAEA provoked this explosive nationalist response. The first was a statement by the IAEA Board of Governors on June 19, 2003, that called on Iran to rectify shortcomings in regard to its reporting of nuclear activities and to accept the Additional Protocol without any conditions. The second was a board resolution in September 2003 that formally requested that Iran "sign, ratify and fully implement the Additional Protocol," along with a second and even more stringent demand that Iran "suspend all further uranium enrichment activities." The September resolution gave Iran less than two months to satisfy the board that it was taking "corrective measures" and threatened to report Iran to the UN Security Council if it failed to do so.[84]

In the context of the US invasion of Iraq only a few months earlier, those demands suggested to many inside and outside Iran that the United States was threatening to launch a war against Iran to force it to abandon its nuclear program. The demands and threat clearly implied in them provoked a political crisis in Iran, polarizing the political elite between those who were primarily concerned about convincing the West that Iran did not have any intention of obtaining nuclear weapons and those who were determined to defy what they regarded as a threat to Iran's independence.

Some officials were convinced that Iran was being pressured to capitulate to demands that would sacrifice its sovereignty and independence. Privately, the supreme leader's adviser on foreign affairs, the former foreign minister Velayati, likened the Additional Protocol to the 1828 Treaty of Turkmenchay, which had ceded a large part of what was then Iranian territory to Russia following the Russo-Persian War. Hossein Shariatmadari, the editor of *Kayhan*, who was also a political adviser to Khamenei, was among those political figures calling for withdrawal from the NPT to assert Iran's right to a nuclear program. There was an intense political debate over whether signing the Additional Protocol was a necessary adjustment in policy or an act of "treason."[85]

---

84. Mousavian, *Iranian Nuclear Crisis*, 68, 73; "Resolution adopted by the Board, September 12, 2003," GOV/2003/69, 3.

85. Mousavian, *Iranian Nuclear Crisis*, 69, 81; Rouhani speech.

That nationalist reaction made it very difficult for Ayatollah Khamenei to find a way to respond without appearing to bow down to aggressive Western demands or triggering a dangerous confrontation. In October 2003, Rouhani, who was responsible for nuclear negotiations with the West, worked out a compromise with the United Kingdom, France, and Germany under which Iran agreed to sign the Additional Protocol while insisting on its absolute right to enrich uranium. But harsh criticism from nationalists continued through 2004 and 2005. The hard-liners' position that Iran should reject the Additional Protocol appears to have had far more popular support than the pragmatic view that Iran should accept it as part of a broader package deal. Supporters of the hard-line position likened their campaign against bowing to these Western demands to the issue that had prompted Iran's biggest nationalist mobilization of the 20th century, the oil nationalization movement led by Mohammad Mossadegh in the early 1950s.[86] (Every March 20 is still celebrated in Iran as the anniversary of Iran's nationalization of British oil interests there, following years of struggle against British and US pressures in opposition to such a move.)

Ever since the external pressure on Iran to cease its enrichment began in 2003, Iranian public support for Iran's right to enrich uranium has been virtually unanimous. A 2009 opinion survey, for example, showed it as high as 98 percent.[87] That situation of almost complete consensus about Iran's nuclear rights has made it politically impossible for any Iranian government to agree to a demand for a permanent halt to uranium enrichment. During the negotiations with the Europeans from 2003 to 2005, senior Iranian officials said in private conversations that the government would have collapsed overnight if it had gone along with the European demand that Iran give up its right to enrich by agreeing to end enrichment indefinitely.[88]

That same near unanimity had an obvious impact on electoral politics as well, creating a dynamic similar to the Cold War US pattern of non-incumbent presidential candidates portraying incumbent presidents as soft on communism. During the 2005 presidential election campaign, candidate Mahmoud Ahmadinejad accused his opponent, former president Rafsanjani, of favoring far-reaching concessions to the Western powers that would give up Iran's nuclear rights. In 2007, after Ahmadinejad had consolidated his position as president, he even arrested former nuclear negotiator

---

86. Homeria Moshirzadeh, "Discursive Foundations of Iran's Nuclear Policy," *Security Dialog* 38, no. 4 (December 2007): 521–543.

87. Sara Beth Elson and Alireza Nader, *What Do Iranians Think?* (Santa Monica: CA: Rand Corporation, National Defense Research Institute, 2011), 11.

88. Interview with an Iranian who had private conversations with top national security officials over several years and who requested anonymity, February 7, 2006.

Hossein Mousavian, who was a key ally of Rouhani and Rafsanjani, on trumped-up charges of "espionage."[89]

The nuclear program has not only been invested with the symbolism of Iranian independence and sovereignty in the face of foreign encroachment, it has also become a source of national pride in scientific-technological prowess. That development was fueled in part by the fact that the uranium conversion facility and the centrifuges and the rest of the equipment for the enrichment facility were designed and built without foreign assistance, except for the basic blueprints. The AEOI appealed to Iranian pride by describing these facilities as an Iranian scientific-technical accomplishment that foreign states had told Iranian scientists and engineers was beyond them. In a newspaper interview, AEOI vice president Mohammad Saeedi recalled, "When we started nobody believed we could develop an indigenous nuclear technology," and even the Iranian scientists "did not know if they were capable of doing this."[90]

Iranian ambassador to the IAEA Ali Asghar Soltanieh, who had been an official in the nuclear program under the shah, said in a 2009 interview, "Nuclear energy has an advantage. Nuclear technology is a meeting point of all disciplines with high standards. Nuclear grade standard is always the best." Mastering the precise standards of nuclear energy, he said, had given the entire scientific sector in Iran a major boost in confidence. "Scientists are believing in themselves more. . . . In many scientific areas, Iran is among the top ten."[91] Iran's nuclear program was indeed a decisive factor in the leap forward in the country's scientific-technical sector that followed the decision to launch an independent capability for conversion and enrichment. A global study in 2010 showed that Iran's production of scientific-technical research, as measured by its output of scientific and technical publications, had increased faster than any other country's in the previous decade, and that nuclear-related fields had led the way by growing the fastest.[92]

By systematically eliminating the key historical facts and real Iranian calculations from the picture, American and Israeli officials have produced

---

89. For Mousavian's account of the arrest and the broader political context, see *Iranian Nuclear Crisis*, 279–87.

90. Farideh Farhi, "'Atomic Energy Is Our Assured Right': Nuclear Policy and the Shaping of Iran's Public Opinion," in Judith S. Yaphe, ed., *Nuclear Politics in Iran* (Washington, DC: Institute for National Security Studies, National Defense University, May 2010), 8.

91. Author's interview with Ambassador Ali Asghar Soltanieh, Vienna, September 6, 2009.

92. Science-Metrix, *30 Years in Science: Secular Movements in Knowledge Creation* (Montreal: Science-Metrix, 2010), 5; Deborah MacKenzie, "Iran Showing Fastest Scientific Growth of Any Country," *New Scientist*, February 18, 2010.

a caricature of an Iranian leadership obsessed with obtaining nuclear weapons. That systematic failure of both governments to apprehend the truth was no accident: it was a function of the political and bureaucratic interests that have driven both US and Israeli policies toward the Iranian nuclear program for two decades. We now turn in the next two chapters to a thorough examination of the unacknowledged but crucial factors underlying the US-Israeli manufacture of the Iran nuclear crisis.

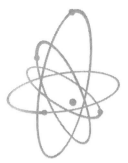

# 4

# US Political Origins
# of the Nuclear Scare

## An Opening to Tehran Falls Through

The end of the Iran-Iraq War and the death of Ayatollah Khomeini in 1989 brought the most far-reaching political change in Iran since the founding of the Islamic Republic in 1979. President Khamenei was selected by the Assembly of Experts as the new supreme leader of the regime, and Majlis speaker Rafsanjani replaced Khamenei as the chosen candidate for the presidency in the July 1989 election. Rafsanjani's victory in that election brought to power a pragmatic conservative who was openly committed to integrating Iran into the global economic system. Rafsanjani spoke English even more fluently than his Berkeley-educated brother and believed Iran needed to convince the West to invest in the Iranian economy.[1]

Along with the end of the Iran-Iraq War in late 1988, the ascendance of Rafsanjani was the first obvious opportunity to shift US Iran policy from open enmity to some form of working relationship. President George H. W. Bush recognized the opportunity and pledged in his inaugural address on January 20, 1989, that Iran's "assistance" in the liberation of US hostages being held by militant groups in Lebanon would be "long remembered," adding, "Goodwill begets goodwill." Bush then asked UN Secretary General Perez de Cuellar to convey a message to Rafsanjani: Bush was ready to improve US-Iran relations if Iran used its influence in Lebanon to free the US hostages. National security adviser Brent Scowcroft recalled later that Bush was not willing to negotiate directly with Iran over the hostages, but

---

1.   Elaine Sciolino, "Rafsanjani Sketches Vision of a Moderate, Modern Iran," *New York Times*, April 19, 1992, 1.

that he was prepared to "reach out subtly" to Iran through that language. "It was a signal," said Scowcroft. "A gesture: you do something nice for us, and I will do something nice for you."[2]

In October 1989, the Bush administration issued a top-secret national security directive on policy toward the Persian Gulf that said the United States "should continue to be prepared for a normal relationship with Iran on the basis of strict reciprocity." It said the process of normalization had to begin with Iran's ending its "support for international terrorism" and freeing the hostages in Lebanon. It cited a number of conditions for full normalization of relations, including "improving relations with neighbors" and "improving its human rights record," but it suggested, by implication, that at least a thaw in relations short of normalization could take place without those conditions being realized.[3] That policy appears to have reflected recognition on the part of Secretary of State James Baker that Iran, which was much less hostile to Israel than it was to Iraq, might share some political interests in the region with the United States.[4] The August 1991 "National Security Strategy of the United States" again left the door open to "an improved relationship with Iran," provided Iran "makes clear it is lending no support to hostage-taking or other forms of terrorism."[5]

Giandomenico Picco, the UN negotiator sent to meet with Rafsanjani, repeated Bush's vow to reciprocate Iran's help in freeing the hostages. In 1991, Rafsanjani set about actively working to obtain the release of hostages held by Shi'a militants in Lebanon with whom Iran had maintained close ties, using secret intermediaries and, in early December 1991, a personal visit to Beirut by Iranian foreign minister Ali Akbar Velayati. That visit was followed on December 4, 1991, by the release of the last American hostage.[6]

After that, Bush and Scowcroft proposed to undertake a reciprocal gesture, in keeping with Bush's promise in his inaugural address nearly three years earlier. In a meeting with UN mediator Picco in mid-January 1992, Scowcroft said it might be possible to take Iran off the terrorist list, reduce economic sanctions, and compensate Iranians for the July 1988 shootdown of an Iranian civilian Airbus by the US Navy, which had killed all 290 Iranian passengers and crew. Scowcroft told Picco he believed a decision

2. "Iran and the West: The Pariah State," BBC documentary, February 2009, http://www.youtube.com/watch?v=wLjRkrTxkzY.

3. National Security Directive 26, "U.S. Policy toward the Persian Gulf," October 2, 1989, http://www.fas.org/irp/offdocs/nsd/nsd26.pdf.

4. Flynt Leverett and Hillary Mann Leverett, *Going to Tehran* (New York: Metropolitan Books, 2013), 339–40.

5. "National Security Strategy of the United States," August 1991, http://nssarchive.us/?page_id=52.

6. Author's interview with Giandomenico Picco, the UN diplomat who worked with Iran to help free the hostages, December 8, 2006.

might be made in early March. Picco kept his personal notes of the meeting, from which he quoted in an interview with the author.[7]

When Picco met Scowcroft again on February 25, 1992, Scowcroft told him that the administration was still considering allowing the sale of some airplanes and parts and easing other economic sanctions. But on April 2, Scowcroft telephoned Picco to tell him that it was now unlikely that there would be any lifting of economic sanctions, because Iran was guilty of terrorism abroad.[8] And in a meeting with Picco on April 10, Scowcroft said that there would be "no goodwill to beget goodwill" after all.[9]

What happened to Bush's reciprocal gesture? Many years later, Scowcroft described the meeting that he and Bush had held with other "principals" in the administration—the secretaries of state and defense and the CIA director—to discuss the proposed gesture to Iran. Bush indicated that he was "sympathetic," according to Scowcroft's account, but "everyone else said Iran is behaving so badly in so many different ways that to reward them by lifting sanctions . . . is just impossible for us." The senior National Security Council (NSC) official on the Persian Gulf, Bruce Riedel, recalled, "The problem, as I told Gen. Scowcroft in that meeting, was that Iran was now deeply engaged in other acts of terrorism that made it very, very difficult to do anything to improve the relationship." Scowcroft's explanation was simple: "I lost the argument."[10]

The more detailed account Scowcroft gave to UN mediator Picco in April 1992, however, suggests that a deeper set of political dynamics drove the refusal to make any reciprocal gesture to Iran. Scowcroft indicated that the decision was related to "new intelligence" that supposedly indicated that Iran was embarking on a new course of terrorist actions and military aggressiveness. Scowcroft told Picco that the new intelligence showed that Iran had made a policy decision to follow "a different road" from one that would have allowed improved relations with Washington. He referred to an alleged assassination of an Iranian national in Connecticut by Iranian agents and to intelligence reports that Iran would use "Hezbollah types" in Europe and elsewhere to respond to Israel's assassination of Hezbollah leader Abbas Mussawi in southern Lebanon in February. But Scowcroft said the intelligence also indicated that Iran was intent on "rearmament" and that it was trying to acquire nuclear weapons.

---

7. This account of the initial meeting and subsequent meetings between Picco and Scowcroft is based on these notes, as read to the author by Picco in a telephone interview January 25, 2009. See also Gareth Porter, "Is Gates Undermining Another Opening to Iran?" Inter Press Service, January 28, 2009.

8. Giandomenico Picco, *Man Without a Gun* (New York: Times Books, 1999), 285.

9. Author's interview with Picco, January 25, 2009.

10. "Iran and the West: The Pariah State."

But Scowcroft cited no intelligence of an actual terrorist attack by Iran, except for the claim of an Iranian assassination of someone who was not identified somewhere in Connecticut. And that claim was apparently either a mistake or a deliberate ruse by someone seeking to justify the refusal to make any reciprocal gesture to Iran, because no such assassination was ever registered in the FBI's central database of incidents relevant to its work.[11] Although he reported the anticipation of future terrorism, Scowcroft did not suggest that Iran was behind the bombing of the Israeli Embassy in Buenos Aires on March 17, 1992.

It is no accident that the characterization of Iran as a sponsor of terrorism and a WMD proliferator began to surface immediately upon the return of Robert Gates as CIA director, after he had served as deputy national security adviser under Scowcroft since August 1989. On November 23, 1991, just two weeks after Gates became CIA director, a "senior administration official" was quoted in the *Los Angeles Times* as saying that relations with Iran would remain in the "deep-freeze," mainly because of Iran's "continued support for international terrorism" and its pursuit of WMD capabilities. The official maintained that if the United States made a gesture to Tehran in response to the freeing of American captives, Rafsanjani would "come under severe domestic political pressures to rebuff any American overture."[12]

That comment about Rafsanjani and a possible gesture toward Iran could only have come from someone in the inner circle of the administration knowledgeable about the Bush-Scowcroft plan. As the *New York Times* had reported three months earlier, there had been no interagency or high-level meetings on Bush administration policy toward the hostage issue, and the only officials who were kept informed were Bush, Secretary of State Baker, Scowcroft, and Scowcroft's deputy, Gates.[13]

In his public testimony before congressional committees in early 1992, moreover, Gates portrayed the Islamic Republic as a threat to the security of the Persian Gulf and to US interests. In testimony before the Senate Armed Service Committee in January, Gates provided a litany of charges against Iran that implicitly argued against any move to improve relations.

---

11. Personal communication to the author from an FBI source who could not be identified, because he was not authorized to speak to the press, October 24, 2013. The source looked in the FBI's main database, which would have included any political assassination in the United States, for any record of an assassination of any kind in Connecticut during 1991 or 1992, and found nothing that could have been the basis of Scowcroft's reference.

12. Norman Kempster, "U.S. Bent on Keeping Iran Ties in Deep-Freeze Diplomacy," *Los Angeles Times*, November 23, 1991, 18.

13. Patrick E. Tyler, "Iran Taking Lead in the Bargaining to Free Hostages," *New York Times*, August 18, 1991, 1.

"Despite the apparent pragmatism of President Rafsanjani," he said, Iran "still poses a potential threat to its smaller neighbors and to a free flow of oil through the Gulf." He maintained that Tehran was continuing to "support terrorism as an instrument of state policy, despite its role in securing the release of the hostages" and that it had "embarked on an ambitious effort to develop its military and defense industries, including programs for weapons of mass destruction."[14]

In his testimony before the House Armed Services Committee in late March, Gates reiterated the same twin themes of Iranian pursuit of terrorism and WMD, but this time he was more explicit about nuclear weapons. He declared that Iran "is developing a capability to produce weapons of mass destruction" and "seeking to acquire a nuclear weapons capability." Gates asserted that the intelligence community expected Iran "probably to promote terrorism and other active measures aimed at undermining progress toward Israeli-Palestinian reconciliation." Despite the fact that the testimony came nearly two weeks after the bombing of the Israeli Embassy in Buenos Aires, however, Gates did not suggest that Iran was behind that bombing. To complete the picture, he reminded the committee members that Iran "has not abandoned the goal of one day leading the Islamic world and reversing the global dominance of Western culture and technology."[15]

What members of Congress and the press could not have known was that the Gates portrayal of Iran as an aggressive terrorist state bent on nuclear weapons distorted the actual assessment of the intelligence community on Iran—sometimes subtly, sometimes not. A national intelligence estimate (NIE) on Iran completed on October 17, 1991, three weeks before Gates returned to the CIA as director, has since been declassified, and it concluded that President Rafsanjani's foreign policy had reflected the dominance of "pragmatism" over "ideological purity" and that Iran had been "gradually turning away from the revolutionary excesses of the past decade . . . toward more conventional behavior."[16]

Contrary to Gates's assertion that Iran represented a threat to the security and stability of the Gulf, the NIE concluded that Iran would not seriously threaten US interests over the two-year period covered by the estimate. It cited both the "grave weakness" of the Iranian economy and

---

14. Threat Assessment, Military Strategy and Defense Planning: Hearings on January 22, 1992, before the Senate Armed Services Comm., 102nd Cong., 2nd sess., statement by CIA Director Robert M. Gates, 12–14, at http://www.loc.gov/law/find/nominations/gates/00059133123_excerpt.pdf.

15. "CIA Warns of Chemical Threat by Iran," *Houston Chronicle*, March 28, 1992, 1.

16. National Intelligence Estimate 34–91, "Iran under Rafsanjani: Seeking a New Role in the World Community?" October 1991, http://www.foia.cia.gov/sites/default/files/document_conversions/89801/DOC_0000602664.pdf.

the fact that Iranian military forces had "limited capabilities" and were "less able to harm vital U.S. interests" than they had been in the past. The estimate also said both President Rafsanjani and Supreme Leader Khamenei believed that Iran's interests lay in better relations with the West.[17]

Although the estimate's section on Iran's nuclear program was deleted from the declassified document, the main thrust of the assessment is clear from a *New York Times* report shortly after the estimate was circulated within the administration: the NIE had characterized the Iranian nuclear program as disorganized and still in its initial stage of development. The *Times* story further revealed that "some administration officials" believed the NIE "underestimates the scope of Iranian intentions."[18] That was presumably a reference to Gates, still at that moment the de facto NSC coordinator on intelligence matters and the one official with a known stake in a clear-cut conclusion that Iran had embarked on a nuclear weapons program.

On the terrorism issue as well, Gates had substituted his own views for those of the intelligence community. In contrast to his suggestion that the intelligence community had concluded that Rafsanjani's government would "probably promote terrorism," the NIE had actually concluded that Iran was "unlikely to conduct terrorism directly against U.S. or Western interests during the next two years, but it is supporting radical groups that might do so."

The possibility that the White House had authorized Gates to publicly cite intelligence on Iran that would be used as an argument against any reciprocal gesture can be ruled out. He began his campaign to demonize Iran before the last US hostage had been released from Lebanon in early December—something the White House would not have countenanced. The aim was evidently to force the president's hand in regard to Iran policy.

Gates declared in congressional testimony that Iran had "embarked on an ambitious effort to develop its military and defense industries, including programs for weapons of mass destruction."[19] Then two months later, he told a congressional committee, "We judge that Tehran is seeking to acquire a nuclear weapons capability."[20] Gates's substitution of his own judgment

17. Kempster, "U.S. Bent on Keeping."

18. Elaine Sciolino, "Report Says Iran Seeks Atomic Arms," *New York Times*, October 31, 1991, A7.

19. Threat Assessment, Military Strategy and Defense Planning hearings, statement by Gates, 12.

20. Regional Threats and Defense Options for the 1990s: Hearings on March 27, 1992, before the Defense Policy Panel, House Armed Service Comm., 102nd Cong., 2nd sess., statement by CIA Director Robert M. Gates, 317, http://www.loc.gov/law/find/nominations/gates/007_excerpt.pdf.

for that of the national intelligence estimate on Iran in his testimony would have been no surprise to those who had worked under Gates as deputy director for intelligence and then deputy director of central intelligence under Director William Casey. Intelligence analysts recalled him as Casey's enforcer in bullying analysts to toe the CIA director's policy line in assessments involving the Soviet Union and Central America. A number of CIA intelligence analysts later recalled that Gates had let analysts know that he expected their papers to be consistent with the "party line," and that those who had dared to write analyses that were not supportive of the policy had often gotten "nasty" memos from Gates.[21] And when the analysts wouldn't write what Gates wanted, he sometimes simply changed it unilaterally, as he did to produce an intelligence assessment to justify the Iran-Contra operation.[22]

But why was Gates so eager to prevent a step toward improvement of relations with Iran? One explanation for his hostility toward Iran is that he blamed then president Rafsanjani for having revealed the 1986 secret visit of NSC staff to Iran in connection with the Iran-Contra plan—an episode that almost cost Gates his career. As deputy director of central intelligence, Gates had been Casey's close ally during the Iran-Contra affair and one of the few Reagan administration officials who knew about the 1985 US offer of arms to Iran in return for the release of US hostages held in Lebanon that later morphed into a way to funnel arms to the Nicaraguan Contras. Gates was nominated for CIA director in early 1987, but he withdrew his name after it became clear that he would not be confirmed because of questions raised by other witnesses about his veracity.[23]

He had been forced to take jobs as an assistant to the president and deputy national security adviser that did not require confirmation. Gates was apparently still bitter about having been deceived by Iranians—Rafsanjani in particular—who the Israelis had suggested were "moderates." Graham Fuller, who served as national intelligence officer for the Middle East and South Asia under Gates during most of the 1980s, recalled that, after Iran-Contra had been revealed, Gates had constantly repeated in meetings with

21. John A. Gentry, *Lost Promise: How CIA Analysis Misserves the Nation* (Lanham, MD: University Press of America, 1993), 74–76.

22. Jennifer Glaudemans, a CIA Soviet analyst at the time, testified in 1991 that Gates had altered the 1985 draft National Intelligence Estimate on which she had worked to conclude that Moscow considered the prospects for increasing influence in Iran "quite good." The original draft she had helped write, however, had said that Soviets viewed their prospects of gaining influence in Iran as "negligible." Jennifer Glaudemans, "Has Gates Learned His Lesson?" *Los Angeles Times*, November 21, 2006.

23. Senate Select Committee on Intelligence, Nomination of Robert M. Gates to be Director of Central Intelligence, Report, October 24, 1991, Senate Executive Reports, Exec. Rept. 102-19 (Washington, DC: Government Printing Office, 1993).

analysts, "The only moderate Iranian is one who has run out of bullets."[24] In conversation with Secretary of State George Shultz in 1987, Gates, then acting director of the CIA, made it sound like that view was coming from his analysts. "Our people are outraged at the idea of 'moderates' there [in Iran]," he told Shultz.[25] Now Rafsanjani was making another bid for an opening to the United States, and Gates was evidently eager to shoot it down.

But the Gates opposition to the planned Bush gesture to Iran involved more than his personal feelings about Rafsanjani and the regime in Tehran. In the context of its adjustment to the end of the Cold War and the threat from the Soviet Union, the CIA had a very large institutional interest at stake in treating Iran as a new, high-priority threat to US security interests—especially as a state threatening to have a uranium enrichment program, which was automatically treated as a "nuclear weapons capability," as Gates had put it. The CIA leadership had begun the search for substitutes for the Soviet threat as early as 1988. The Soviet Union had absorbed a large proportion of CIA budgetary resources at the height of the Cold War, and before the collapse of the Soviet Union, the agency had begun making major adjustments in its allocations of resources. By fiscal year 1990, only 15 percent of those resources were focused on the Soviet Union, according to Gates.[26] The CIA was trying to position itself to convince Congress that new threats required shifting vastly increased commitments of intelligence collection and analytical assets to other targets that had replaced the Soviet threat. And once again, nuclear proliferation was its single biggest argument for such a shift.

Gates's predecessor as CIA director, William H. Webster, had quickly identified the proliferation of weapons of mass destruction and long-range ballistic missiles as the most promising new threat with which to absorb human and budgetary resources formerly focused on the Soviet Union and its allies. As early as December 1988, Webster had begun arguing that the "proliferation of advanced weapons" was the most serious security threat on the horizon. "By the year 2000," Webster warned, "at least fifteen developing countries will either have produced or be able to produce their own ballistic missiles." And 20 countries would be producing chemical weapons,

---

24. Porter, "Is Gates Undermining."

25. George Shultz, *Turmoil and Triumph: My Years as Secretary of State* (New York: Charles Scribner's Sons, 1993), 867.

26. Robert M. Gates, "Statement on Change in CIA and the Intelligence Community," April 1, 1992, 34, http://www.gwu.edu/~nsarchiv/NSAEBB/NSAEBB144/document%2018.pdf. The statement was presented to a joint session of the Senate Select Committee on Intelligence and the House Permanent Select Committee on Intelligence. See note 34 below.

he said, some of which would be able to put chemical warheads on ballistic missiles.[27]

Webster made a series of speeches on the threat of proliferation of missiles and weapons of mass destruction in late 1990 and early 1991. In a speech in March 1991, he warned, "There are a number of serious dangers inherent in nuclear proliferation," the most obvious of which was the "danger that nuclear weapons might be used in regional conflicts." The New York Times had reported that the speeches represented "one of the most public campaigns ever undertaken by a Director of Central Intelligence" on a single issue.[28] But despite Webster's attempt to establish proliferation as the new equivalent to the Soviet threat, pressures continued to build in Congress for severe cuts in the CIA budget as well as far-reaching intelligence reforms. It was because of the threat of major CIA budget cuts that Webster announced his intention to leave the agency in May 1991.[29]

One month after Gates took over as CIA director in November 1991, the presidents of Russia, Ukraine, and Belarus dissolved the Soviet Union and created the Commonwealth of Independent States on December 8, 1991. That brought to a formal end the state that had provided the rationale for the extraordinary spending on national security for decades. Two days after that event, Gates declared in testimony to a House Defense Policy Panel, "The old verities that have guided this country's national security policies for the last 45 years have disappeared in an historical instant."[30] Gates continued the campaign begun by Webster to sell Congress on the need to maintain existing levels of budget and manpower for the agency based in large part on the threat of proliferation of weapons of mass destruction. In his testimony before the Defense Policy Panel in December 1991, Gates said the proliferation of nuclear, chemical, and biological weapons and their delivery systems was "foremost" among the new post-Cold War challenges. He told the panel that 20 states already had or were in the process of acquiring such weapons,

---

27. Michael Klare, *Rogue States and Nuclear Outlaws* (New York: Hill and Wang, 1995), 21.

28. Steven Engelberg, "C.I.A.'s Chief Campaigns Against Missile-Making by Third World," *New York Times,* March 31, 1989, A6; William Overend, "Soviet Spying Increasing, Webster Says," *Los Angeles Times*, March 31, 1989, 15.

29. Douglas F. Garthoff, *Directors of Central Intelligence as Leaders of the U.S. Intelligence Community, 1946–2005* (Washington, DC: Center for the Study of Intelligence, Central Intelligence Agency, 2005), 187, 191; Michael Wines, "CIA in Search of a Role," *New York Times,* May 9, 1991, A1.

30. Potential Threats to American Security in the Post Cold War Era: Hearings on December 10, 1992, before the Defense Policy Panel, House Armed Services Comm., 102nd Cong., 1st sess., statement by CIA Director Robert M. Gates, 4, http://www.loc.gov/law/find/nominations/gates/006_excerpt.pdf.

and that the "accelerating proliferation" of such weapons was "probably the gravest concern."[31]

Meanwhile, Gates had taken advantage of his position as deputy national security adviser to devise an ingenious solution to the political problem of reducing the pressure for cutting the agency's budget. He drafted a national security review memorandum, NSR-29, providing a mechanism by which policymakers could specify what intelligence they needed from the CIA and the intelligence community. Signed by the president November 15, 1991, one week after Gates left the NSC staff to take over at the CIA, the memorandum noted, "Many non-Soviet issues have assumed greater importance for the Intelligence Community in recent years" and called for policymakers at relevant departments and agencies to submit their priorities for intelligence to the NSC by March 1992, which would then be translated into a national security directive to guide the CIA's prioritization of resources. It was the best argument he could have devised to ward off congressional cuts in the CIA's budget. As Gates explained to a CIA audience in December, the process he had set in motion would prove to Congress that his allocations were based not on "bureaucratic self-justification" but on "the expressed needs of national security policymakers."[32]

Gates knew that the military leadership viewed the proliferation of nuclear weapons and other weapons of mass destruction as the one issue that could be presented as a threat comparable to the old Soviet menace. "With the diminution of the threat from the Soviet Union, technical and human resource collection and analytic talent through the community is being refocused on this [proliferation] threat," he told the Senate Armed Services Committee in January 1992. The intelligence community had the role of "alerting policymakers to the existence of new programs or advances in established programs in special weapons areas," Gates said.[33] And Gates told senators about a new "Nonproliferation Center," which he described as combining intelligence assessment and policy coordination functions on the proliferation threat. He said the center included "senior officials from several agencies" who would "better formulate and coordinate intelligence activities in support of U.S. government policies." And he cited the need for a bigger investment in human intelligence assets to provide "early warning" on proliferation threats.[34]

---

31. Ibid., 4–5.

32. Garthoff, *Directors of Central Intelligence*, 202–3, 212.

33. Threat Assessment, Military Strategy and Defense Planning hearings, statement by Gates, 66.

34. Weapons Proliferation in the New World Order: Hearings on January 15, 1992, before the Senate Governmental Affairs Comm., 102nd Cong, 2nd sess., testimony of CIA Director Robert M. Gates, 14–15.

Gates had identified Iran as a primary example of the threat for which the CIA's services were needed. In an appearance before the first-ever joint session of Senate and House Intelligence Committees on April 1, 1992, he revealed a strategy for fending off deep budget cuts revolving around proliferation, Iran, and the Persian Gulf. He pointed to a long list of "problems and dangers all over the world" that would "continue to engage America's attention," beginning with "instability and the fragility of reform in the former Soviet Union, the proliferation of nuclear, chemical and biological weapons and ballistic missiles in more than 20 countries," and "the rearmament of Iran." Although he did not accuse Iran explicitly of having a nuclear weapons or WMD program, he mentioned "nuclear programs in Iran and Algeria." He repeated once again what had become his mantra—that "proliferation is probably our highest priority" and that the CIA had "made substantial new investment in that."

Gates then proceeded to make his main pitch to the intelligence committees. "I think it is incumbent on us, if we are going to ask to receive essentially the same level of resources that we have to satisfy you that we are spending them wisely and that we are not just continuing blindly down paths that we have followed in the past." When Senator Robert Kerrey suggested that no current or future threat was comparable to that of the Cold War Soviet threat, Gates invoked the supposed threats to US oil access from Iraq and Iran. "When the United States is deeply dependent for its way of life on imported oil," Gates argued, "what goes on in Iran and Iraq in the Persian Gulf area becomes very important in terms of our national security and national wellbeing."[35]

The "rearmament of Iran" was a code phrase used by Gates to suggest that Iran was bent on using military power to dominate the region. But the foreign diplomats in Tehran following Iran's military with whom *New York Times* correspondent Elaine Sciolino talked in April 1992 scoffed at the Gates argument. They told her that Iran's rearmament effort was nothing more than a minimum defensive effort. One diplomat pointed out that Iran had to rebuild "almost from ground zero," and that Iraq remained far stronger than Iran militarily, largely because the Iranian air force lacked spare parts and the navy had hardly improved over the 13 years of the regime's existence. Another said reports of Iran's military buildup were "highly exaggerated" and called the estimated $2 billion a

---

35. S. 2198 and S. 421 to Reorganize the United States Intelligence Community: Joint Hearing on April 1, 1992, before the Senate Select Comm. on Intelligence and the House Permanent Select Comm. on Intelligence, 102nd Cong., 2nd sess., testimony of CIA Director Robert M. Gates, 10, 32, 34, 36.

year it was spending for defense "peanuts" compared to what Iran needed militarily.[36]

Gates was not alone in conjuring up a new threat from Iran as part of the painful adjustment to the loss of the Soviet threat. The Pentagon had been working on that challenge for years. By 1987, after the emergence of Mikhail Gorbachev as head of the Soviet Communist Party, the proportion of Americans who said they feared the Soviet Union, which had stood at 64 percent in 1983, had declined to 31 percent.[37] There was talk in Congress and even among some former Pentagon officials who were independent of its institutional interests of the need for deep cuts in the military budget: former secretary of defense Robert S. McNamara and former assistant secretary of defense Lawrence Korb said in December 1989 that the budget could be cut in half over five years.[38]

As early as May 1987, the vice director of the Joint Staff for strategic plans and policy, Air Force Maj. Gen. George Lee Butler, concluded that the Cold War was already over and began pushing for redefining US security interests in terms of threats from regional adversaries.[39] One way regional states could be substituted for the Soviet threat was to define the issue in terms of the proliferation of weapons of mass destruction. All the military services, including the bureaucracy responsible for nuclear weapons, found ways to relate their operations to that threat. In congressional testimony in June 1990, Secretary of Defense Richard Cheney articulated the argument that the threat of WMD proliferation required the maintenance of Cold War levels of US nuclear weapons. After the 1991 Gulf War and revelations about the extent of Iraq's nuclear weapons program, Cheney issued a top-secret order to the military to target potential proliferators in plans for nuclear operations. The air force seized on the proliferation rationale to expand its roles and missions. Gen. Butler, by then head of the air force's Strategic Command, declared in 1993, "Our focus now is not just the former Soviet Union but any potentially hostile country that is seeking weapons of mass destruction."[40]

---

36. Elaine Sciolino, "Counting Iran's New Arms Is the Easy Part," *New York Times*, April 26, 1992, A2.

37. Miroslav Nincic, "America's Soviet Policy: Patterns of Incentives," in William Zimmerman, ed., *Beyond the Soviet Threat: Rethinking American Security Policy in a New Era* (Ann Arbor: University of Michigan Press, 1993), 151, fig. 1.

38. David E. Rosenbaum, "Pentagon Spending Could Be Cut in Half," *New York Times*, December 13, 1989.

39. Lorna S. Jaffee, "The Base Force," *Air Force Magazine*, December 2000, 56–57.

40. Hans Kristensen, "Targets of Opportunity," *Bulletin of Atomic Scientists*, September-October 1997, 22–23.

The generals responsible for the Middle East also recognized the need to find a replacement for the alleged Soviet threat that had always been used to justify a US war plan for the region. The Central Command, which had responsibility for everything from Egypt all the way to Central Asia, had been established in 1983 with the mission of stopping the Red Army from crossing the Zagros Mountains and seizing the precious oil fields of Iran. But the military officers responsible for the region had long viewed the war plan that had been drawn up to stop a Soviet invasion of Iran as a sham. "We'd used the operating plan for years, but most generals knew it made no sense and would eventually be junked," recalled Gen. H. Norman Schwarzkopf, who had been named Central Command chief in 1988. "Nobody except a few stubborn hard-liners believed that we'd go to war against the Soviets in the Middle East."[41]

When Schwarzkopf took over the Central Command, his first move was to try to persuade the Pentagon bureaucracy to scrap the whole idea of preparing for a Soviet invasion of Iran. Schwarzkopf figured that Iraq was the "most plausible enemy" for a Middle East war plan, and he was prepared to demand that either a new regional war plan against Iraq be adopted for his command or that the command itself be shut down.[42] Before the Berlin Wall fell in October 1989, the newly installed chairman of the Joint Chiefs of Staff Colin Powell authorized Schwarzkopf to shift the focus of the Central Command war plan from a Soviet Union threat to Iran to an Iraqi invasion of Saudi Arabia. When the Central Command produced a new war plan for defeating Iraqi forces in Kuwait and Saudi Arabia, some staff officers who had long seen Saddam as a US ally against Iran viewed it as an effort to find a substitute for the loss of the Soviet threat.[43]

Another element in the Pentagon plan for saving its budget from being reduced to a fraction of its previous size was to substitute the capability to fight two wars simultaneously against regional adversaries for the previous rationale of being able to fight a war against the Soviets in what was dubbed the Regional Defense Strategy. President George H. W. Bush approved the new rationale for military spending in spring 1990 and presented it in a speech on August 2, 1990.[44]

---

41. H. Norman Schwarzkopf with Peter Petre, *It Doesn't Take a Hero* (New York: Bantam, 1993), 331.

42. Schwarzkopf, *It Doesn't Take a Hero*, 331–32.

43. Diane T. Putney, *Airpower Advantage: Planning the Gulf War Air Campaign, 1989–1991* (Washington, DC: Air Force History and Museum Program, US Air Force, 2004), 10–12.

44. George H. W. Bush, remarks at the Aspen Institute Symposium in Aspen, CO, August 2, 1990, http://www.presidency.ucsb.edu/ws/?pid=1873.

He gave the speech on the same day as Saddam Hussein's invasion of Kuwait. Bush and his key advisers, defense secretary Cheney and national security adviser Scowcroft, quickly decided to make the invasion of Kuwait a *casus belli*. When the Arab states, including the Saudis, who supposedly needed to be defended from Saddam, sought to forge a political solution to the conflict, Bush resisted the idea. Bush believed Saddam's army could be easily defeated, and he wanted to rebuild political support for a continued global US military role by fighting a decisive war against a weak regional foe.[45]

The easy US victory over Iraqi forces in Operation Desert Storm in February 1991 was to be the template for future US wars under the Regional Defense Strategy. Two weeks after the end of the war, Cheney declared that Operation Desert Storm "presages very much the type of conflict we are most likely to confront again in this new era." He said the Pentagon and the military services would be targeting other "regional powers with modern armies, sophisticated attack aircraft and integrated air defenses" in its military strategy.[46]

Gates also knew that the combination of the collapse of the Soviet Union and the Gulf War had led the Bush administration to adopt the strategic assessment—written by Undersecretary of Defense Paul Wolfowitz and Cheney—that the United States was now in a much stronger position in the Middle East/Persian Gulf region to assert its interests and those of Israel. That viewpoint was clearly reflected in the drafting of defense policy guidance for fiscal years 1994–99 that had begun in September 1991, in which Wolfowitz aide Lewis "Scooter" Libby played a key role. One Libby draft argued that the war had strengthened US ties with "moderate states" in the region, and that "Arabs and Israelis have for the first time in many years met to discuss peace." The draft referred to "limiting the proliferation of weapons of mass destruction" and "stemming the flow of militarily significant technology to potential adversaries" as "long-term defense policy goals."[47] By early 1992, the tone of the Pentagon had become decidedly more confident and even openly aggressive. As Joint Chiefs chairman

---

45. George Bush and Brent Scowcroft, *A World Transformed* (New York: Vintage, 1998), 317–21, 353–54. Bush later celebrated what he cited as having "kicked the Vietnam syndrome once and for all." George H. W. Bush, remarks to the American Legislative Exchange Council, March 1, 1991, *Public Papers of the Presidents of the United States*, bk. 1, 1991, 195–97.

46. Statement by Secretary of Defense Richard Cheney before the House Foreign Affairs Committee, March 19, 1991, quoted in Michael T. Klare, "A New Military Strategy for Washington?" *Le Monde Diplomatique*, November 1997.

47. "Defense Policy Guidance, FY 1994–99," draft, March 30, 1992, 3, 10, http://www.gwu.edu/~nsarchiv/nukevault/ebb245/doc06a.pdf.

Powell famously characterized the new US post-Cold War military posture, "I want to be the bully on the block."[48]

The new Pentagon analysis of the region had obvious implications for policy toward Iran. During Operation Desert Storm, Iran had communicated to the United States that it was pleased with the weakening of Saddam's forces, and Secretary of State Baker and other senior officials had considered bringing Iran into the regional political-diplomatic order, according to former top advisers to Baker. But the Wolfowitz-Libby analysis suggested that the United States was now in a position to dominate the regional order, so there was no longer any need to make any effort to deal diplomatically with Iran, as had been assumed when the Bush administration first declared its openness to improving relations with Iran in 1989. Senior aides to Baker later said he accepted the new Wolfowitz-Libby analysis of the region.[49] Henceforth, the administration would treat Iran simply as a regional adversary whose power in the region could be contained by unilateral US policy, and its nuclear program would be treated as one of the primary national security challenges faced by the United States.

Gates could be confident, therefore, that the meeting convened by Scowcroft in March 1992 to discuss a reciprocal gesture to Iran would support the position Gates had staked out even before he had become CIA director. Cheney and Baker had already accepted that there should be no opening to Iran. And Bruce Riedel, the senior NSC staff specialist on the region who recalled confirming the alleged intelligence on Iranian terrorism at the meeting, had been a protégé of Gates at the CIA.[50] The argument by Riedel that Iran was engaged in "new terrorism" that ruled out any improvement of relations was a more convenient explanation for the decision to scrap the promise that Bush had made in his inaugural address than the new geopolitical appraisal and the needs of the major national security organizations.

## Clinton and Iran: Proliferation Plus Israel

The Clinton administration went even further than the Bush administration in singling out Iran as its primary adversary in the Middle East. That ramping up of pressure on Iran by the Clinton administration was still driven by the same bureaucratic incentives that had appeared at the end of the Cold War, but it shifted into overdrive because it was linked to support

---

48. David Armstrong, "Dick Cheney's Song of America," *Harper's*, October 2002.

49. Leverett and Leverett, *Going to Tehran*, 339–40.

50. Personal communication to the author from 18-year CIA veteran Philip Giraldi, May 1, 2013.

of the Israeli government's drive to portray Iran as the greatest threat to peace in the world.

Even before Bill Clinton entered the Oval Office in January 1993, his national security team had already decided to elevate the issue of proliferation in national security policy. The first expression of that priority was the creation of a separate Directorate of Nonproliferation and Export Controls in the National Security Council staff. The new director presided over all interagency meetings on proliferation issues, including the drafting of a presidential decision directive on proliferation and export controls, which was then the subject of a speech by Clinton at the UN General Assembly in September 1993.[51] From the beginning of the administration, the nonproliferation specialists in the White House and State Department became major players, with significant influence over the formulation of policy toward Iran.

But it was the Pentagon that was most active in exploiting the WMD proliferation issue to expand its bureaucratic reach. Secretary of Defense Les Aspin undertook a "Bottom Up Review" beginning in March 1993, from which he drew the conclusion that of all the new post-Cold War dangers, "the one that most urgently and directly threatens Americans at home and American interests abroad is the new nuclear danger"—that is, the danger of proliferation of nuclear weapons. In December, Aspin announced what he called the Defense Counter-proliferation Initiative, the main thrust of which was to "develop new military capabilities to deal with the new threat." It was explicitly based on the premise that prevention of proliferation through denial would not be sufficient. Aspin declared that the Defense Department would acquire new weapons and new strategies for military operations to destroy such weapons. The chairman of the Joint Chiefs of Staff and regional commanders would develop plans for dealing with weapons of mass destruction in the hands of adversaries. The perception was widespread outside the United States that the Pentagon was gearing up for a strategy of preventive and/or preemptive attacks against suspected WMD facilities.[52] Some observers suggested, however, that Aspin was merely repackaging existing Defense Department programs as a response to the loss of the Soviet enemy in order to maintain congressional funding for those activities.[53] In their

---

51. Robert S. Litvak, *Rogue States and U.S. Foreign Policy: Containment after the Cold War* (Washington, DC: Woodrow Wilson Center Press, 2000), 37. Litvak was the first director of the Proliferation Directorate at the NSC, from 1993 to 1997.

52. Remarks by Secretary of Defense Les Aspin at the National Academy of Sciences, Committee on International Security and Arms Control, December 7, 1993, in US Senate Committee on Governmental Affairs, *Nuclear Proliferation Handbook* (103rd Cong., 2nd sess.), 198–203.

53. Litvak, *Rogue States*, 39.

"National Military Strategy" for 1994, the Joint Chiefs of Staff identified the spread of weapons of mass destruction as the leading military threat facing the United States as well. And the regional commanders integrated attacks on WMD targets into their respective war plans.[54]

Now that it had taken on proliferation as a threat for which it should adopt military plans, the Pentagon gave new prominence to Iran in its overall justification for the continuation of the US military's global role. An analysis of the global political-military situation for the remainder of the 1990s prepared by the Joint Staff in May 1993, apparently as a basis for a PowerPoint presentation for congressional briefings, portrayed Iran as the major threat to dominate the Middle East. It attributed to Iran the "ultimate aim" of a "widespread, militant Islamic resurgence and the replacement of Western influence throughout a substantial part of the third world while dominating the Persian Gulf." The paper predicted that Iran would become "more aggressive in the Persian Gulf and perhaps elsewhere" by "the end of the decade if not sooner."[55]

The interests of the Pentagon and the military in portraying Iran as a new threat justifying preparations for war in the Middle East dovetailed with the Clinton administration's move to align its Iran policy with that of the Israeli government of Prime Minister Yitzhak Rabin. That decision was a result of the Rabin government's formulation of a new policy of raising worldwide alarm about Iran's alleged nuclear ambitions and use of terrorism. When Clinton entered the White House, Rabin and his foreign minister, Shimon Peres, immediately pressured him to join Israel in treating Iran as "Enemy Number 1."[56]

But Clinton's adoption of the new Israeli line toward Iran began even before his election, when he decided to position himself as more explicitly pro-Israel than the Bush administration had been. He had chosen as his adviser on the Middle East during the election campaign Martin Indyk, an Australian citizen who was a professional partisan of Israeli interests without any claim to academic expertise or professional experience on the Middle East. Indyk had been an adviser on international media and communications to hard-line Likud Party prime minister Yitzhak Shamir

---

54. Government Accountability Office, "Weapons of Mass Destruction: DOD's Activities to Combat Weapons Use Should be More Integrated and Focused," GAO NSI-AD-00-97, May 2000, 26.

55. Joint Staff, "The Global Threat in the 1990s," May 1993, with cover letter from director of the Joint Staff, Vice Admiral P. C. Macke, which refers to a related slide show, "Challenge to Global Security in the 1990s," an unclassified document held in the library of the Center for Defense Information, now part of the Project on Government Oversight.

56. Clyde Haberman, "Israel Focuses on the Threat Beyond the Arabs—in Iran," *New York Times*, November 8, 1992, A18.

and then deputy director of research for the American Israel Public Affairs Committee (AIPAC), the powerful lobbying organization that was known for taking positions reflecting the Likud Party line. Indyk had been the co-founder of the Washington Institute for Near East Policy in 1985, alongside the wife of the chairman emeritus of AIPAC Lawrence Weinberg, and Indyk was named the institute's first executive director. The idea behind the institute, as Indyk explained to the *National Journal* later, was to give the semblance of independence from Israel to longer "academic" writings— obviously with the intent of fully supporting Israeli policies.[57]

Preparing Clinton for his first meeting with Prime Minister Rabin in October 1992, Indyk argued that the collapse of the Soviet Union had weakened the Arab enemies of Israel and that all of Israel's neighbors were now negotiating with Israel—the same point made by Paul Wolfowitz and Cheney aide Lewis Libby in their controversial defense policy guidance paper. "To capitalize on the moment," Indyk told Clinton, he needed only to "put his immense influence as leader of the dominant power behind Rabin as he moved forward." Clinton could achieve peace in his first four years in office, he assured the candidate. Clinton responded that he wanted to do that.

Indyk had a similarly simplistic formula for dealing with Iran. Since both Iraq and Iran were "hostile to our interests," he argued, Clinton should "work to contain them while we pressed ahead with Arab-Israel peacemaking." This time Clinton responded with a bit of post-Cold War imperial bluster. Containing them was not a "tough enough policy," Indyk recalls him as saying. "We had to find a way to change their behavior or change the regime."[58]

After Clinton's election victory, he named Indyk as his special assistant as well as senior director for Near East and South Asia on the NSC staff. Indyk was far more than what his titles indicated, however. He acted as the administration's main policymaker on the Middle East rather than coordinating interagency meetings, as NSC staff had done in the past.

One of the earliest and most consequential policy decisions to come out of the Clinton administration was announced in a speech by Indyk in May 1993 that restated what he had told Clinton during the campaign. Indyk rejected a balance-of-power approach to Iran and Iraq because of "the antagonism that both regimes harbor towards the United States and

57. Grace Halsell, "Clinton's Indyk Appointment One of Many from Israel Think Tank," *Washington Report on the Middle East*, March 1993, 9. On AIPAC's record of hewing to Likud Party views, see Trita Parsi, *Treacherous Alliance: The Secret Dealings of Israel, Iran and the U.S.* (New Haven, CT: Yale University Press, 2007), 183.

58. Martin Indyk, *Innocent Abroad: An Intimate Account of American Peace Diplomacy in the Middle East* (New York: Simon and Schuster, 2009), 16, 31.

its allies in the region" and because "we don't need to rely on one to balance the other." The operational significance of that approach, as Indyk made explicitly clear, was that Iran was to be subject to the same kind of punitive measures as Iraq had been. Because Iran had not been put under "the kind of international regime that has been imposed on Iraq," said Indyk, a "structural imbalance" existed between the pressures on the two countries, which are thus "tilted in favor of Iran, with very dangerous consequences."[59] So the real point of the speech was to urge the international community to join the United States in treating Iran more like it did Iraq.

Thus a new Iran policy, dubbed "dual containment," which responded fully to Israeli desires, was formulated and presented by an NSC staffer who had come out of Israel's unofficial lobby in Washington, soon after Israel had begun urging such an approach on the United States. No wonder the State Department's policymaker on Middle East, Robert Pelletreau, later recalled that it was "pretty much accepted in Washington" that the policy had originated in Israel.[60] Reflecting the reality that the speech was not the result of an interagency process, Indyk acknowledged in a later interview, "People like to say 'Indyk's speech wasn't cleared.'"[61] Indyk's predecessor as NSC director for the region, Robert Litvak, observed that the speech was a case of the "linkage between foreign policy and domestic politics" becoming "the key determinant" of the administration's policy toward Iran.[62] In other words, the harsh new US policy toward Iran was being driven by Israel's ability to manipulate American politics through its powerful domestic lobbying arm.

Having signed on to the Israeli position on Iran, the Clinton administration proceeded to pressure US allies not only to allow no exports of technologies that could be used by Iran for its nuclear program, which the United States had already been doing, but also to cut off all loans, investments, and arms sales. The rationale was that Iran supported terrorism and pursued nuclear weapons. After visiting Israel, Secretary of State Warren Christopher declared Iran an "international outlaw" and "dangerous country." Clinton administration officials told the *New York Times* that the isolation of Iran would only end "if Tehran halts its support for terrorism,

---

59. Martin Indyk, "The Clinton Administration's Approach to the Middle East," speech to the Soref Symposium, Washington Institute for Near East Policy, May 18, 1993, at http://www.washingtoninstitute.org/policy-analysis/view/the-clinton-administrations-approach-to-the-middle-east.

60. Parsi, Treacherous Alliance, 171.

61. Daniel Pipes, "Interview with Martin Indyk: Perspective from the White House," *Middle East Quarterly*, March 1994.

62. Litvak, *Rogue States*, 63.

curtails its military buildup, stops its subversion of other governments and ends its quest for nuclear weapons."[63]

In line with the new policy, the Clinton administration went beyond what Robert Gates had said about Iranian intentions to acquire nuclear weapons. Christopher suggested in a May 1995 press briefing that intelligence clearly pointed to a covert nuclear weapons program. "Based upon a wide variety of data," he said, "we know that since the mid-1980s, Iran has had an organized structure dedicated to acquiring and developing nuclear weapons."[64]

But what the intelligence had shown was that Iran was intent on acquiring enrichment technology—which by definition constituted a "nuclear weapons capability"—not on acquiring nuclear weapons. In March 1996, CIA Director John M. Deutch said, "A wide variety of data indicate that Tehran has assigned civilian and military organizations to support the production of fissile material for nuclear weapons." Deutch then went on to explain what that meant: "We judge that Iran is actively pursuing an indigenous nuclear weapons capability."[65] Christopher had deliberately misrepresented the intelligence assessment to make his desired political point.

The Clinton administration made the issue of Russia's agreement with Iran to help rebuild its nuclear reactors at Bushehr one of its top priorities for the first summit meeting between Clinton and Russian president Boris Yeltsin in April 1993. Yeltsin rebuffed the US pressure to cancel the Bushehr contract, but in early 1995, as the United States began preparing for another Clinton-Yeltsin summit meeting in May, US officials escalated pressure for the cancellation of the agreement to reconstruct Bushehr and to provide other reactors to Iran. In early April 1995, Secretary of Defense William Perry went to Moscow primarily for that purpose, taking with him a US intelligence report asserting that Iran had a "crash program" to build nuclear weapons. Intelligence officials admitted that the report was aimed at combating the effect of a recent Russian intelligence report that concluded that Iran was not intent on building nuclear weapons, reversing a 1994 conclusion that had attributed nuclear "ambitions" to Iran.[66]

63. Douglas Jehl, "U.S. Seeks Ways to Isolate Iran," *New York Times*, May 27, 1993, A1.

64. Office of the Spokesman, "Press Briefing by Secretary of State Warren Christopher on the President's Executive Order on Iran," US Department of State, May 1, 1995.

65. Permanent Subcommittee on Investigations of the Senate Comm. on Government Affairs, testimony of CIA Director John M. Deutch, March 20, 1996, https://www.cia.gov/news-information/speeches-testimony/1996/dci_testimony_032096.htm.

66. Steven Erlanger, "Russia Says Sale of Atom Reactor Is Still On," *New York Times*, April 4, 1995; Steven Greenhouse, "U.S. Gives Russia Secret Data on Iran to Discourage Atom Deal," *New York Times*, April 4, 1995.

Just three weeks before the May 1995 summit meeting, Alexei Yablokov, an environmental adviser to Yeltsin who opposed the proposed nuclear deals with Iran, published an article in the Russian newspaper *Izvestia* providing details of an agreement reached in January between Iran and the head of Minatom, the Russian atomic energy organization, that included a commitment to discuss a centrifuge plant, among other items.

The Clinton administration was determined to use the leak to stop not only the proposed centrifuge plant but also the contract on Bushehr, which had nothing to do with centrifuges. The official US position was that Iran might not turn the spent fuel from the reactor over to the Russians but instead accumulate weapons-grade plutonium. But that argument put Washington at odds with the IAEA. Bushehr was a light-water reactor, and the IAEA had helped many countries with light-water reactors and did not regard them as a proliferation threat. The IAEA's specialists regarded light-water reactors as "proliferation resistant," primarily because in order to remove the fuel from one for any reason, the reactor must be shut down, thus making it very easy to detect any diversion. By 2001, the IAEA had almost 200 light-water reactors under safeguards agreements that provided for procedures to assure against any diversion of the plutonium waste into weapons production.[67]

Privately, in fact, US officials acknowledged that the type of plutonium produced by Bushehr and the small research reactor Russia had promised to Iran was far less likely to be used in nuclear weapons than plutonium from heavy-water reactors. Indeed, the United States was leading an international consortium to provide a light-water reactor to North Korea as a more proliferation-proof substitute for heavy-water reactors.[68] Furthermore, Iran's representative to the IAEA had declared as early as October 1992 that Iran was willing to accept additional safeguards on the two reactors to be supplied by Russia, and had "no objections" to returning spent fuel from the reactors to Russia.[69]

US ambassador to Russia Thomas Pickering sent a cable to Washington in early 1995, suggesting that the United States offer a deal on Bushehr to the Russians: the United States would not oppose Russia's work on rebuilding Bushehr if Moscow could provide guarantees that Russia would control all the spent fuel, and that Iran would not be able to get into reprocessing. But Pickering never received an answer from Washington. The reason, he believed, was that the nonproliferation specialists in the

---

67. Yousry Abushady, "Can Light Water Reactors be Proliferation Resistant?" IAEA-SM-367/15/08, no date shown (circa 2001).

68. Erlanger, "Russia Says Sale."

69. Mark Hibbs, "Iran Would Return Nuclear Spent Fuel, Accept Stringent Safeguards," *Nuclear Fuel*, October 12, 1992, 5.

administration did not want any compromise on the issue.[70] The NSC
director for nonproliferation, Daniel Poneman, later confirmed that he
and others thought the Bushehr deal made by Iran with the Russians "as
an energy deal makes no sense. So it only makes sense as a stalking horse
for a weapons effort."[71]

The real motive for the United States in pressuring Russia to cut off aid
to the Bushehr project was not that plutonium that would be produced
by those reactors could be used for nuclear weapons but that they would
enhance the "nuclear expertise" of the Iranians and legitimize the Iranian
nuclear program. The rehabilitation of Bushehr would involve large numbers of Iranian personnel working with nuclear technology and would
provide significant formal training for graduate-level students, which was
unacceptable to both the Clinton administration and to Israel.[72] The US
position thus came down to a demand that Iran give up the right to have
the same nuclear expertise as dozens of other countries.

In January 1999, the Clinton administration played its ultimate card
with the Russians, threatening to ban Russian contracts with US companies
for launching commercial satellites on Russian rockets if Russia failed to
curb technology transfers that helped Iran develop long-range missiles and
nuclear weapons.[73] But the Russians rebuffed that threat, and the Clinton
administration never pushed the issue actively again.

Reflecting both the hostility toward Iran within the national security
bureaucracy and the influence of the Israeli line on its Iran policy, the
Clinton administration also adopted the same a priori assumption that
Iran was a threat to the issue of terrorism. The CIA's Counter-Terrorism
Center and the FBI were already inclined to suspect Iran and/or Hezbollah
of being responsible whenever a major terrorist incident took place. In
the case of the terror bombing of Pan American World Airways flight 102
over Lockerbie, Scotland, in December 1988, for example, the Counter-
Terrorism Center had simply assumed that Iran had used Palestinian
operatives to carry out the bombing in retaliation for the shoot-down of
an Iranian civilian airliner earlier that year, killing all the civilians and crew.

---

70. Interview with Ambassador Thomas Pickering, January 8, 2013.

71. James M. Goldgeier and Michael McFaul, *Power and Purpose: U.S. Policy toward
Russia after the Cold War* (Washington, DC: Brookings Institution, 2003), 179.

72. Stuart Goldman, Kenneth Katzman, and Carl E. Behrens, "Russian Missile Tech-
nology and Nuclear Reactor Transfer to Iran," Congressional Research Service, updated
July 29, 1998, 13; Author's interview with Keith Weissman, former staff member of
AIPAC specializing on Iran, January 17, 2013.

73. Daniel Williams, "U.S., Russia Trade Gibes over Iran," *Washington Post*, January 15,
1999, A1.

Only in mid-1990 did the investigation begin to focus on Libya and finally turn up evidence of responsibility.[74]

Under the Clinton administration, however, the existing tendency to suspect Iran first became even more pronounced. After the World Trade Center bombing on February 26, 1993, administration officials fed media speculation about Iranian or Hezbollah responsibility with briefings reminding reporters of its official view that Hezbollah was the "most aggressive and lethal" terrorist group in the world. They asserted that it had been responsible for several "bombings and assassinations" over the previous year in the Middle East, Europe, and Latin America, including the March 1992 car bombing of the Israeli Embassy in Buenos Aires.[75]

It is not clear, however, that the US intelligence community had reached any such conclusion about the Israeli Embassy bombing. Cables from the US Embassy in Buenos Aires in the first week following the explosion had indicated that at least one bomb had definitely exploded inside the embassy itself and reported that anti-Semitic right-wing Argentine military officers, far from condemning the bombing, had blamed the government of President Carlos Menem for having provoked it by his pro-American policies and had begun using it to demand changes in government.[76] And one month after the embassy bombing, when Scowcroft met with UN hostage negotiator Picco, he had not suggested that Iran was suspected of organizing that terror bombing.[77]

Reflecting the Rabin government line, officials of the Clinton administration suggested to the news media within its first few weeks that the problem of terrorism was linked to Shiite "fundamentalism," as though Hezbollah's attacks on Israelis in Lebanon over more than a decade had been caused by irrational religious extremism and had nothing to do with the Israeli military occupation of the country. And they said the problem was expanding across the globe. The *Los Angeles Times* even quoted one State Department official as saying that Hezbollah terrorism extended to "every continent except Antarctica."[78]

---

74. Ronald J. Ostrow and Robin Wright, "U.S. Tackling Blast Probe on Unprecedented Scale," *Los Angeles Times,* March 4, 1993.

75. R. Jeffrey Smith, "Experts: Islamic Extremists Post an Aggressive Threat," *Washington Post,* March 17, 1993, A25; Robin Wright, "Experts See Signs Global Terrorism Will Escalate," *Los Angeles Times,* March 17, 1993, A1; Knut Royce, "Blast Motive Elusive/ Without It Probers Can't Call It Terrorism," *Newsday,* March 24, 1993, 7.

76. Cables from the US Embassy in Buenos Aires to the State Department on March 18, 20, and 23, 1992. State Department archives of declassified documents on Argentina, http://www.state.gov/m/a/ips/c35445.htm.

77. Author's interview with Giandomenico Picco, January 25, 2009.

78. Smith, "Experts: Islamic Extremists"; Wright, "Experts See Signs"; Royce, "Blast Motive Elusive."

After another terrorist bomb went off at the main Jewish community center in Buenos Aires on July 17, 1994, the same political dynamic drove the US response. That same day, Israeli prime minister Rabin declared, "The trail leads to an Iran-backed international infrastructure to carry out terrorist acts" and called for a worldwide effort to combat "this venomous snake and smash its skull." Christopher blamed the bombing on "those who want to stop the peace process in the Middle East." Two months later, the State Department coordinator for counterterrorism, Philip Wilcox, announced that the United States had "mounting evidence" of Iran's guilt in the Buenos Aires bombing.[79]

In fact, however, no such evidence had been found, nor would it be over the next few years. William Brencick, who was then chief of the political section in the US Embassy in Buenos Aires and the primary liaison with Argentines and Americans involved in investigating the bombing, told me, "I think our perspective on the case was probably related more to our enmity [toward Iran] than to the evidence." US officials had "lots of assumptions," he said, "but no hard evidence to connect those assumptions to the case."[80] Ron Goddard, then the deputy of chief of mission in Buenos Aires, recalled that he and other embassy officials had "suspected very seriously that Hezbollah was involved," but investigators had found nothing to link the bombing to Iran. "The whole Iran thing seemed kind of flimsy," Goddard told me.[81] James Bernazzani, the head of the FBI's Hezbollah Office, was sent to Buenos Aires in late 1997 to help the Argentine investigators on the case, reflecting the administration's assumption that Hezbollah was involved. But Bernazzani acknowledged years later that the investigation turned up no real evidence of Iranian involvement during his work on the case, and that what was regarded as evidence by Argentine investigators was essentially falsehoods.[82]

The Clinton administration's policy toward Iran reflected the mutually reinforcing interests of the two most powerful entities involved: the US national security bureaucracy—especially the Pentagon—and the Israeli government and its powerful lobby in the United States. For their part, the Israeli governments of the 1990s defined Iran as a mortal threat to the

---

79. Reuters dispatch from Jerusalem, *Buenos Aires Herald*, July 20, 1994; Sergio Kiernan, *Atrocity in Buenos Aires: The AMIA Bombing, One Year Later* (New York: American Jewish Committee, 1995), 29–30n4.

80. Author's interview with William Brencick, political counselor, US Embassy in Buenos Aires, 1994–97, June 16, 2007.

81. Author's interview with Ron Goddard, May 18, 2007.

82. Gareth Porter, "Bush's Iran/Argentina Terror Frame-Up," *Nation*, February 4, 2008; Alexei Barrionuevo, "Inquiry on 1994 Blast at Argentina Jewish Center Gets New Life," *New York Times*, July 18, 2009, A8.

existence of the Jewish state for reasons that had little or nothing to do with Iranian policy. The real reasons were related more to the need to manipulate US policy and Israeli domestic opinion. We now turn to the disparity between the ostensible rationale for Israel's Iran nuclear scare campaign and the real calculus underlying that campaign, which is a key to understanding the manufactured crisis to come in the next decade.

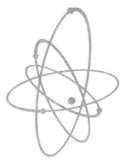

# 5

# Israeli Political Origins
of the Nuclear Scare

## Rabin Creates an Iranian Nuclear Threat

Soon after Labor Party leader Yitzhak Rabin was elected prime minister
in June 1992, his government adopted a new rhetorical stance toward
Iran that marked a fundamental turning point in Israeli policy. The
new government's line referred to Israel's "struggle against murderous
Islamic terror" and the alleged threat of Shi'a fundamentalism. Rabin
and Foreign Minister Shimon Peres created a new office in the Foreign
Ministry called the Peace in the Middle East Department to carry out a
global campaign to isolate Iran politically by portraying Iran and Shi'a
fundamentalism as the biggest threats to peace in the world. Rabin
declared publicly that Iran "has megalomaniac tendencies in regard to the
Middle East based on spreading Islamic fundamentalism in the region."
He said Iran was "building up its military and developing weapons of
mass destruction." Iran did not represent an "immediate threat," he said,
but a "medium-range one."[1]

Rabin was quite specific about how and when the threat would materi-
alize. He predicted in December 1992 that Israel would face "a large-scale
threat of ground-to-ground missiles equipped with non-conventional
warheads within 3 to 7 years." And in January 1993, he warned that Iran
"now has the appropriate manpower and resources to acquire nuclear
weapons within the next ten years," and said, "It will happen unless there

---

1. Michael Roten, "Rabin: We Are Ready for Any Eventuality," *Jerusalem Post*, January
15, 1993, 2.

is an appropriate international effort to prevent Iran from achieving its ends."[2]

In early 1995, Rabin government officials raised the alleged nuclear threat from Iran to an even more prominent position in their anti-Iran propaganda and even began suggesting that it might be necessary to use military force to destroy it. In January 1995, an unidentified official in Tel Aviv called the potential for an Iranian nuclear weapon "the most serious threat" facing Israel. The official said Iran could have a bomb in about five years—a much shorter estimate than either Rabin or his national security advisers believed. And the official also threatened that if the program was not halted, Israel would be "forced to consider attacking Iran's nuclear reactors," just as it had done against Saddam Hussein's Iraq in 1981.[3] A few months later, the British newspaper the *Independent* reported that the Rabin government was "considering whether to attack Iranian nuclear facilities," even though Israeli security officials did not believe an attack like the air raids on Iraq's Osirak reactor would be successful in the Iranian case.[4] The Bushehr reactor had not yet been rehabilitated after successive Iraqi bombings of the reactor during the war, so it wasn't even clear what the targets for such an attack would have been.

In 1996, after Rabin was assassinated by a right-wing Israeli extremist, the threatening rhetoric was raised several more notches. The government spokesman went on record in an interview with the *Times* of London saying that it was now the "working assumption" that a coalition led by the United States would launch a "preemptive strike" on Iran to prevent it from obtaining a "nuclear capability." The spokesman explicitly likened the situation to that of 1981, "when we bombed the Iraqi nuclear plant." When you are on the "front lines," he said, "you have to take what appears harsh action before a threat can be realized."[5]

This escalating Israeli rhetoric, culminating in an explicit threat of preventive war against Iran to ensure that it could not have a functioning nuclear program, appeared to herald the first serious crisis over Iran's nuclear program. But it was not at all what it appeared. The ostensible Israeli threat was based on a double deception: the overall propaganda line

---

2. Douglas Davis, "Major: Rabin Brings 'New Source of Hope,'" *Jerusalem Post,* December 10, 1992, 2; Dan Izenberg, "Rabin: Iran Potentially Greater Threat than Iraq," *Jerusalem Post,* January 21, 1993.

3. Chris Hedges, "Iran May be Able to Build an Atomic Bomb in 5 Years, U.S. and Israeli Officials Fear," *New York Times,* January 5, 1995, A1.

4. Patrick Cockburn, "Israel Targets Iranian Nuclear Plans for Raids," *Independent* (London), May 22, 1995.

5. Christopher Walker, "Israel Sees Iran as Next in Line for Punishment," *Times* (London), April 19, 1996.

about Iran as the biggest threat to Israel did not reflect the Israeli intelligence appraisal, and Israel's senior national security strategists were not contemplating preventive war against Iran.

The reality behind the artificial hyping of the Iranian nuclear threat was that Israeli intelligence considered Iran only a second- or even third-level risk to the security of Israel. Iran was not even on the list of priority issues for Israeli intelligence in the early to mid-1990s. That list of security priorities included the Palestinian intifada, the intentions of Syria and Iraq, and, as less immediate threats, Libya and Egypt, according to the Mossad director at the time, Shabtai Shavit.[6]

The leadership of the Israel Defense Forces (IDF) was similarly unconvinced that Iran represented a serious threat. The Israeli military viewed Iraq, Syria, and Lebanon as more serious threats than Iran, and it still held the view that Iran and Israel had more shared strategic interests than interests in conflict—particularly given Iran's fundamental hostility toward Saddam Hussein's Iraqi regime.[7] That relatively relaxed view of Iran reflected the influence of what Israeli strategists called the "periphery doctrine," which had dominated Israeli policy during the shah's regime and through the 1980s. It held that Iran's conflict with the Sunni Arab regimes in general and Iraq in particular was more important than its conflict with Israel. The periphery doctrine was discarded as the official government view by Rabin in 1992, but it remained quite influential in Mossad and some Likudist circles.[8]

Israeli cooperation with Iran was especially close during the shah's regime. In 1958, Israel, Iran, and Turkey established an intelligence cooperation alliance called Trident, which involved coordination of counterintelligence as well as intelligence programs.[9] In the late 1970s, after the Arab refusal to sell oil to the West over US military aid to Israel during the 1973 war had benefited Iranian oil exports, Iran and Israel cooperated in a $1.2 billion scheme called Project Flower to jointly develop advanced missile systems, which might be launched from submarines and perhaps eventually even fitted with nuclear warheads.[10]

---

6. Yossi Melman and Meir Javadanfar, *The Nuclear Sphinx of Tehran: Mahmoud Ahmadinejad and State of Iran* (New York: Carroll and Graf, 2007), 151–52, 270nn1–2. One of the co-authors interviewed former Mossad chief Shavit on December 17, 2006.

7. Dalia Dassa Kaye, Alireza Nader, and Parisa Rosha, *Israel and Iran: A Dangerous Rivalry* (Santa Monica, CA: RAND, 2011), 21–22.

8. Parsi, *Treacherous Alliance*, 195–96.

9. Ibid., 11–13; remarks by Yossi Alpher, a senior Mossad official who worked on programs to advance the "periphery doctrine" in the 1970s and 1980s, at the International Institute for Strategic Studies, Washington, DC, May 4, 2013.

10. Parsi, *Treacherous Alliance*, 74–76.

But even after the overthrow of the shah, Israel and Iran continued military cooperation during the Iran-Iraq War, based on their common enmity toward Saddam's Iraq. It had to be covert, because Iran could not acknowledge its dependence on Israel at a time when Ayatollah Khomeini was excoriating Israel. The secret initiative to provide arms to Iran in return for the release of US hostages held by Iran-allied Shiite forces in Lebanon actually began with a proposal to President Ronald Reagan's national security adviser, Robert C. McFarlane, by the director general of Israel's Foreign Ministry, David Kimche, in spring 1985. Israeli prime minister Shimon Peres intervened in February 1986 to urge the Reagan administration to go ahead with the secret offer.[11] In 1987, Rabin, then minister of defense, criticized US policy for its pro-Saddam tilt, noting that Iran had been a friend of Israel for 28 of its 38 years in existence. Why, Rabin asked, could that not happen again once the "crazy idea of Shiite fundamentalism" no longer dominated the regime?[12]

The death of Khomeini in 1989 renewed the hope among Israeli strategists, including Rabin himself, that they could reach a modus vivendi with Iran based on the periphery doctrine. And even after Iraq's defeat in 1991, Israeli national security officials still viewed Iraq as far more threatening, especially given its chemical and nuclear weapons programs.[13] Yossi Alpher, who had been responsible for actually implementing the periphery doctrine as a Mossad official and was then an adviser to Defense Minister Rabin, reaffirmed in a December 1989 television interview that Iraq, which was still the main enemy, was getting stronger, and that Israel had an interest in supporting Iran in its continued confrontation with Iraq and other Arab states.[14] And even after Rabin became Prime Minister in late 1992, Israeli intelligence and the defense ministry allowed Israeli companies and middlemen to sell military goods to Iran.[15]

Rabin viewed the collapse of the Soviet Union and the defeat of Saddam's army as creating a more benign security environment for Israel in general, both because of Iraq's weakness and the Arab regime's loss of superpower support.[16] Furthermore, Rabin apparently did not really

---

11. Robert C. McFarlane, with Zofia Smardz, *Special Trust* (New York: Cadell and Davies, 1994), 17–27; Parsi, *Treacherous Alliance*, 116–121.

12. Efraim Inbar, *Rabin and Israel's National Security* (Washington, DC: Wilson Center Press, 1999), 138–39.

13. Parsi, *Treacherous Alliance*, 168.

14. Ibid., 131.

15. Dan Raviv and Yossi Melman, *Spies against Armageddon: Inside Israel's Secret Wars* (Sea Cliff, NY: Levant Books, 2012), 3.

16. Michael Roten, "Bully of Baghdad Can No Longer Fight," *Jerusalem Post*, January 15, 1993, 5; Inbar, *Rabin and Israel's National Security*, 134–40. This was also the gist

believe that Iran represented a mortal threat to Israel even in the middle term. He suggested privately that Iran would not be able to acquire a nuclear weapon for another 10 to 15 years—two to three times longer than he had asserted publicly two years earlier.[17]

For Rabin, invoking an extraordinary new threat from Iran had an immediate domestic political objective: deflecting Israeli animosity away from the Palestinians and providing political cover for Rabin's moves for peace with the Palestine Liberation Organization (PLO). The need to nego-tiate with the Palestinian resistance organization was the central thrust of Rabin's national security policy. Rabin's official strategic formulation was that peace negotiations with the Palestinians were necessary to resolve Israel's "inner circle of threat" so that it would be strong enough to face the "outer circle of threat" from Iran's nuclear program and its alleged promo-tion of Shi'a extremism. Later, belligerently anti-Iran Israelis would argue that the strategy was driven by a genuine fear of an aggressive Iran.[18] But Yossi Alpher, who became an aide to Rabin during the period the prime minister was applying his Iran/Palestinian strategy and would become an adviser to Prime Minister Ehud Barak in 1999, has made it is very clear that it was Rabin's interest in opening talks with the PLO that drove the new policy toward Iran. As Alpher recalled in an interview, "In 1993–94, Rabin justified his Palestinian policy by arguing that it would strengthen Israel in dealing with Iran."[19]

Mark Heller, a senior researcher at the Jaffee Center for Strategic Studies at Tel Aviv University, confirmed that the purpose of portraying a threat from Iran in alarming terms was to "help the Rabin Government with Israelis who harbored doubts about the peace talks with the Palestine Liberation Organization." That required portraying the twin threat of Iran and Shiites in the region in the most lurid terms possible. The argument the Rabin government was making, Heller said, was "if you don't make peace with these guys, look what's coming next—Islamic fundamental-ists with nuclear arms behind them."[20] A senior adviser to Rabin, Itamar Rabinovich, later argued that "the threat was real, it wasn't invented," but

of the analysis presented to US presidential candidate Bill Clinton by Martin Indyk, who clearly was getting his cues from the Rabin government, in preparing him to meet Rabin in fall 1992, in Indyk, *Innocent Abroad*, 15–16.

17. Kaye, Nader, and Rosha, *Israel and Iran*, 21. The authors cite an interview with an "Israeli analyst" in Tel Aviv in August 2010.

18. Yossi Klein Halevi and Michael B. Oren, "Israel's Worst Nightmare," *New Republic*, February 5, 2007.

19. Author's interview with Yossi Alpher, June 25, 2012.

20. Clyde Haberman, "Israel Eyes Iran in the Fog of Nuclear Politics," *New York Times*, January 15, 1995, 4.

he admitted to historian Trita Parsi that it was exaggerated for political purposes. Efraim Inbar, of the Begin-Sadat Center for Strategic Studies at Bar-Ilan University in Israel, who wrote an admiring account of Rabin's national security policy, was more candid. "Rabin played the Iran threat more than it was deserved in order to sell the peace process," he said.[21]

The provision of political cover for negotiations with the PLO was not the only unacknowledged political function of the Iranian threat campaign. Especially at the beginning, Rabin was also interested in negotiating with Israel's Arab neighbors, and inflating the threat from Iran was aimed at appealing to Arab regimes that did not trust Iran, particularly those that were pro-Western. The idea was to convince the Arab regimes that they shared with Israel what Dennis Ross, Bill Clinton's Middle East coordinator at the time, called "a common threat in Iran and fundamentalism." Yossi Alpher, reflecting the Rabin government's thinking, commented in May 1993, "If you are looking for a silver lining in the Iran threat, it may be that it could be a unifying factor in moving Israel and its Arab neighbors closer in finding a way to deal with that threat."[22] It was not a new idea: the Reagan administration had tried but failed to convince the Likud government of Prime Minister Yitzhak Shamir to seek a "strategic consensus" with the "moderate" Arab regimes against Iran.[23]

Rabin's new political line on Iran also served two strategic objectives in relation to US policy: to induce the United States to use its power to eliminate the Iranian nuclear program through force or the threat of force and to enhance the value of Israel as a strategic ally of the United States in the region. When Rabin called for an "appropriate international effort to prevent Iran from achieving its end," he was acknowledging that Israel itself was limited in its ability to use military force against Iran, and that it would be up to the United States to use its superior military power to threaten Iran over the issue of its nuclear program. Even as Israel was making the alleged threat from Iran a leitmotif of its foreign policy, Israeli officials and political leaders admitted privately that they hoped to avoid having to invest the billions of dollars that would be needed if Israel were to seriously engage in a military competition with Iran.[24]

One of the ways Israel could get the United States to increase the pressure on Iran was to argue that Iran was just a few years away from getting a nuclear bomb. The public Israeli estimate that Iran would be able to get

21. Parsi, *Treacherous Alliance*, 170, 180.

22. Jon Immanuel, "Newsline with Joseph Alpher," *Jerusalem Post*, May 19, 1993, 2.

23. Parsi, *Treacherous Alliance*, 169.

24. David Hoffman, "Israel Seeking to Convince U.S. That West Is Threatened by Iran," *Washington Post*, March 13, 1993, A14.

a nuclear weapon within five years was a ploy to push the United States to adopt a more coercive approach to the Iranian nuclear program. When Defense Secretary William Perry met with Rabin in Israel in January 1995, the Israeli and US estimates of the "years to an Iranian bomb" were sharply divergent—at least for public consumption. After the meeting, Perry and Rabin agreed publicly on a range of 7 to 15 years. But Perry hinted strongly that the United States had pushed for the longer end of the estimate, saying the Iranians had "many, many years" to go.[25]

Later in 1995, the Israelis used what they claimed was new intelligence about the Iranian nuclear program to try to persuade the United States to take a more aggressive posture toward it. Maj. Gen. Yaakov Amidror, then head of research and assessment for the IDF, later recalled that he and a delegation of military intelligence analysts had tried and failed in 1995 to convince their American counterparts they had "found the first signs that the Iranians were going nuclear."[26]

But in 1995, Mossad still considered the Iranian nuclear program to be a relatively low risk to Israeli security, according to then Mossad director Shavit. He recalled later that his "personal trigger" in regard to becoming concerned about Iran's nuclear program was when Iran began to "increase the range of its missiles." The Iraq threat did not "justify the enlargement of the missile range to more than 1,000 kilometers," Shavit told the interviewer.[27]

But Iran had no missile with that kind of range in 1995. In mid-December 1994, Rabin himself accused North Korea of supplying Iran with missiles that had a range of only 300 miles (485 kilometers).[28] It was not until 1996 that the Israeli press reported that Iran had received ten Nodong missiles from North Korea.[29] Even then, Israeli experts believed that Iran was experiencing "major problems and delays in creating a domestic missile production capability," according to American analyst Michael Eisenstadt, who consulted with Israeli government specialists.[30]

The Israeli attempt to move the US intelligence community toward a more alarmist posture in 1995 was a complete failure. "At the end of our

25. Haberman, "Israel Eyes Iran."

26. Maj. Gen. Yaakov Amidror, "The U.S. National Intelligence Estimate on Iran and Its Aftermath," Jerusalem Center for Public Affairs, March 9, 2008, http://jcpa.org/article/the-u-s-national-intelligence-estimate-on-iran-and-its-aftermath-a-roundtable-of-israeli-experts-3/.

27. Melman and Javadanfar, *Nuclear Sphinx*, 151–52 and 155–56.

28. Parsi, *Treacherous Alliance*, 184, 323n81.

29. Michael Elleman, *Iran's Ballistic Missile Capabilities*, 21.

30. Michael Eisenstadt, *Iranian Military Power: Capabilities and Intentions* (Washington, DC: Washington Institute for Near East Policy, 1996), 30.

discussions," Amidror recalled, "the U.S. side gave us the impression that they were thinking to themselves, 'After we Americans finish off Iraq as an enemy of the State of Israel, then you Israelis are going to build a new threat because you cannot live without such a threat.'"[31] Amidror's remark suggests that US Defense Intelligence Agency analysts, like others in the US intelligence community, understood that the Israelis were exaggerating the evidence of Iranian nuclear intent in order to advance their political interests.

Apart from justifying the Rabin government policy of negotiating with the Palestinians and pushing the United States to take a more confrontational stance toward Iran, the creation of a new Iran threat responded to another Israeli strategic political problem. The end of the Cold War had rendered irrelevant a fundamental long-term Israeli political-diplomatic strategy of convincing Washington that Israel was its indispensable ally against its adversaries in the Middle East. Israeli security officials and political leaders revealed in interviews in early 1993 their fear that the demise of the Soviet Union had eliminated one of Israel's most potent assets in its relationship with the United States: its role as the main bulwark in the Middle East against Soviet expansionism. "There was a feeling in Israel that, because of the end of the Cold War, relations with the U.S. were cooling and we needed some new glue for the alliance," recalled Efraim Inbar. Inflating the Iran threat served to create a new regional adversary to replace the Soviet Union in that Israeli strategy.[32]

The idea of Israel as indispensable ally generated a host of political and economic benefits to the Jewish state, not the least of which was to persuade the United States to continue to give it wide latitude in its negotiations with the Palestinians. Even as Rabin was using the Iran threat to provide the political cover for those negotiations in early 1993, his government was anxious about being pushed by the United States to make compromises with the Palestinians that Israel would not accept. Rabin government officials were making the argument to their American counterparts, both directly and through visiting US Jewish groups, that Washington should reduce its pressure on Israel in the negotiations with the Palestinians and Arab governments. The message being conveyed was "Don't push us," because a bad agreement resulting from US pressure on Israel would increase the danger to the West from Iranian-sponsored Islamic fundamentalism.[33]

31. Amidror, "U.S. National Intelligence Estimate."

32. Inbar quote from Parsi, *Treacherous Alliance*, 170; Michael Parks, "Israel Sees Self Defending West against Militants," *Los Angeles Times*, January 2, 1993, 13.

33. Parks, "Israel Sees Self Defending."

## Netanyahu Abandons the Iranian Threat

Just a little over two weeks after Likud Party chairman Benjamin Netanyahu took over as prime minister of Israel in June 1996, he gave a speech to a joint session of the US Congress in which he adjusted only slightly the rhetorical approach taken by the Labor government about the threat from Iran. The major difference was that Netanyahu did not distinguish between Iran and Iraq, treating both as equally dangerous. Still, Netanyahu appeared to agree with Labor's alarmist view of the Iranian nuclear program, declaring that if either of the "despotic" regimes in Iraq or Iran acquired nuclear weapons, it would have "catastrophic consequences not only for my country and not only for the Middle East but for all mankind." Netanyahu went on to declare that "time is running out" for preventing Iran or Iraq from acquiring such weapons and called for "immediate and effective prevention." The *Times* of London suggested that the reference recalled Israel's bombing of the Iraqi nuclear reactor at Osirak in 1981.[34]

But just as the Rabin government's worldwide propaganda campaign about the Iranian threat did not reflect the actual views of Israeli national security strategists and intelligence analysts, Netanyahu's rhetoric did not represent the real strategic thinking about Iran in the new Likud government. Netanyahu had not concluded that Iran was a serious threat to Israel, because he was still conducting a major policy review on the issue.

It was a highly unusual policy review: Netanyahu received two competing assessments on Iran. The first, from Gen. Amos Gilad, the head of the intelligence branch of the IDF, portrayed Iran's missile program as a serious threat to Israel, going so far as to predict that Iranian missiles would be able to hit Israel by 1999. But Gilad was known in intelligence circles to have a "personal vendetta" against Iran, and to embrace an extreme view of the Islamic Republic. He represented a distinctly minority view within IDF intelligence. Most intelligence analysts there agreed that although Iran presented a threat to Israel, the threat was also limited by the nature of Iranian politics. They viewed the future of the Islamic regime as far from certain, even in the short run. A "national assessment" by IDF intelligence, which had already been completed, had rejected the alarmist view of Iran by Gilad, who had written the first draft. The final draft had concluded that Iran might have nuclear weapons as early

34. Speech by Prime Minister Benjamin Netanyahu to joint session of Congress, July 10, 1996, http://www.mfa.gov.il/MFA/MFAArchive/1990_1999/1996/7/PM%20 Netanyahu-%20Speech%20to%20US%20Congress-%20July%2010-%201996.aspx; *Times* (London), July 10, 1996.

as 2005, but that the Islamic hard-liners would likely already have been replaced by then.[35]

The other assessment, from Mossad, Israel's international intelligence agency, suggested that Iran's missile program was driven by fear of Saddam's Iraq rather than by a determination to target Israel. The Mossad view, presented by Uzi Arad, the head of the intelligence analysis side of the organization, reflected the continued adherence of Israeli intelligence officials to the periphery doctrine. He argued that Iran's ballistic missile program had begun during its eight-year war with Iraq, in which Iraqi missiles had hit its population centers—including, ultimately, Tehran—and that Iran's air force had remained woefully weak. Mossad's analysts believed that Iran's progress in ballistic missiles had been limited by its economic weakness, lack of scientific and technical skills, and heavy dependence on foreign technology, which made it vulnerable to denial strategies. Arad also argued that the Labor government had been provoking unnecessary conflict with Iran by claiming that there was an existential threat to Israel and by suggesting that it might be necessary to use force against Iran if the program continued to develop.[36]

Just around the time Netanyahu was considering his Iran policy options, the Mossad arguments suggesting a lack of urgent concern about the Iranian missile program were reflected in a study published by the Washington Institute for Near East Policy, which usually mirrors the thinking of Israeli national security strategists. The analysis of the Iranian missile program by Michael Eisenstadt emphasized the Iranian experience of being victims of Saddam's missile attacks on Iranian cities in 1988, which had contributed to the crisis in morale. Eisenstadt suggested that Iran might view the missile program "as a way to compensate for the weakness of its air and defense forces." He also made the point that Israeli threats to attack the Iranian nuclear program had "lent additional impetus to Iranian effort to acquire long-range missiles such as the North Korean Nodong-1 that are capable of reaching Israel."[37]

In the end Netanyahu sided with Mossad against Gilad. He dialed back the anti-Iran rhetoric of the previous Labor government and even quietly sought a modus vivendi with Iran in the first months of his term in office. Then he chose Uzi Arad, the Mossad intelligence director who had made the more convincing argument on Iran, as his national security adviser.[38]

---

35. Scott Ritter, *Target Iran* (New York: Nation Books, 2006), 23.
36. Parsi, *Treacherous Alliance*, 193–96.
37. Eisenstadt, *Iranian Military Power*, 27–28.
38. Parsi, *Treacherous Alliance*, 196–200.

The domestic Israeli political context gave Netanyahu reason to end Labor's public demonization of Iran. Unlike Rabin, Netanyahu had no immediate political need for a propaganda campaign built around the theme of Iran as the major threat to Israel because he had no intention of negotiating with the Palestinians. The Likud Party was formed in 1973 out of a union between Menachem Begin's Herut movement and other small Jewish nationalist organizations. Herut was in turn based on Ze'ev Jabotinsky's Revisionist Zionism and its determination to achieve "Greater Israel." The Likud Party platform, adopted in 1977, was emphatic on the point: "Judea and Samaria," it said, in biblical references to the West Bank, "will not be handed to any foreign administration; between the sea and the Jordan there will be only Israeli sovereignty."[39]

Netanyahu was dead set against carrying out the Oslo Accords requirement for Israel to negotiate with the Palestinians to "establish a Palestinian Interim Self-Government Authority" pending a final settlement.[40] He declared in his July 1996 speech to the US Congress that Jews had the "right to live anywhere" in "Judea and Samaria."[41] That meant that he had no intention of agreeing to withdraw Israeli troops from the occupied territories, which would have to be a central element of any agreement. He had no reason to continue the Labor government's demonization of Iran to justify its seeking to reach a settlement with the PLO. In fact, because Netanyahu intended to focus the Israeli public on the Palestinians as the main enemy, any focus on Iran would distract from that effort. "Blaming the Iranians for Palestinian terrorism would be counterproductive to his message that terror was coming from the Palestinians," recalled Keith Weissman, who was then working for AIPAC and thus getting regular briefings on the government's thinking.[42]

In 1997, however, Netanyahu began to reverse the public stance he had adopted in 1996, and ultimately shifted to a more belligerent tone toward Iran. What ostensibly triggered the shift in Netanyahu's policy was not a dramatic new development in Iran's nuclear program but what Israeli military intelligence claimed was a major program of assistance to the Iranian ballistic missile program by the Russian government. But in fact, the shift was consistent with Mossad's view that Iran remained vulnerable to a strategy of denial because of the relative weakness of its scientific and engineering capabilities. The return to the threat rhetoric that Netanyahu

39. Likud Party platform (1977), http://www.jewishvirtuallibrary.org/jsource/Politics/LikudPlat1977.html.
40. "Declaration of Principles on Interim Self-Government Arrangements," September 13, 1993, at http://news.bbc.co.uk/2/hi/middle_east/1682727.stm.
41. Speech by Netanyahu to joint session of Congress.
42. Quoted in Parsi, *Treacherous Alliance*, 199.

had rejected in 1996 reflected a new opportunity for Israel to use American power to carry out such a denial strategy. It was prompted in large part by a major shift in US domestic politics on the issue of a ballistic missile defense system that provided a powerful incentive for Netanyahu to take a more aggressive stance toward Iran's missile program.

While the Netanyahu government was experimenting with a low-profile policy toward Iran from mid-1996 to early 1997, the primary national security issue in Washington was the Republican right-wing attack on a 1995 CIA estimate on the ballistic missile threat to the United States. That estimate had concluded that there would be no such threat to the United States from Iran, Iraq, or North Korea for at least 15 years. In 1996, both the missile-defense lobby in Congress and the Republican Party's neo-conservative foreign policy elite, which was close to Netanyahu and the Likud government in Israel, were seeking to reverse that judgment. The Republican-controlled Congress set up a commission, led by former White House chief of staff Donald Rumsfeld, that would present an alternative to the CIA's estimate on the ballistic missile threat.

The new tilt in US politics toward an alarmist view of Iranian missile programs in general offered Israel a potent new form of leverage on Russia to stop any assistance to Iran and slow the Iranian missile program as well as the nuclear program—and perhaps even a new source of leverage on the Clinton administration's policy toward the Oslo Accords. In late 1996, Israeli military intelligence began accusing the government of Russian president Boris Yeltsin of knowingly allowing technology transfers to the Iranian missile program and helping the Iranians develop a medium-range ballistic missile that could reach Tel Aviv. In October 1996, General Gilad, who had lobbied Netanyahu unsuccessfully for a hard line against Iran, told a group of US officials in Washington that Russian missile specialists were shuttling back and forth between Russia and Iran and that Russian companies were involved in every aspect of the development of the new Iranian medium-range missile. Gilad suggested that the technological assistance to Iran was an official Yeltsin government policy, portraying the development of the Iranian Shahab-3 missile as a joint Russian-Iranian project.[43]

Gilad returned to Washington in January 1997 to give a detailed briefing on the alleged Russian policy of helping Iran build a new medium-range missile to Leon Fuerth, Vice President Al Gore's national security adviser. The Israeli military intelligence official charged that a Russian entity had

---

43. Kenneth Timmerman, *Countdown to Crisis: The Coming Nuclear Showdown with Iran* (New York: Three Rivers, 2006), 198–200; "Russia Said Developing Ballistic Missiles with Iran," Channel 2 TV (Jerusalem), February 10, 1997, FBIS FTS199700527001231, May 29, 1997.

sold Iran "detailed instructions on how to construct the Soviet SS-4 ballistic missile," and that information on that Soviet missile's RD-214 engine had been transferred to the Iranian missile program. Gore then confronted Prime Minister Victor Chernomyrdin with the information received from Gilad in February 1997.[44]

Israeli minister of industry and trade Natan Sharansky, a former political prisoner in the Soviet Union who had emigrated to Israel in 1986, lobbied key members of Congress on the alleged Russian export of nuclear and missile technology to Iran.[45] And in early 1997, Netanyahu became personally involved in selling the new argument to President Clinton. He told Clinton that Russian missile technology to Iran threatened Israeli security, and that because of that technology, Iran could potentially launch missiles against Western Europe in the future. He even argued that Iran would eventually build a missile that could reach the Atlantic Coast of the United States.[46]

The Israeli campaign involved leaking what appeared to be particularly damning pieces of intelligence on the Russians' alleged technology assistance to the Iranian missile program. In September 1997, the right-wing *Washington Times* reported that Israeli officials had shown US intelligence officials a copy of a $7 million contract between a Russian company called NPO Trud and the Iranian missile program covering "transfer of equipment related to the SS-4 medium-range missile." And an Israeli intelligence report was said to have included a list of 12 Russian ministries, research institutes, and companies allegedly involved in the transfer of missile technology to Iran, as well as the names of top Russian officials supposedly conniving in the sales.[47]

The Israeli lobbying, leaks of sensational stories to the news media, and congressional hearings based in large part on Israeli intelligence reports led in October 1997 to the introduction in the Senate of a bill called the Iran Missile Proliferation Sanctions Act, which mandated economic sanctions against any state that sold missile technology to Iran and was explicitly aimed at getting the Clinton administration to pressure the Russian government to halt its alleged technology assistance to Iran's missile and

---

44. Robin Wright, "Russia Warned on Helping Iran's Missile Program," *Los Angeles Times*, February 12, 1997, A1, A6.

45. Strobe Talbott, *The Russia Hand: A Memoir of Presidential Diplomacy* (New York: Random House, 2002), 258.

46. "PM on Iran Missile Threat to US," *Qol Israel* (Jerusalem), February 26, 1997, FBIS FT 19970625004069, June 25, 1997.

47. Bill Gerz, "Russia, China and Iran's Missile Program," *Washington Times*, September 10, 1997.

nuclear programs.[48] Netanyahu visited Washington in January 1998 to push the legislation, which passed both houses by overwhelming margins in mid-1998.[49]

Eventually it became clear, however, that the Israelis had vastly exaggerated the extent of the Russian technology transfer to Iran's missile program as well as the degree of official connivance in it, and that the most spectacular allegation of technology transfer was simply not true. A Russian research institute had assisted Iran with a guidance package for the Shahab-3, and the Aerodynamics Institute had sold plans for a wind tunnel.[50] But Russians as well as others involved in investigating the charges concluded that Russian technology sales to Iran were largely confined to dual-use materials and did not include the most sensitive Russian technology.[51] Scott Ritter, who had been on the UN weapons-inspection team in Iraq, likened the kind of goods sold to Iran by Russian companies to what was being sold to Iraq during the same period. "Old equipment destined for the scrap heap, or mothballed material long forgotten in the inventory was now sold by enterprising black marketeers," Ritter argued.[52]

Contrary to the claim in Israeli intelligence reports, the $7 million contract between NPO Trud and the Iranian missile program was not for components of the SS-4 or its engine. According to later reports, the contract didn't specify any particular technology, but the company later learned that Iran was trying to obtain turbopumps for rocket engines. There was no possibility, however, of Iran getting SS-4 technology from NPO Trud, because that company had never been involved in developing or producing the SS-4 or its engine.[53]

Although hundreds of Russian engineers had ended up working in Iran, a later inquiry by the *Washington Post* found that they were lower-level engineers, not top specialists in Russian missiles. "These guys are useful at the level of basic research, not advanced development," Steven Zaloga, a

---

48. Iran Missile Proliferation Sanctions Act of 1997, S. 1311, 105th Cong., 1st sess. (1997), http://thomas.loc.gov/cgi-bin/query/z?c105:S.1311: ; Iran Missile Proliferation Sanctions Act of 1997, report together with additional views (to accompany H.R. 2709), 105th Cong., 1st sess., Rept. 103–305 (1997).

49. Talbott, *Russia Hand*, 260–261.

50. Michael Eisenstadt, "Russian Arms and Technology Transfers to Iran: Policy Challenges for the United States," *Arms Control Today*, March 2001.

51. Michael Dobbs, "A Story of Iran's Quest for Power: A Scientist Details the Role of Russia, *Washington Post*, January 13, 2002, A1.

52. Ritter, *Target Iran*, 24–25.

53. Federation of American Scientists, "Shahab-5/IRSL-X-3, KOSAR/IRIS," http://www.fas.org/nuke/guide/iran/missile/shahab-5.htm; C. P. Vick, "Shahab-5/Kosar/the Simorgh 3, 4 & 5 Series," May 25, 2010, Global Security, http://www.globalsecurity.org/wmd/world/iran/shahab-5.htm.

US defense consultant on military technology, told the *Post*. A department head at the Moscow Aviation Institute, Vadim Vorobei, said that the Iranian program of bringing Russian engineers to the country was not transferring sensitive Russian technology, but rather was aimed at convincing the world that Iran had "a lot of Russians . . . working for them and everybody else should be scared by it."[54] In other words, the hiring of Russians was part of an Iranian effort to appear more advanced in its missile program than it really was for deterrence purposes.

The highly successful Israeli campaign to portray a deliberate Russian program of assistance to Iran in building an intermediate-range ballistic missile was a preview of the way Israel would deploy intelligence reports on Iran's nuclear program. The Israeli reports invariably featured speculative and often far-fetched interpretations of the evidence that were passed off as hard intelligence. Asked later by the *Washington Post* about claims about Russian assistance that were subsequently discredited, Uzi Arad said the Israelis had "evidence that is sufficient to convince us," and they were "not obligated to prove anything to the Russians."[55]

The Israeli campaign of intelligence reports on the Russian government and the Iranian missile program appears to have served multiple Israeli strategic aims. The Israelis hoped increased US pressure on the Russians to cut off assistance to the Iranian program by Russian engineers and private companies would reduce the ability of future Iranian missiles to reach Israel effectively. But the Israeli campaign policy had other potential political benefits for the Likud government. It could help take the pressure off Netanyahu from the Clinton administration over Israel's implementation of the Oslo Accords. Clinton had been pushing Netanyahu to agree to a larger withdrawal from the occupied territories than Netanyahu was willing to accept. One way the focus on Iranian missiles reduced US pressure on Israel was by "changing the channel," as David Makovsky of the Washington Institute for Near East Policy put it.[56] It forced the administration to spend more time and energy responding to Netanyahu's demand on Russia and Iranian missiles and less on the Palestinian issue.

The effect of the Israeli campaign to influence Congress, meanwhile, was to put at risk the close US cooperation with the Yeltsin government in Moscow on key security issues that was the lynchpin of the Clinton administration's Russia policy and, arguably, of its foreign policy in general. By late 1997, Strobe Talbott, Clinton's main adviser on Russia, was worried that the Israeli campaign in Congress was succeeding in taking

54. Dobbs, "Story of Iran's Quest."
55. Ibid.
56. Parsi, *Treacherous Alliance*, 207.

away the administration's flexibility on the question of sanctions against the Yeltsin government. And by early 1998, Talbott had concluded that the policymakers were "losing control of our policy to an assertive and hostile Congress."[57]

That Israeli chokehold on the administration's Russia policy through its ability to influence key Republican congressional figures would make it more difficult for the Clinton administration to pressure the Likud government to make concessions to the Palestinians on withdrawal from the West Bank and other issues. Some US officials viewed the Israeli campaign to convict the Yeltsin government of helping Iran build ballistic missiles as part of Netanyahu's strategy for resisting US pressure to negotiate in good faith with the Palestinians. As one State Department official said, "If Israel can hold the Russia relationship hostage, the Clinton administration may be unable to manage US policy in the Middle East, including the peace process."[58]

After Netanyahu had established Israel's political leverage on the Clinton administration through Russia policy, the conflict between Netanyahu and the administration became more acute. In early May 1998, after 14 months of no progress in the Israeli-Palestinian negotiations, the Clinton administration proposed a plan calling for Israel to withdraw its troops from an additional 13 percent of the West Bank, which would have brought Palestinian control to 40 percent of the territory. But Netanyahu was very reluctant to go along with the demand. He was afraid he could not keep his governing coalition together if he agreed. The National Religious Party, which was closely aligned with Israeli settlers living on what had been Palestinian land, threatened to vote no confidence if Netanyahu went beyond withdrawal from 9 percent of the West Bank.[59]

Two weeks after the Clinton proposal was made public, the Senate passed, 90–4, a bill that imposed sanctions against Russia unless it agreed to take much more active steps to stop the alleged leaking of missile technology to Iran. Clinton quickly vetoed the bill, but he still had to avoid an easy congressional override of the veto. In a "carefully choreographed compromise" between the Clinton and Yeltsin administrations, the Russian government immediately took new measures against entities that had been accused of aiding Iran's missile program, and the Clinton administration

---

57. Talbott, *Russia Hand*, 258, 261.

58. Joseph Fitchett, "Israeli Reaction to Iran's Buildup Is Heightening Nuclear Fears in Mideast," *International Herald Tribune*, December 19, 1997, 6.

59. Doug Struck, "Netanyahu Says U.S. 'Cannot Dictate to Us,'" *Washington Post*, May 7, 1998, A30; Rebecca Trounson, "Breakthrough Could Be Near in Mideast," *Los Angeles Times*, June 6, 1998; Itamar Rabinovich, *The Lingering Conflict: Israel, the Arabs, and the Middle East, 1948–2012* (Washington, DC: Brookings Institution Press, 2012), 80.

came up with a formula that it hoped would satisfy Congress involving "trade restrictions" on entities the Russian government was sanctioning.[60] But the administration knew it had to have Israeli help in getting House speaker Newt Gingrich to accept a version of the bill that preserved some flexibility in sanctioning Russia, and the Israelis agreed to help.[61] A former adviser to Rabin, Itamar Rabinovich, noting how Netanyahu was able to mobilize a number of key members of Congress, including Gingrich, to support his position, observed that there was "no precedent for this level of Israeli involvement in US domestic politics."[62]

Despite that new political leverage on the administration, Netanyahu accepted Clinton's insistence on the 13 percent withdrawal at the Wye River Conference with PLO leader Yasser Arafat in October 1998. After starting to carry it out, however, Netanyahu halted the withdrawal process as he began to prepare for general elections for the Knesset and for the prime minister's position in May 1999. Netanyahu's loss to the Labor Party's Ehud Barak ended his experiment in using alarmist claims about Iranian nuclear and missile programs and hints of a military option to manipulate US policy. But his successor continued the rhetorical line on Iran that both Labor and Likud governments had embraced.

## Netanyahu Returns to Threats against Iran

The final stage of Netanyahu's evolving Iran policy was a new campaign of military threats toward Tehran. After the delivery in November 1997 of the first of 25 advanced US F-151 fighter planes, which had been chosen because of their longer range and larger payload, the Netanyahu government began to raise the possibility of a preemptive attack on Iran if the missile and nuclear programs continued to advance. Netanyahu referred on several occasions to Israel's 1981 attack on Iraq's Osirak reactor without explicitly linking it to Iran. Meanwhile, word was being leaked to the press that military planners were studying the options of hitting Iranian missile plants or assassinating foreign scientists alleged to be working at the facilities. The government also circulated rumors through diplomatic channels that an attack on an Iranian missile facility was imminent, while communicating through diplomatic channels that a preventive strike would be launched by the end of 1998 if there was no change in Iran's

60. Talbott, *Russia Hand*, 273.

61. Michael Dobbs, "How Politics Helped Define Threat," *Washington Post*, January 14, 2002, A1.

62. Itamar Rabinovich, "A Price to Pay," *Jerusalem Post*, May 15, 1998, 8.

missile-development program. US officials privately called the tactic, which avoided direct, public threats, a "bluff."[63]

Netanyahu combined the threats with a new rhetorical line, claiming that Iran represented "the most serious threat since 1948." That was the statement Netanyahu made at a January 1998 meeting sponsored by Labor Party Knesset member Efraim Sneh, who was taking the most aggressive posture toward Iran in the country. And in conversations with US officials, Netanyahu began using the term "existential threat" to describe Iran's missile program.[64] That kind of rhetoric and the threats that were conveyed to the Iranians represented precisely the policy that Netanyahu's advisers had warned Netanyahu 18 months earlier was causing Iran to view Israel as a potential adversary.

The timing of the turn back to threats—even if made indirectly rather than being stated by officials of the Netanyahu government—suggests that once again, Israeli belligerence toward Iran was actually serving an entirely different Israeli interest. In this case, the purpose appears to have been to fend off a US-Iranian rapprochement that seemed like a distinct possibility at that point. It came after reformist Mohammad Khatami, elected president of Iran unexpectedly in May 1997, sent obvious signals that he was interested in improving relations with the United States. In his first months in office, Khatami had named a new foreign minister, former UN ambassador Kamal Kharrazi, and other cabinet ministers who were attacked by hard-line conservatives as lacking "hatred toward America," and Khatami also began speaking publicly about a "dialogue of civilizations," saying Iran would have relations with "any state that respects our independence." And former Iranian officials with ties to the regime were dispatched to Washington to contact a wide range of US officials with the message that rapprochement between Iran and the United States was possible if Washington was interested.[65]

Watching that process, the Netanyahu government was determined to do whatever it could to prevent any warming of US-Iranian relations from occurring.[66] The tactic of threatening Iran at a time when the Khatami government had made no move indicating hostility toward Israel appears to have been aimed at provoking a public anti-Israel reaction from Iran that

63. Fitchett, "Israeli Reaction"; Christopher Walker, "Israel Steps Up Plans for Air Attacks on Iran," *Times* (London), December 9, 1997, 14.

64. Jim Hoagland, "Hammering at Russia," *Washington Post*, January 8, 1998, A21.

65. Kenneth M. Pollack, *The Persian Puzzle: The Conflict between Iran and America* (New York: Random House, 2004), 312–16.

66. Matthew Campbell and Uzi Mahnaimi, "Iran's Mullahs on Brink of a Nuclear Bomb," *Sunday Times* (London), December 21, 1997, 13; "Netanyahu Working to Prevent U.S. Policy Shift on Iran," *Haaretz* (Tel Aviv), December 15, 1997.

would make it more difficult for the Clinton administration to respond positively to Khatami's apparent interest in a thaw in relations.

But instead of lashing out with aggressive rhetoric toward Israel, Iran gave a carefully modulated response to the Netanyahu government's threats. Iranian strategists were not in a position to raise tensions with Israel by issuing military counterthreats. The Iranian missile that the Netanyahu government was hyping as a threat to Israel would not even be ready for its first flight test until July 1998—and then it turned out to be a failure. Iran's defense strategists were still struggling to find a formula for a deterrent to an Israeli attack.

A few days after the Iranian missile flight test in 1998, Iranian defense minister Ali Shamkhani said in an interview with a Saudi newspaper that a military strike against Iran by the United States or Israel was "unlikely in the foreseeable future." Then he repeated it for emphasis: "At the moment, this is unlikely." In August 1998, Khatami declared that Iran's intermediate-range missile, the Shahab-3, "had been developed to defend against Israel and not Iran's neighbors." Khatami suggested that the Israelis could still influence Iran's decision on deployment by clearly backing off its threat to attack Iran's nuclear reactor, saying, "At the moment we do not have any plans to produce these missiles, but if we feel the need, we would do so."[67] If the Israeli tone toward Iran changed, Khatami implied, Iranian-Israeli relations could return to the status quo that existed before the Israeli threats; if not, Iran would be forced to take steps to prepare for a possible war with Israel.

The British press reported that the Khatami government tried to follow up with a diplomatic probe the following spring. Iran asked the British government to facilitate contact with Israel to discuss arms control measures between the two countries. An Israeli official confirmed that there had been a "hint" of Iranian interest in direct talks in April, but Israel apparently had not expressed any interest in such talks, and Iran immediately denied the report as "baseless."[68]

The carefully measured Iranian response appears to have confirmed the skepticism of some within Netanyahu's own party about the wisdom of aggressive gestures toward Iran. When Sneh, a retired brigadier general in the IDF, called for a preemptive strike against Iran in September 1998, the Likud Party chairman of the Knesset Foreign Affairs and Defense

---

67. Anthony H. Cordesman, *Iran's Military Forces in Transition: Conventional Threats and Weapons of Mass Destruction* (Westport, CT: Greenwood, 1999), 252.

68. Robin Allen, Judy Dempsey, Mark Huband, and David Wighton, "Iran Moves to Open Dialog with Israel," *Financial Times* (London), June 21, 1999, 6; Patrick Cockburn, "Tehran Seeks Arms Talks with Israel," *Independent* (London), June 21, 1999, 11; "Iran Denies Report over Talks with Israel," Xinhua, June 21, 1999.

Committee, Uzi Landau, warned that such "unnecessary chatter" could increase the likelihood of Israel being targeted by Iranian missiles. [69] But in mid-1999, the Netanyahu government fell after Likud's loss in a general election, and in July 1999, Sneh was named deputy minister of defense in the new Labor government.[70] The message from Sneh's remark for Iran's national security strategists would certainly have been that Iran needed to accelerate work on the Shahab-3 missile.

Although the new government of Ehud Barak came to power with more rhetoric about the threat from Iran, Israeli intelligence was still saying essentially what it had said under previous governments: Israeli security interests would not be served by a confrontation with Iran. In 2000, the director of Mossad, Ephraim Halevy, was still basing his assessment of Iran on a residual form of the periphery doctrine. Although he estimated that Iran would be capable of having a nuclear weapon by 2010, he did not believe there was any way to prevent it if Iran chose to do so. Halevy believed that Israel should nevertheless seek to explore an accord for mutual coexistence with Iran, even if it were only tacit rather than explicit, in the face of what he called a "Sunni ocean" in the region representing the primary danger for both countries.[71]

The history of the origins and early development of Israel's Iran nuclear scare and threat to attack Iran over its nuclear and missile programs highlights a pattern in which both the Rabin and Netanyahu governments deliberately exaggerated the threat from Iran, in sharp contradiction with the Israeli intelligence assessment. The ruse served a variety of political interests, most of which were related to the manipulation of US policy in the region. Both Rabin and Netanyahu sought to get Washington to take on the task of forcing Iran to abandon its nuclear program in part to ensure that Washington would still regard its alliance with Israel as a central fixture of its Middle East policy. Both Rabin and Netanyahu also used hints of Israeli military action against Iran as part of the conscious construction of an Iranian nuclear scare at a time when Tehran had not yet decided to focus on Israel as an adversary.

---

69. Douglas Davis, "Iran: Military Buildup Is Needed to Counter Israel," *Jerusalem Post*, August 2, 1998, 3; "Iran Unveils Missile, Has Plans for More," *Milwaukee Journal*, September 27, 1998, 16; "Iran's New Medium-Range Missile Prompts Fierce Debate in Israel," *Oregonian* (Portland, OR), September 28, 1998, A5.

70. "Ephraim Sneh, MK," Israeli Parliament (Knesset) website, http://www.knesset.gov.il/mk/eng/mk_eng.asp?mk_individual_id_t=94.

71. Alain Chouet, "Why Iran Will Have the Bomb," European Strategic Intelligence and Security Center, Background Analysis, March 5, 2007, http://alain.chouet.free.fr/import/Iran0_EN.pdf, 7. Chouet was former head of the French intelligence service, DGSE.

The consequences of the Israeli policy of inflating a threat from a nuclear Iran to achieve other objectives were far-reaching. Although the Israeli threat of war against Iran did not reflect the government's actual intent, Iranian officials were obliged to take it seriously. By suggesting a militarily aggressive stance toward Iran, however disingenuously, the Labor and Likud governments quite unnecessarily made Israel a military adversary that would eventually be targeted by Iranian missiles. The deceptive Rabin and Netanyahu policies established a template that would be followed by every Israeli government after them and would become a central element in the manufactured crisis.

6

# Choosing Regime Change
# Over Diplomacy

## Bush Administration and Regime Change

After the Natanz facility was revealed in mid-2002, the George W. Bush administration's policy toward Iran's nuclear program appeared on the surface to be aimed at forcing Iran to give up the program, thus continuing the thrust of the Clinton administration's policy. But like so much of the politics and policies surrounding the issue, that public posture was a cover for a rather different policy. The administration was actually less concerned about the Iranian nuclear program than about delegitimizing the Iranian regime. And that ambition for regime change distorted the Bush policy toward the nuclear issue, perversely skewing it toward provoking Iran to accelerate its enrichment program.

The administration's strategy in the Middle East was based on the firm conviction that the Islamic regime in Iran would fall within a few years as part of the broader redrawing of the political map of the region that the neoconservatives were planning. From 2003 to 2005, the Bush administration's foreign policy was dominated by its project for overthrowing Saddam Hussein and turning Iraq into a base for projecting US power into the rest of the Middle East. The result was expected to be a string of regime changes in those countries that had not been de facto allies of the United States. Dennis Ross, the first fellow at the Washington Institute for Near East Policy after it was set up in 1985 and thus privy to the thinking of the neoconservative strategists, told journalist Jeffrey Goldberg in 2002 that the Iraq operation would "legitimize American led 'regime change' in the Middle East." And it would leave Iran surrounded by pro-American governments in Kabul,

Baghdad, and Istanbul.[1] Iran was targeted as the biggest prize of all in the regime change strategy.

That strategy was first laid out in a paper sent by Secretary of Defense Donald Rumsfeld to Bush on September 30, 2001, calling for the administration to focus not on taking down Osama bin Laden's al-Qaeda network but on establishing "new regimes" in a series of states by "aiding local peoples to rid themselves of terrorists and to free themselves of regimes that support terrorism." It was issued as "Strategic Guidance for the Defense Department" on October 3, 2001—just three days after it had gone to the president. That document, drafted by Undersecretary of Defense Douglas Feith in consultation with the Joint Staff at the Pentagon, said that the Defense Department would seek to isolate and weaken those states and to "disrupt, damage, or destroy" their military capacities—not necessarily limited to WMD. The document included as a "strategic objective" a requirement to "prevent further attacks against the U.S. or U.S. interests"—language so broad as to justify plans to use force against virtually any state that was not a client of the United States.[2]

The list of states that Rumsfeld and Deputy Secretary of Defense Paul Wolfowitz wanted to take down included Iraq, Iran, Syria, Libya, Sudan, and Somalia, according to a general working in the Pentagon who passed it on to Gen. Wesley Clark in November 2001. After a public appearance in 2008, Feith revealed to this writer that all six countries were on the list for regime change in the Pentagon paper.[3]

Feith was part of a tight-knit group of neoconservatives at the Pentagon and on Vice President Cheney's staff. The Pentagon group included David Wurmser, who was the most vocal and passionate advocate for regime change in Iraq, Iran, and Syria, and Wolfowitz. The group within Cheney's office included John Hannah and Scooter Libby, both of whom subscribed to the regime change strategy. They all believed strongly that a show of the effectiveness of US military power would shake the foundations of the regime in Iran, according to Hillary Mann Leverett, who was coordinator for the Persian Gulf and Afghanistan on the National Security Council staff in 2002 and 2003.[4]

1. Jeffrey Goldberg, "A Reporter at Large: In the Party of God (pt. 1)," *New Yorker*, October 14, 2002.

2. Douglas J. Feith, *War and Decision: Inside the Pentagon at the Dawn of the War on Terrorism* (New York: Harper, 2008), 81–85.

3. Gareth Porter, "Pentagon Targeted Iran for Regime Change after 9/11," Inter Press Service, Antiwar.com, May 6, 2008.

4. Gareth Porter, "For Neocons, Iran Aim Is Still Regime Change," Inter Press Service, October 30, 2007; Interview with Hillary Mann Leverett, McLean, VA, March 14, 2013.

Wurmser and his colleagues regarded the 1999 student protests in Iran—the largest political protests since the 1979 revolution—as evidence that the population was seething with revolt against the regime. "They believed most Iranians were ready for secular democracy," recalled Leverett. National security adviser Condoleezza Rice was also intrigued by the prospects for regime change in Iran. The main difference between her and the vice president's office was that she didn't want the administration to talk about it openly, whereas Cheney's advisers wanted to "put regime change on a banner," Leverett recalled. And the idea resonated with Bush. "I remember hearing the president talking about this," said Leverett. "He said one of the reasons for doing Iraq was if you created democracy in Iraq, it would empower people in Iran who wanted democracy."[5]

The neoconservatives did not view regime change in Iran as proceeding independently of US military power, according to Leverett, but they expected that it would require less violence than was necessary to remove Saddam Hussein in Iraq.[6] They believed, however, that it would be necessary to use force to remove the Bashar al-Assad regime in Syria, which was a key ally of Iran, and thus strike a crucial blow to Iran's prestige, as Wurmser asserted in an interview after leaving the administration. Wurmser and the other regime change advocates also insisted that the United States had to be prepared to make war on Iran if and when the time came to do so.[7] Meanwhile, the regime change advocates were content to wait for the political changes by force in Baghdad and Damascus to have their mobilizing effect in Iran.

Rice viewed President Mohamed Khatami, the surprise winner of the 1997 election, as the "Gorbachev" of Iran who was trying to reform the regime while keeping it from falling apart, according to Leverett. The regime change strategy required a search for the Iranian "Yeltsin" who would actually dissolve the Islamic state and declare a secular liberal republic. But the neoconservatives never identified anyone who could conceivably play that role. Cheney himself was actively involved in pursuing the objective of regime change in Iran, according to Leverett, who was tasked with writing a National Security Presidential Memorandum on the subject. In 2002, Cheney even met secretly with the shah's son, former prince Reza Pahlavi, who the Vice President's Office believed could be useful in undermining a regime seen as on the verge of collapse.[8]

---

5. Interview with Hillary Mann Leverett.
6. Porter, "For Neocons."
7. Toby Harnden, "US 'Must Break Iran and Syrian Regimes,'" *Telegraph* (London), October 5, 2007.
8. Interview with Hillary Mann Leverett.

The neoconservatives were uniquely impervious to realities on the ground in the region. Leverett recalled being "astounded" to hear the advocates of regime change in the administration suggest as late as 2005 that the situation in Iraq was on track to help destabilize Iran, even though US intelligence and the US military command in Iraq had concluded that the Iraqi resistance to the occupation was continuing to grow. That extreme confidence of the neoconservatives in their utopian analysis of Iran and the rest of the region only waned in late 2005, after which neoconservatives began arguing openly for all-out war against Iran.[9]

The neoconservative project for regime change in the Middle East required that the administration reject any form of cooperation with Iran, even if it concerned an objective that was ostensibly very important to the United States. The State Department responded to the 9/11 attacks with a strategy that involved cooperation with Iran and Syria, on intelligence sharing and possibly joint operations against al-Qaeda. But in December 2001, the neoconservatives, with Wolfowitz in the lead, vetoed any such cooperation before the issue reached the most senior officials in the administration. The rules for dealing with Iran and Syria excluded any cooperation with them against al-Qaeda. Iran was not to be treated as a sovereign equal, regardless of the circumstances. The regime change policy had trumped what was supposedly a primary interest of the United States.[10]

Then, at the beginning of May 2003, came an Iranian diplomatic move that no one in Washington had anticipated: a two-page detailed proposal for direct US-Iranian negotiations on the full range of issues that divided them, sent to the White House through the Swiss ambassador in Tehran, Tim Guldimann. The Iranians offered to negotiate on their nuclear program and their policy toward Israel, Hezbollah and Palestinian armed groups, Iraq, and cooperation on al-Qaeda. But they wanted the United States to negotiate an end to its "hostile behavior," including removing Iran from the US "axis of evil" and terrorism lists and ending all economic sanctions. And finally, they wanted US "recognition of Iran's legitimate security interests in the Persian Gulf." The Iranians proposed three parallel working groups to negotiate "road maps" for three sets of issues: weapons of mass destruction, terrorism and regional security, and economic cooperation.

But the Bush administration's undeclared commitment to regime change in Iran ruled out any possibility of exploring a diplomatic engagement with Iran. According to Flynt Leverett, former senior director

---

9.  Porter, "For Neocons"; Reuel Marc Gerecht, "To Bomb, or Not to Bomb," *Weekly Standard* (New York), April 24, 2006.

10.  Gareth Porter, "Burnt Offering," *American Prospect*, June 2006, 20–23.

for Middle East affairs on the NSC staff, only a few days after the receipt of the letter, Secretary of State Colin Powell was instructed that there would be no reply to the proposal, except to dispatch a message of displeasure with the Swiss ambassador for having passed on the message. Not a single interagency meeting had been convened to discuss the matter before the decision was made, Leverett pointed out.[11]

Bush still had not called off a meeting in Geneva between the presidential envoy to Afghanistan, Zalmay Khalilzad, and Iranian ambassador Mohammad Javad Zarif scheduled for later in May, one of a series of meetings taking place in Geneva. But Rumsfeld and Cheney exploited a terrorist bombing in Riyadh on May 12, 2003, to close down that diplomatic channel. Rumsfeld declared, "We know there are senior al Qaeda in Iran . . . presumably not an ungoverned area." In fact, US intelligence believed there were border areas of Iran where the government's control was very limited and where al-Qaeda cadres could easily hide, but Rumsfeld and Cheney persuaded Bush that Iran was aligned with al-Qaeda, and he agreed to cancel the meeting with Zarif scheduled for May 21.[12]

The policy of refusing any engagement with Iran had far-reaching implications for the Bush administration's handling of the issue of Iran's nuclear program. In rejecting a diplomatic understanding with Iran, the administration was revealing its disinterest in heading off a full-fledged enrichment program by Iran unless it was accomplished through force. "They were not really interested in trying to keep Iran's enrichment program in check," Hillary Mann Leverett recalled, because the neoconservative view was, "We were going to be on the march, so it didn't matter if they enriched." In one conversation with Leverett in 2003, people in Cheney's office made it clear that they didn't want to focus on the nuclear issue, because, as they explained, "After regime change, we may not want to oppose possession of nuclear weapons by Iran."[13]

## The Europeans Intervene Diplomatically

What the Bush administration wanted in 2003 was to head off any agreement between Iran and the IAEA, which would enhance Iran's legitimacy and inhibit the administration's freedom of action to bring about regime change. That was the task given to John Bolton, undersecretary of state for arms control and international security and the administration's main policymaker on proliferation.

---

11. Porter, "Burnt Offering," 24.
12. Ibid.
13. Interview with Hillary Mann Leverett.

Before joining the administration, Bolton had hitched his wagon to the interests of Israel, and especially of the right-wing Likudists. A longtime member of the Advisory Board of the Jewish Institute for National Security Affairs, Bolton supported the Iran regime change policy. His special assistant from early 2002 to late 2003 had been David Wurmser.[14] From Bolton's office, Wurmser had moved to the office of Vice President Cheney, where he had even more influence over US policy in the Middle East.

From mid-2003 on, Bolton was determined to move the Iran issue out of the IAEA to the UN Security Council."[15] The idea was to prevent IAEA director general Mohamed ElBaradei from reaching an agreement with Iran, blurring Iran's status as part of the "axis of evil." But it was also aimed at clearing the path to regime change by force, if necessary. "I just wanted to finish checking the boxes (first the IAEA and then the Council)," Bolton wrote in his memoirs, "either to get the real and substantial support we needed or to show the 'multilateralists' that we had tried their route and were now going outside the UN system to do what we needed to do." The Israelis were warning him that Iran was getting close to "the point of no return" when it would have mastered the entire nuclear fuel cycle, and at that point, "we could not stop their progress toward nuclear weapons without using force."[16]

But both ElBaradei and the three leading European Union states—the United Kingdom, France, and Germany, sometimes referred to as the EU-3—were determined to avoid having the Iran nuclear issue taken to the Security Council. ElBaradei had already made himself a thorn in the side of the Bush administration. At a UN Security Council meeting shortly before the invasion of Iraq, ElBaradei had delivered a stinging refutation of the Bush administration's claims about Saddam Hussein's nuclear weapons program, based on the IAEA's investigations.[17] Bolton knew that ElBaradei would seek to frustrate his plan; he viewed ElBaradei as "more interested in trying to cut a deal than in faithfully reporting what IAEA inspectors were telling him" and disparaged the IAEA as "the UN's nuclear watchpuppy."[18]

ElBaradei's August 26, 2003, report provided no accusation against Iran on which to base a demand for referral to the Security Council.[19] Bolton

14. Jim Lobe, "New Cheney Adviser Sets Syria in His Sights," Inter Press Service, October 20, 2003.

15. John R. Bolton, *Surrender Is Not an Option* (New York: Threshold Editions, 2007), 136.

16. Ibid., 153, 140.

17. Mohamed ElBaradei, "The Status of Nuclear Inspections in Iraq: An Update," statement to the UN Security Council, March 7, 2003, http://www.iaea.org/newscenter/statements/2003/ebsp2003n006.shtml.

18. Bolton, *Surrender*, 135.

19. GOV/2003/63, August. 26, 2003, 9.

nevertheless wanted the resolution adopted at the September meeting of the IAEA Board of Governors to include language calling for referral in November. He ordered Ambassador Ken Brill, the US permanent representative to the IAEA, to lobby for it. But the three most important European allies were not in agreement. The US invasion and occupation of Iraq, which the administration believed had created great fear in the minds of the Iranians, also made the United Kingdom, France, and Germany unwilling to cooperate with Bolton's strategy on Iran.

A few days before the board was to meet in Vienna on September 8, Bolton learned that the EU-3 would not support him on referral to the Security Council, although they promised that they would "lay the basis" for such a move. The resolution that was approved by the board requested that ElBaradei "submit a report in November 2003 or earlier if appropriate, on the implementation of this resolution, allowing the Board to draw definitive conclusions." The resolution also called on Iran to "remedy all failures identified by the Agency and cooperate fully with the Agency to ensure verification of compliance with Iran's safeguards agreement by taking all necessary actions by the end of October 2003."[20]

Under that threat of being brought before the Security Council, Hassan Rouhani, now Iran's nuclear policy chief, negotiated the Tehran Declaration with the foreign ministers of the United Kingdom, France, and Germany on October 21, 2003. Iran pledged to sign the Additional Protocol, the revised IAEA safeguards agreement mandating much more intrusive inspections and reporting requirements, and to suspend enrichment and reprocessing activities.[21] The Europeans were offering in return to block the Americans from taking Iran to the Security Council. "The Europeans did not want to see that case go to the UN Security Council and cause another crisis in the region," Rouhani recalled later. "They promised us they would resist and would not allow that case to go to the UN Security Council."[22] British foreign minister Jack Straw and German foreign minister Joschka Fisher told Rouhani that their objective in negotiating with Iran was to serve as a "human shield" against an American or Israeli attack on Iran's nuclear facilities, which they clearly viewed as a possible result of the US move to take Iran to the Security Council.[23] That objective was

20. GOV/2003/69, September 12, 2003, "Resolution Adopted by the Board on 12 September 2003," 2–3.

21. "Statement by the Iranian Government and Visiting EU Foreign Ministers," October 21, 2003, http://www.iaea.org/newscenter/focus/iaeairan/statement_iran21102003.shtml.

22. Rouhani speech.

23. Mousavian, *Iranian Nuclear Crisis*, 103; ElBaradei quotes Straw and Fisher as telling him the same thing. See *Age of Deception*, 131.

only implied in the text, which said the European ministers believed that "full implementation of Iran's decisions, confirmed by the IAEA's Director General, should enable the immediate situation to be resolved by the IAEA Board."

The European agreement with Iran was an obvious setback for the Bolton strategy, and it was compounded by ElBaradei's report in early November, which detailed Iranian failures to report nuclear material and activities but concluded, "There is no evidence that the previously undeclared nuclear materials and activities . . . were related to a nuclear weapons program."[24] Senior US officials let it be known that they were "outraged" at ElBaradei's conclusion, and Bolton said it was "impossible to believe."[25]

The Bush administration tried to pressure other governments to support its strategy to shift the Iran file to the Security Council. At a meeting with the Europeans and other delegations a few days before the start of the meeting, Secretary of State Powell leaked to the news media that he had lambasted a European draft resolution as "totally inadequate" because it lacked a "trigger mechanism." The United States was demanding language that would automatically commit the board to finding Iran to be "noncompliant" and sending the issue to the Security Council if Iran failed to meet certain conditions. Powell said the United States would prefer that the board pass no resolution rather than the unacceptable European version. But in the end, only three countries—Canada, Australia, and Japan—were willing to support the US position.[26]

The board resolution said merely that if "any further serious Iranian failures come to light," the board would "meet immediately to consider, in the light of the circumstances and of advice from the Director General, all options at its disposal, in accordance with the IAEA Statute and Iran's Safeguards Agreement," making no reference to referral to the Security Council.[27] In one of the many unexpected consequences of the extreme aggressiveness of the US invasion and continued occupation of Iraq, the Europeans had stood up to US pressure on the Iran issue.

Iran and the EU-3 reached a follow-up agreement on February 24, 2004, in which Iran pledged to suspend not only introduction of gas into centrifuges but also the manufacture of centrifuge parts and

24. GOV/2003/75, November 10, 2003, 9–10.

25. Sonni Efron and Maggie Farley, "New Discord Rises between U.S. and Allies," *Los Angeles Times*, November 19, 2003; Paul Richter, "U.S. Questions UN Findings on Iran Bid for Nuclear Arms," *Los Angeles Times*, November 13, 2003.

26. Peter Slevin, "U.S. Criticizes Europe's Iran Plan," *Washington Post*, November 19, 2003; David E. Sanger, "Nuclear Board Said to Rebuff Bush over Iran," *New York Times*, November 20, 2003.

27. GOV/2003/81, November 26, 2003, 3.

assembly of centrifuges, and the Europeans pledged to seek the closure of the Iran nuclear dossier in the June meeting of the board. But then the IAEA discovered that Iran had omitted the fact that it had received the designs for a more efficient centrifuge, called P-2, as distinct from the more rudimentary P-1 centrifuges, in its declaration to the IAEA in October. That created renewed suspicions on the part of the Europeans. Another source of tension was Iran's acceleration of centrifuge assembly between the agreement in late February and early April, when the suspension of enrichment activities was to go into effect. Still another irritant was the public inauguration of Iran's uranium conversion facility in Esfahan on March 28. As a result, the Europeans drafted a resolution in advance of the June board meeting indicating that they were no longer firmly committed to resisting a referral of Iran to the Security Council.[28]

That development might have led to a move to send Iran to the Security Council by the end of 2004, had Iran not come up with another diplomatic proposal for the EU-3 in late July: a "framework of mutual guarantees" involving the achievement of long-term strategic cooperation through confidence-building steps.[29] That proposal elicited a somewhat ambiguous European diplomatic response. In October, the foreign policy chief of the European Union, Javier Solana, went to Washington with a proposal for a two-stage plan that required Iran to "suspend all enrichment and reprocessing-related activities in a comprehensive and internationally verifiable manner." The proposed plan specified that the suspension would be "indefinite, until we reach an acceptable long-term agreement." Only if Iran were to comply with that demand for an open-ended suspension of enrichment would the EU "reaffirm the right of Iran to develop research, production and use of nuclear energy for peaceful purposes without discrimination in conformity with Article 2 of the NPT." The proposal also envisioned a later stage of economic and security cooperation in which Iran's relations with the West, including the United States, would be "normalized." But if Iran did not comply, the EU would support the referral of the Iran nuclear issue to UN Security Council.[30]

28. Mousavian, *Iranian Nuclear Crisis*, 121–37, 143; Rouhani recalled later that the Europeans suspected Iran of having an undeclared site where P-2 centrifuges were being assembled. See Rouhani speech.

29. Mousavian, *Iranian Nuclear Crisis*, 139–40.

30. Quotes are from the document tabled by the EU at a G-8 meeting in Washington, as reported by Agence France-Presse, October 21, 2004. Other details about the document are from Robin Wright, "Europeans to Press Iran on Nuclear Plans," *Washington Post*, October 16, 2004, A18. See also Mousavian, *Iranian Nuclear Crisis*, 145–46.

The EU proposal was not acceptable to Iran, because it called for a suspension without a time limit and defined the "objective guarantees" of the peaceful nature of Iran's nuclear program as meaning "stopping" the program. But on November 15, 2004, after several rounds of intensive negotiations, the Europeans and Iran signed the Paris Agreement, which included compromises that made the text acceptable to Iran: First, the suspension would continue only "while negotiations on a long-term agreement are underway," thus giving Iran the power to terminate both the negotiations and the suspension. Second, the European governments explicitly acknowledged that Iran's suspension was "a voluntary confidence building measure and not a legal obligation." Third, it included Iranian language that the agreement would "provide objective guarantees that Iran's nuclear program is exclusively for peaceful purposes." That language was a way of committing the EU-3 to negotiations on ways to guarantee that Iran's independent fuel-cycle activities were not being used to support a weapons program.[31]

The Paris Agreement eased the pressures that Bolton and the United States had been building up for moving the Iran file to the Security Council. But the agreement had one fundamental flaw that both sides recognized: the most important actor of all in a long-term settlement of the issue, the United States, was not only absent from the negotiations but hostile to them. The EU-3 couldn't substitute for the United States in reaching a longer-term accommodation with Iran that would give it an incentive to curb its enrichment program. As an Iranian diplomat involved in the talks observed, "The EU doesn't know what it can offer absent U.S. permission, and absent U.S. assurances, we don't know what we can deliver."[32]

The three EU governments were equally aware that, without US backing, the negotiations were likely to fail. In the months preceding the Paris Agreement, they had been telling American contacts that they wanted the United States to be willing to enter the diplomatic game at an early stage, and that in the meantime, it was important for the United States to communicate to the Iranians that it would be willing to "put cards on the table at some stage."[33] But the Bush administration was determined that the EU-3 engagement should go no further. Two days after the Paris Agreement

31. Text of Paris Agreement, November 15, 2004, INFCIRC/637, November 26, 2004, http://www.iaea.org/Publications/Documents/Infcircs/2004/infcirc637.pdf.

32. International Crisis Group interview with Iranian diplomat, January 2005, "Iran: Is There a Way Out of the Nuclear Impasse?" Middle East Report 51, International Crisis Group, February 23, 2006, 2.

33. William Drodziak, Geoffrey Kemp, Flynt Leverett, and Christopher J. Makins, "Partners in Frustration: Europe, the United States and the Broader Middle East," policy paper, Atlantic Council, September 2004, 10–11.

was announced, Powell, on a refueling stop on his way to Santiago, Chile, told reporters he had seen "information" suggesting Iran had been "working hard" to match a ballistic missile with a nuclear weapon.[34]

Powell's remarks were widely viewed in Washington as part of a US effort to undercut the EU-Iranian agreement. As recently as mid-October, in preparation for the G-9 meeting that dealt with the EU proposal to Iran, Powell had approved the "script" Bolton had given him calling for a hardening of the EU proposal to Iran. It was Vice President Cheney who had approved the gist of Bolton's script before it went to Powell.[35] And the State Department deputy spokesman, clearly following a policy ordered by the White House at Bolton's behest, pushed the line that Iran had a covert nuclear weapons program. While acknowledging that there were "differences of opinion" on whether Iran had a covert nuclear weapons program—an allusion to the IAEA assessment—he said, "We believe the arguments stack up in our favor. We will continue to press this case."[36]

## Bolton's Satellite Photo Ploy

In early 2004, Bolton gave the IAEA satellite imagery of specific sites at Iran's Parchin military complex that he claimed had features making them appropriate for hydrodynamic tests on an implosion-type nuclear weapon—tests that simulate the conditions of an actual nuclear weapon using high explosives but no fissile material.[37] He wanted the IAEA to demand an inspection of the sites at Parchin based on the satellite photos, even though they clearly did not constitute evidence that Iran had conducted any such tests.

Bolton's strategy for the IAEA board to support a referral of Iran to the Security Council was keyed to using what he called "Iran's continued intransigence" to build a case that it was hiding a nuclear weapons program. The August 2003 inspection of Kalaye Electric Company, which had revealed Iran's repainting and retiling of the room to which the agency had been previously denied access, "was precisely the kind of dissembling and concealment that demonstrated Iran was trying to hide something," as

---

34. Robin Wright and Keith Richburg, "Powell Says Iran Is Pursuing Bomb," *Washington Post*, November 18, 2004, AO1.

35. Bolton, *Surrender*, 160–61. Bolton says nothing at all in his memoirs about the Bush administration's response to the most dramatic development in the Iran issue, the Paris Agreement, perhaps because he seeks to portray Powell as undermining his own hard line on EU-Iran negotiations. Ibid., 158–64.

36. Alec Russell, "Briefing Frenzy in Washington over Iran Nuclear Fear," *Telegraph* (London), November 20, 2004; Barry Schweid, "Analysis: Echoes of Iraq in Case vs. Iran," Associated Press, November 19, 2004.

37. Seymour M. Hersh, "The Next Act," *New Yorker*, November 27, 2006.

Bolton later recalled.[38] Parchin was Iran's military technology testing base, and Bolton evidently expected that Iran's military would never agree to allow the IAEA to go poking around that complex, regardless of whether it was doing any research related to nuclear weapons there. Iran's refusal of the IAEA request for an inspection of the sites in question would thus dramatize Iran's "intransigence" in regard to allegations about possible nuclear weapons-related activities.

In July 2004, ElBaradei authorized IAEA communications with the Iranians, conveying the agency's interest in visiting the sites at Parchin depicted in the images.[39] But ElBaradei issued two quarterly IAEA reports on Iran on June 1 and September 1, 2004, that made no reference to Parchin.[40] After the June report came out without calling for an inspection of Parchin based on the satellite photos, Bolton persuaded the Bush administration to adopt a policy of actively seeking to replace ElBaradei as director general of the IAEA rather than letting him serve a third term.

Bolton called ElBaradei's American deputy, David Waller, in August to tell him that the United States wanted ElBaradei to step down in mid-2005 rather than serve a third term, citing the seldom-used rule limiting the tenure of UN agency heads to two terms. Bolton promised effusive words for ElBaradei's service if he agreed to step down. But ElBaradei, who had been thinking of leaving the IAEA for personal reasons, was infuriated that Bolton and the US administration would "presume to dictate whether I ran for a third term." He decided to stay on after all, both to obtain a mandate to work on multilateral diplomacy on Iran and, as he put it in his memoirs, to "stand up against U.S. bullying." Over the next few months, the State Department tried to get several figures from Brazil, Argentina, Japan, and Australia to run against ElBaradei, but in the end no other government would support the US move against him.[41]

Meanwhile, US intelligence tapped ElBaradei's phone, hoping to get evidence that he had acted inappropriately in relations with the Iranians. No such evidence was ever found, but Reuters correspondent Louis Charbonneau later recalled that "several diplomats from a Western nation" had showed him what they claimed were transcripts of conversations between ElBaradei and the Iranian ambassador which they said showed he had "overstepped his authority."[42]

---

38. Bolton, *Surrender*, 136, 140.

39. ElBaradei, *Age of Deception*, 139; Pierre Goldschmidt, personal communication to the author, March 4, 2004.

40. GOV/2004/34, June 1, 2004; GOV/2004/60, September 1, 2004.

41. ElBaradei, *Age of Deception*, 180–81.

42. Dafna Linzer, "IAEA Leader's Phone Tapped," *Washington Post*, December 12, 2004, 1; Louis Charbonneau, "Rice on WikiLeaks Spy Charges: We're Just Diplomats," Reuters, November 29, 2010.

Despite the utter failure of the US effort to remove ElBaradei as director general, the Bush administration continued to oppose him right up to the first official consideration of his serving another term by the IAEA Board of Governors in late April 2005. But not a single member of the board was willing to join with the United States in opposing ElBaradei at that meeting.[43]

Soon after the Bush administration adopted a policy to unseat ElBaradei, Bolton leaked the satellite imagery of Parchin he had previously given to the IAEA to ABC News and to the Institute for Science and International Security (ISIS). On September 15, ABC News reported, "The US government and the IAEA have questions about a military site with suspected ties to the country's nuclear program." It quoted an unnamed State Department official as saying the United States "suspects nuclear activities at some of [Iran's] facilities" and that the suspicions "focus on possible testing of high explosives." The IAEA had requested permission from Iran to visit the facility more than a month earlier, ABC said, but Iran had "ignored the request," according to "US and UN sources."

ABC said it had been given images showing a building in Parchin's "high-explosive test area" that could permit testing of explosions relevant to a nuclear weapon. But later in the story, ABC acknowledged that the images did not indicate whether the testing conducted there was for the development of a nuclear weapon or merely for conventional high explosives. The story quoted the former head of the Defense Threat Reduction Agency at the Defense Department, Jay C. Davis, as saying, "Neither the design of the facility nor the nature of the tests is unique to nuclear weapons."[44]

On the same day, ISIS published a series of seven satellite images of different sites at the Parchin complex on its website, along with a commentary that indicated that ISIS Executive Director David Albright had been briefed by Bolton's staff on their analysis of the images. The images ISIS published conveyed nothing about the likelihood of work related to nuclear weapons. Albright and a co-author referred to the site singled out by ABC as being "a logical candidate for a nuclear weapons-related site" but acknowledged that some facilities at the site appeared to be "more suited to armaments research or rocket motor testing." The only basis for suggesting that it might be the site of nuclear weapons-related tests was that it included some buildings "suited to conduct high explosive testing."[45]

---

43. George Jahn, "U.S. Opposes Reappointment of Chief U.N. Nuclear Inspector, Prompting Agency to Defer Decision," Associated Press, April 27, 2005.

44. Jacqueline Shirer and Jonathan Karl, "Suspicions Arise about Iran's Nuclear Program," ABC News, September 15, 2004.

45. David Albright and Corey Hinderstein, "Parchin: Possible Nuclear Weapons-Related Site in Iran," Institute for Science and International Security, September 15, 2004.

Other buildings on the site had no apparent relationship to such testing, according to the authors; another site nearby might or might not have had a high-explosives bunker that could be used for various purposes. And they dismissed the argument by "some analysts" that the excavation at a separate site might include tunneling as irrelevant to the purpose of the site. The overall tenor of the commentary was one of skepticism about the official line from Bolton's office that there was any substantive basis for suspicion of nuclear weapons testing at Parchin.

But Bolton understood that the caveats expressed by ISIS would essentially drop out of any story of his statement citing the photographs and casting further doubt on Iran's nuclear intentions. In comments to George Jahn of the Associated Press attributed to a "senior U.S. official," Bolton cited the publication of the satellite imagery by ISIS as alarming new evidence of Iran's covert nuclear weapons program. And according to Jahn's story, the official had "accused the UN nuclear watchdog of suppressing information on Parchin in its latest report on Iran," calling it "a serious omission."[46]

Behind Bolton's charge were apparent differences between ElBaradei and the IAEA deputy director general for safeguards, Pierre Goldschmidt, over what to do with Bolton's satellite photographs. ElBaradei recognized that Bolton was pushing the agency to request access to one of Iran's most sensitive military sites on the basis of "information" that wasn't evidence of Iranian nuclear weapons testing at all. The September report said, "The Agency has discussed with Iran authorities open source information relating to dual use equipment and materials which have application in the conventional military area and in the civilian sphere as well as in the military sphere. The Agency welcomes Iran's willingness to discuss these topics." But it did not mention Parchin by name, or the satellite photos, or the fact that the agency had requested a visit to Parchin.[47] And ElBaradei declared at a news conference during the September board meeting, "We do not have any indication that this [Parchin] site has any nuclear related activities."[48]

Goldschmidt, who had been IAEA deputy director general for safeguards since 1999, would neither confirm nor deny for this book that an explicit reference to concerns that nuclear-related testing might have taken place at Parchin had been included in an earlier draft of the September

46. For two different versions of the Jahn story, see George Jahn, "Iran: U.S.-Europe to Demand Iran Nuclear Tech Freeze," Associated Press, *Tulsa (OK) World*, September 17, 2004 and Jahn, "U.S. Accuses Iran of Working on N-bomb," Associated Press, *Dawn* (Karachi), September 17, 2004.

47. GOV/2004/60, September 1, 2004, 8.

48. "IAEA Says No Sign of Nuclear Activity at Suspect Iran Site," Agence France-Presse, September 17, 2004, http://www.spacewar.com/2004/040917163425.ohd9s7ce.html.

report but were taken out by ElBaradei.[49] However, Goldschmidt's first paper for the Carnegie Endowment for International Peace after leaving the IAEA in June 2005 clearly indicated that he suspected that Iran might be hiding nuclear testing at Parchin and that he opposed ElBaradei's position at the September 2004 board meeting. The essay expressed regret about the fact that the IAEA's existing mandate required that it "find at least traces of nuclear material at an undeclared facility that can be associated beyond doubt to equipment, material or activities that could only be relevant to manufacturing nuclear weapons." That standard, he suggested, was one that the IAEA "would be hard-pressed to meet."

Goldschmidt wrote that any equipment that might be used either for conventional or nuclear weapons "would most likely to be located at secret military sites," which he suggested would be "difficult, if not impossible" for the IAEA to access quickly enough to find the incriminating evidence before it could be removed. And he specifically cited the "Parchin site in Iran" as an example of the problem. "It is therefore essential," Goldschmidt concluded, "for the IAEA to look for any *indication* that a non-nuclear weapon state *may be* undertaking activities that could signal the existence of a nuclear weapons program and to report such findings to the Board of Governors" (italics in original).[50] Goldschmidt's argument was evidently a response to ElBaradei's denial that there had been any such indication of Iranian nuclear weapons-related activity at Parchin. His essay hinted strongly that he had pushed for the IAEA to report mere suspicions of a nuclear weapons program based on information that was far from being evidence of such activity.

Two months after denying any evidence of Iranian nuclear weapons activity, however, ElBaradei gave in to pressure from the United States and from Goldschmidt to go public with the information that Bolton and Goldschmidt had wanted in September report. The November IAEA report included the same paragraph as the September report, but this time it also said the agency had requested in October that its inspectors be allowed to visit Parchin.[51]

## The IAEA Inspections at Parchin

The IAEA request to visit Parchin was qualitatively different from previous IAEA inspection trips to Iran. Asking to visit sites on a military reservation where Iran undertook testing of various weapons systems would require

---

49. Personal communication to the author from Pierre Goldschmidt, March 4, 2013.

50. Pierre Goldschmidt, "The Urgent Need to Strengthen the Nuclear Non-Proliferation Regime," Carnegie Endowment for International Peace, January 2006.

51. GOV/2004/83, November 15, 2004, 22.

some understandings with Iran about how to minimize the risks to Iranian national security. And Iranian policymakers suggested that those satellite photos did not represent a valid basis for requesting to visit one of its most sensitive military sites. "They should have evidence that there are nuclear activities," an unnamed Iranian official told the *New York Times* in early December, "not just, 'We heard from someone that there is dual-use equipment that we want to see.'"[52]

Nevertheless, Iran did not refuse the request, which came at a time when it was eager to demonstrate its transparency to the IAEA as well as to the Europeans. The IAEA sent a note on October 26 proposing "specific modalities" for such a transparency inspection, and Iranian officials agreed to meet with Heinonen, then Goldschmidt's deputy for Iran and the Middle East, in Vienna on January 7, 2005, to discuss the issue.[53]

What happened at the January 7 meeting and in the IAEA inspection a week later is now the subject of conflicting accounts by Goldschmidt and Heinonen. In his presentation to the board on March 1, 2005, Goldschmidt said, "Out of the four areas identified by the Agency to be of potential interest, the Agency was permitted to select one area."[54] That wording suggested that Iran had explicitly denied access to three of the four sites that the IAEA had wanted to visit, and the IAEA inspection was described in an Associated Press article on the board meeting—presumably on the basis of Goldschmidt's remarks—as a "severely restricted visit" to Parchin.[55]

But in 2012, Heinonen, who actually discussed the modalities of the inspection visit with the Iranians at the January 7 meeting, provided a dramatically different account of the details of the IAEA to which Iran had agreed. In an interview with Scott Peterson of the *Christian Science Monitor*, Heinonen recalled:

> Parchin is a fairly large geographical area. I think there are hundreds of buildings when you put them all together. So they divided it actually into sectors, and it's easy to divide because the way the valleys and the mountains are there, so you get four distinct areas.

52. William J. Broad, David E. Sanger, and Elaine Sciolino, "Arms Inspectors Said to Seek Access to Iran Site," *New York Times*, December 2, 2004, A1.

53. "Statement to the IAEA Board of Governors by Mr. Pierre Goldschmidt, March 1, 2005," Iran Watch, http://www.iranwatch.org/international/IAEA/iaea-goldschmidt-statement-030105.htm. Hereafter cited as Goldschmidt statement, March 1, 2005. The same text is also found in GOV/2005/67, September 2, 2005, 10.

54. Ibid.

55. "Iran Says It Fears Leaked Nuclear Information," Associated Press, March 2, 2005.

Then we agreed that we—we wanted actually to take, to go differently. But they wanted four areas. First you select the area, then you
select the buildings. The selection did not take place in advance, it
took place just when we arrived, so all of Parchin was available. You
would just take one sector, and then from that sector you know,
when we drove there, and arrived, we told them which building.[56]

Dividing the entire facility into quadrants and giving the IAEA team permission to select several buildings to be inspected within the quadrant
of its choice would have resulted in very different results from allowing
the agency to visit only one of four areas of interest to the agency, as
Goldschmidt had suggested. A satellite image of the entire Parchin complex
that identifies the area of "Possible Nuclear Weapons Development" sites
shows that the sites shown on the ISIS site and said to have possible high-
explosives facilities were not only within the same quadrant of Parchin
but were all located within the same roughly one square kilometer in an
estimated 25 to 42 square kilometers (15 to 25 square miles) of the entire
complex.[57]

Rather than denying access to most of the sites the IAEA wanted to
see, as Goldschmidt's description suggested, the parameters that Iran
had insisted on, according to Heinonen, appear to have actually allowed
the IAEA to inspect most if not all of the sites in which the agency had
expressed interest.

Goldschmidt insisted to the author that Heinonen had not reported
such an Iranian plan to him. "I never heard when I was at the Agency
that Iran had divided the Parchin site into four quadrants or sectors,"
Goldschmidt said.[58] Goldschmidt explicitly acknowledged in his report to
the board, however, that the agency had "selected five buildings" and that
the inspectors "had free access to those buildings and their surroundings."[59]
That sounds very much like what Heinonen described. Goldschmidt
recalled that he depended on the agency's expert on satellite imagery,
Fredric Claude, to choose the locations in which the agency was primarily
interested, and that he was not aware of how far apart those locations were.
Goldschmidt also said his primary concern was that Heinonen and Claude

56. Notes of an interview by Scott Peterson with Olli Heinonen, March 19, 2012,
provided to the author by Peterson, March 17, 2013. See also Scott Peterson, "Iran's
Parchin Complex: Why Are Nuclear Inspectors So Focused on It?" *Christian Science
Monitor*, April 20, 2012. The published story does not have the full quotation from
Heinonen.

57. The satellite image is on the Global Security website, http://www.globalsecurity.
org/wmd/world/iran/parchin-2-002.htm.

58. Personal communication to the author from Pierre Goldschmidt, March 26, 2013.

59. Goldschmidt statement, March 1, 2005.

had revealed what sites they wanted to visit at the January 7 meeting, so there was no real "surprise" about where the IAEA wanted to visit when the inspection took place later that month.[60]

The inspection of the five buildings and surrounding grounds chosen by Heinonen and Claude produced no indication that any of them had been used for anything related to nuclear weapons. The IAEA took environmental samples from all five sites to test for any substance that could have been used for hydrodynamic or hydrostatic testing of nuclear designs. All the tests came back negative.[61]

During the January 14 inspection, Heinonen requested a second visit to Parchin the second week in February to inspect another area of the military facility. The initial response from Iran on February 27 was a flat rejection of the request. It said, "The expectations of the Safeguards Department in visiting specified zone and points in Parchin complex are fulfilled and thus there is no justification for any additional visit."[62]

ElBaradei argued to Iran that he needed another round of inspections. "I can't convince the international community with one inspection," he reportedly told the Iranians.[63] Further action on the issue was delayed until after Iran elected Mahmoud Ahmadinejad as its new president in June 2005, and a new government could be formed. On October 31, 2005, the new secretary of Iran's Supreme National Security Council, Ali Larijani, finally met with Heinonen and agreed to a second inspection visit to Parchin. ElBaradei's report said only that Larijani had agreed to give the inspectors access to "buildings requested within the area of interest." That description was consistent with the parameters Iran had prescribed to Heinonen in January. But this time Larijani posed a significant condition: the IAEA had to agree that it would be the last time it would request such transparency visits to Parchin. Heinonen promised that if the inspectors found nothing suspicious, the Parchin file would be closed permanently, according to the Iranian account.[64]

During the second inspection the following day, November 1, Claude chose five more places from the map and satellite images to be inspected. Once again, environmental samples were taken at each site, and again they all tested negative for any substance that might have been used in hydrodynamic

60. Personal communication to the author from Pierre Goldschmidt, March 31, 2013.

61. GOV/2005/67, September 2, 2005, p. 10.

62. Goldschmidt statement, March 1, 2005.

63. "How ElBaradei Closed Parchin File, Opened by Amano?" IRNA, November 19, 2011, Raja News.

64. GOV/2005/87, November 18, 2005, 4; "How ElBaradei Closed Parchin File."

or hydrostatic tests.[65] Thus the IAEA had inspected and done sampling at 10 specific sites of its choosing at Parchin in the two visits. For the next six years, the IAEA did not suggest the need to inspect any site at Parchin or raise the possibility that there were any suspect sites in the complex. ElBaradei and the Safeguards Department did indeed close the Parchin file. But in late 2011, the IAEA demanded access to the site once again, based on a claim by Israel that a cylinder for nuclear-related tests had been installed at Parchin in 2000, and a new political drama began around that demand.

## Rice Brings the Europeans under Control

A crucial turning point in the negotiations between Iran and the EU-3 came in the first months of the second George W. Bush administration and the new secretary of state, Condoleezza Rice. Her first foreign trip as secretary—February 3–11, 2005, along with her primary negotiator with the Europeans, Undersecretary for Political Affairs Nicholas Burns—was spent working on bringing the British, French, and German governments into line with US policy on Iran's nuclear program.[66]

After Rice returned to Washington, Burns continued to negotiate with the EU-3 through February and early March. He wanted them to commit to rejecting any enrichment activities by Iran and, if Iran refused to accept that condition for an agreement, to supporting the referral of Iran to the Security Council.[67] By early March, Burns had secured the French Foreign Ministry's support for its demand for the exclusion of enrichment. As one French official said, "We consider that the only 'objective guarantee' of the exclusively peaceful nature of Iran's nuclear program is the effective cessation of all activities leading to the production of nuclear material."[68]

The Europeans wanted the United States to back their talks with Iran by providing real political, economic, and security benefits. But as indicated by Rice on March 11, the only concessions they could wrest from the Bush administration were to drop the US objection to Iran's application to join the World Trade Organization and to approve a license for spare parts for

---

65. GOV2005/87, 4.

66. Burns was not identified as the primary negotiator during Rice's trip, but he acknowledged in a later interview that he had been the primary "liaison" with the European foreign ministries on Iran. Interview with Undersecretary of State Nicholas Burns, *Der Spiegel*, December 20, 2005.

67. Robin Wright, "U.S. Wants Guarantees on Iran Effort," *Washington Post*, March 4, 2005, A12.

68. French Foreign Ministry official Philippe Errera, interview with International Crisis Group, "Iran: Is There a Way Out of the Nuclear Impasse?"

Iranian commercial aircraft.[69] Based on previous Iranian statements to the Europeans, it was evident that the Iranians would consider that proposal an insult in the context of the negotiations on its enrichment program.

At the conclusion of those negotiations, Burns was confident that the Europeans were now fully aligned with US policy, meaning they would not make any deal with Iran allowing enrichment of any kind. "The Europeans are now with us," he told the *New York Times*, speaking as "the senior US official" who had been negotiating with the Europeans, "in the view that we could never monitor [Iran's] enrichment activity reliably enough to ensure that Iran was not producing bomb-grade uranium." An argument had been going on quietly between European officials and the Bush administration over whether Iran could be singled out politically for denial of the right to enrich, but Burns now declared triumphantly, "That argument is now over."[70]

That Burns argument was specious: the IAEA was perfectly capable of detecting any effort by Iran to divert fissile material for enrichment to bomb-grade levels, as the Obama administration would eventually acknowledge explicitly. And US intelligence was capable of detecting any "secret" site where centrifuges were being introduced before they could become operational, as its detection of the Natanz and Qom enrichment sites in 2002 and 2009 demonstrated.

The Europeans fell into line with the United States mainly because they had entered into the negotiations in the vain hope that Washington would enter the talks and offer some substantive concessions. Instead, the Bush administration was continuing to pursue its policy of ensuring that Iran could not reach any agreements that would enhance the legitimacy of the Islamic regime. That objective had been pursued more effectively by taking Bolton, who was intensely disliked by the Europeans, out of his policymaking role on Iran and nominating him to be ambassador to the United Nations.

The European position toward Iran also hardened because the fears of the British, French, and Germans of a US war against Iran had dissipated. "At the beginning, they thought if we went to the UN Security Council, we would have a new crisis and a war in the region," nuclear negotiator Hassan Rouhani recalled in late 2004. "However, today the possibility that we will have a war if we go to the UN Security Council seems remote." The US had

---

69. Rice interview with Reuters, March 11, 2005, 1, http://merln.ndu.edu/archivepdf/syria/State/43319.pdf.

70. David E. Sanger and Steven R. Weisman, "US and EU Forge Joint Strategy on Iran Talks," *International Herald Tribune*, March 12, 2005, 1.

become bogged down in Iraq, Rouhani observed, and was in no position to threaten Iran.[71]

The collapse of the European diplomatic venture with Iran was foreshadowed at a meeting in Paris on March 23, when Iran made one last attempt to reach an accord with the Europeans on a deal that would provide concrete "objective guarantees" against diversion of nuclear material into a weapons program. The Iranian plan included commitments to "limitation of the extent of the enrichment program to solely meet the contingency fuel requirements of Iran's power reactors" and to "immediate conversion of all enriched Uranium to fuel rods to preclude even the technical possibility of further enrichment."[72] The latter offer was particularly significant because Iran did not have the capability to fabricate such fuel rods itself, so it implied that either the low-enriched uranium would have to be shipped to another country for conversion or done under international auspices within Iran. Once the fuel rods were fabricated, Iran would not be able to reconvert them into uranium that could be enriched to higher levels without great difficulty and without being easily detected; in the meantime, Iran would be forgoing the accumulation of a stockpile of uranium that could eventually be enriched to weapons-grade levels. What the Iranians wanted in return, Ambassador Mousavian told a foreign academic, was security guarantees and the lifting of economic sanctions imposed by the United States.[73]

The Iranian proposal was an extraordinary concession to Western concerns about the Iranian nuclear program. Coming at a time when Iran still had not enriched a single kilogram of uranium and was starting with a clean slate, the plan would have provided verifiable evidence that Iran was not seeking a nuclear weapon. "All of us were impressed by the proposal," recalled the UK's permanent representative to the IAEA, Peter Jenkins, who was on the British delegation at the March 23 meeting. The European delegations called for a break to discuss it among themselves, according to Jenkins, and then pleaded for more time to consider the Iranian proposal further.[74]

---

71. Rouhani speech.

72. Permanent Mission of Iran to the United Nations, "Unnecessary Crisis: Setting the Record Straight about Iran's Nuclear Program," November 18, 2005, in Payvand Iran News, November 22, 2005, http://www.payvand.com/news/05/nov/1211.html.

73. Mustafa Kiraboglu, "Good for the Shah, Banned for the Mullahs: The West and Iran's Quest for Nuclear Power," Middle East Journal 60/2 (Spring 2006): 231.

74. This account of the European response to the Iranian proposal is from the author's interview with Peter Jenkins, former UK permanent representative to the IAEA, June 5, 2012. His account was first published in Gareth Porter, "US Rejected 2005 Iranian Offer Ensuring No Nuclear Weapons," Inter Press Service, June 6, 2012.

But Jenkins knew that the result was foreordained by the previous US-European understanding, and that no proposal, no matter how forthcoming, was acceptable to the British government if it involved any Iranian enrichment. "I knew in my heart of hearts that this was a waste of time—that it would not fly," recalled Jenkins. "The British objective was to eliminate entirely Iran's enrichment capability."

That was also the official objective of the EU-3. The formal proposal from the EU at that same Paris meeting—a direct result of the understanding reached with Rice and Burns—called for an indefinite suspension of enrichment by Iran, not limited to the duration of the negotiations themselves. The Iranians made clear to the EU-3 both before and during that meeting that they could not agree to any loss of their right to enrich, Jenkins recalled. But the Europeans made no move to adjust their diplomatic strategy.

It was not only pressure from the Americans and the dissipation of European fears of war over Iran that made the EU-3 so inflexible diplomatically. Equally or more important was the fact that the Europeans shared the Bush administration's assessment that Iran was negotiating from a very weak bargaining position. Like the Americans, they believed the Islamic Republic's leaders were too desperate for an agreement with the West to refuse what they acknowledged was an unattractive deal being offered by the EU-3. A few years later, after Iran had gone on to build a major stockpile of enriched uranium, one of the European foreign ministry political directors who carried out most of the negotiations with Iran admitted to an Iranian acquaintance that the EU-3 had made a serious miscalculation in 2005. "We were so shortsighted," said the European. "We thought we had you in a corner." He recalled that EU-3 officials had been convinced that Iran was so afraid of being taken to the Security Council that it would finally give in to the EU, even though it would not obtain much benefit in doing so.[75]

The Europeans were assuming that the Iranians' warning about their right to enrichment as a red line was merely their opening negotiating position, according to Jenkins. "I don't think we realized fully in March 2005 that Iran was not prepared to give up enrichment as the price of a settlement," he recalled. "We believed that if we could come up with sufficient incentives and scare Iran with the threat of referral to the Security Council, they would give in."

---

75. Personal communication to the author from an Iranian source who had the conversation with the European diplomat, and who asked to remain anonymous, March 12, 2013.

The Europeans were confident enough of their superior bargaining position that they hoped to string the Iranians along by leading them to believe they were considering the March 23 offer. As a European official had said the week before the meeting, "Iran right now has suspended its activities, verified by inspections. That means we don't have to be in such a hurry."[76] A European diplomat leaked to a news agency several days later that the Europeans were "thinking about the Iranian proposal," even though that proposal was "not really acceptable." But another European diplomat, who was not in on the plan, revealed that the leak was a ploy. "Our hands are tied," said the diplomat, referring to a strictly limited enrichment program. "We'd lose the Americans if we agreed to it."[77]

European diplomats also revealed that part of the reason for stringing the Iranians along by not rejecting the Iranian proposal immediately was that the EU-3 did not want to undermine candidates running for president of Iran in the June election who would favor increased engagement with the West.[78] That was an obvious reference to former president Hashemi Rafsanjani, who was a leading candidate in the June election and who had let it be known that he was willing to cooperate with Europeans on cessation of uranium enrichment, while retaining "the right to the technology."[79]

Iranian foreign minister Kamal Kharrazi publicly warned on the eve of a pivotal Iran-EU meeting in London on April 29 that Iran would not accept "delay tactics" by the EU-3. "If talks with the European Union are not successful tomorrow," he said, "negotiations will collapse and we will have no choice but to start the uranium enrichment program."[80] At the April 29 meeting, the Iranian delegation tried to convey the political pressures Iranian negotiators were under from hard-line nationalist political forces at home, charging they had been "tricked" into accepting the suspension of enrichment. The Iranian team also told the Europeans that the supreme leader had ordered Rouhani to resume the operations of the uranium conversion facility, in the hope of using that threat to increase pressure on the Europeans to present a plan that would allow the talks to continue. Meanwhile, the head of the National Security and Foreign Policy

---

76. Steven R. Weisman, "Europe and U.S. Agree on Carrot-and-Stick Approach to Iran," *New York Times,* March 12, 2005.

77. Reuters dispatch, March 30, 2005.

78. Louis Charbonneau, "Chirac Pushes EU to Drop Hard Line on Iran—Diplomats," Reuters, April 13, 2005.

79. Rafsanjani's adviser, Mohammed Atrianfar, told the International Crisis Group in an interview on May 27, 2005, that Rafsanjani would "stop uranium enrichment," but other Iranians doubted that he would agree to the EU-3 demand for such a cessation. "Iran: Is There a Way out of the Nuclear Impasse?", 2.

80. Nazila Fathi, "Iran Hints Talks on Ending Its Nuclear Program Are Near Collapse," *New York Times,* April 29, 2005.

Committee of the Iranian Majlis, Alaeddin Boroujerdi, demanded the termination of the negotiations with the EU-3, asserting they "don't have the necessary capacity and powers to reach an understanding with the Islamic Republic of Iran."[81]

After having confidently followed the US lead in March, the Europeans began to get cold feet in May. European political directors asked Burns the day before a meeting with Rouhani in Geneva on May 25 for more flexibility to negotiate with Iran. Burns, taken by surprise, was categorical that the United States expected the Europeans to demand the "dismantlement" of Iran's nuclear program, including the uranium conversion facility. The Europeans tried to satisfy both the Americans and the Iranians by taking the position that uranium conversion could not be accepted in the short run, but that they would leave the door open for such work in the future.[82] To convince the Iranian nuclear chief that they were now serious, the EU-3 said they were prepared to offer guarantees on a series of issues as part of an agreement, including full support for provision of nuclear plants, assurances of long-term fuel supplies, gradual removal of restrictions on dual-use equipment exports to Iran, and Iranian security.

But the Europeans, who were evidently gambling on a Rafsanjani victory in the presidential election, also asked Rouhani for three more months to come up with a final proposal. Rouhani compromised by giving them two more months to develop a complete proposal, but repeated three times during the meeting that Iran would reject any proposal that excluded enrichment. That decision meant that the proposal would not be handed over until after the Iranian election.[83] Supreme Leader Ali Khamenei, disillusioned with the lack of any benefit after six months of a suspension of enrichment by Iran, effectively pulled the plug on the negotiations.

Then came a development that none of the negotiators had expected: Rafsanjani, who had been favored to win the June presidential election, was defeated by the much less well-known former mayor of Tehran, Mahmoud Ahmadinejad. The European hopes for a multistage process of negotiation with Iran, based on the assumption that Rafsanjani would be able to make some accommodations to European interests, were in ruins. But the Iranian negotiators, who were close to Rafsanjani, were also taken by

---

81. "Iran Hardliners: Stop Nuke Negotiations," Associated Press, Fox News, May 8, 2005.

82. Dafna Linzer, "Europeans Open Talks With Iran on Nuclear Program," *Washington Post*, May 25, 2005.

83. Mousavian, *Iranian Nuclear Crisis*, 169–71.

surprise. German foreign minister Joschka Fisher observed privately that Iranian diplomats were "in shock" about Ahmadinejad's victory.[84]

The proposal that the EU-3 gave to Iran on August 8 had no chance of being accepted, and the Europeans knew it. It demanded a complete and permanent end to Iran's enrichment-related activities and offered noting except the "prospect" of economic, political, and security cooperation in the future. A European diplomat acknowledged at the time that the proposal was deficient but explained that it "was never meant to be our final offer. That was the first offer in what we thought would be a long, drawn-out negotiation."[85] The Europeans, constrained by the Bush administration's rejection of real diplomacy, had counted heavily on both general Iranian weakness and the supposed willingness of Rafsanjani to accommodate the West on enrichment. With the end of the negotiations and Ahmadinejad's victory, the Iranian diplomatic stance became much harder, and the Iranian march to uranium enrichment became inevitable. In April 2006, Ahmadinejad announced that Iran had successfully enriched uranium and had thus become a "nuclear power."

---

84. WikiLeaks cable 05BERLIN2235, US Embassy in Berlin to State, "FM Fischer on Iran," July 1, 2005.

85. Interview by International Crisis Group, Brussels, September 20, 2005, in "Iran: Is There a Way Out of the Nuclear Impasse?", 3.

# 7

# The IAEA Comes Up Empty

On October 16, 2003, after Iran had been forced to acknowledge the last of its nuclear secrets to the IAEA, Iran's new nuclear policy coordinator, Hassan Rouhani, met with IAEA director Mohamed ElBaradei and committed Iran to provide full disclosure of all its nuclear activities in the past.[1] From then until 2008, the official purpose of the investigation by the IAEA's Safeguards Department was to verify that all of the declarations Iran was required to make providing detailed chronologies of its decisions were accurate and complete. In theory, at least, once the investigation had established the completeness and accuracy of its declarations, Iran's Safeguards Agreement would be subject to the same routine IAEA inspection as other member states.

But the political reality was, as usual, very different from the formal IAEA posture. ElBaradei viewed the process as a potential contribution to a diplomatic resolution of the nuclear issue. The deputy director general for Safeguards, Goldschmidt, and his deputy for Iran, Heinonen, on the other hand, suspected that the Iranian nuclear program was probably a cover for nuclear weapons work. They expected the investigation to lead to evidence of such work.

For the United States and Israel, the main problem was how to prevent ElBaradei from achieving the goal of verifying that the Iranian nuclear program was peaceful. The United States "didn't want Iran to cooperate with the IAEA," recalled Hillary Mann Leverett, the former Bush administration National Security Council staff specialist on Iran.[2] The United States and Israel influenced the course of the investigation by feeding intelligence to the Safeguards Department that reinforced the suspicions of Goldschmidt

---

1. GOV/2003/75, November 10, 2003, 4.
2. Interview with Hillary Mann Leverett, March 14, 2013.

and Heinonen that Iran was continuing to conceal its military nuclear program.

Tehran was engaged in negotiations with the British, French, and German governments aimed at frustrating the US strategy for moving the Iran file from the IAEA to the Security Council, which provided an incentive to cooperate with the investigation as fully as possible. ElBaradei reported in September 2004 that the agency was making "steady progress in understanding the program" and that it had already concluded its investigation of two issues: Iran's laser-enrichment activities and its uranium conversion.[3]

But the two verification issues that the IAEA identified in 2004 as most important to its overall evaluation of the Iranian nuclear program were the uranium contamination found on centrifuge components and Iran's suspected work on P-2 centrifuges from 1995 to 2002.[4] On both those issues, as well as others, IAEA reports initially pointed to evidence that appeared to indicate Iran had carried out nuclear activities that could signal an intention to develop a nuclear weapon. Information pointing toward an innocent explanation, on the other hand, was not included in the reports. It was as if prosecutors in a criminal case before a court were allowed to issue official reports periodically on behalf of the court informing the public of the most damning evidence but saying nothing about any of the evidence put forward by the defense. And as if the IAEA's reports did not skew the presentation of the evidence sufficiently, the Bush administration and its allies actively leaked specious stories on the evidence to a passive news media.

## Contamination, Procurement, and Centrifuges

The IAEA reported in November 2003 that the environmental samples taken at Kalaye Electric Company in August 2003 and at Natanz previously had revealed the presence of high-enriched uranium (HEU) particles and low-enriched uranium (LEU) particles that were not consistent with the nuclear material in Iran's declared inventory. Although Iran insisted that the contamination found in the samples could not have been the result of its own tests, because the centrifuges had never been used to enrich above 1.2 percent, the Safeguards Department was clearly suspicious of the significance of the contamination.[5]

---

3. GOV/2004/60, September 1, 2004, 10.
4. GOV/2004/60, 10–11.
5. GOV/2003/75, November 10, 2003, 3, 7.

Media coverage of that initial report did not play up the contamination issue, but only because the main theme of the report was that there was no evidence that Iran had been working on a nuclear weapon. In a departure from the usual sensationalized coverage of agency findings, stories on the report either ignored the information about the HEU contamination or treated it in a more neutral fashion.[6]

The next IAEA report, released in February 2004, returned to the contamination issue, and this time it made the political implications much clearer. The environmental samples, it said, showed LEU and HEU that "called into question the completeness of Iran's declarations about its centrifuge enrichment activities" and "there remain a number of discrepancies and unanswered questions." The report framed the technical issue in the starkest terms: "Environmental samples showing uranium enriched to 36% U-235 have come almost entirely from one room in the Kalaye Electric Company workshop, which seems to be predominantly contaminated with that material. Only negligible traces of 36% enriched uranium have been found on imported centrifuge components." Then it commented, ominously, "The level of contamination suggests the presence of more than just trace quantities of such material."[7]

This time the storyline in news media coverage was dramatic: Iran stood accused of having produced high-enriched uranium in secret. The *New York Times* headlined, "Fuel Traces for N-Arms Found in Iran." The *Washington Post* reported that environmental samples had shown "the presence of uranium enriched to 25 times the level acknowledged by Iran" and said the IAEA had suggested that Iran "may have enriched uranium on its own" contrary to its denials.[8]

In a June 2004 report, the IAEA again cast doubt on the possibility that the 36 percent HEU found in the samples could be attributed to foreign-made parts: "It is unlikely, based on the information currently available, that the Agency will be able to conclude that the 36 percent uranium 235 contamination found at Kalaye and Farayand was due to the components from the State in question." It stated in conclusion, "Other possible explanations remain under study," which clearly suggested that it suspected Iran

6. Joby Warrick and Glenn Kessler, "IAEA Criticizes Iran's Nuclear Enrichment Program, Long Secret," *Washington Post*, November 11, 2003, A5; Associated Press, "UN: No Evidence Iran Trying to Make Weapons," *Dubuque Telegraph-Herald* (Dubuque, IA), November 11, 2003.

7. GOV/2004/11, February 24, 2004, 6–7.

8. William J. Broad and David E. Sanger, "Fuel Traces for N-Arms Found in Iran," *New York Times*, February 25, 2004, A4; Peter Slevin and Joby Warrick, "Iran Faulted on Nuclear Declaration," *Washington Post*, February 25, 2004, A18.

of having had an enrichment program that included much higher enrichment than it had admitted.[9]

The proponents of military confrontation with Iran were gleeful. In testimony before Congress in June 2004, John Bolton derided Iran's explanation for the contamination. Iran had "said it had not enriched uranium more than 1.2 percent," Bolton declared. "Later when the evidence of uranium enriched to 36 percent was found, it attributed the contamination to imported centrifuge parts."[10]

By late summer, however, it was an open secret among diplomats in Vienna that the Safeguards Department had concluded internally that the HEU contamination had indeed come from centrifuge technology Iran had imported, not from its own enrichment activities. That conclusion was leaked to *Jane's Defence Weekly* and then reported by the *Washington Post*. The sources, described as "diplomats and experts working on the Agency's investigation" said the IAEA had determined on the basis of the data it already had obtained from Pakistan that the traces of 56 percent HEU, which had not been mentioned in the IAEA's reports, came from the equipment Iran had purchased from middlemen who had connections with Pakistan's A. Q. Khan network, but that the 36 percent HEU had come from Russian centrifuge parts.[11]

A September 2004 report on the origin of the HEU contamination conceded that the Iranian explanation for the contamination appeared to be correct. "The Agency's analysis to date has shown that most of the contamination found at Kalaye Electric Company workshop and Natanz correlates reasonably with HEU contamination found on imported components," said the report. Referring to "correlations and model enrichment calculations based on the enrichment process in another possible country of origin," the agency now conceded it "appears plausible" that the uranium particles it had found in the two locations "may not have resulted from enrichment of uranium at those locations." In other words, the evidence now appeared to exonerate Iran. Nevertheless, the report again ended by stating, "Other explanations for this and the LEU contamination continue to be investigated."[12]

A November 2004 report suggested that Goldschmidt and Heinonen were still hoping to blame the contamination on secret Iranian enrichment. It asserted that contamination caused by imported centrifuge parts was

---

9. GOV/2004/34, June 1, 2004, 6.

10. Dafna Linzer, "No Proof Found of Iran Arms Program," *Washington Post*, August 23, 2005, A1.

11. Dafna Linzer, "Findings Could Hurt US Effort on Iran," *Washington Post*, August 11, 2004, A16.

12. GOV/2004/60, September 1, 2004, 6.

"one possible explanation" but that other possibilities were being investigated, "including the possibility of the contamination having resulted from undeclared enrichment activities conducted by Iran, from imported uranium not declared to the Agency and/or contaminated equipment imported from sources other than those known to the Agency." It said it would not draw any "final conclusion" until "further investigation."[13]

The "further investigation" was done by a panel of scientists from the United States, France, Japan, and Russia that soon began meeting secretly to analyze the environmental sampling data from Iran. Over the next few months, that panel "definitively matched" samples of HEU from the locations in Iran with contamination on other centrifuge equipment coming from Pakistan, US and foreign officials told the *Washington Post*. IAEA officials close to ElBaradei were reported to be eager to get the conclusion of the scientific panel out in order to cut short the Bush administration's exploitation of the issue in support of its hard-line refusal to engage Iran diplomatically on its nuclear program. The *Post* quoted a "senior official" of the agency, who had discussed the findings on condition of anonymity, as saying, "The biggest smoking gun that everyone was waving is now eliminated with these conclusions."[14]

A September 2005 IAEA report made no mention of the international scientific panel. But it did refer to the environmental swipes on centrifuge parts from another member state that "tend, on balance, to support Iran's statement about the foreign origins of most of the observed HEU contamination." The threat of further investigation of explanations based on safeguards violations by Iran in the previous report was never repeated.[15]

In February 2006, the agency reported it had found new evidence supporting the foreign origins of the contamination from samples taken in December 2005 from a centrifuge that had been obtained by another member state from the procurement network used by Iran.[16] Yet in spite of the weight of evidence indicating that the issue had been resolved, the language of IAEA reports indicated that the Safeguard Department was going to keep the file open in order to maintain leverage on Iran with regard to other issues. In an April 2006 report, the authors appeared to link the unresolved status of the contamination issue to information on the enrichment program in general. "Since it will be difficult to establish a definitive conclusion with respect to the origin of all the contamination," it said, "it is essential for the Agency to make progress in ascertaining the

13. GOV/2004/83, November 15, 2004, 8–9.
14. Linzer, "Findings Could Hurt US Effort on Iran."
15. GOV/2005/67, September 2, 2005, 4.
16. GOV/2006/15, February 22, 2006, 2–3.

scope and chronology of Iran's centrifuge enrichment program." And in June, the contamination issue was linked to the full implementation of the Additional Protocol, which Iran had just stopped implementing February 6, 2006—two days after the IAEA Board of Governors passed a resolution requesting ElBaradei to report to the UN Security Council that Iran must cease all enrichment-related activities.[17]

Meanwhile, the contamination investigation had merged with a separate investigation into the Physics Research Center (PHRC), which Iran never denied was a Defense Ministry-related organization, and its alleged role in procuring dual-use technology related to uranium enrichment. When the PHRC was first brought to public attention in 2003, it was not in connection with nuclear weapons. The Mujahedeen-e-Khalq's political front, NCRI, had charged that the PHRC was working on biological weapons, evidently because it had been renamed the Biological Studies Center.[18] But Heinonen later wrote that it was a "set of procurement information about the PHRC which prompted [the IAEA] in 2004 to raise the first questions on the role of the military in Iran's nuclear program."[19] Heinonen was referring to a set of telexes on procurement requests from Sharif University between 1990 and 1994, many of which used a telex number at the PHRC and some of which involved dual-use technologies that could be used in a gas centrifuge enrichment program.[20] US and/or Israeli intelligence, which had long interpreted those telexes to mean that the Iranian military was involved in a nuclear program, shared the telexes with the IAEA during its investigation.[21]

17. GOV/2006/38, June 8, 2006, 1–2. Iran's decision to suspend implementation of the Additional Protocol is referred to in GOV/2006/15, February 27, 2006, 6. The resolution of the IAEA Board of Governors of February 4, 2006, is in GOV/2004/14, February 4, 2006.

18. Gary Samore, ed., *Iran's Strategic Weapons Programme: A Net Assessment* (New York: Routledge, 2005), 44.

19. David Albright and Olli Heinonen, "Opening the Door to a Solution with Iran," ISIS Reports, Institute for Science and International Security, May 9, 2012.

20. The information in the telexes involving the effort to procure technologies and material that might be used in a uranium enrichment program was detailed in Herbert Krosney, *Deadly Business: Legal Deals and Outlaw Weapons* (New York: Four Walls Eight Windows, 1993), 261–65. For some details on the background of the telexes and an argument, without actual evidence, that the PHRC was using Sharif University to obtain the items for a covert military nuclear program, see David Albright, Paul Brannan, and Andrew Stricker, "The Physics Research Center and Iran's Parallel Military Nuclear Program," Institute for Science and International Security, February 23, 2012. The Albright argument was then covered as proven fact in Joby Warrick, "Formerly Secret Telexes Reveal Iran's Early Use of Deceit in Nuclear Program," *Washington Post*, February 22, 2012.

21. The first allusion in an IAEA report to the information in the telexes and the role of the PHRC in procurement, which is indirect, is GOV/2011/65, November 11, 2011, 8 and annex, 5.

When the agency acquired satellite photos of the site at Lavisan-Shian in Tehran where it thought the PHRC was located, however, it found that the entire area had been razed. All of the buildings had been destroyed and the topsoil removed beginning in November 2003. The IAEA had made no request to Iran for information about the PHRC, however, until after the June 2004 Board of Governors' meeting, at which US ambassador Kenneth Brill said the site had been connected with alleged nuclear-related activities and that the razing of the site had been meant to hide the evidence of the PHRC's nuclear work from the IAEA. Brill asserted that the topsoil had been removed, although an unnamed IAEA official was quoted as saying the inspection "produced no proof that any soil had been removed at all."[22] Iran agreed to let IAEA inspectors carry out environmental sampling of the site within two weeks. The sampling found no evidence of any nuclear material, but the IAEA report said detecting such material in the soil would be "very difficult in light of the razing of the site."[23]

Iran had explained in response to the agency's initial inquiry about Lavisan-Shian that the site had been razed because the municipality had demanded its return from the Ministry of Defense. In mid-2005, Iran provided documentary proof that the razing of the Lavisan-Shian site was a result of the municipality's decision rather than the PHRC's past presence there. The IAEA acknowledged that the information Iran had provided "appeared to be coherent and consistent with its explanation."[24]

Iran also told the IAEA that the PHRC had not even existed as an organization since 1998. It had been established in 1989 for the purpose of "preparedness for combat and neutralization of casualties due to nuclear attack." In 1998, according to the Iranian account, the PHRC was replaced by something called the Biological Studies Center, which worked exclusively on "radioprotection." The agency offered no information that conflicted with that account, nor did it suggest that it had found any reason to question it.[25]

Nevertheless, Bush administration officials planted the seeds of a full-blown news media myth about Lavisan-Shian as a covert nuclear weapons site. The essence of the story was the claim, contrary to the facts, that Iran had denied the IAEA access to the site until after it had been bulldozed.[26]

---

22. Reuters, "No Sign of Nuke Work at Suspect Iran Site—Diplomats," September 29, 2004.

23. GOV/2004/83, November 15, 2004, 21–22.

24. GOV/2005/67, September 2, 2005, 10.

25. GOV/2004/83, November 15, 2004, 21–22.

26. Carla Anne Robbins, "Atomic Test," *Wall Street Journal*, March 18, 2005; Alissa J. Rubin, "Report Documents Iran's Reticence on Nuclear Disclosure," *Los Angeles Times*, September 3, 2005, A3.

Seven years after the IAEA had first asked for and almost immediately gotten such access, David Albright of ISIS was still indignant about Iran's allegedly "interfering with the ability of the IAEA to investigate the allegation that the PHRC was involved in nuclear activities."[27]

In February 2006, Iran agreed that IAEA investigators could meet with the former head of the PHRC, identified elsewhere as Sayyed Abbas Shahmoradi-Zavareh, who had simultaneously been a professor at Sharif University. The agency was also allowed to take environmental samples from vacuum equipment with high-pumping speeds located at the university that was shown to them because it had been acquired through the PHRC. When the results of the environmental samples came back, they showed a small number of particles of natural and high-enriched uranium.[28]

That was the point at which the IAEA investigation into the origin of contamination in relation to centrifuge parts merged with its investigation into the PHRC's assumed role in the Iranian nuclear program. In addition to the high-vacuum equipment at the university, the list of dual-use items Heinonen wanted to ask the Iranians about included fluorine (an essential component of uranium tetrafluoride and uranium hexafluoride used in uranium enrichment), fluorine-handling equipment, a balancing machine, mass spectrometers, and magnets, including ring magnets that could be used on uranium centrifuges. Those were the items that had been found in the Iranian telexes that had drawn intense interest in US and European intelligence agencies in the early 1990s.[29]

But by spring 2006, both sides were halting progress on the resolution of specific issues in order to gain leverage on others or on the resolution of the entire package of issues. Iran had begun holding back information on the PHRC until agreement on an overall resolution could be achieved. Meanwhile, the IAEA was deliberately avoiding a resolution of the contamination issue to keep pressure on Iran on the PHRC issue in particular. The PHRC issue remained frozen until mid-2007.

After Iran's failure to mention its acquisition of designs for P-2 centrifuges—a more advanced model than the P-1 it had originally acquired from the A. Q. Khan network—in its October 2003 declaration, Goldschmidt and Heinonen suspected that Iran had a centrifuge program that was more advanced and more extensive than it acknowledged. They

---

27. David Albright and Robert Avagyan, "Further Activity at Suspected Parchin Testing Complex," ISIS Reports, Institute for Science and International Security, May 30, 2012.

28. GOV/2006/27, April 28, 2006, 6. The IAEA report does not identify the individual by name, but Shahmoradi-Zavareh is identified as the former head of PHRC in Albright, Brannan, and Stricker, "The Physics Research Center."

29. Ibid.

believed the AEOI was lying when it explained that no actual work had been done on centrifuges between 1995 and 2002.[30] The AEOI explanation for the lack of work on P-2 centrifuges during the period was shortages of professional resources and the unexpected difficulties encountered in making P-1 centrifuges work. The AEOI also insisted that despite frequent contacts with the intermediaries who had provided the drawings from 1995 through 1999, there were no further discussions with the intermediaries on the P-2 centrifuge.[31]

The European officials with whom Iran was negotiating in 2004 told Iranian nuclear negotiator Hassan Rouhani that they did not believe the Iranian explanation either. Rouhani recalled that when he told the Europeans that the small private-sector facility was the only site active on P-2 centrifuge development, they responded, "You paid so much money for these designs, only to give them to a private individual to work on his small, privately owned workshop?" The Europeans made it clear to Rouhani that they believed the Iranians were carrying out the main activities on the P-2 at a different site.[32]

The IAEA said that the reasons given by Iran for the apparent gap between 1995 and 2002 "do not provide sufficient assurances that there were no related activities carried out during that period." The IAEA found it suspicious that the contractor had been able to make the modifications necessary for the composite cylinders within such a short period after getting the drawings in early 2002.[33]

But the agency was not taking into account some central factors in the Iranian decision-making on centrifuges. One of the reasons underlying the absence of any P-2 program during 1995–2002 was the distrust of the supplier network that the AEOI had developed after several years of frustration with the inferior P-1 components the Khan network had provided in 1987. One of the crucial elements of the AEOI account was that the intermediaries offered to sell Iran actual P-2 centrifuges in 1996, but the AEOI did not pursue the offer because it had been burned so badly by the first deal. As a result, the AEOI had only general engineering drawings to work with in constructing the P-2, rather than detailed manufacturing drawings. The distinction was crucial. The AEOI concluded on the basis of an assessment of the country's technical and scientific expertise that it could not master P-2 centrifuges until it had gained experience working on P-1s. The Iranian claim that a veteran of the P-1 work at the AEOI had signed a contract to

30. GOV/2004/11, February 24, 2004, 8.
31. GOV/2004/60, September 1, 2004, 5.
32. Rouhani speech.
33. GOV/2004/60, 5.

work on a model P-2 centrifuge design in 2002 was supported not only by the contractor in an interview with the IAEA investigators but by the contract reviewed by IAEA inspectors in April 2004 as well as the engineer's logbook and the components he produced, which they were able to examine in detail at his workplace.[34] The AEOI also provided a complete oral translation of the report on its entire research and development process for the P-2, as Goldschmidt later recalled.[35] The IAEA reports of March and June 2004, which cast doubt on the Iranian claim, mentioned the interview with the contractor, but not that additional documentary evidence was provided by the AEOI.[36]

Sometime in the latter half of 2005, the IAEA obtained the report of the 2004 interrogation of Bukhary Sayed Abu Tahir, a member of A. Q. Khan's nuclear supply network, in Malaysia, during which Tahir had claimed that three shipments of one P-2 centrifuge each had been sent to Iran in 1997. An unidentified diplomat leaked that testimony to Agence France-Presse in January 2006.[37] Heinonen confronted Iran with that Tahir testimony in November 2005, and in meetings in Tehran February 12–14, 2006, and the AEOI repeated its insistence that it had not purchased any P-1 or P-2 centrifuge components after 1995. Heinonen decided to go public with the charge, without revealing the source, in the February 2006 IAEA report, which said the agency had "information . . . indicating the possible delivery of P-2 components to Iran by the supplier network."[38]

But Heinonen's decision to publicize an accusation for which no confirming evidence had been found turned out to be a revealing mistake. Tahir could not produce any documentation for the claim, according to both IAEA and US State Department sources.[39] The claim was evidently discredited because after that initial mention of the alleged Iranian purchase of P-2 centrifuge components, it was never referred to again in subsequent IAEA reports.

---

34. "Communication of 13 June 2004 from the Permanent Mission of the Islamic Republic of Iran Concerning the Report of the Director General Contained in GOV/2004/34," June 6, 2004, INFCIRC/630, Attachment, 3.

35. Personal communication to the author from Pierre Goldschmidt, July 2, 2013.

36. GOV/2004/11, February 24, 2004, 8; GOV/2004/34, June 1, 2004, 5.

37. Michael Adler, "Iran 'Received Nuke Shipments,'" Agence France-Press, January 21, 2006.

38. GOV/2006/15, February 27, 2006, 4.

39. Adler, "Iran 'Received Nuke Shipments'"; Gareth Porter, "No Evidence of Secret Enrichment by Iran," Inter Press Service, July 11, 2006.

# The Uranium Metal Document and Plutonium Experiments

In its November 2005 report, the IAEA revealed that among the documents it had obtained from Iran was one "related to the procedural requirements for the reduction of $UF_6$ to metal in small quantities, and on the casting and machining of enriched natural and depleted uranium metal into hemispherical form, with respect to which Iran stated that it had been provided on the initiative of the procurement network and not the request of the Atomic Energy Organization of Iran."[40] But the IAEA did not suggest that the document was a guide to forming a component of a nuclear weapon or single it out as a new issue for verification. It merely mentioned it as one of a number of documents shared by Iran that were relevant to the 1987 offer by the procurement network.

In a pattern replicated often during the IAEA investigation, however, the BBC, depending on unnamed diplomats, described the document as evidence of a nuclear bomb program. The BBC story's lead was, "Iran has passed on to United Nations inspectors documents on how to build a crucial part of a nuclear bomb, the UN's atomic agency says." It quoted "a source familiar with the report" as saying the information amounted to "design information which could be used for a central part of a nuclear bomb."[41]

But the document was nothing of the sort. In a briefing for member states in late January 2006, Heinonen, who had succeeded Goldschmidt as deputy director for safeguards in June 2005, acknowledged that the document was "related to the fabrication of nuclear weapon components" but added, "It did not, however, include dimensions or other specifications for machined pieces for such components."[42] In other words, it was not "design information" for a bomb. The discussion of casting of uranium metal into hemispheres was so general, in fact, that only one and a half pages of the 15-page document were actually devoted to that subject.[43]

The story of how the uranium metal document actually fell into the hands of the IAEA sheds further light on its actual significance. In January 2005, when Iran was still motivated to provide maximum cooperation with

40. GOV/2005/87, November 18, 2005, 2.

41. BBC, "Iran given 'Nuclear Weapon' Data," November 18, 2005.

42. "Developments in the Implementation of the NPT Safeguards Agreement in the Islamic Republic of Iran and Agency Verification of Iran's Suspension of Enrichment-related and Reprocessing Activities," Update Brief by the Deputy Director for Safeguards, January 31, 2006, 2.

43. "Communication Dated 7 March 2006 Received from the Permanent Mission of the Islamic Republic of Iran to the Agency," INFCIRC/672, March 8, 2006, 1–2.

the IAEA, it agreed to allow IAEA investigators to look through boxes of old AEOI files, according to a source familiar with the episode. During the search, the investigators came across the uranium metal document. "As they were going through boxes of papers, it literally fell out," the source recalled.[44] After he had left the IAEA, Heinonen commented in an interview that it was "difficult to figure out why it was there."[45] That comment indirectly acknowledged that if Iran had believed it was a highly sensitive document, it would not have been left in files along with ordinary papers on the enrichment program.

Despite Heinonen's previous straightforward description to diplomats, he shifted his position on the issue in the February 2006 IAEA report. Suddenly the document was treated as a major issue in the investigation. Even though the report admitted there was no indication that Iran had actually used the document, it declared its "existence in Iran" to be "a matter of concern." It said the document was "related to uranium re-conversion and casting which was part of the original 1987 offer by the intermediaries." Furthermore, it said, "The Agency is aware that the intermediaries had this document, as well as other similar documents, which the Agency has seen in another Member State. Therefore, it is essential to understand the full scope of the offer made by the network in 1987."[46]

Heinonen's ostensible reason for suddenly elevating the document was that because Libya had gotten that document as well as bomb designs from the Khan network, therefore Iran could have done the same thing. The real reason, however, can be deduced from the fact that Heinonen had not found the document particularly significant until the Board of Governors, at the insistence of the United States, cited it in a resolution on February 4, 2006, that called on the director general to report Iran to the UN Security Council. The sudden upgrading of the document's importance by Heinonen appears to have been done at the behest of the United States.

What Heinonen had kept out of IAEA reports on the issue, however, was that the intermediaries had given the agency accounts indicating that the 15-page document had been given to Iran without Iran requesting it. Heinonen had interviewed Tahir of the Khan network, who was present when the Iranians purchased the centrifuge designs in Dubai in 1987 and apparently backed up the Iranian claim. Notes of that interview were given to journalists Douglas Frantz and Catherine Collins, who used them as the basis for the story of the transaction recounted in their book. According

44. Personal communication to the author from a Vienna-based diplomat, July 2, 2008.

45. Author's interview with Olli Heinonen, Cambridge, MA, November 5, 2010.

46. GOV/2006/15, February 27, 2006, 4–5.

to that account, after agreeing on the price of centrifuge components and plans, the intermediaries "sweetened the deal" by throwing in the uranium metal document, in the hope of selling the Iranians the technology in the future.[47]

Heinonen confirmed in an interview with me that he had interviewed Tahir as well as other members of the network who were familiar with the deal with Iran. His main argument was that their testimony was inconclusive. "They all told different stories," he said. "We still don't know whether the Iranians asked for it." But when I asked him whether the Khan network sources he had interviewed had contradicted the Iranian claim that the AEOI had not requested such a document, he replied, "They didn't challenge the Iranian assertion."[48]

Heinonen implied strongly, however, that he believed the Khan network people had lied about not having sold any nuclear weapons designs to Iran. "Tahir and the network guys say, 'We don't know anything about nuclear weapons,'" he told me. "The guys in the network—they all try to make the case look better than it is." Heinonen had become fixated on the idea that Iran must have gotten nuclear weapon designs from the network, even though he had found no evidence of it.

The IAEA investigation of Iran's plutonium experiment began after the AEOI admitted at a meeting in late 2003 that it had carried out experiments in irradiating depleted uranium to separate small amounts of plutonium at the Esfahan Nuclear Technology Center from 1988 to 1993. Iran said only 3 kilograms (6.6 pounds) of depleted uranium were irradiated, and estimated that only micrograms—a few millionths of a gram—of plutonium were produced. The IAEA found that the quantity of plutonium was milligrams (thousandths of a gram), rather than micrograms. But it was clear from the minute amounts produced and the absence of any evidence of further work that the experiment was for basic scientific understanding rather than part of a weapons program. The IAEA nevertheless treated it as suspicious because it concluded that the age of the solution was less than 12 to 16 years and that it might have been created more recently than Iran had declared.[49]

Iran insisted that it had conducted no experiments on plutonium separation after 1993. In April 2005, Iran explained that in 1995 and again in 1998, it had purified the plutonium solution and used it to produce plutonium discs, which it emphasized was different from experiments to obtain

47. Douglas Frantz and Catherine Collins, *The Nuclear Jihadist* (New York: Twelve, 2007), 160 and 381.

48. Author's interview with Olli Heinonen, Cambridge, MA, November 5, 2010.

49. GOV/2003/75, November 10, 2003, annex, 5–6.

plutonium. The discs were sent to the agency's lab, and a preliminary assessment appeared to corroborate the Iranian claims.[50]

Before the IAEA was able to assess the Iranian explanation, however, the Bush administration was carrying out another political operation aimed at convincing the public that Iran had been caught red-handed. The *New York Times* ran a story that said, "Iran has admitted that it conducted small-scale experiments to create plutonium, one of the pathways to building nuclear weapons, for five years beyond the date when it previously insisted it had ended all such work, a senior official of the International Atomic Energy Agency is expected to report Thursday." The *Times* reported that it had obtained Goldschmidt's three-page statement to be presented to the Board of Governors at its quarterly meeting, and that he would say that "Iran made the admissions after being confronted with the result of laboratory tests conducted on samples collected from an Iranian nuclear site."[51]

But that wasn't what Goldschmidt's statement to the board actually said. Instead he accurately stated Iran's position that no plutonium experiments had been conducted or plutonium separated since 1993. And he noted that Iran had confirmed in writing what it had told the agency investigators.[52] In a pattern that would be repeated in coverage by the *Times* and other news outlets of the IAEA's ultimate disposition of the entire set of issues, the author of the story was reporting not what was in the document, but what he was being told by his anonymous source.

The leak of the false and misleading information to the *Times* had evidently come from the US delegation to the board meeting. The statement at the meeting by the US representative, Jackie Sanders, a political ally of John Bolton's, said, "Now we learn that Iran continued with plutonium experimentation until at least 1998, five years later." That was the same "five years later" theme as in the story leaked to the *Times*.[53]

Discussions between AEOI officials and agency inspectors in April 2006 failed to resolve the inconsistencies identified by the agency in the Iranian explanation, and the agency declared that it could not "exclude the possibility . . . that the plutonium analyzed by the Agency was derived from

50. GOV/2005/67, September 2, 2005, 7.

51. Richard Bernstein, "Iran Said to Admit Tests on Path to Atom Arms," *New York Times*, June 16, 2005.

52. "Highly Confidential: Statement of the DDG-SG in the June 2005 Board of Governors Meeting," http://www.iranwatch.org/international/IAEA/iaea-goldschmidt-statement-061305.pdf.

53. "Iran Not Forthcoming on Past, Present Nuclear Efforts, US Says," US statement, June 2005 IAEA Board of Governors Meeting, http://iipdigital.usembassy.gov/st/english/texttrans/2005/06/20050616173244frllehctim0.9385797.html#ixzz2OP5T0wK3.

source(s) other than the ones described by Iran."[54] But during further technical exchanges in 2006 and the first half of 2007, it began to become clear to the agency that technical problems rather than Iranian covert production of plutonium had created the inconsistencies. When Iran and the IAEA reached an initial agreement in July 2007 on the still unresolved issues, the plutonium experiments issue was the first to be resolved. Within days of that agreement, Iran provided the quantitative data and other clarifications requested by the IAEA. As a result, the agency revised its estimates of the plutonium abundance that would be expected from such an experiment and concluded that Iran's statements on the experiments were "consistent with the agency's findings." On August 20, 2007, before it resolved any of the other verification issues, the agency declared that it considered the plutonium experiment issue "resolved."[55]

## Polonium-210 and the Gchine Mine

The IAEA discovered in September 2003 from the operating records of the Tehran Research Reactor that bismuth metal samples had been irradiated during the 1989–1993 period, producing polonium-210, a highly radioactive radioisotope. It was not an experiment that Iran was required to report to the agency, because bismuth is not nuclear material. And far from being done covertly, the experiment was recorded in full in the logbook at the research reactor, which was under IAEA safeguards and therefore available to inspectors at any time of their choosing.[56]

Nevertheless, the agency made it one of the major issues under "verification activities" in its March 2004 report, solely on the ground that polonium-210 can be used, in conjunction with beryllium, as a neutron initiator in certain nuclear weapon designs. The agency acknowledged that it could also be used for radioisotope thermoelectric generators, or nuclear batteries.[57] An unnamed Western diplomat fed the *Washington Post* the politically hyped story that the IAEA had discovered Iran had "produced and experimented with polonium, an element useful for initiating the chain reaction that produces a nuclear explosion, according to two people familiar with a report the inspectors will submit."[58]

---

54. GOV/2006/27, April 28, 2006, 5.

55. GOV/2007/48, August 30, 2007, 2–3, attachment, 2.

56. "Comments and Explanatory Notes by the Islamic Republic of Iran on Report of the IAEA Director General (GOV/2004/11)," INFCIRC/628, March 5, 2004, 4.

57. GOV/2004/11, February 24, 2004, 5.

58. Karl Vick, "Another Nuclear Program Found in Iran," *Washington Post*, February 24, 2004, A1.

Iran immediately gave the IAEA access to two of the scientists who had participated in the experiments, one of whom was living outside of Iran and returned specifically to meet with inspectors. The two scientists said that only two bismuth samples had been irradiated, and that polonium-210 had been extracted from only one of the irradiated samples. They said further that the experiment, which had ended in 1991, was basic research on chemical separation of polonium with the development of radioisotope thermoelectric generators in mind, although it was also stated that it had been part of a study about neutron sources. Such neutron sources for industrial applications, Iranian officials noted, were not available to Iran because of restrictions that had been imposed on its technology imports.[59]

Iran provided a copy of the original project proposal requested by the IAEA. The November 2004 report admitted that the agency had no "concrete information that is contrary" to Iran's explanation. Nevertheless, it said the IAEA "remains somewhat uncertain regarding the plausibility of the very limited applications of short-lived Po-210 sources."[60] That remark appeared to suggest that Iran could not possibly have aspired to such advanced applications of neutron sources as radioisotope batteries, which play a key role as power sources for satellites, for example. The authors of the report evidently were not aware of the fact that Iran had begun pursuing a program for constructing a space satellite many years earlier.[61]

After dismissing the Iranian explanation without having any evidence to contradict it, the IAEA made no further reference to the issue until the announcement of the work program in August 2007, suggesting that even Heinonen did not consider the case involving polonium-210 very convincing. Heinonen failed even to mention it in his update brief for member states on his investigation in late January 2006.[62]

The story of the Gchine mine investigation is even more revealing of the broader politics of the Safeguards Department's investigation. In early 2004, the department began to focus, for reasons that it did not explain, on an obscure aspect of Iran's overall nuclear program: Iran's management of the uranium mine at Gchine, near Bandar Abbas in southern Iran. And it was focused even more specifically on the ore-concentration facility

---

59. GOV/2004/11, February 24, 2004, 5; "Comments and Explanatory Notes," 4.

60. GOV/2004/83, November 15, 2004, 18.

61. Federation of American Scientists, "IRIS and Iran's Emerging Space Program," http://www.fas.org/nuke/guide/iran/missile/iris.htm.

62. Update Brief by the deputy director general for safeguards, January 31, 2006.

associated with the mine.[63] The IAEA acknowledged that it had no indication of any undeclared activity in connection with the inquiry.[64]

The mystery of the purpose of the investigation began to unfold in 2005. Goldschmidt said in March 2005 that the purpose was to "better understand the complex arrangements governing the current and past administration of the mine."[65] Only in September 2005 did the agency explain that it "wished to investigate further how a turn-key project for a uranium ore processing plant could have been implemented by a newly founded company, described as having had limited experience in uranium ore processing, in such a relatively short period of time." It was particularly suspicious that this new company could have been able during the period of 2000 and 2001 to "design, procure, build and test the grinding process line for the mill."[66]

Jackie Sanders, the US permanent representative to the IAEA, revealed the real aim of the agency's Gchine inquiry in her official statement to the March 2005 board meeting: "We continue to wonder and to ask whether Iran's military played a role in overseeing that uranium mine and to what purpose."[67] The agency was pursuing what it thought was evidence that the military was using an engineering company as its front to control the Gchine mine.

The first thing the agency requested about Gchine was the original contract between the AEOI and an engineering company named Kimia Maadan for the management of the ore-processing plant at the mine. At a meeting with the IAEA in April 2005, Iran showed the investigators a copy of the July 2000 AEOI contract with Kimia Maadan, which was translated orally for them, as well as a number of documents on the project, including the "as built" drawings provided by the company to the AEOI. During a visit to Iran August 13–18, 2005, IAEA investigators were able to meet with the individual who had taken over the management of the project for the AEOI in 2002. They learned that Kimia Maadan had just been founded and that after initially trying to acquire the items off the shelf and assemble them, the company found that it needed to hire subcontractors to do much

63. GOV/2004/83, November 15, 2004, 2–3.

64. GOV/2005/67, September 2, 2005, 7.

65. Statement to the IAEA Board of Governors by Pierre Goldschmidt, deputy director general for safeguards, March 1, 2005, excerpts at http://www.iranwatch.org/international/IAEA/iaea-goldschmidt-statement-030105.htm.

66. GOV/2005/67, September 2, 2005, 7–8.

67. Statement to the IAEA Board of Governors by Ambassador Jackie Wolcott Sanders, special representative of the president for the non-proliferation of nuclear weapons and US representative to the Conference on Disarmament, March 2, 2005, http://2001-2009.state.gov/t/ac/rls/rm/42901.htm.

of the work. The report implied that the sequence of events was implausible without a deeper explanation. The agency also questioned why no work had been done at the Gchine mine from 1993 to 1999, implying that there was something suspicious about that fact as well.[68] After the September 2005 report, however, the IAEA went silent on the issue, failing to mention the Gchine mine in any of its reports during 2006 or 2007.

## The Work Program

By 2006, progress toward resolution of most of the issues under investigation had become frozen. Iran was holding on to some information it knew it would provide to the IAEA on the PHRC, Gchine, and other issues in order to negotiate an eventual deal that would bring the entire process to an end. The agency, for its part, was clearly refusing to publish information it had on some issues—the contamination issue being the clearest and most important example—that would have shown Iran's innocence.

Meanwhile, ElBaradei was eager to negotiate a deal with Iran to resolve all the remaining issues. But it was not until June 26, 2007, that Ali Larijani, the secretary of Iran's Supreme National Security Council, told ElBaradei in a face-to-face meeting that Iran was ready to work out a plan to resolve the outstanding issues. Negotiations on the details of the plan began within days, and after three meetings with Larijani in July, Iran and the IAEA reached full agreement on August 21, 2007, on a "work program" aimed at finally clarifying all unresolved issues.[69]

The official text of the agreement provided that the work program covered "all remaining issues" which were identified specifically in the agreement and "confirmed that there are no other remaining issues and ambiguities regarding Iran's past nuclear program and activities." The agency also agreed that it would provide Iran with "all remaining questions" on the issues covered, and that Iran would have no more questions to answer after that. And most important of all, the agency agreed that once the plan was implemented, the implementation of safeguards in Iran "will be conducted in a routine manner."[70]

The agreement was very specific about the order in which the issues would be discussed and committed the two sides to resolve them within three months. That turned out to be unrealistically short, but it reflected the confidence in Tehran that Iranian officials could quickly satisfy the investigators that their suspicions had been misplaced. Looming over the

---

68. GOV/2005/67, September 2, 2005, 7–8.

69. ElBaradei, *Age of Deception*, 256–57; GOV/2007/48, August 30, 2007, 1.

70. GOV/2004/48, August 30, 2007, attachment, 4.

negotiations, however, was a much more explosive issue that could nullify the effect of resolving all those issues covered by the work program: a collection of documents purporting to be from an Iranian research project on nuclear weapons that the United States, Israel, and their European allies were charging Iran had carried out between 2001 and 2003. Originally the IAEA had called the program that was alleged in those papers the "Green Salt" project, but in 2007, it began calling them the "alleged studies."

The IAEA had tried to make the "alleged studies" one of the "outstanding issues" for which Iran would take responsibility for helping to resolve, but the Iranian negotiators refused. The paragraph in the work program agreement on the "alleged studies" said Iran considered the documents as "politically motivated and baseless" but agreed "as a sign of good will and cooperation with the Agency" to "review and inform the Agency of its assessment." The agency pledged, for its part, to provide "access" to the documents in its possession on three elements of the studies. That deliberately ambiguous language would allow the Safeguards Department to argue that allowing Iran to look at the document but not to have a copy to study fulfilled the IAEA's obligation.

The history of centrifuge work was the first issue on the agenda for resolution, beginning with the 1987 deal between Iran and the Khan network for P-1 centrifuge designs. Iran had firmly denied that there was any military involvement with regard to the decision to purchase P-1 centrifuge technology from the intermediaries in 1987. To support its contention, the AEOI produced a copy of a confidential communication from the president of the AEOI to the prime minister on February 27, 1987, which the prime minister approved on March 5, 1987. On the basis of that documentation and interviews with Iranian officials and the supply network, the IAEA concluded, "Iran's statements are consistent with other information available to the Agency concerning Iran's acquisition of declared P-1 centrifuge enrichment technology in 1987."

The agency also conceded for the first time that the evidence supported Iran's assertion that it had not worked on developing P-2 centrifuges from 1993 to 1999. "Based on visits made by Agency inspectors to the P-2 workshop in 2004, examination of the company owner's contract, progress reports and logbooks, and information available on procurement enquiries," the report said, "the Agency has concluded that Iran's statements on the content of the declared P-2 R&D activities are consistent with the Agency's findings."[71]

That was a roundabout way of acknowledging that Iran had been telling the truth from the beginning. The report referred to only one piece of

---

71. GOV/2004/58, November 15, 2007, 5.

information provided by Iran in November 2007: a copy of the contract with the engineer for the manufacture of a rotor tube. But Iran had said in an official communication to the agency more than three years earlier that it had provided that document along with all the other materials to the inspectors in early 2004.[72]

The IAEA report also finally withdrew the agency's earlier claim that it had information from the intermediary network that two shipments of P-2 centrifuges had been sent to Iran during the period in question. It stated, "The Agency does not have credible procurement related information pointing to the actual acquisition by Iran of P-2 centrifuges or components during this period" then added, in parentheses, "An earlier indication which appeared to support this (GOV/2006/15, para. 18) could not be substantiated."[73]

On the issue of the source of HEU contamination found on high-vacuum equipment at a technical university (which has since been identified as Sharif University, although it was not identified in the IAEA report), Iran provided crucial additional information. Sayyed Abbas Shahmoradi-Zavareh, a former head of the PHRC who was teaching at the university, had been asked to procure the equipment for the Physics Department for its projects in coating optical mirrors, optical lasers, laser mirrors, and similar devices, according to the Iranian account. But when the equipment arrived at the university in 1991, it was found to be incomplete and to have some wrong parts, and only some parts were ever used in the university and outside. The contamination had occurred, according to AEOI, in 1998, when a technician testing used centrifuge components from Pakistan at an AEOI laboratory needed the vacuum service of the university to repair a pump. Some of the imported vacuum-equipment items had been used in that repair operation, it said, and as a result, it contaminated the equipment.

The IAEA investigators were able to interview both the person who had requested the repair and the Sharif University technician who used the equipment in question to do the repair. Finally, they were able to examine the pump that had been repaired and take a swipe sample, and they compared the signatures from that sample with that of the centrifuge parts originating in Pakistan. The analysis of the signatures was the clinching evidence that the Iranian account had been accurate. The IAEA declared in a February 2008 report that the question "is no longer outstanding at this stage." Then it added, "However, the Agency continues, in accordance

---

72. "Communication of 13 June 2004 from the Permanent Mission of the Islamic Republic of Iran," 3.

73. GOV/2007/58, November 15, 2007, 4.

with its procedures and practices, to seek corroboration of its findings and to verify this issue as part of its verification of the completeness of Iran's declarations."[74] Again, the file was closed, but the IAEA was claiming the authority to reopen it at any time, contrary to the work program agreement.

Because of the role of Shahmoradi-Zavareh in procuring the vacuum equipment and the fact that he had been head of the PHRC, however, Heinonen carried out a separate investigation on what a report referred to as "Procurement activities by the former Head of PHRC." Heinonen had been primarily interested in that topic all along because of the belief of intelligence analysts stretching back well over a decade that the trail of those items procured by the former PHRC head was linked to a separate military program. But the information that Iran provided to the IAEA on Shahmoradi-Zavareh's procurement activities revealed that the intelligence analysis had been wrong from the start. Iran showed that the dual-use items long believed to represent evidence of a military hand in the nuclear program were in fact procured for entities other than the PHRC itself— mainly for educational use.[75]

The AEOI produced multiple forms of documentary evidence to support its assertion that the high-vacuum equipment had been requested by Sharif University for its Vacuum Technique Laboratory, specifically for use in experiments by its students on evaporation and vacuum techniques for producing thin coatings. The evidence included instruction manuals on the experiments, internal communications, and shipping documents related to the procurement of the equipment.

As for magnets that the analysts were sure had been for gas centrifuges, it turned out that the procurement had been requested by the Physics Department of the university in order for students to carry out "Lenz-Faraday experiments." Again, the AEOI was able to provide instruction manuals on those experiments, the request for funding that included a request to approach the head of the PHRC, and the invoice for cash sales from the supplier. The balancing machine that Shahmoradi-Zavareh attempted to procure on two occasions was for the Mechanical Engineering Department of the university, in order for students to measure vibrations and forces in rotating components. Iran again proved that explanation by turning over laboratory experiment procedures, the requests for the procurement of the machine, and the letter confirming the completion of the purchase. And IAEA inspectors found the balancing machine in question at the Mechanical Engineering Department.

---

74. GOV/2008/4, February 22, 2008, 2–3.

75. The following account of the information provided by Iran is based on GOV/2008/4, February 22, 2008, 3–4.

As for the 45 cylinders of fluorine gas that Shahmoradi-Zavareh had attempted to procure—and that Western intelligence had found so suspicious—it had been requested by the Office of Industrial Relations of the university for its research on the chemical stability of polymeric vessels. The AEOI produced the request from that office to buy fluorine and communications between Shahmoradi-Zavareh and the president of the university about the rejection of the request for the fluorine by the supplier.

Iran acknowledged that in one case, Shahmoradi-Zavareh did help the AEOI with procurement of a $UF_6$ mass spectrometer, because the AEOI was constrained by US-sponsored restrictions on technology that could be used for a nuclear program. But the documentation presented showed that Shahmoradi-Zavareh had undertaken that procurement task at the request of the dean of the university, who had approached him in 1988, which was the year before the PHRC was established. Shahmoradi-Zavareh was then head of the Mechanics Workshop of the Shahid Hemmat Industrial Group, which worked on the ballistic missile program for the Defense Ministry. He had tried to procure the mass spectrometer, but without success.

The IAEA response to this devastating blow to Heinonen's thesis about the PHRC as an agent of the Iranian military carrying out a covert nuclear program employed some tortured circumlocution. "The replies were not inconsistent with the stated use of the equipment," the IAEA report concluded. Then it signaled the IAEA's intention to continue to investigate the PHRC "in connection with the alleged studies."

On the polonium-210 issue, Iran turned over new documents that it had been withholding until agreement on a resolution of all the issues. The IAEA report described them as "additional copies of papers and literature searches that had formed the basis for the request for approval of the project . . . copies of the project proposal, the meeting minutes and the approval document from the Scientific Advisory Committee of TNRC," the Tehran Nuclear Research Center. The IAEA declared the question "no longer outstanding at this stage," but then added the same language it had added to nearly all the other issues it had agreed to consider resolved, claiming the authority to continue to "seek corroboration of its findings and to verify this issue as part of its verification of the completeness of Iran's declarations."[76]

On the Gchine mine and ore-processing facility, Iran provided new and more detailed documentation to prove that Heinonen's suspicions about who had been running them were unwarranted. The AEOI also explained why it had expended resources on the Saghand uranium mine in Yazd province in the 1993–2000 period rather than on Gchine. It turned over

---

76. Ibid., 4.

the budget, five-year plans, contracts with foreign entities, and studies and reports on the issue showing that Saghand was estimated to have far more uranium than Gchine, and that there was not enough money in the government's 1994–98 five-year plan for the AEOI to finance work on both mines. It was only in the subsequent five-year budget that adequate funding was provided for Ghine.

Documents given to the IAEA investigators also proved that Kimia Maadan was not a front for the Iranian military but had actually been created by the AEOI itself in May 2000 solely to design, equip, and put into operation the ore-processing plant at Gchine. They revealed that the core staff of Kimia Maadan consisted of about half a dozen experts who had previously worked for the AEOI's Ore Processing Center and that the conceptual work and know-how used by Kimia Maadan to carry out the contract had been generated by AEOI itself. The documents, some of which had already been shared with the investigators before, proved to the satisfaction of the IAEA that the planning for and work on the Gchine mine and the ore-processing plant on which Kimia Maadan worked had always been under the full control of the AEOI.[77]

The Iranian documents had disproven the Israeli-inspired suspicion that Kimia Maadan was merely a cat's-paw for the Iranian military. The IAEA declared that it considered the issue "no longer outstanding at this stage." But having acknowledged that IAEA "uncertainties" had been proven wrong, the report then added that the agency "continues to verify this issue as part of verification of the completeness of Iran's declarations." So the issue was closed, but it could be opened at any time.

The resolution of the uranium metal document issue had appeared for more than two years to hinge on Iran's turning over a copy of the document itself to the IAEA. On November 8, 2007, Iran gave the agency a copy of the document, which the agency had argued it needed to be able to finally establish the "full scope of the 1987 offer" document. The November 2007 report said nothing about closing the file on the issue of the document. But ElBaradei sent a letter to Iran the same day the copy of the document was received, stating, "Iran delivered the 15-page document related to the procedures for conversion of uranium and its casting. This closes the u-metal issue of the Work Plan." In another letter on November 30, ElBaradei confirmed the earlier decision, saying that the agency "confirms that this section of the Work Plan is completed."

Iranian nuclear negotiator Saeed Jalili quoted from that letter and a similar one on the P-1/P-2 issue in claiming at a meeting with EU foreign policy chief Javier Solana on November 30 that both the uranium

---

77. Ibid., 5–6.

metal and centrifuge issues were now closed. But Heinonen, who was being pressed by the anti-Iran coalition not to close any issues, assured Ambassador Simon Smith of the United Kingdom that the letters "were not intended to be categorical" and that the agency could still revert to the P-1/P-2 issues again in resolving the uranium contamination issue.[78]

Meanwhile, the news media produced highly distorted stories on the uranium metal document that added yet another layer to the false narrative surrounding it. On November 13, two days before the official release of the IAEA report on the first round of the work program, a European diplomat briefed reporters on the Iranian provision of a copy of the uranium metal document to the IAEA. Once again, the diplomat ignored the distinction that had been made in the agency's own reports between showing specifically how to machine uranium metal into hemispheric forms and describing the steps in a general way. The result was another round of stories that led the public to believe that Iran had been withholding a blueprint for a nuclear device from the IAEA. The Associated Press story, which came out the same day as the briefing, reported that Iran finally "handed over long-sought blueprints showing how to mold uranium into the shape of warheads, diplomats said Tuesday."[79] The *New York Times* reported the following day, "After years of stonewalling, Iran has given the UN watchdog agency a document showing how to cast uranium metal into hemispheres to form the core of an atom bomb, European officials said Tuesday."[80] In fact, it was no such sinister nuclear weapons design, and Iran had obviously been waiting to turn it over until it could do so as part of a deal that would close the file on the "unresolved issues."

But despite two letters from ElBaradei declaring the issue closed, Heinonen, who was under pressure from the United States and its allies on the board not to close any issues, took action to keep it open. He sent the document to the government of Pakistan and reported in the November report on the work program that the agency was "seeking more information." Heinonen publicly reopened the file in the February 2008 IAEA report. The agency, it said, was "still waiting for a response from Pakistan on the circumstances of the delivery of this document in order

78. The letters from ElBaradei to Iran are quoted in "Explanatory Comments by the Islamic Republic of Iran on the Report of the IAEA Director General (GOV/2008/08) to the September Board of Governors," INFCIRC/737, September 28, 2008, 5; WikiLeaks Cable 07UNVIENNA742, US Embassy Vienna to State Department, "Likeminded Ambassadors Regroup Post-NIE," December 7, 2007.

79. Associated Press, "Iran Turns Over Nuclear Warhead Blueprints," November 13, 2007.

80. Elaine Sciolino, "In Gesture, Iran Provides Nuclear Document," *New York Times*, November 14, 2007.

to understand the full scope and content of the offer made by the network in 1987."[81]

Although it satisfied Heinonen's allies in the United States and other IAEA delegations, his fixation on Pakistan was also related to his belief that the Pakistani government might have agreed to provide Iran with nuclear weapons technology. "We still don't know what [the Pakistani government] knew about the deal," he said in an interview with me three years later. And then he made a comment that suggested why he had been so interested in investigating the possibility that Pakistani officials had been involved. "If there was a military dimension," he said, "most likely it was on a government-to-government level." When I interviewed him again by phone a few days later, he brought up the Pakistani government angle again. "In the end was this a government-to-government deal?" he asked rhetorically. "Were there high-level officials who had agreed?"[82]

During a briefing in May 2008 for member state delegations on the "alleged studies" documents, which was evidently geared to the interests of his Western allies, Heinonen brought up the uranium metal document again. He called Iran's possession of the document "alarming" according to a Western diplomat. "He essentially said there was no reason why a country would need to possess such a document unless they wanted to produce uranium hemispheres for a nuclear weapon," the diplomat reported.[83] Although false and misleading information about IAEA board meetings given to the media by unnamed diplomats had become a standard feature of the IAEA investigation, the report was probably accurate given the views Heinonen expressed later.

The polonium-210 issue was resolved in a two-day meeting January 20–21, 2008, at which the agency's questions sent in a September 15 letter were answered. To support its explanation that the project was basic research for enhancing knowledge with no immediate application, but with the potential application to nuclear batteries in mind, Iran presented meeting minutes, the approval document from the Scientific Advisory Council of the Tehran Nuclear Research Center, and a complete copy of the reactor

---

81. GOV/2008/4, February 22, 2008, 4.

82. Author's interview with Olli Heinonen, November 5, 2010; telephone interview with Heinonen, November 10, 2010. In a bizarre twist to the story of the IAEA investigation, the November 2011 report's annex stated, "In an interview in 2007 with a member of the clandestine nuclear supply network, the Agency was told that Iran had been provided with nuclear explosive design information." See GOV/2011/65, November 8, 2011, Annex, 8. In the two interviews with me lasting over two hours, Heinonen, who would have been involved in any such 2007 interview, did not even hint at any such claim by a member of the Khan network.

83. Agence France-Presse, Vienna dispatch, "IAEA 'Alarmed' by Iran's Alleged Nuclear Weapons Work: Diplomat," May 29, 2008.

logbook for the period covered by the experiment. The IAEA declared the issue "no longer outstanding at this stage" while adding the same boiler-plate language asserting the authority to continue to investigate as it saw fit.

Despite the fact that the IAEA had conceded on every issue the two sides had agreed would be resolved in the work program, coverage of the report by the two most influential US newspapers managed to convey a story that was exactly the opposite. The *Washington Post* story by Robin Wright completely ignored the substantive content of the report and portrayed it instead as unresponsive to the IAEA probe. According the *Post*, the IAEA said Iran "did not fully answer questions or allow full access to Iranian personnel."[84] What the report actually said, however, was "Iran has provided sufficient access to individuals and has responded in a timely manner to questions and provided clarification and amplification on issues in the context of the work plan."[85] Instead of reporting the conclusions reached on the issues covered in the report, the article quoted US ambassador Gregory L. Schulte's comment that the "key thing" in the report was that "Iran's cooperation was selective and incomplete."

The *New York Times* story similarly portrayed the report as a failure of Iran to cooperate, citing "new but incomplete disclosures about its past nuclear activities." Elaine Sciolino and William J. Broad said the report "made it clear that even while providing some answers, Iran has continued to shield many aspects of its nuclear program." Ignoring the report's clear acknowledgment of the veracity of the Iranian accounts of the 1987 offer and the handling of the P-2 centrifuge issue, Sciolino and Broad instead quoted an unnamed "senior official linked to the nuclear agency" as saying he "would not call" the centrifuge file "closed."[86]

After the February 2008 IAEA report acknowledged that it found no fault in the Iranian declarations on the rest of the work plan issues, the *Post* again found a way to support the Bush administration's verdict on the outcome. While making passing reference to the fact that Iran had "provided answers to most questions about its nuclear past"—but without noting that the agency had found the answers consistent with its own information—Joby Warrick and Robin Wright followed the US propaganda line once more and asserted that the only important issue was Iran's failure to address the "alleged studies" documents. This time the *Post* quoted US ambassador to the United Nations Zalmay Khalilzad, saying, "Yes they have answered some questions and made some progress on some issues. But

84. Robin Wright, "US to Seek New Sanctions Against Iran/ UN Report Faults Iran's Input on Nuclear Program," *Washington Post*, November 16, 2007, A22.

85. GOV/2007/58, November 15, 2007, 8.

86. Elaine Sciolino and William J. Broad, "Report Raises New Doubts on Iran Nuclear Program," *New York Times*, November 16, 2007, A10.

these are not the central issues, and on the most central issues of the past, there is no progress. In fact things are getting worse."[87]

Coming at a critical juncture in the effort to build up a sense of crisis over Iran's nuclear program, the two IAEA reports should have reversed the process by making it clear that the IAEA had found nothing over its four years of investigation to indicate that Iran's nuclear activities were somehow related to a covert weapons program. But the coverage of the *Post* and the *Times* unambiguously supported the political momentum of the developing nuclear scare by avoiding the crucial facts in the two reports in favor of reporting the propaganda line of the Bush administration and those in the IAEA with a similar political slant.

## Pressuring ElBaradei

The United States and its allies on the IAEA Board of Governors were unhappy with ElBaradei's work program with Iran from the beginning. They feared that it would give Iran an opportunity to reduce international pressures by convincing the IAEA secretariat of its explanations for the issues under investigation. After the announcement of the work plan agreement, the United States, United Kingdom, France, and Germany warned ElBaradei in a démarche that it was not permissible for the work plan to result in the "normalization" of the Iran file.[88] That implied that they expected ElBaradei to simply reject or gloss over evidence that emerged in the course of the investigation of various issues showing that the activities questioned by the IAEA had not been part of a nuclear weapons program.

The November 2007 director general's report on the progress achieved in the first round of the work plan confirmed the fears of the United States and its allies that the resolution of all of the remaining issues was now likely unless diplomatic pressure could head it off. US ambassador Schulte worried that Iran would indeed provide sufficient evidence to resolve all the remaining issues except for the "alleged studies." In a cable to Washington on December 7, he wrote, "We need to ensure that the Director General does not close those issues or even declare that Iran's information is 'not inconsistent with' the Agency's findings as he has with the plutonium and centrifuge issues."[89]

At a meeting of "like-minded" member states (the United States, the European three, Australia, Canada, and Japan) in Vienna on December 7,

---

87. Joby Warrick and Robin Wright, "US Seeks Support for Sanctioning Iran, Nuclear Issues Unresolved, IAEA Says," *Washington Post*, February 23, 2008.

88. WikiLeaks cable 08UNVIENNA31, US Embassy Vienna to State, "Time to Kill the Work Plan?" January 17, 2008.

89. WikiLeaks cable 07UNVIENNA742.

diplomats expressed consternation that ElBaradei had gone too far toward closing the books on the first two issues. UK Ambassador Smith was upset that ElBaradei's letters to Iran on the P-2 centrifuge and uranium metal document issues had gone further than the language used in the report to the board, which gave the IAEA freedom to return to them when they chose. The nuclear counselor at the US mission, Geoffrey R. Pyatt, said he was worried that the IAEA secretariat might deal with the remaining outstanding issues in the same way it had the P-1/P-2 centrifuge and uranium metal document issues: by declaring what he called Iran's "non-answers" to be "consistent" with information it had collected.[90]

Schulte said he had "emphasized" to ElBaradei "the importance of pushing Iran for a confession"—an admission that it had secretly worked on a nuclear weapon—in the context of the work plan. In demanding pressure for a "confession," Schulte was reflecting the Bush administration's eagerness to take advantage of the conclusion in the national intelligence estimate that had just been completed that Iran had been conducting a covert nuclear weapons research and development program from 2001 to 2003 but halted it abruptly. President Bush had said Iran had to "come clean" on its nuclear program, and Undersecretary of State John Negroponte then explained, "They've got to acknowledge that they had such a weapons program."[91]

That complaint was a tacit admission that the IAEA had failed to find any evidence for any of the suspicions it had raised from 2004 through 2007. By mid-January, when the "like-minded" diplomats reassembled, they were even more convinced that all the remaining unresolved issues would be reported effectively closed by ElBaradei in his February report. The German chargé d'affaires told the group that Iran had provided "extensive documentation" on the contamination issue connected with the PHRC and that there had been no "substantial discussion" of the "alleged studies." Australian ambassador Peter Shannon warned that the director general's report might well be a "dud," which would negatively affect the prospects for agreement within the group of five permanent Security Council members plus Germany (P5+1) on a new Security Council resolution. Confirming that danger, Schulte said the goal now was to get such a resolution early in February before ElBaradei's report was finished.

Schulte took the lead in calling for strong pressure on ElBaradei to back off the course he was on. He wanted the like-minded group to remind ElBaradei of "our expectation that Iran be held to a higher standard."

90. Ibid.
91. Transcript, Newsmaker interview with John Negroponte, PBS Newshour, December 5, 2007.

Schulte suggested that "inspectors" were "grumbling about [ElBaradei's] closing issues for political reasons."[92] What Safeguards Department officials had explained to Israeli ambassador Israel Michaeli, however, was that the "general mood" was to "close issues if it came to a matter of judgment rather than hard facts."[93] But the "like-minded" group was only interested in keeping Iran under suspicion of covert work on nuclear weapons. The French chargé d'affaires said that demarches should be sent to ElBaradei from each of the board member's capitals before his report was finished, warning him that "normalization" of the Iran file through the work plan was "unacceptable."

Ambassador Shannon suggested that the usefulness of the work plan, which he said had been "trouble" from the beginning, was coming to an end, and that it might be time to put pressure on ElBaradei to terminate it. Schulte agreed that the board "must reassert its authority on the DG [director general], who needs to be reminded that he represents the Board." He also remarked that the board's membership was now more "auspicious" for such a move than it had been in the past, referring to the departure of several states that had supported Iran's position from the board and their replacement by more compliant states.[94] Two weeks later, Pyatt told the Israeli ambassador that if the United States had indications that ElBaradei was preparing to "declare the work plan 'completed,'" it would tell him that was unacceptable.[95]

Those statements were mostly bluster, aimed at maintaining the Western diplomats' sense of their power over the IAEA. In early February, two weeks before the ElBaradei report was expected, Schulte reported to the State Department that the secretariat had "more or less closed all the other issues." He said the United States and its European allies were now in agreement that "everything hinged on the DG's treatment of the 'alleged studies.'" Schulte suggested that the United States and its like-minded allies should now be prepared to raise the stakes in the political game with ElBaradei. "We must . . . warn the DG in very stark terms," he wrote, "that the IAEA's integrity and his own credibility are at stake, and that any hint of whitewash of Iran's weapons activities would cause irreparable harm to the Agency's relationship with major donors."[96]

92. WikiLeaks cable 08UNVIENNA31.

93. WikiLeaks cable 08UNVIENNA55, US Embassy Vienna to State, "Israel in the Dog House with DG," January 31, 2008.

94. WikiLeaks cable 07UNVIENNA31.

95. WikiLeaks cable 08UNVIENNA55.

96. WikiLeaks cable 08UNVIENNA64, US Embassy Vienna to State, "Maintaining Pressure on Iran at the March Board," February 5, 2008.

Schulte was referring to the ultimate weapon available to the United States and its allies in trying to control ElBaradei. Nine months earlier, Schulte had passed on a threat from Secretary of State Condoleezza Rice that if ElBaradei continued to create obstacles to US diplomatic strategy on the Iranian nuclear program, the United States "could treat the IAEA budget like that of the Universal Postal Union."[97] Schulte vowed that the United States would seek to "diminish the value of the IAEA and the work plan as a 'pressure relief valve' for Iran" and to make it clear that the Security Council and the IAEA Board of Governors—not ElBaradei—"must make a final decision on whether to return Iran to 'routine' verification." He vowed to "reassert Board authority over the DG and dispense with the work plan."

The diplomatic pressure on ElBaradei and Heinonen did have an impact on the IAEA position on the status of the issues and of Iran's file. ElBaradei did not prevent Heinonen from adding language at the end of the agency's conclusion on each issue asserting that it was free to return to the issue if and when it chose. That was, of course, a direct violation of the explicit wording of the work program agreement.

The most important tool of the US-led coalition to keep Iran in the dock as accused party at the IAEA, however, was the "alleged studies." Ambassador Schulte and his allies were insistent that the main function of the IAEA was now to press Iran hard on the basis of those documents. Under pressure from the United States and its anti-Iran coalition, the IAEA was about to shift to a much more openly partisan role, combining investigator, prosecutor, and judge in regard to the intelligence documents alleging a covert nuclear weapons program in Iran. But the IAEA—which had revealed publicly in early 2003 that the infamous Niger uranium letter that had been cited by the Bush White House to justify war on Iraq was a fake—should have undertaken a serious investigation of the "alleged studies" documents. Instead, the agency became part of the scheme to use those documents to help build a case for more serious sanctions against Iran.

# 8

# The Mystery of the
# Laptop Documents

## An Iranian "Curveball"?

Sometime during summer or fall 2004, the US government came into possession of a large cache of documents purporting to be from an Iranian
research program on nuclear weapons. Totaling more than a thousand
pages, the documents showed studies on a redesign of the Iranian ballistic
missile's reentry vehicle, high-explosives testing for a nuclear weapon detonator, and a bench-scale uranium conversion system—all of which were
purportedly done from 2001 through 2003. The documents were reportedly brought out of Iran on a purloined laptop computer, giving them the
patina of having come straight out of a clandestine Iranian nuclear weapon
program.

From the beginning, the documents were enveloped in a fog of mystery
about how they had been obtained in Iran—if they had indeed come from
within the country—and who had brought them out. At first, the intelligence community seemed to be genuinely in the dark about their provenance. Stories about the documents over the next year failed to penetrate
the mystery of the source of the documents.[1] The *New York Times* reported
in November 2005 that US officials had "largely refused to provide details

---

1.  Carla Anne Robbins, "Atomic Test: As Evidence Grows of Iran's Program, U.S. Hits
Quandary," *Wall Street Journal*, March 18, 2005, A1; Michael Adler, "US Briefs on Alleged Iranian Nuclear Warhead Work: Diplomats," Agence France-Presse, October 9,
2005; William J. Broad and David E. Sanger, "Relying on Computer, U.S. Seeks to Prove
Iran's Nuclear Aims," *New York Times*, November 13, 2005.

of the origins of the laptop computer beyond saying that they obtained it in mid-2004 from a longtime contact in Iran."[2]

But David Sanger of the *Times* was eventually given a more detailed explanation for the papers. The source was an Iranian engineer or scientist who had been recruited to be a spy at an international scientific conference, according to the story, and in 2003–4, the spy obtained the documents from a secret nuclear weapons project on which he had been working and stored them on a laptop computer. But he began to worry that he was under suspicion by Iran counterintelligence and gave the laptop to his wife, who was then able to get out of the country with their children and give the laptop to the US government. Sanger was told that the US government never learned whether the spy was imprisoned or killed.[3]

But that dramatic tale of successful penetration of what was said to have been Iran's most secret nuclear project, its ultimate discovery, and the narrow escape of the wife and children with the laptop full of sensitive nuclear documents was highly suspicious. Intelligence agencies never divulge such details about a source, even if the source has already been compromised, and the detail about the source being recruited at an international scientific conference would have been particularly damaging had it been true. Sanger attributed it to a "former intelligence official."[4]

But there were other versions of the story as well. One version had the spy stealing the laptop with all of the documents already on it from a participant in the secret nuclear weapons project whom Germany's Federal Intelligence Service (the BND) had tried unsuccessfully to recruit as an informant.[5] Then, a few years later, yet another version of the story appeared, identifying the spy not as a scientist or engineer but as an Iranian businessman with contracts with the Iranian government for the construction of buildings related to the nuclear program, who had been recruited by the BND. In the final and most highly embellished version of the origins of the documents, the spy was even given the code name "Dolphin."[6]

The stories were all suspect, but the last one was even more ludicrous than the others because of the lack of a credible link between getting contracts for pouring concrete and access to what was being billed as Iran's equivalent to the Manhattan Project. A former intelligence official who was following the reporting on the laptop documents at the time the

---

2.  Broad and Sanger, "Relying on Computer."

3.  Sanger, *Inheritance*, 65–66.

4.  Ibid., 66.

5.  Dafna Linzer, "Strong Leads and Dead Ends in Nuclear Case Against Iran," *Washington Post*, February 8, 2006, A14.

6.  Eric Follath and Holger Stark, "The Birth of a Bomb," *Der Spiegel*, June 17, 2010.

*Der Spiegel* story was published recalled that he never saw any reporting suggesting that there was a well-placed German spy. "It would have been a spectacular triumph," he told me, "but it was apparently made up to confuse people."[7]

The latter two versions both involved a link to the German intelligence agency. By early 2005, the connection between the source and the BND was widely accepted. In the first, longer story on the laptop documents, the *Wall Street Journal* reported that "an intelligence source, solicited with German help," had provided the documents to the US government.[8]

Officials sometimes deflected questions about the provenance of the documents by suggesting that it couldn't be discussed because it involved someone whose fate was still unknown. As one former US intelligence official explained to the author, "The laptop stuff was unusually sensitive, because it involved the safety of somebody's life."[9] Had that actually been true, however, there would not have been so many different versions of the origins of the documents peddled to the news media.

Very early on though, an entirely different possibility was being discussed among some intelligence officials. It came a few days after Secretary of State Colin Powell told reporters in mid-November 2004 about "information" that the Iranians were "working hard" on putting missiles together with "a weapon," which he clearly implied was nuclear.[10] Officials interviewed by the *Washington Post* said they "did not know the identity of the source or whether the individual was connected with the Iranian armed opposition group Mujahedeen-e-Khalq."[11]

The fact that nothing was known about the source of the documents within the intelligence community itself was highly significant, especially since it had already been sensitized to the danger of a self-interested source peddling information that could be used as the basis for policy decisions. That had happened in the case of the Iraqi source given the code name "Curveball" who spun a tale of Iraqi mobile bioweapons labs that turned out to be nonexistent. It was even more significant that some intelligence officials were already thinking about the possibility that the MEK could be behind the laptop documents.

---

7. Author's interview with a former US intelligence official who asked not to be identified, September 20, 2011.

8. Robbins, "Atomic Test."

9. Author's interview with a former US intelligence official who insisted on anonymity, Washington, DC, March 2, 2012.

10. Sonni Efron, Tyler Marshall, and Bob Drogin, "Powell's Talk of Arms Has Fallout," *Los Angeles Times*, November 19, 2004.

11. Dafna Linzer, "Nuclear Disclosure on Iran Unverified," *Washington Post*, November 19, 2004.

Then came an explicit warning from a senior German political appointee about the MEK origins of the documents. Karsten Voigt had been a Social Democratic Party member of parliament for more than two decades and was the party spokesman on foreign policy in the Bundestag before being appointed coordinator of German-North American cooperation in the German Foreign Office in 1998. He had been in that position ever since. Voigt told the the *Wall Street Journal* that the laptop documents had been provided by "an Iranian dissident group" and that the United States and Europe "shouldn't let their Iran policy be influenced by single-source headlines."[12]

Although it must have raised eyebrows within some circles in Washington and in European capitals, there was no media follow-up to Voigt's statement. But three years later, Voigt's assertion was confirmed by a second source close to the German chancellor and foreign minister. "I can assure you," the source told me, "that the documents came from the Iranian resistance organization."[13]

The MEK and its front organization NCRI, had long been listed as a terrorist organization by the US government and had been putting out information about Iranian nuclear weapons work for years, much of which had been demonstrably false. The assertion by two German sources that the laptop documents had come from that group suggested that the stories that had been put out to explain the origins of the documents had been aimed at covering up the actual story of how they came into US hands.

Karsten Voigt retired from the Foreign Office in 2010, and agreed three years later to tell me how and why he had warned publicly in 2004 about the MEK having provided the laptop documents.[14] Voigt said he was told about the source of the laptop documents by senior officials of the BND. "It was not a formal briefing but a conversation with my contacts," Voigt recalled. The senior BND officials were concerned, he said, about Colin Powell's remarks about intelligence on mating a missile with a nuclear warhead, which the BND immediately recognized as a reference to the laptop documents. "They didn't like the way it was being used by the United States," Voigt said.

Voigt's BND contacts knew all about the documents, Voigt said, because the individual who had delivered the papers was a source, though not a full-time agent, for the BND. Furthermore, the BND had reached a negative conclusion about the trustworthiness of the source. "They

---

12. Alex Keto, Geraldo Samor, and Carla Anne Robbins, "Bush Pushes His Top Priorities at APEC Meeting," *Wall Street Journal*, November 22, 2004.

13. Author's interview with a source close to the German Foreign Ministry who insisted on anonymity, Washington, DC, September 15, 2007.

14. Author's interview with Karsten Voigt, March 13, 2013.

believed the source was doubtful," said Voigt, because they knew he was affiliated with the MEK.

The BND was acutely aware of the danger of the United States relying on an informant with a personal or political interest in convincing Western governments that the Iranian regime had weapons of mass destruction. "We had such a situation in the Iraq war," Voigt recalled. The memory of the infamous Curveball—an Iraqi who had told elaborate stories of Iraqi mobile bioweapons laboratories that were used by Bush administration officials to support the WMD rationale for war—was still very fresh in the minds of BND officials. Only a few months before the BND had received the intelligence documents from its sometime source on Iran, it had finally agreed to allow a CIA official to interview Curveball.[15]

Curveball had not been a BND agent either, but the intelligence agency had interviewed him as an Iraqi refugee in Germany and passed on reports of his accounts about mobile bioweapons labs in Saddam's Iraq. As BND officials continued to interrogate him, however, they began to find "inconsistencies and discrepancies" in his account. When CIA director George Tenet asked the BND directly in December 2002 whether the White House could use Curveball's information for public statements, it signaled to the Germans that the Bush administration was planning to cite the Iraqi defector's claims to justify war in Iraq—a war that the government of German chancellor Gerhardt Schroeder strongly opposed. The response from August Hanning, the head of BND, was a signed, two-page letter to Tenet warning that the Curveball testimony was "unconfirmed and untested." Hanning later said the letter warned, "Please be cautious about using this source." Nevertheless, Powell cited Curveball's testimony as the centerpiece of his February 2003 UN Security Council speech making the case for war. Senior BND officials involved in the Curveball issue had been aghast at Powell's exploitation of information from a source about whom they had specifically warned the CIA. Those same senior BND officials, including Hanning, were still in place in November 2004.[16]

When BND officials read about Powell's off-the-cuff remarks to reporters referring indirectly to information in the laptop documents, they were afraid that the same thing was happening again. Schroeder's government was opposed to a US war in Iran, and Powell had made the remarks almost immediately after the German government had negotiated, along with France and the United Kingdom, an agreement with Iran aimed at

---

15. Bob Drogin, *Curveball* (New York: Random House, 2007), 265–71.

16. Ibid., 85–99, 134–38, 159–60, 281–82; Hanning quote is from "The Spies Who Fooled the World," BBC *Panorama*, March 23, 2013.

ensuring that the United States would not move the Iran nuclear issue into the UN Security Council.

The BND officials with whom Voigt met immediately after the Powell remarks didn't tell him explicitly that they wanted him to go public with the message that the source of the information was unreliable. But Voigt was a unique figure in the German government; he was known to be inter-acting constantly with Americans in the executive branch, Congress, and the think-tank community. He believed that the BND officials were expect-ing him to get out the word to Americans about the connection between the MEK and the new documents. "They tell you, 'this is confidential,' but you get the story," Voigt said.

After Voigt pointed publicly to the MEK as the source of the informa-tion that had been cited by Powell and warned against relying on it to make policy toward Iran, no one from the US government contacted him to inquire about what he knew and how he knew it. Powell later said he was never informed that the BND had doubts about the source of the laptop papers, according to his former chief of staff, Lawrence Wilkerson.[17] One former senior US intelligence officer said he was unaware that any such warning was passed on to the CIA, but that it would probably have been done on the basis of personal relationships at the senior level, so the rest of the agency would not know about it.[18]

## Reasons for Doubt

It is a well-known principle in the intelligence community that when infor-mation or documentation appears precisely at the right moment to answer key strategic questions, it should be regarded with caution, because it is likely to have been planted deliberately to influence policy. The fact that the laptop documents fell into US hands at the moment that Washington needed evidence to accuse Iran of a covert nuclear weapons program reminded some intelligence analysts of that maxim. "Even with the best intelligence," one official told the *New York Times*, "you always ask yourself, 'Was this prepared for my eyes?'"[19]

As soon as the intelligence analysts began studying the laptop docu-ments closely, they began to see several things that raised red flags. One source familiar with the attitude toward the documents in the intelligence

---

17. Personal communication to the author from Karsten Voigt, March 30, 2013; per-sonal communication to the author from Lawrence Wilkerson, Powell's chief of staff in 2004, April 6, 2013.

18. Personal communication to the author from a former senior intelligence officer who insisted on remaining anonymous, March 25, 2013.

19. Broad and Sanger, "Relying on Computer."

community told the *Los Angeles Times* that some administration officials were "surprised" that Powell had gone public with intelligence that was so "weak" and therefore "was not supposed to be used."[20]

The first thing that struck analysts was the odd combination of elements included in the purported Iranian nuclear weapons program. The documents portrayed only three types of activities: studies on the redesign of the reentry vehicle of the Shahab-3 missile to accommodate what appears to be a nuclear weapon, a pair of "flow sheets" showing a process for uranium conversion, and a set of experiments on exploding bridge wire technology (EBW) broadly similar to that used on early designs for the US atomic bomb. But there was nothing about all the other issues that would have to be researched for a full-fledged nuclear weapons program—nothing about covert enrichment or about designing and testing components of a nuclear device. David Albright at ISIS, who had talked with analysts who had read the documents, said they were puzzled. "Why these three things?" he wondered, "Why not other projects?"[21] In a later interview with the *New York Times*, Albright asked, "Is it part of a plan to develop a weapon that can fit on a nuclear missile? And if so, why are so many parts missing?"[22]

Robert Kelley had been the IAEA's senior weapons inspector in Iraq twice and had long been involved in tracking foreign nuclear weapons programs. In 2005, he quickly made his way through the entire collection of documents at IAEA headquarters. What struck him more than anything else was the sudden appearance of the "flow sheets" on uranium conversion after hundreds of pages of computer printouts on other subjects. "That was two or three pages that wasn't related to anything else in the package," he recalled. "It was on a different topic, and you just wondered, was this salted there for someone to find?"[23]

Another troubling feature of the documents was that they contained no evidence that the three different projects were in communication with one another. "So how could the documents be in the same collection?" Albright asked. He expressed doubt that the documents could have come from a single laptop computer as had been suggested by the official story of their provenance.[24] If the documents had been on the same computer, he observed, the owner should have had access to a wide range of documents on the entire program, including communications among different parts

20. Efron, Marshall, and Drogin, "Powell's Talk."

21. Author's interview with David Albright, September 15, 2008.

22. David E. Sanger, "Nuclear Agency Says Iran Has Used New Technology," *New York Times*, February 23, 2008.

23. Scott Peterson, "Iran Nuclear Report: Why It May Not Be a Game-Changer After All," *Christian Science Monitor*, November 9, 2011.

24. Author's interview with Albright, September 15, 2008.

of it. But instead the collection contained only a few quite unrevealing documents on administrative details from individual projects.[25] In light of that deficiency, the fact that a couple of documents had handwritten notes that made references to work in other projects was all the more suspicious.[26]

An even more serious problem bothered Albright. Why, he wondered, was the research in the technical documents "so primitive"? Albright's intelligence source had apparently impressed on him the shoddiness of the numerous attempts to get the size, weight, and diameter of the reentry device right while accommodating what appeared to be a nuclear weapon. "The reentry vehicle study isn't very good work," Albright said.[27] Albright even questioned the *New York Times* on its failure to report that fact. In a November 2005 exchange with William J. Broad about an article he and David Sanger had written on what they had called the "warhead documents," Albright said he was "curious to know why you did not report on the technical flaws in the work by this group of engineers. Did your sources not tell you about these flaws of this missile group?"[28]

Perhaps the main reason some intelligence analysts were so concerned about the technical flaws in the reentry vehicle schematics was that Sandia National Laboratories, one of the major US government-funded nuclear weapons laboratories, had reportedly done computer simulations of the data shown in the drawings and found them deficient. The simulations had shown, in fact, that none of the 18 efforts shown in the drawings would have worked.[29]

Both independent and US government analysts also noticed something else that raised a fundamental question about the documents on redesign of the reentry vehicle of the Shahab-3: the reentry vehicle depicted in the schematics did not match the one on the missile that Iran had flight tested in August 2004. Albright pointed out in his letter to the *New York Times* in November 2005 that the documents didn't appear to reflect the new Iranian missile. He pointed out that based on the photographs of the 2004 test launch, a nuclear warhead would have to be about 600 millimeters

25. See GOV/2008/15, May 26, 2008, annex, 1–2.

26. The handwritten notes on a letter that was clearly genuine are referred to indirectly in GOV/2008/15, annex, 1.

27. Author's interview with Albright, September 15, 2008.

28. Letter from David Albright to William J. Broad, November 15, 2005. The correspondence between Broad and Albright was in a PDF along with other correspondence between Albright and the *Times*. The link was provided by Jeffrey Lewis, "ISIS Against the Gray Lady," Arms Control Wonk, November 18, 2005, http://lewis.armscontrolwonk. com/archive/866/isis-against-gray-lady. The link to the PDF no longer works, apparently reflecting Albright's own decision to withdraw it, but the author copied the Albright letter as a Word document before it was withdrawn.

29. Linzer, "Strong Leads," A14.

in diameter to fit in the reentry vehicle. The bomb design that had been provided to Libya by the A. Q. Khan network, however, was about 900 millimeters in diameter. He questioned whether Iran could "build such a small warhead anytime soon" and said it raised the question whether Iran had developed the new missile and reentry vehicle "with a non-nuclear mission in mind."[30] In an interview with *Arms Control Today,* an unnamed former State Department official made the same observation about the mismatch between the new Iranian missile and the bomb technology presumed to be available.[31]

A second alleged clandestine nuclear research project shown in the papers involved a "process flow chart" for a bench-scale system for conversion of uranium ore for enrichment, purportedly by the Kimia Maadan company in May 2003. But when Iranian officials were shown the flow chart, they immediately spotted multiple technical errors in it, as Iranian ambassador Ali Asghar Soltanieh told me in September 2009.[32] The technical flaws were so unambiguous, in fact, that the head of the IAEA Safeguards Department, Olli Heinonen, acknowledged in his February 2008 briefing that the diagram had "technical inconsistencies."[33]

The serious technical errors in the reentry-vehicle and uranium conversion studies were highly relevant to the question of their authenticity, because the primary reason cited by US officials for judging them as most likely being authentic was the level of technical knowledge allegedly shown in them. David Sanger quoted one administration official as saying, "All the information was so sophisticated and so technical that it would be very difficult for someone to fabricate."[34]

Although other analysts were allowed to examine the laptop documents, it was the scientific and weapons specialists at the Weapons Intelligence, Nonproliferation, and Arms Control Center (WINPAC), the CIA's center for expertise on weapons of mass destruction (succeeding the NPC), who were responsible for determining their authenticity. Paul Pillar, who was then the national intelligence officer for the Middle East and South Asia, recalled later that his own input into the assessment was relatively small.

30. David Albright response to the *New York Times* article, November 13, 2005; Albright reply to William J. Broad, November 15, 2005, copy in author's personal files.

31. Paul Kerr, "Questions Surround Iran's Nuclear Program," *Arms Control Today*, March 2006.

32. Author's interview with Ali Asghar Soltanieh, Vienna, September 7, 2009.

33. "Briefing Notes from February 2008 IAEA Meeting Regarding Iran's Nuclear Program"(Technical Briefing by the Deputy Director General for Safeguards: "Alleged Studies on Weaponization," February 25, 2008), ISIS Reports, Institute for Science and International Security, April 11, 2008, 4.

34. Sanger, *Inheritance,* 67.

"There was some back and forth," Pillar said, but he "didn't have enough minutes in the day to go through technical raw reporting."[35]

The question of the documents' authenticity was apparently never completely resolved. US intelligence sources told the *Washington Post* that US intelligence "considers the laptop documents authentic but cannot prove it" and "cannot completely rule out the possibility" that they were forged.[36]

## Telltale Signs of Fraud

The most politically potent documents in the collection were those purporting to show efforts to redesign the reentry vehicle of an Iranian missile, supposedly as part of a project with the code name "Project 111."[37] When Robert Joseph, US undersecretary of state for arms control and international security, made a formal presentation on the documents to leading IAEA officials in Vienna in July 2005, he gave special attention to the redesign schematics as evidence that Iran was seeking to fit a nuclear weapon into its Shahab-3 missile.[38]

But as Heinonen confirmed in an interview, the schematics all showed the original Shahab-3 missile.[39] Iran had already decided years earlier to abandon that missile design in favor of an improved design with a very different nosecone. In mid-2004, Iran flight tested the new missile with a reentry vehicle that had a "triconic" or baby-bottle shape, rather than the less aerodynamic dunce-cap-shaped nosecone on the original Shahab-3 missile.[40]

Whoever did those drawings aimed at showing efforts to fit a nuclear weapon in the nosecone of Shahab-3 missile clearly did not know that a new missile was being developed that would have a reentry vehicle with a very different shape. The first flight test of the redesigned missile in mid-August 2004 took place after the entire collection of documents had either been delivered or were on their way to be delivered. Before that test, no information was available to tip off foreign intelligence analysts that the Iranians were developing an improved missile with a different warhead, according to Michael Elleman, the author of the most authoritative study

---

35. Author's interview with Paul Pillar, October 25, 2012.

36. Linzer, "Strong Leads," A14.

37. The main documents associated with "Project 111" and the other projects shown in the laptop documents are described briefly in GOV/2008/15, May 26, 2008, annex 1, 1–2.

38. Broad and Sanger, "Relying on Computer."

39. Author's interview with Olli Heinonen, Cambridge, MA, November 5, 2010.

40. Michael Elleman, *Iran's Ballistic Missile Capabilities: A Net Assessment* (London: International Institute for Strategic Studies, 2010), 23–24. Elleman is listed as "contributing editor" but is in fact the author.

of the Iranian missile program to date.[41] Iranian military strategists had cleverly disguised the fact that they had abandoned the Shahab-3 in order to maximize its deterrent value. Iran had announced in early 2001 that the Shahab-3 had entered "serial production"; then, in July 2003, very soon after the US invasion of Iraq, Iran pronounced the Shahab-3 "operational." The Elleman study points out, however, that the announcement was obviously aimed at persuading Washington and Tel Aviv that Iran already had an operational missile capability. The study concludes that it is "very dubious" that the missile ever went into "serial production."[42]

I asked Heinonen, who became a senior fellow at Harvard University's Belfer Center for Science and International Affairs after leaving the IAEA, how Iran's alleged secret nuclear weapons research program could have worked so hard at redesigning the reentry vehicle of a missile that the Iranian military had already abandoned in favor of an improved model. Heinonen suggested that the missile engineers working for the head of the project had been ordered to redesign the older Shahab-3 model before the decision was made by the missile program to switch to a newer missile with a different reentry vehicle design, and that it couldn't change its work plan once it was decided.[43] But the evidence shows that the redesign of the missile had begun as early as 2000. The CIA's national intelligence officer for strategic and nuclear programs, Robert D. Walpole, testified in 2000 that the Iranian defense minister had already announced the development of the Shahab-4, which the minister characterized as more capable than the Shahab-3.[44]

Iran had compelling reasons for abandoning the old Shahab-3 design: it had failed repeatedly in three flight tests between 1998 and 2000. And it had a range of only 800 to 1,000 kilometers (500 to 620 miles) with a conventional payload, and therefore could not reach more than a small portion of Israel. On the other hand, the redesigned missile flight-tested in 2004 could carry a payload of conventional high explosives close to 1,000 miles, bringing all of Israel within the reach of an Iranian missile for the first time.[45]

41. Author's interview with Michael Elleman, Washington, DC, September 20, 2010.

42. Elleman, *Iran's Ballistic Missile Capabilities*, 23.

43. Author's interview with Heinonen, November 5, 2010.

44. Hearing on September 21, 2000, before the International Security, Proliferation and Federal Services Subcommittee, Senate Committee on Governmental Affairs, 106th Cong., 2nd sess., prepared statement of Robert D. Walpole, https://www.cia.gov/news-information/speeches-testimony/2000/schindler_WMD_092200.htm.

45. Elleman, *Iran's Ballistic Missile Capabilities*, 23, 25. One of Israel's top specialists on Iranian missiles, Uzi Rubin, noted soon after the August 2004 flight test that the new missile would carry about 15 percent more propellant, increasing its range to 1,450 kilometers, or 900 miles. Alon Ben-David, "Iran Unveils Redesigned Shahab missile," *Jane's Defence Weekly*, September 27, 2004.

The decision to replace the Shahab-3 with an improved version with a completely redesigned reentry vehicle was already made long before the alleged covert nuclear weapon program described in the intelligence documents was said to have gotten under way, according to Elleman.[46] The decisive evidence that Heinonen's explanation for the mismatch could not be true is the fact that the alleged warhead development program was not even organized until early 2002, and the earliest date on any of the documents on missile reentry vehicle redesign is August 28, 2002.[47] Obviously Iran's Defense Ministry did not decide to order a complete redesign of the Shahab-3, with particular attention to the reentry vehicle, in 2000 and then—two years later—order missile designers to redesign the reentry vehicle for the older missile it had decided not to produce in the future, in order to accommodate a nuclear weapon.

Heinonen had another explanation for the anomaly, however. He argued that the group working on the schematics of the reentry vehicle had no connection with the regular Iranian missile program but was working for Dr. Mohsen Fakhrizadeh, who was named in the intelligence collection as the man in charge of the entire nuclear weapons research program. "It looks from that information that this group was working with this individual," said Heinonen. "It was not working for the missile program."[48]

Heinonen offered no reason, however, why the purported missile-engineering group would have been working in complete isolation from the country's missile program, or why the head of the alleged effort to integrate a nuclear weapon into Iran's intermediate-range ballistic missile would not have been informed about an improved missile that had already been in the works for more than two years. And his explanation is contradicted by another purported internal document: a one-page letter from the "project executive" to the Shahid Hemmat Industrial Group dated March 3, 2003, "seeking assistance with the prompt transfer of data" for the work on redesigning the reentry vehicle.[49] The Shahid Hemmat Industrial Group had been responsible for the development of the Shahab-3 and the rest of

---

46. Author's interview with Michael Elleman, Washington, DC, November 6, 2010. For more information on this point, see Gareth Porter, "Laptop Papers Show Wrong Missile Warhead," Inter Press Service, November 19, 2010.

47. "Excerpts from Internal IAEA Document on Alleged Iranian Nuclear Weaponization," ISIS Reports, Institute for Science and International Security, October 2, 2009, 3; GOV/2008/15, May 26, 2008, annex, 2.

48. Author's interview with Heinonen, November 5, 2010.

49. GOV/2008/15, May 26, 2008, annex, 1.

Iran's ballistic missile program.[50] The document clearly portrays a project that is dependent on an entity that was the heart of Iran's missile program.

Another clear giveaway that the intelligence documents were not genuine involves a project code given to one of the subprojects under what was called "Project 5," which dealt with uranium mining and conversion. The subproject on conversion, often referred to as the Green Salt project, was given the code name "Project 5.13," according to Heinonen's February 2008 briefing for member states. A second subproject involving ore processing at the Gchine mine, he said, was given the code name "Project 5.15."[51]

Both of those subprojects, according to the laptop documents, had been carried out by Kimia Maadan, which Heinonen had already identified as a front for the military in 2004 (see chapter 7). The "alleged studies" documents thus appeared to confirm Heinonen's existing suspicions about Kimia Maadan as a front for the military.

But what Heinonen had failed to notice about the ore-processing facility project at the Gchine mine bearing the code name Project 5.15 was that the project had actually been initiated by the civilian Atomic Energy Organization of Iran more than two years before the earliest date assigned to the existence of the alleged Iranian secret weapons research program. The February 2008 IAEA report acknowledged that Iran had provided detailed documentation showing that an AEOI "decision to construct a UOC [uranium ore concentration] plant at Gchine, known as 'project 5/15,' was made August 25, 1999."[52] That date for the beginning of the ore-concentration project was at least a year and a half before the earliest date for the start of the alleged secret nuclear weapons program given by US officials briefing other states on the documents.[53]

When I raised the contradiction with Heinonen, he registered disbelief at first. "Who says Project 5.15 was created two years earlier?" he asked me. I pointed out that the mid-1999 date of the decision to create the ore-concentration project at Gchine was in the February 2008 IAEA report. He admitted that he didn't recall the specifics of the timeline on Kimia Maadan, but then added, as if to explain the problem away, "We have a lot more information about Kimia Maadan that we didn't include in our

50. Testimony of Pat O'Brien, assistant secretary, Office of Terrorist Financing and Financial Crimes, US Department of the Treasury, Senate Committee on Banking, Housing, and Urban Affairs," June 22, 2006, http://www.treasury.gov/press-center/press-releases/Pages/js4331.aspx; "Hemmat Industrial Complex," Global Security, http://www.globalsecurity.org/wmd/world/iran/tehran-hemat.htm.

51. "Briefing Notes from February 2008 IAEA Meeting," 3.

52. GOV/2008/4, February 22, 2008, 5.

53. Adler, "US Briefs on Alleged Iran Nuclear Warhead Work."

reports." Six days later, when I brought up the contradiction again in a telephone interview, he said, "That one I have trouble answering."[54]

Iranian officials who were shown documents on the "alleged studies" in early 2008 immediately noticed another anomaly: none of them had any security markings or official stamps showing the date of receipt or the seals of the sending office. Iran's permanent representative to the IAEA, Ali Asghar Soltanieh, recalled in a September 2009 interview that he pointed out these anomalies to an IAEA delegation in Tehran in spring 2008 and brought it up repeatedly in meetings of the Board of Governors. According to Soltanieh, that complaint had never been challenged.[55]

A senior IAEA official interviewed in September 2009 said the lack of such markings is not a "killer argument," because the governments that had provided the documents could claim they had taken the markings out before passing them on to the IAEA for security reasons.[56] Such markings are commonly removed when documents are shared with another government or international organization. The reason for the removal is to deny the state of origin of the document the knowledge of which copy was acquired, on the ground that it could reveal the source that had provided the document. But the IAEA could have insisted on at least being shown the original documents to verify that they did, in fact, have such markings and official stamps on them when they were first obtained. After all, when the IAEA investigated the Niger uranium document cited by the George W. Bush administration as part of its justification for invading Iraq, it was anomalies in the "form, format, contents and signature" of the document that gave it away as a fabrication.[57]

Heinonen suggested that the reason the documents didn't have such confidentiality markings was that they had been taken by an intelligence agent straight from the computer on which they had been typed.[58] But that explanation raises even more serious questions about the documents. To obtain such documents, a spy would have needed access to one or more servers related to the entire alleged program. And if that were the case, the collection would have included a far wider range of documents than

54. Author's interview with Heinonen, November 5, 2010; telephone interview with Heinonen, November 11, 2010.

55. Author's interview with Ali Asghar Soltanieh, Vienna, September 6, 2009; IN-FCIRC/737, "Explanatory Comments by the Islamic Republic of Iran on the Report of the IAEA Director General (GOV/2008/38) to the September Board of Governors," September 28, 2008.

56. Author's interview with a senior IAEA official, Vienna, September 6, 2009, on condition that the official could only be identified as a "senior official."

57. Transcript of Mohammed ElBaradei's UN presentation, March 7, 2003, CNN, http://www.cnn.com/2003/US/03/07/sprj.irq.un.transcript.elbaradei/.

58. Interview with Heinonen, November 5, 2010.

were actually found contained in it. And Heinonen's explanation fails to account for the fact that official communications supposedly coming from the Defense Ministry and addressed to officials under its authority had no stamps or seals of any kind.

## Clues Pointing to Israel

The fact that the MEK was instrumental in conveying the laptop documents to US intelligence is a clue that leads ultimately to Israel as the original source of the collection. As discussed earlier in this book, Israel had used the MEK to "launder" intelligence that it wanted to get out to the public but didn't want to have attributed to Israel's Mossad, including, most notably, the intelligence on Natanz and Arak in 2002. Israel had also supported the MEK in other ways, providing assistance to broadcasts by the NCRI from Paris into Iran, according to another Iranian exile group. An Israeli diplomat confirmed to a reporter for the *New Yorker* that Israel had found the MEK "useful" but would not elaborate.[59]

Israel was more highly motivated than any other state to mount such an effort to convince the world that Iran had an active nuclear weapons program. And the Israeli government is known to have had an active program to influence in particular the US intelligence assessment of the Iranian nuclear program, as it had done in the case of its assessment of Saddam Hussein's WMD. The Israeli program was started in summer 2003 with the creation of a new unit of Mossad, its international intelligence agency, to generate stories in the Western media by briefing reporters on covert Iranian efforts to obtain nuclear weapons, according to Israeli officials. As part of the program, Mossad sometimes passed on documents it said had come from Israeli spies inside Iran.[60]

Mossad was also engaged in a broad campaign to shift US policy toward a more openly confrontational stance with Iran. Although there were figures in the State Department—notably Secretary of State Powell—and in the CIA who resisted such a shift, the George W. Bush administration offered Israel the best opportunity it had ever enjoyed to use purported intelligence documents to accomplish such a policy shift. At the time Mossad would have been working on the project in 2002–3, it had multiple points of access that it could use to obtain sensitive US intelligence data and to introduce Israeli intelligence claims into the administration's

---

59. Connie Bruck, "Exiles," *New Yorker*, March 6, 2006.

60. Frantz and Collins, *Nuclear Jihadist*, 296–97. The authors state that their account of the Israeli campaign to influence political attitudes toward Iran's nuclear program was based on interviews with "high-ranking Israeli military, intelligence and foreign ministry officials." Ibid., 394.

policymaking process, including John Bolton at State, Paul Wolfowitz at Defense, John P. Hannah (a protégé of Dennis Ross) at the NSC, and Lewis Libby, Vice President Cheney's chief of staff and national security adviser.[61] Top Israeli intelligence officials frequently went to Washington to brief top Bush administration officials.[62]

CIA director George Tenet and the CIA's intelligence directorate, however, were extremely skeptical of Israeli intelligence products on Iraq and Iran. After each Israeli intelligence briefing, the agency's intelligence division issued reports that tended to contradict the information from Mossad.[63] According to one journalistic account from a pro-Israel source, Tenet believed that US satellite reconnaissance data was being processed and analyzed by Israeli intelligence before US intelligence had even made its own assessment, and that it was being used to sway the US Congress. Tenet had complained to Israeli officials on more than one occasion that Mossad had planted an agent high in the Bush administration. Israeli officials said that Tenet regarded Mossad's reports as aimed at pressuring US intelligence and the Bush administration to adopt the Israeli line that Iran was approaching the "point of indigenous capability" to build a nuclear weapon—a position that Bolton had already accepted—and thus maneuver the United States into a military confrontation with Iran. In late 2003, according to the account, Tenet decided to withhold some intelligence on Iran's nuclear program, especially information from US satellite reconnaissance, from Israel.[64]

Two former CIA officers said the story is consistent with what they knew about Tenet's views of Israeli intelligence. Paul Pillar, former national intelligence officer for the Middle East, thought that the story about Tenet's reducing cooperation because he believed Israeli reporting and analysis was aimed at pushing the US closer to war with Iran rang true. "It sounds exactly like the kind of conclusion he would have reached," Pillar said.[65] Flynt Leverett, who had been an analyst at the CIA before working at the National Security Council, recalled, "I know there were times Tenet would

---

61. On Hannah's close ties to Ross, see Douglas Jehl, "In Cheney's New Chief, a Bureaucratic Master," New York Times, November 2, 2005. On Libby's role in promoting the interests of Sharon's government, see John Kampfner, Blair's Wars (New York: Free Press, 2003), 187. On Wolfowitz's regular meetings with Israeli intelligence officials and his intervention to support their assessments, see James Risen, State of War (New York: Free Press, 2006), 73.

62. Risen, State of War, 72.

63. Ibid., 72–73.

64. "CIA Reduces Exchange with Israel," Middle East Newsline, September 1, 2004, http://www.jonathanpollard.org/2004/090104b.htm.

65. Author's interview with Paul Pillar, October 25, 2012.

play a bit of hardball with the Israelis. When he felt they were being provocative, he would restrict or modify some cooperation."[66]

But during the time in 2003 when the documents were being created, the Israelis almost certainly learned that the Tenet problem would be removed in 2004 if not earlier. As early as May 2003, Tenet had told White House chief of staff Andrew Card that he was considering resigning, although he had not yet decided, and within months, Tenet heard that the Bush administration was talking with the chairman of the president's Foreign Intelligence Board about taking the position. In April 2004, Tenet informed the White House he would resign after an excerpt from Bob Woodward's book *Plan of Attack* published in the *Washington Post* quoted Tenet as calling the Iraqi WMD case a "slam dunk."[67] Tenet resigned two months later, and although the date on which the laptop documents were given to US intelligence has never been revealed, no source has ever dated it earlier than summer 2004.

Another intriguing piece of evidence of Israeli provenance of the documents is the assertion by the Israeli authors of a new book on Mossad that Mossad "had procured" the collection of laptop intelligence documents in 2004 and had "shared it with other Western intelligence agencies."[68] That claim conflicts with the accounts given by US intelligence sources that the United States obtained the papers from an Iranian source, as well as with the BND account earlier in this chapter. But it appears to reflect a need on the part of Israeli officials to boast of a role in what has been a big political success against Iran, even at the risk of linking the documents to Mossad.

The most convincing evidence that Mossad was behind the laptop documents, however, is the fact that certain information that the Israelis were passing on to the IAEA in 2003–4 was clearly based on intelligence information that later turned up in the collection of documents transmitted by the MEK. One of the very first decisions made by Goldschmidt and Heinonen of the IAEA Safeguards Department about the investigation into the history of Iran's nuclear program in early 2004 was to look into mining and ore concentration at the Gchine mine.

It was a mysterious line of inquiry, since it had nothing to do with Iran's declarations. The Safeguards Department did not have its own sources of intelligence to guide it to such an obscure issue. It depended on foreign intelligence agencies to provide it with such information. And it was launched a year and a half before the "alleged studies" documents

---

66. Author's interview with Flynt Leverett and Hillary Mann Leverett, March 14, 2013.

67. George Tenet, *At the Center of the Storm* (New York: HarperCollins, 2007), 477–85.

68. Raviv and Melman, *Spies Against Armageddon*, 9.

were shared with the IAEA and several months before the documents were passed to US intelligence.

Only one foreign intelligence agency would have steered the IAEA Safeguards Department to inquire into the Gchine mine and the contractual arrangements surrounding the ore-processing plant there. Mossad had begun sharing its intelligence on Iran's nuclear program at regular meetings with Goldschmidt and Heinonen in the crucial period from August 2002 to early 2003, as former UN weapons inspector Scott Ritter was informed by "sources close to the IAEA"—the phrase traditionally used by journalists to refer to IAEA officials.[69] That intensive intelligence sharing was continuing during the period leading up to the IAEA decision to launch its investigation into the Gchine mine.

Mossad was able to tip off the IAEA about Kimia Maadan's role at Gchine because it had obtained a May 23, 2003, letter to Kimia Maadan from another Iran engineering company that Kimia Maadan had contacted about a programmable logic controller, which could be used for uranium enrichment or conversion, among its many applications. Mossad was always looking for evidence of Iranian imports of dual-use technology, and surveillance and penetration of Iranian engineering and high-tech firms by dedicated agents would have been one of the primary ways Mossad collected such intelligence.

Once it had become aware of Kimia Maadan's role in procuring dual-use technology, Mossad would have starting asking questions about the firm and would have learned quickly about its contract with AEOI for the Gchine ore-concentration operation, which would not have been a particularly sensitive matter. That pathway from the May 2003 letter to Gchine provides a logical explanation for what was otherwise an inexplicable IAEA interest in ore concentration and its conviction that Kimia Maadan was a front for the Iranian military.

That same May 2003 letter that led Mossad and the IAEA to focus on the Gchine mine and its ore processing appeared in the "alleged studies" papers as one of two documents on the Green Salt project in the list published by the IAEA in May 2008.[70] Mossad obviously decided to make the May 2003 letter a pivotal document in the laptop-documents collection. The fact that the authenticity of the letter itself would certainly be clearly established by IAEA would be crucial in giving the entire collection of documents credibility. And the link between the May 2003 letter and uranium conversion inspired the idea for making Kimia Maadan the key actor in a uranium

69. Scott Ritter, *Target Iran* (New York: Nation Books, 2007), 57-58.
70. GOV2008/15, May 26, 2008, annex, 1.

conversion subproject portrayed in the documents. The process flow sheet for bench-scale uranium conversion showed Kimia Maadan as the author.

The same letter was also used to show interconnections among different parts of the purported Iranian covert nuclear program that otherwise were not shown in the laptop documents. The May 2003 letter that appeared in the collection had extensive handwritten notes that included a "reference to the leadership of the project concerning the missile reentry vehicle," according to the IAEA.[71] The letter from the engineering firm that Iran later turned over to the IAEA, however, had no handwritten notes on it, as was mentioned by Heinonen in his February 2008 briefing and confirmed to me by a senior IAEA official in 2009.[72]

In recent years, David Albright has defended claims by the IAEA based on information from Israel. But in September 2008, he said in an interview that he could not deny that Israel fed information to the MEK on Natanz and Arak in order to get the information out to the public. Then he added, "Later, after 2002, the Israelis certainly were doing that, and you have to ask yourself could the documents be theirs?"[73]

## Olli Heinonen's Trap

After the Bush administration gave the IAEA a set of the laptop documents in mid-July 2005, the documents sat in a safe at the agency's Vienna headquarters for months without any systematic review. Meanwhile senior officials of the agency had very different views of the collection. Director General ElBaradei made little secret of his skepticism about their authenticity. Two Israeli journalists learned from sources at the IAEA in 2005 and 2006 that "some senior officials" at the agency regarded the laptop documents as having been fabricated by a Western intelligence agency.[74] In November 2005, ElBaradei told the New York Times he was bound to "follow due process, which means I need to establish the veracity, consistency and authority of any intelligence and share it with the country of concern." In the case of the laptop documents, ElBaradei said, "That has not

---

71. GOV/2008/4, February 22, 2008, 6; GOV2008/15, May 26, 2008, annex, 1.

72. "Briefing Notes from February 2008 IAEA Meeting," 4; interview with a senior IAEA official, Vienna, September 6, 2009.

73. Author's interview with David Albright, September 15, 2008.

74. Yossi Melman and Meir Javadanfar, The Nuclear Sphinx of Tehran (New York: Carroll and Graf, 2007), 142–43. For further evidence of skepticism toward the documents at senior levels of the agency, see ElBaradei, Age of Deception, 279–80; Bob Drogin and Kim Murphy, "UN Calls US Data on Iran Nuclear Aims Unreliable," Los Angeles Times, February 25, 2007.

happened."[75] He was referring to the refusal of the Bush administration to allow the agency to share any of the documents with Iran.

Heinonen, on the other hand, seemed to have no consistent view about the authenticity of the documents. Although he never claimed publicly that the documents were authentic during his tenure as deputy director general, Heinonen told the Israeli newspaper *Haaretz* in 2012, "We concluded that much of it was evidently authentic."[76] In an interview with this writer a month later, however, he downplayed the "alleged studies" collection. "It's not evidence," he said. "It's just a lead. I would not try to say this is evidence."[77] That inconsistency suggests that Heinonen was not concerned about whether the documents were authentic. He was ready to use them to pursue his objective of proving that Iran was pursuing a covert nuclear weapons program, regardless of their origins.

With the completion of the work program in early 2008, the focus of Heinonen's attention shifted to confronting the Iranians with the intelligence documents. On January 27–28 and February 3–5, 2008, Heinonen brought to a meeting with Iranian officials hard copies of the documents on a bench-scale uranium conversion process and on exploding bridge wire (EBW) experiments, as well as a single computer image showing a schematic layout of the inner cone of a missile re-entry vehicle. But Iran was not allowed to take any of the documents outside the room or copy them.[78] Even though they were not given the documents to study, the Iranians pointed out at those meetings that some of the organizations and some of the individuals named in the documentation, for example, were nonexistent. After three more rounds of meetings in April and May, Iran submitted a 117-page paper that detailed the Iranian case that the documents were fabricated.[79]

ElBaradei remained highly skeptical about the documents. He raised the necessity for "due process" in verifying their authenticity at the March 2008 meeting of the Board of Governors and returned to the subject at the June 2008 meeting.[80] An agency source told me later that summer that during the process of writing different drafts of the May report, some IAEA

75. Broad and Sanger, "Relying on Computer."

76. Yossi Melman, "Behind the Scenes of UN Inspection of Iran," *Haaretz* (Tel Aviv), October 22, 2010.

77. Author's interview with Heinonen, November 5, 2010.

78. Interview with Ali Asghar Soltanieh by Mohammad Kamaali, June 29, 2008, Campaign against Sanctions and Military Intervention in Iran, http://www.campaigniran.org/casmii/?q=node/5439.

79. GOV/2008/15, May 26, 2008, 4–5.

80. Mohamed ElBaradei, "Introductory Statement to the Board of Governors," June 2, 2008.

officials wanted to make it clear that the IAEA was "not in a position to authenticate the data."[81]

But ElBaradei's position on the issue was notably absent from the May 2008 report in which the documents were the central issue. Instead, the report reflected the viewpoint of Heinonen. That report marked a shift to a more aggressive role by Heinonen in close collaboration with the United States and its allies on the issue. During and after the work plan negotiations, Heinonen had assured angry US and like-minded diplomats that he had been "skeptical" about ElBaradei's trip to Tehran and "unsatisfied" with Iran's explanations on some issues, including what he characterized as an "improbable story" on the contamination issue (despite the fact that the technical evidence precluded any other outcome).[82]

Heinonen had also assured the US mission that he supported the US refusal to provide copies of the intelligence documents to Iran. At a meeting of experts of the P5+1 group in April 2009, the German deputy chief of mission suggested that some board members regarded denying copies of the documents to Iran as a "hindrance" to the "verification process." But Heinonen "dismissed" the need for such sharing, arguing that "Iran had been given repeated ample access to the information, but still claims only that they are 'forgeries,'" according to the embassy reporting cable on the meeting.[83]

Heinonen's explanation suggested that the denial policy was justified by Iran's refusal to accept the authenticity of the documents. That position was consistent with US ambassador Schulte's insistence that the objective of the next phase of the IAEA's work should be to force Iran to "fully disclose" its past nuclear weapons program and make a "confession."[84] If the idea was to demand, in effect, that Iran accept the authenticity of the documents, then it had to be prevented from obtaining any information that might be used to support its position that they were fabricated. By March 2008, Schulte was reporting that the IAEA secretariat "appears divided between those, like Heinonen, who want to press ahead on the weaponization investigation, and others"—clearly referring to ElBaradei and his allies—"who want to use passage of [UN Security Council Resolution]

81. Author's interview with an IAEA source who insisted on anonymity, August 5, 2008.

82. WikiLeaks Cables, 08UNVIENNA20, US Embassy Vienna to State, "ElBaradei Sees Progress from Tehran Trip," January 14, 2008; 08UNVIENNA98, US Embassy Vienna to State, "Likeminded Ready to Draft a Board," February 15, 2008.

83. WikiLeaks Cables, 09UNVIENNA192, US Embassy Vienna to State, "P5+1 Experts' Meeting Useful Mechanism," April 29, 2009.

84. WikiLeaks Cables, 08UNVIENNA98, February 15, 2008; 07UNVIENNA742, US Embassy Vienna to State, "Likeminded Ambassadors Regroup Post-NIE," December 7, 2007.

1803 as an excuse to slow roll the Iran account for the rest of 2008."[85] The US mission would later refer to the "close and constructive relationship we have had with Heinonen" and ask him to remain as deputy director after ElBaradei's departure in October 2009.[86]

The May 2008 report introduced a new formula explaining why the laptop documents should be considered credible: "This information, which was provided to the Agency by several Member States, appears to have been derived from multiple sources over different periods of time, is detailed in content and appears to be generally consistent."[87] That boilerplate language would be repeated in subsequent reports like a mantra that was not subject to debate or discussion.

Heinonen and his allies were trying to sidestep the authentication issue. A senior IAEA official explained to me why the language in the May report was disingenuous. "There are intelligence-sharing networks," the official said. "So one can't rule out that one organization shared it with others. That gives us 'multiple sources consistent over time.'"[88] The United States and Germany, which had the documents first, had obviously shared them with the other friendly governments so that it could be claimed that the papers were provided by "multiple sources."

The May report also unveiled a new political ploy in regard to the "alleged studies" documents. It claimed that Iran "did not dispute that some of the information contained in the documents was factually accurate, but said the events and activities concerned involved civil or conventional military applications."[89] French ambassador François-Xavier Deniau had referred to the same argument at a meeting of P5+1 ambassadors two months before the IAEA report. "Iran has acknowledged some of the studies while claiming that they were for non-nuclear purposes," Deniau had declared.[90] That remark could only have been made on the basis of discussions involving Heinonen and Schulte about how to portray Iran's position on the documents in subsequent IAEA reports.

---

85. WikiLeaks Cables, 08UNVIENNA185, US Embassy Vienna to State, "P5+1 Consider 'What Next?'" March 27, 2008. UN Security Council Resolution 1803, passed on March 3, 2008, called on all states to "exercise vigilance" about aid to or trade with Iran or financial dealings with Iranian banks, http://www.iaea.org/newscenter/focus/iaeairan/unsc_res1803-2008.pdf.

86. WikiLeaks Cables, 09UNVIENNA322, US Embassy Vienna to State, "IAEA Leadership Team and U.S. Influence," July 7, 2009.

87. GOV/2008/15, May 26, 2008, 4.

88. Author's interview with senior IAEA official, Vienna, September 7, 2009.

89. GOV/2008/15, May 26, 2008, 4.

90. 08UNVIENNA185, March 27, 2008.

The Bush administration and its allies and Heinonen were in agreement on the need to keep maximum pressure on Iran by showing that Iran was refusing to cooperate with the agency's investigation. They also agreed that they could best do that by demanding access to Iranian documentation and specialists regarding its conventional explosives work and its redesign of the Shahab-3. In order to justify such a demand, Heinonen came up with the tactic of claiming that Iran had already conceded that the documents contained some information that was accurate. Thus the IAEA would merely be asking Iran to "clarify" the question of what was accurate and what was false in the intelligence documents. "In light of the discussion on 14 May 2008," said the report, "the Agency is of the view that Iran may have additional information, in particular on high explosives testing and missile related activities, which could shed more light on the nature of these alleged studies and which Iran should share with the Agency."[91]

The new IAEA tactic cleverly exploited a statement that was literally true but highly misleading. After the May 2008 report, Iran sent an official document to the IAEA explicitly denying the IAEA's suggestion that it had conceded that anything in the "alleged studies" documents was accurate except for already publicly known facts. "It is evident that anybody who intends to forge a document uses real names to show the material more convincing and internally consistent," said the Iranian response.[92] Nearly four years later, after Heinonen had left the agency and the tactic was no longer in play, the agency finally confirmed the truth of Iran's denial: the IAEA report of November 2011 acknowledged that what Iran had "confirmed" was "some of the information . . . such as acknowledgement of names of people, places and organizations."[93] But the news media paid no attention to the 2008 Iranian denial, and Heinonen and his Western allies could be confident that the tactic would not be revealed as a deception. In 2011, moreover, the IAEA acknowledgment of the brazen misrepresentation of Iran's position in earlier reports also went unnoticed in the news media.

Heinonen's language on the issue of Iran's high-explosives work was also clearly intended to invite the reader to make a false inference. "Concerning the alleged work to design and build an EBW detonator and a suitable detonator firing unit," the report said, "Iran acknowledged that it had conducted simultaneous testing with two to three EBW detonators with a time precision of about one microsecond. Iran said, however,

---

91. GOV/2008/15, 4–5.
92. INFCIRC/737, "Explanatory Comments." The Iranian response refers to specific paragraphs in GOV/2008/38, September 15, 3–5.
93. GOV/2011/65, November 8, 2011, annex, 2.

that this was intended for civil and conventional military applications."[94] That carefully constructed pair of sentences left the clear impression that Iran was acknowledging that it had carried out the EBW detonator work detailed in one of the "alleged studies" documents. In fact, Heinonen had revealed to IAEA member governments in a briefing on February 25, 2008, that the "alleged studies" document described experiments in which EBW detonators were fired at a rate of 130 nanoseconds—nearly eight times faster than the one microsecond rate of the EBW detonators that Iran had acknowledged having used for nonnuclear applications.[95]

The September 2008 report returned to the idea that Iran had admitted to the accuracy of some information in the documents. It insisted that Iran had not done enough to respond to the documents, "particularly in light of the fact that, as acknowledged by Iran, some of the information contained in it was factually accurate." And it asserted that Iran had "confirmed the veracity of some of the information." It repeated the conclusion from the previous report "that Iran might have additional information, in particular on high explosives testing and missile related activities, which could shed more light on the nature of the alleged studies." The report insisted that Iran should "identify and clarify those elements of the documentation which it considered to be factually correct, and to specify those aspects considered by Iran to have been fabricated." And it specifically requested meetings with Iran to discuss the details of its EBW and Shahab-3 missile programs.[96]

But Iran had actually given the agency detailed evidence in 2008 that its EBW program could only have been for conventional weapons. It had turned over a Farsi-language document that provided the technical specifications for its detonator development program. Iran had also provided two conference papers co-authored by researchers at Malek Ashtar University of Technology and the Air Defense Industries Group of Tehran discussing the development of EBW technology in Iran, obviously in the context of anti-aircraft and/or anti-ship missile systems. None of that documentation was mentioned by the agency in its 2008 reports, which would have given the lie to the claim of Iranian refusal to provide relevant information. But in November 2011, once the deception was no longer needed, the IAEA acknowledged that Iran had provided the documentation at the time the agency was saying it was not responding adequately to the documents.[97]

---

94. GOV/2008/15, May 26, 2008, 4.
95. "Briefing Notes from February 2008 IAEA Meeting," 5.
96. GOV/2008/38, September 15, 2008, 3–5.
97. GOV/2011/65, annex, 8.

In 2008, the IAEA was also demanding "discussions with Iranian experts on the contents of the engineering reports examining in detail modeling studies related to the effects of various physical parameters on the re-entry body from the time of the missile launch to payload detonation." The agency said it had offered to "discuss modalities that could enable Iran to demonstrate credibly that the activities referred to in the documentation are not nuclear related, as Iran asserts, while protecting sensitive information related to its conventional military activities."[98]

But a senior IAEA official confirmed in a 2009 interview that the agency was indeed asking Iran to turn over classified documentation on the Shahab-3 reentry vehicle. "We want them to explain to us that the design studies are not for nuclear weapons," said the official. "We're saying, 'You say you've done re-entry vehicle re-engineering [on Shahab-3], so show us some documentation.'" Asked whether this request would not compromise Iran's national security secrets, the official said, "Yes, there will have to be some compromise on their part, because the charges are serious. If someone is accused of nefarious crimes, it is in their interest to share a little of their security to show they are baseless."[99]

As intrusive as it was on Iran's military security, moreover, the demand for such secret data on the Shahab-3 would not have proven Iran's innocence, as one European diplomat acknowledged in an off-the-record conversation in 2009. "I don't think it would help a lot to get the specific plans of Shahab-3," the diplomat said. "They could be working on other studies and we wouldn't know about it."[100]

Heinonen and his US, Israeli, and European backers were determined to ensure that Iran would not escape the political pincer effect that had been created by the Security Council and the IAEA. On the one side, Iran was subject to UN Security Council resolutions punishing it through economic sanctions in part because it was refusing to come clean with the IAEA. On the other side, the IAEA was not going to offer any route to clearing up the accusations.

The effectiveness of the trap was sealed by the Iranian rejection of the IAEA's bid to obtain information on Iranian conventional weapons and missile design. After the IAEA demand for such intrusion into Iran's military security in the meetings in August, Iran expressed its concern to ElBaradei in a September 5, 2008, letter that "sensitive information related to conventional military and missile-related activities would be

98. GOV/2008/38, 5.

99. Author's interview with senior IAEA official, Vienna, September 6, 2009.

100. Gareth Porter, "Nuclear Agency Demanding Iranian Missile Blueprints," Inter Press Service," September 19, 2009.

compromised." After those meetings, Iran refused to participate in any further meetings on the "alleged studies" issue.[101]

Heinonen and his American allies had found a perfect way to spin the laptop documents to ensure that the facts could not intrude on their campaign of international pressure on Iran to force it to end its nuclear program. The strategy began with the pretense that Iran had admitted that the documents were accurate, at least in part. Heinonen and the IAEA blandly decried Iran's refusal to come clean, while hiding the actual Iranian response. But the strategy then led to demands for information about Iran's conventional military programs that Heinonen and his allies knew would close the door to Iranian cooperation. That was precisely the point. The Iranian boycott of the investigation became a new reason for the United States and its allies to accuse Iran of refusing to cooperate.

That IAEA strategy, coordinated with the Bush administration and its allies, opened the way for a cascade of new IAEA claims of an Iranian weaponization program, beginning in 2009 and based on another round of documents provided by Israel. The new phase of the campaign was conceived and driven by the Israelis to create an even more acute crisis over Iran's nuclear program. With ElBaradei no longer willing to restrain Heinonen on the wording of IAEA reports, the Israelis were now positioned to get the IAEA to endorse the idea that Iran had been continuing to work covertly on nuclear weapons not only before but even after 2003.

---

101. GOV/2008/38, September 15, 2008, 4; GOV/2008/59, November 19, 2008, 4.

# 9

# Intelligence Failure

The US intelligence community should have blown the whistle on the laptop documents from the start, given their murky origins and multiple signs of fraud based on contradictions with verifiable facts. The failure of the system to prevent the use of those documents as the basis for the far-reaching international campaign of isolation and punishment of Iran parallels the failure of the system to prevent the political exploitation of the fabricated tale of Iraqi bioweapons labs in the run-up to the Iraq war.

Unlike the intelligence failure on Iraq, which has been the subject of detailed official studies, the failure on Iran has yet to be acknowledged. But a series of deeply flawed intelligence assessments on weapons of mass destruction in Iran over many years have displayed the same institutional and cognitive distortions that led the intelligence community to mistakenly express confidence in the existence of programs of weapons of mass destruction in Iraq. The intelligence assessments on both countries reflected deep-seated predispositions on the part of a major component of the intelligence community to find evidence of WMD programs. In fact, the same group of intelligence analysts was making similar mistakes—and in some cases virtually the same mistakes—on the parallel WMD issues in both Iraq and Iran during the 2001–7 period. And the root of the problem of false positives in both Iraq and Iran WMD assessments was the influence of incentives for intelligence analysts to tilt toward assessments that they had reason to believe would be rewarded by the system.

The Robb-Silberman Commission, created by President George W. Bush to investigate the intelligence failure on Iraq, found no evidence of political pressure to alter assessments on Iraq, and, not surprisingly, no analysts admitted to shaping intelligence judgments in order to serve "policymaker preferences." But the commission did find that "some analysts" were influenced by the knowledge that the administration had very decided views on policy toward Iraq and that "challenges to it—or even refusals to find its confirmation—would not be welcome."[1] The overall "policy climate" in regard to Iraqi WMD, as Paul Pillar, the national intelligence officer for the Middle East and South Asia from 2000 to 2005, called it, had a pervasive influence on the intelligence community's expectations and behavior on Iraq. It effectively "politicized" it, Pillar said, primarily by the effect of policymakers' directing attention to certain questions in ways that predisposed the collectors and analysts to the preferred answers. "When policymakers repeatedly urge the intelligence community to turn over only certain rocks," Pillar observed, "the process becomes biased." By concentrating resources on those questions, he said, the intelligence community "eventually produces a body of reporting and analysis that, thanks to quantity and emphasis, leaves the impression that what lies under those same rocks is a bigger part of the problem than it really is."[2]

The Robb-Silberman Commission report shows that collectors and analysts were well aware of what they were expected to find under those rocks in Iraq. The commission learned from the analysts themselves how that dynamic had worked in regard to the question of an Iraqi chemical warfare program. What analysts had believed was an increase in the number of suspected Iraqi chemical facilities turned out to be simply the effect of the collectors having been directed to more than double the amount of satellite imagery of such "suspect facilities" in 2001–2 compared to the total in 2000.

That mistake then rippled outward to cause other errors. Analysts told the commission that the images had shown trucks transshipping materials to and from ammunition depots, including suspected chemical weapons sites. The conclusion that Iraq had restarted chemical weapons production was based on nothing more than the increased number of images of such movements of trucks to and from suspected sites, which had been interpreted as possible movement of chemical munitions.[3] The commission concluded that Iraq had actually destroyed all of its undeclared chemical weapons stockpile in 1991, that it was not producing any chemical agents, and that its infrastructure for chemical production was in "far worse shape" than the intelligence community had believed. The commission found abundant evidence that the intelligence community had come to believe

1.  Commission on the Intelligence Capabilities of the United States Regarding Weapons of Mass Destruction, report to the president, March 31, 2005, ch. 1, 188. Hereafter cited as Commission Report to the President.

2.  Paul R. Pillar, "Intelligence, Policy and the War in Iraq," *Foreign Affairs*, March–April 2006.

3.  Commission Report to the President, ch. 1, 122–26.

that Iraq had a chemical weapons program based on nothing more than a predisposition to believe that one existed.[4]

The problem that Pillar and the Robb-Silberman Commission described from different angles is familiar to intelligence professionals. A former senior intelligence official recalled a striking example of that effect during the first Gulf War when intelligence analysts were tasked with finding Iraqi Scud missiles in Kuwait. "There were hundreds of reports of Scuds in Kuwait," he recalled. "Imagery interpreters were finding the Scud TELs [transporter-erector-launchers] everywhere. We even had human sources saying they saw TELs. It happened all the time." But no Scuds were ever actually confirmed in Kuwait, the official said, because there weren't any. "Anybody who knew anything about Saddam would have known that he would not have put them there."[5]

Other veterans of intelligence analysis recalled that a similar problem arose after the creation of the Nonproliferation Center (NPC) in September 1991 as an intelligence organization within the CIA committed specifically to assessing evidence of WMD programs. CIA Director Robert M. Gates described the role of the new center as "alerting policymakers to the existence of new programs or advances in established programs in special weapons areas."[6] The expectation that the targeted countries were indeed proliferating nuclear weapons was built into the structure and culture of the new center.

Thomas Fingar, who was head of the State Department's Bureau of Intelligence and Research in 2004–5 and was deputy director of national intelligence for analysis in 2005–8, said the problem of expectations as an influence on performance affected both the NPC and the CIA's Counterterrorism Center, which was organized in 1986. "Because of the interest in CP [counterproliferation] and CT [counterterrorism], that's what guys are told to go after," said Fingar. The problem, as Fingar summed it up, is, "You get the answer to the question you ask. Pavlov's dog knows you answer the question and you get money." Fingar was suggesting that analysts were expected to produce evidence of target countries' activities in nuclear proliferation or terrorism. There was "nothing inherently evil about that," he said. "That's just the way it worked."[7]

---

4. Commission Report to the President, ch. 1, 117.

5. Author's interview with a former senior intelligence official who demanded anonymity, January 2, 2013.

6. Threat Assessment, Military Strategy and Defense Planning: Hearings on January 22, 1992, before the Senate Comm. on Armed Services, 102nd Cong., 2nd sess., statement by CIA Director Robert M. Gates, 34.

7. Author's interview with Thomas Fingar, Oxford, UK, February 7, 2013.

The 100 analysts concentrated in the NPC at its founding in 1991 were experts on the technical analysis of weapons of mass destruction and on investigating potential foreign suppliers of WMD, particularly nuclear-related technology. They had no training or interest in analyzing the political and policy context of the proliferation issue in question. Not surprisingly, that orientation shaped their judgments about proliferation issues. The former senior intelligence official recalls the effect of bringing together analysts who specialized in weapons and proliferation and lacked the training, knowledge, and motivation to address the policy context of WMD issues. "They didn't know how to fit WMD into the national doctrine and strategy of the target country," he recalled. "Naturally they're going to find that [the proliferation threat] is true in that country."[8]

Ellen Laipson, who was the national intelligence officer for the Near East and South Asia from 1990 to 1993, had a similar view of the effect of the creation of the NPC. "It's a self-validating concept," she said. "You put more resources into an issue; then you're going have more to say about that." A significant part the NPC's work, she recalled, was meeting the Pentagon's appetite for technical intelligence on WMD. "The military has its own requirements and planning culture that is independent of political decisions," Laipson said. The weapons specialists were "interested in capabilities," according to Laipson. "They believed a lot in what we can know from the technical state of the program" and viewed politics as "a separate exercise," Laipson said. "We had weapons analysts looking at the procurement strategy and the size of their buildings," she recalled. "At what point does that have its own logic?"[9]

Fingar saw the same bifurcation in the intelligence assessment process. "The guys closely linked [to] stopping proliferation acquired a predisposition to see malign intentions—to infer as the most likely that which was malign," he said, whereas, "Regional guys tended to have a wider mix of assessments, different levels of confidence."[10]

Iran's nuclear program was the main proliferation issue assessed by the intelligence community in the immediate aftermath of the creation of the NPC. The CIA initiated a national intelligence estimate (NIE) on Iran's foreign policy, which included an assessment of the Iranian nuclear program, just around the time the NPC was organized in September 1991. A central factor in determining the substance of the estimate was that Gordon Oehler, the national intelligence officer for science and technology,

---

8. Interview with former senior intelligence official who demanded anonymity, January 2, 2013.

9. Author's interviews with Ellen Laipson, February 1, 2009 and February 4, 2013.

10. Interview with Fingar.

had overall responsibility for the assessment and the weapons analysts at NPC had the task of writing the first draft of the estimate.

That meant that weapons analysts would dominate the estimate on the nuclear program from beginning to end. Laipson recalled that she was only a "supplementary player" on the issue in the 1991 estimate. She had an opportunity to comment on the outline that was adopted for the estimate, but she was not a substantive contributor to the draft. In fact, she did not even read the draft of the estimate until it had gone to an interagency committee. The regional analysts "were in the room," she recalled, "but in the third chapter and only on the few lines on the political context."[11]

In 1990, Western intelligence began intercepting telex messages from Sharif University in Tehran and the Physics Research Center, which had connections to the Ministry of Defense, attempting to procure several dual-use items that could be utilized in uranium enrichment. The telexes included orders for ring magnets, fluoride and fluoride-handling equipment, a balancing machine, a mass spectrometer, and vacuum equipment.[12] Since by definition the dual-use items might equally have been procured for nonmilitary purposes, they could not be conclusive evidence of any military role in enrichment, much less a covert military nuclear program. But intelligence analysts tasked with finding evidence of proliferation regarded those procurement efforts by a figure who had defense connections as prima facie evidence of a military-run nuclear program. (See chapter 7 for details on that intelligence.)

In its waning days, the George H. W. Bush administration pushed for curbing all nuclear technology transfers to Iran on the basis of what officials said was intelligence indicating "a suspicious procurement pattern."[13] That was an obvious reference to the telexes from Sharif University. For the next decade, those telexes would buttress the view of the NPC and, after 2001, of the CIA's Weapons Intelligence, Nonproliferation, and Arms Control Center (WINPAC) that Iran was determined to obtain nuclear weapons. But in late 2007 and early 2008, Iran finally gave the IAEA detailed documentary evidence showing that the items in question were actually procured for and used by academic departments of Sharif University, and the IAEA did, in fact, find the equipment in use at the university. The most important supposed evidence for the official view of the intelligence community that Iran was

11. Author's interview with Ellen Laipson, February 13, 2013.

12. Herbert Krosney, *Deadly Business: Legal Deals and Outlaw Weapons* (New York: Four Walls Eight Windows, 1993), 263–65.

13. Steve Coll, "US Halted Nuclear Bid by Iran," *Washington Post*, November 17, 1992.

pursuing a "nuclear weapons capability," if not a nuclear weapon, was finally disproved.[14]

## Reversing the Burden of Proof: Chemical and Biological Weapons

The Robb-Silberman Commission discovered that the analysts working on weapons of mass destruction in Iraq had effectively reversed the normal analytic practice of evaluating the degree to which the evidence proved the existence of a WMD program and instead required proof that it did *not* exist. Analysts at WINPAC explained to the commission that because of Iraq's history of deception on its nuclear program, and the evidence that it was trying to produce components that could be used in a uranium enrichment program, "they could not envision having reached the conclusion that Iraq was not reconstituting its nuclear program." The analysts told the commission they could imagine doing so only if a "well-placed reliable human source" had provided specific information to that effect.[15]

That shift in the burden of proof on WMD programs, which aligned with the self-interest of the analysts in the circumstances described above, helps to explain why WINPAC analysts insisted that evidence that was full of contradictions and anomalies led them to such a firm conclusion. That same dynamic, driven by the same set of perverse incentives, had a similarly distorting effect on the intelligence assessments on Iran. The distorting effect is most clear-cut in the CIA's assessment of the alleged Iranian chemical and biological weapons programs from the early 1990s until 2007.

An incident in August 1993 illustrates the tendency of WINPAC's predecessor, the NPC, to assume confidently that Iran was running a chemical weapons program despite the absence of any real evidence of its existence. Someone provided information to US intelligence that Iran had purchased thiodiglycol, which is used in making mustard gas, and thionyl chloride, which is a precursor of nerve gas, from a Chinese firm, and that it was being carried on a specific ship from a Chinese port. US warships demanded to inspect the cargo of the Chinese ship before allowing it to reach its destination.

Possession of those two chemicals was not even prohibited under the Chemical Weapons Convention, which had been opened for signature in January 1993. Both chemicals have numerous civilian applications, but thiodiglycol is a Schedule 2 chemical under the convention, and thionyl chloride is a Schedule 3 chemical, which were to be declared for monitoring

---

14. GOV/2008/4, February 22, 2008, 3–4.
15. Commission Report to the President, ch. 1, 168–69.

and on-site verification once the convention went into effect.[16] The Clinton administration would have had no legal basis under the convention to hinder the commercial transfer of the chemicals.

But in this case, the Chinese Foreign Ministry, which denied the US assertion about the ship's cargo, offered to have a third party inspect it. The United States refused and kept the Chinese ship on the high seas for 20 days, according to the Chinese account, before an agreement was reached on the terms of the inspection. When it finally took place, the inspection showed that no such chemicals were present. The United States refused to apologize to China, however, on the grounds that it had acted on its intelligence in good faith.[17] During 1995, Iran bought several factories for industrial chemicals as well as pesticides and herbicides from China. The CIA's NPC, still clinging to the Defense Intelligence Agency position that Iran had a chemical weapons program during the Iran-Iraq War, leapt to the conclusion that Iran was making a major effort to build up that program. Obviously referring to those factories, Oehler, by then the director of the NPC, testified in November 1995 that Iran "is spending large sums of money on long-term capital improvements . . . which tells us that Tehran fully intends to maintain a chemical weapons capability well into the future."[18] But by that criterion, any industrial chemical sector anywhere in the world could be defined as a "chemical weapons capability."

The NPC soon began conjuring up a full-fledged Iranian chemical weapons program in regularly published assessments. From 1997 through 2002, the regular "721" report to Congress on proliferation of WMD and missile systems written by the NPC and, from 2001 on by WINPAC, contained boilerplate language saying, "Iran has manufactured and stockpiled chemical weapons, including blister, blood and choking agents and the bombs and artillery shells for delivering them."[19]

But the report for the first half of 2003, released in November 2003, began a retreat from such confident language, claiming only that Iran "likely has already stockpiled blister, blood, choking, and probably nerve

16. See Article 6, "Activities Not Prohibited under This Convention," Convention on the Prohibition of the Development, Production, Stockpiling and Use of Chemical Weapons and on their Destruction.

17. Patrick E. Tyler, "No Chemical Arms Aboard Chinese Ship," *New York Times*, September 6, 1993.

18. R. Jeffrey Smith, "Chinese Firms Supply Iran with Gas Factories, U.S. Says," *Washington Post*, March 8, 1995.

19. See unclassified reports to Congress on "Acquisition of Technology Relating to Weapons of Mass Destruction and Advanced Conventional Weapons," 1997–2003, CIA webpage on "Recurring Reports," at https://www.cia.gov/library/reports/archived-reports-1.

agents."[20] The report for the second half of 2003, which wasn't released until November 2004, retreated from the "likely has" language to the much more uncertain "may have" in referring to the stockpiling of "blister, blood, choking, and possibly nerve agents." The report for 2004, which was not released until May 2006, eliminated any reference to stockpiles of chemical weapons, confining itself to the claim that Iran "continued to seek production technology, training, and expertise from foreign entities that could further Tehran's efforts to achieve an indigenous capability to produce nerve agents." Thus it admitted, by implication, that it could not claim an active chemical weapons program in Iran.

No further 721 reports were published until 2008, when a report was released covering 2006. That report evidently came after a prolonged struggle within the analytical community over the issue. The report stated, "While Iran is a party to the Chemical Weapons Convention (CWC), it continues to seek production technology, training, and expertise from foreign entities that could advance a CW program. We judge that Iran maintains a small, covert CW stockpile."[21]

WINPAC executed a parallel retreat from the earlier assessment of what its predecessor, the NPC, had described in the 721 reports as a nascent biological weapons program. "Its biological warfare (BW) program began during the Iran-Iraq war," said the 1997 report, "and Iran may have some limited capability for BW deployment." Outside assistance to Iran's biotech sector is "difficult to prevent, given the dual-use nature of the materials and equipment being sought and the many legitimate end uses for these items." That statement was prefaced by a sentence about Iran continuing to acquire dual-use biotech equipment from abroad, "ostensibly for civilian uses."

The same statement was repeated in the annual 721 reports for 1998 and 1999. In the first semiannual report for 2000, however, the NPC qualified that language. Instead of suggesting that the biotech equipment being acquired by Iran was part of a bioweapons program, the report equivocated, saying, "We judge that this equipment and know-how could be applied to Iran's biological warfare (BW) program." That implied uncertainty about whether it was actually being applied to such a program, and it introduced

---

20. The retreat of WINPAC's analysts from their claims of an Iranian chemical weapons program is detailed in Markus K. Binder, "Iran's First Generation Chemical Weapons Evaporate, As Certainty Declines in U.S. Intelligence Reports," WMD Insights, February 2008, 19–26.

21. Unclassified Report to Congress on the Acquisition of Technology Relating to Weapons of Mass Destruction and Advanced Conventional Munitions, January 1 to December 31, 2006, http://ncpc.dni.gov/files/Acquisition_Technology_Report_030308.pdf.

a note of uncertainty into the origins of the alleged program, suggesting that Iran "probably" began the program during the Iran-Iraq War.

By September 2003, when the report for the second half of 2002 was released, WINPAC was beginning to backpedal still further from its initial position, assessing only that Iran "probably" had an "offensive BW program." In the 2003 report, released in late 2004, it was no longer even certain about Iran's capability for bioweapons, assessing that Iran "probably" had the capability to "produce at least small quantities of BW agents." Then the 2004 report, released in 2006, failed for the first time to make any reference to a biological weapons program in Iran. And in 2008, the retreat from the NPC's original position culminated in an acknowledgment in the report covering 2006 that the NPC no longer believed Iran had such a biological weapons program. "Our assessment of Iran's biotechnology infrastructure," it said, "indicates that Iran probably has the capability to produce large quantities of some Biological Warfare (BW) agents for offensive purposes, if it made the decision to do so."[22]

Thus by 2006, the alleged Iranian biological weapons program, which had been touted as the most active chemical weapons program in the Third World, had faded by stages into nonexistence in the NPC/WINPAC assessments. There was no suggestion that Iran had made a reversal of policy on either chemical or biological weapons. Instead, it appears the CIA weapons analysts' conclusions that Iran had chemical and biological weapons programs, like its conclusions on Iraq's alleged WMD programs, simply didn't hold up and had to be abandoned. The timing of WINPAC's retreat on both chemical and biological weapons from that stance between 2003 and 2006 suggests that it began as a result of the irrefutable evidence that WINPAC had been dead wrong in its assessment of WMD in Iraq and continued after 2004 as a result of pressure from CIA directors Porter Goss and Michael V. Hayden and other intelligence officials to identify assumptions, characterize sources of information, and specify limits of confidence in both judgments and the underlying information. Those new analytic standards, formally required beginning in 2007, were widely discussed and applied beginning in 2005, according to Thomas Fingar, former chairman of the National Intelligence Council, which is responsible for all national intelligence estimates.[23]

The NPC and then WINPAC had made self-serving assumptions about presumed chemical and biological programs in Iran from 2001 on, and

---

22. See unclassified reports to Congress on "Acquisition of Technology," 1997–2003, CIA webpage on "Recurring Reports"; Unclassified Report to Congress on the Acquisition of Technology, January 1 to December 31, 2006.

23. Personal communication to the author from Thomas Fingar, May 23, 2013.

their analysts were empowered to play the dominant role in the assessment process not only by the internal distribution of power within the CIA but by a wider political and policy climate. That structural bias in intelligence on Iran inevitably shaped intelligence assessments about Iran's nuclear program as well.

## The Iran Intelligence That the CIA Suppressed

The covert CIA operative known only as "Doe" in legal documents about his case was no ordinary American spy. Born in the Middle East, he was fluent in Farsi as well as in Arabic. "He could sit in a cafe in Beirut and chat with a local intelligence source without drawing attention from hostile intelligence agencies," the operative's lawyer, Roy Krieger said. The CIA told him he would be given an intelligence medal in recognition of his service.[24]

Yet despite his value as a covert operative in regard to WMD in the Middle East, Doe charged that he was put under intense pressure by powerful figures in the agency because they did not welcome what he had been told about WMD in the Middle East. The story of Doe sheds new light on a crucial aspect of the distortion of the US intelligence assessment on Iran's nuclear program. It shows how the bureaucratic interests of key CIA officials determined the fate of strategically important "humint" (human intelligence) on the Iranian nuclear program.

Doe began working for the CIA as a contract covert operations agent in 1982, and for the agency's Counter-Proliferation Division (CPD) in 1995. Between 1995 and 2001, he established relationships with several intelligence sources he considered knowledgeable and reliable. But information from those sources, which he then reported to his managers, led to a serious conflict between the operative and officials of the agency's Directorate of Operations. The conflict ultimately resulted in a lawsuit brought by the operative in 2004 against then CIA director Goss and two other senior CIA officials: Director of Operations James Pavitt and the unnamed director of the CPD. One of the episodes described in very guarded terms in the lawsuit involved intelligence on the Iranian nuclear program that the CIA did not want to be passed on to the intelligence community or policymakers. And because of that lawsuit, the important story of that intelligence on the Iranian nuclear program can now be told.

A court filing in the lawsuit included a paragraph recounting the specific episode that occurred in 2001 involving an individual whom Doe characterized as "a highly respected human asset." Four lines obviously related to the source's nationality and what he told Doe were redacted from

---

24. Author's interview with Roy Krieger, January 19, 2013.

the court document at the demand of the CIA.[25] The initial press coverage of the case in 2005 was based on the assumption that the paragraph in question as well as others in the legal complaint were related to Iraq.[26] But that assumption was mistaken. Doe told Krieger that the "asset" was Iranian, according to Krieger, and that what the Iranian told him was that the Iranian government "had never intended to weaponize" the enriched uranium it was planning to produce.[27] That information was consistent with the history of the Iranian program that can be reconstructed from all available sources, but it conflicted with what the hawks on Iran in the Bush administration wanted to see in the NIE.

Doe immediately reported the information provided by his Iranian source to his supervisor, according to the court filing. The supervisor, in turn, met with Pavitt and the chief of the CPD about the information. After that meeting, Doe was instructed not to prepare any written report on the matter. His superiors assured him that Pavitt and the chief of the CPD would personally brief the president (then George W. Bush) on the intelligence—an assurance suggesting the extremely significant nature of the information the source had supplied. But Doe learned from his own sources in the agency headquarters that no such briefing ever occurred, and he believed that as a result, the president was being "misled by the withholding of vital intelligence." The chief of the CPD then tried to put pressure on Doe to terminate his relationship with his sources. He "advised Plaintiff," according to the court pleading, "that his promotion to GS-15 and receipt of the Special Intelligence Medal had been approved by Defendant Pavitt but were being withheld until Plaintiff removed himself from further handling of this asset."[28]

That was not the only occasion on which the CIA either ordered Doe to change his intelligence reporting on matters related to weapons of mass destruction or prevented the report from being circulated to intelligence analysts or policymakers. His complaint to the court outlined four other episodes between 2000 and 2002 in which officials of the CPD explicitly rejected his reporting on WMD. After the first of those four other episodes in 2000, Doe was informed by his managers that his report "did not support

25. Second Amended Complaint, Doe v. Hon. Porter Goss, et al., Civil Action 1:04-cv-02122-GK, November 15, 2005, 6, http://www.expose-the-war-profiteers.org/archive/legal/2005/20051115.pdf.

26. James Risen, "Spy's Notes on Iraqi Aims Were Shelved, Suit Says," *New York Times*, August 1, 2005.

27. Author's interview with Roy Krieger, January 6, 2009; personal communication to the author from Krieger, January 17, 2013; author's interview with Krieger, January 21, 2013.

28. Second Amended Complaint, 6–7.

the earlier assessment," according to the court filing.[29] They were apparently referring to the assessment by weapons analysts at the NPC in 2000 that the allegation made by the infamous Iraqi source known as Curveball that Iraq had mobile bioweapons labs was credible. Doe was informed that if he didn't alter his report, "it would not be received well by the intelligence community"—meaning the Counter-Proliferation Division and Pavitt.

The intelligence on Iran's nuclear intentions that Doe had tried to introduce into the US intelligence system also represented a threat to the interests of the heads of the CPD and the Operations Division at the CIA. They were not neutral actors on the question of intelligence about the Iranian nuclear program. The CPD was not only involved in managing and coordinating the collection of intelligence on Iranian WMD from various sources; it was also engaged in active covert operations aimed at sabotaging the Iranian nuclear program. Its most ambitious effort in that regard was Operation Merlin, the story of which was later recounted by James Risen of the *New York Times*.[30] The CPD sent a former Soviet nuclear engineer who had defected and was living in the United States and on the Operations Directorate's payroll to Vienna in early 2000 with the mission of giving the blueprints for a nuclear device to Iran's permanent mission there. The trick underlying the operation was that one critical detail in the original blueprints from Soviet scientists was changed so that the device wouldn't work, and the theory was that the CIA would be able to obtain valuable information about the status of Iran's nuclear weapons program by observing the Iranian response to the supposedly flawed bomb plans. But the CPD managers had failed to anticipate that a well-trained scientist might spot the flaw—as the Russian scientist did instantly—and find a way to correct it.

Operation Merlin put the CPD in a situation of serious conflict of interest. It was supposed to be managing its operatives and their intelligence networks to obtain the most accurate information possible on Iran's capabilities and intentions in regard to its nuclear program. But Operation Merlin was obviously based on the premise that Iran was actively pursuing nuclear weapons and that it would be better to try to slow the Iranian drive to possess an effective weapons design by feeding Tehran a flawed design. If the director of the CPD and Pavitt had gone to President George W. Bush in 2001 with the substance of the report from the Iranian source, they would have been admitting that what they had been telling the president

29. Ibid., 6.

30. James Risen, *State of War: The Secret History of the CIA and the Bush Administration* (New York: Free Press, 2006), 194–212.

for the previous year appeared to have been completely wrong and that Operation Merlin was an unnecessary risk.

Pavitt and the head of the CPD both had a powerful incentive, therefore, to prevent the crucial intelligence that had been obtained by Doe from circulating within the US intelligence community and among policymakers. After yet another incident in 2001 in which the CPD refused to disseminate a report on intelligence regarding WMD in Iraq that one of Doe's source had passed on to him, a colleague of Doe's warned him that CIA management was planning to "get him" for continuing to defy them by filing reports at odds with prevailing CIA positions on WMD in the Persian Gulf. But in 2002, Doe filed yet another report after a meeting with an intelligence source and again was told by a senior desk officer at the CPD that he must change his reporting. And once again, after he refused, he was told to cease contact with the source.[31]

The CIA operations directorate began retaliating against Doe in 2003, initiating an investigation into an allegation that the operative had sex with a female intelligence source. And several months later, just five days after Doe started work at a new position at the CIA, he was placed on administrative leave and told that he would not get the promotion or the intelligence medal. In 2004, the CIA's Office of Inspector General told Doe that he was being investigated for having diverted money for payment of intelligence sources to his own use, and while the investigation was still ongoing, he was fired for unspecified reasons.[32] In April 2005, however, Doe was told that the investigation of him had ended without any finding of wrongdoing, according to the court filing.[33]

In 2004, Doe initiated his lawsuit against Goss, Pavitt, and the unnamed head of the CPD, claiming a series of wrongful CIA actions against him in retribution for his reporting on WMDs. The CIA sought to have it dismissed on technical grounds unrelated to the substance of the case, but the US district court in Washington, DC refused to dismiss all the counts of the civil suit.

The CIA refused to comment on the substance of the case when the *Washington Post* reported on it in July 2008. The CIA's spokesman said, "It would be wrong to suggest that CIA managers direct their officers to falsify the intelligence they collect or to suppress it for political reasons. That's not our policy. That's not what we're about."[34] But the CIA did not deny that

---

31. Second Amended Complaint, 8.

32. Ibid., 8–9.

33. Ibid., 10.

34. Joby Warrick, "Ex-Agent Says CIA Ignored Iran Facts," *Washington Post*, July 1, 2008, A02.

Doe had in fact been promised special recognition for his work as well as a promotion before the episodes involving his reporting on the Curveball bioweapons lab claim and the dramatic information on the charge of a covert Iranian nuclear program. Nor did the agency deny that Doe had been subjected to two investigations that would not normally have been mounted against someone whose espionage was of such central importance.

Furthermore, the agency effectively confirmed the close relationship between Doe and the Iranian source, as well as the source's importance. In 2007, the CIA insisted that Doe could not appear in court, nor could the news media be within blocks of the law office where he and Krieger would participate in a status conference by telephone. The reason, as explained by Krieger, was that the CIA was worried that if his photograph or a sketch of him were to become public, it would endanger "one of our most valued assets," because the "asset" was so closely associated with Doe.[35] Furthermore, Doe learned independently of the CIA that the valued source had been "exfiltrated" out of Iran to the United States by 2007.[36]

By 2009, after the case had dragged on for five years, Doe, who had no job, was unable to raise the tens of thousands of dollars that would have been necessary to continue the litigation. He was forced to end the suit, and because of the agency's insistence that the valued source's life would be threatened by any public appearance, Doe was unable to go public with his story.[37] The result was that the story of the CIA and the crucial missing intelligence on Iran's nuclear intentions has never come to light until now.

## The WINPAC Factor

Beginning in 1997, the CIA's Nonproliferation Center sent a series of unclassified reports to Congress on the status of WMD in Iran and other targeted countries suggesting suspicions of Iran's nuclear intentions but refraining from charging flatly that it had a nuclear weapons program. In 1997 and 1998, the reports offered the same boilerplate language: "Tehran continues to seek fissile material and technology for weapons development and has set up an elaborate system of military and civilian organizations to support its effort." And in another paragraph the reports said that Iran's nuclear technology infrastructure "would be useful in supporting nuclear weapons research and development." But they did

---

35. Chitra Ragavan, "Ex-Agent Ties Firing to CIA Pressure," *U.S. News and World Report*, February 9, 2007.
36. Interview with Krieger, January 6, 2013.
37. Interview with Krieger, January 21, 2013.

not explicitly declare that Iran had decided to go beyond having a nuclear weapons capability.[38]

In its report for the first six months of 1999, however, the NPC added a sentence that referred explicitly to "Iran's nuclear weapons research and development program." That shift in language to an explicit accusation that Iran had a program for weapons research and development coincided with the decision by the CIA to revise its 1995 NIE on the ballistic missile threat from Iran and North Korea under heavy political pressure from Congress, reflecting the strength of the missile defense lobby.

The George W. Bush administration gave further impetus to that accusation by the CIA. CIA director George Tenet created WINPAC in early 2001 by reorganizing all the NPC weapons analysts into an even larger center of analytical capability on proliferation issues. It represented the complete centralization of all the CIA's technical weapons specialists into a single office. And it was staffed with a large number of young, inexperienced weapons analysts, most of whom had been in the CIA for less than five years.[39]

John Bolton "put Iran on the front burner as of May 2001," according to one of his deputies, Paula DeSutter. At a meeting with top Russian officials, Bolton also pushed Moscow to end its nuclear cooperation with Iran—the same diplomatic objective the Clinton administration had pursued for years.[40]

Those developments set the stage for the 2001 National Intelligence Estimate on the nuclear program. Bolton did not want his pressure on Iran to be weakened by an NIE that left doubt on whether Iran was conducting a nuclear weapons program, and he knew that WINPAC was the key to a clear-cut conclusion on the issue. As former national intelligence officer Paul Pillar recalled, WINPAC was "the principal locus of analytic horsepower" on nuclear weapons within the CIA, which meant that it would do "most of the work on the NIE."[41]

At Bolton's request, Fred Fleitz, a former CIA counterintelligence officer who was then on the WINPAC staff, was assigned to work in his office as "the acting Chief of Staff" while simultaneously performing "liaison

38. See unclassified reports to Congress on "Acquisition of Technology," 1997–2003, CIA webpage on "Recurring Reports," https://www.cia.gov/library/reports/archived-reports-1.

39. On the establishment of WINPAC, see Kathleen M. Vogel, *Phantom Menace or Looming Danger?: A New Framework for Assessing Bioweapons* (Baltimore: Johns Hopkins University Press, 2012), 20. The description of the young WINPAC analysts is in Peter Eisner and Knut Royce, *The Italian Letter* (New York: Rodale, 2007), 120–21.

40. Kenneth R. Timmerman, *Countdown to Crisis* (New York: Three Rivers, 2005), 261; Bolton, *Surrender*, 54–59.

41. Author's interview with Paul Pillar, October 25, 2012.

functions for the Agency and Mr. Bolton," as Fleitz described it. Bolton also established direct relationships with the analysts at WINPAC, according to the head of WINPAC, Alan Foley. "He invited them down for briefings, and that sort of thing," Foley told the Senate Foreign Relations Committee, and "even took one on a trip abroad."[42]

And the person supervising the analysts was Robert D. Walpole, the national intelligence officer for strategic and nuclear programs and formerly a weapons analyst in WINPAC's predecessor, the NPC. Walpole's role was critical to the outcome, Pillar said, because "Who has the lead can make a difference in what gets in the estimate."[43]

Walpole had already presided over an estimate that had fallen prey to political pressures, directing the 1999 ballistic missile threat NIE.[44] And in 2003, in the run-up to the war in Iraq, Walpole would loyally defend before Congress the WINPAC analysts' argument that the infamous Iraqi aluminum tubes purchased by the Saddam Hussein regime in 2001 must have been intended for uranium enrichment—an argument that most analysts recognized was contradicted by the technical evidence.[45]

In the work on the 2001 NIE on Iran's nuclear program, WINPAC's technical analysts wrote not only about Iran's capabilities in regard to possible nuclear weapons but also the crucial section on Iran's nuclear intentions, according to Pillar. "Those immersed in science and weapons programs would have a tendency to infer intentions from what they see in the program," he observed, which meant that they concluded that Iran was intent on obtaining nuclear weapons.[46] But there was no direct evidence for the intention to go to weaponization. "We're talking about things that are a matter of inference, not direct evidence," Pillar said.[47]

After the first draft was complete, when Pillar and other Iran specialists could comment on the draft, they offered a dramatically different view, according to Pillar. Most of them believed that the Iranian regime had not made a decision to build nuclear weapons and that Iran's decision

42. Fleitz and Foley were interviewed by the Senate Foreign Relations Committee staff in 2005 in conjunction with Bolton's nomination to be ambassador to the United Nations. The original record of the interviews is not available; the quotes are in Marcy Wheeler ("emptywheel"), "What Do We Learn about Fred Fleitz from the Bolton Testimony?", *The Next Hurrah* (blog), September 24, 2005, http://thenexthurrah.typepad.com/the_next_hurrah/2005/09/what_do_we_lear.html.

43. Author's interview with Paul Pillar, January 27, 2009.

44. On the CIA's retreat from its 1995 NIE under political pressure, see Michael Dobbs, "How Politics Helped Redefine Threat," *Washington Post*, January 14, 2002, A1.

45. Michael Isikoff and David Corn, *Hubris: The Inside Story of Spin, Scandal and the Selling of the Iraq War* (New York: Crown, 2006), 117–19.

46. Interview with Pillar, October 25, 2012.

47. Interview with Pillar, April 26, 2013.

on manufacturing nuclear weapons would be especially influenced by US policy—particularly whether the United States pursued an aggressive policy toward Iran or was willing to offer security assurances to Tehran. Citing pragmatic arguments made by Iranian officials against possession of nuclear weapons, they suggested that Iran was pursuing a "hedging strategy" aimed at having the technical know-how and capability to acquire nuclear weapons but refraining from doing so for an indefinite period of time. But the WINPAC analysts tended to be uninterested in such arguments. "Some of them would say, 'Don't give me that Iranian-decision-yet-to-be-made approach. They've already decided!'" Pillar recalled.[48]

The summary of the conclusions to be published at the beginning of the estimate were decided in an interagency meeting to achieve consensus on the final product. Because two dramatically different points of view had been expressed during the discussion of the draft, the participants either had to agree to compromise language or to register fundamental disagreement on the conclusions. No one wanted the latter, so they had to work out a way to combine the key points of both sides.

"You have these tussles over what the upfront section should look like," Pillar said. He described a process of argument and negotiation at interagency meetings focused on the order of key sentences representing the two competing conclusions. The side that prevailed got its conclusions into the very first two sentences, Pillar said, whereas the competing conclusion might only appear in the third paragraph.[49] That final determination of the order in which the key findings were be summarized was crucial to the impact of the estimate, because the analysts understood that senior officials would be primarily looking at the conclusions, not the supporting information and analysis.

The outcome of the final meeting on the 2001 estimate was a clear-cut victory for the WINPAC line over the alternative that had been advanced by Pillar and some other regional and country analysts. The language used in the paragraphs summarizing the main conclusions has not been made public, but the title of the NIE leaves no room for doubt about which view prevailed: "Iran Nuclear Weapons Program: Multifaceted and Poised to Succeed, but When?"[50]

By the time work on a successor NIE on the Iran nuclear program began in early 2005, the political context of intelligence assessment had changed from that of 2001 in several ways: WINPAC had emerged as the

---

48. Interview with Pillar, January 27, 2009.

49. Interview with Pillar, October 25, 2012.

50. Paul K. Kerr, *Iran's Nuclear Program: Status,* Congressional Research Service, September 19, 2009, 16n86.

major player in the 2002 NIE on Iraq WMD and had ultimately been proven wrong; the laptop documents had come into the hands of US intelligence in 2004; and a new set of analytic standards to guide intelligence was being widely discussed within the intelligence community as a result of the Iraq NIE debacle, although it had not yet been officially promulgated. But analytical differences still remained on Iran's nuclear intentions: WINPAC analysts were poised to reaffirm their previous assessments about the Iranian nuclear program, and Pillar and other country and regional analysts were still making the argument that Iran had not made any decision to weaponize and was engaging in a "hedging" strategy.[51]

WINPAC had pushed the Curveball testimony and the aluminum tubes allegation against the judgments of most other analysts outside WINPAC.[52] And even after Curveball was revealed to be a fabricator, the management of WINPAC still refused to recant its position on the source because its own credibility was staked on that position. WINPAC management accused one analyst, who had changed his mind about Curveball and called for an official reassessment, of "making waves" and being "biased." The analyst was treated like a pariah at WINPAC and was finally forced out of the organization.[53]

The 2002 Iraq NIE disaster did have some influence on the way the WINPAC analysts interacted with regional and country analysts. "There was a lot of cross talk between the political and technical [analysts]—a lot more than before Iraq," recalled Pillar. One of the results of that greater interaction was that the 2005 NIE included analysis that provided alternative explanations for nuclear activities that Iran had not reported to the IAEA and that the authors of the draft had interpreted as evidence of a covert nuclear weapons program, according to sources cited by the *Washington Post*.[54]

But that didn't change the overall conclusion of the estimate, which was what policymakers read and what would be reflected in policy statements. "Being willing to listen is not the same as what are we were going to come up with as to the bottom line," Pillar said.[55] The first sentence of the key

51. Interview with Pillar, October 25, 2012; personal communication to the author from Pillar, January 14, 2013.

52. Vogel, *Phantom Menace or Looming Danger?*, 17, 33, 38, 55, and 59; Drogin, *Curveball*, 130–32, 138–40, 142, and 147; Isikoff and Corn, *Hubris*, 37–41, 130, 165–66; Eisner and Royce, *Italian Letter*, 121–24.

53. Drogin, *Curveball*, 151–52; Commission Report to the President, 193–94.

54. Dafna Linzer, "Iran Is Judged 10 Years from Nuclear Bomb," *Washington Post*, August 2, 2005.

55. Interview with Pillar, October 25, 2012.

conclusions in the 2005 estimate was that the analysts assessed "with high confidence that Iran currently is determined to develop nuclear weapons despite its international obligations and international pressure, but we do not assess that Iran is immovable."[56]

The WINPAC view of Iran's intentions had again clearly prevailed over that of the political analysts, but it was now qualified somewhat by the former. Pillar noted that despite the confidence expressed in the lead sentence that Iran was "determined to develop nuclear weapons," no evidence had come to light of any Iranian nuclear weapons design work. Pillar later concluded that he and the national intelligence officer for strategic weapons and WMD had "done a kind of a crappy job of bridging the two views."[57]

"The most important consideration" in the discussion among analysts on the draft estimate, Pillar said, was "still the nuts and bolts of what is happening on the ground as far as what [the weapons analysts'] sources are telling them."[58] But it wasn't merely human intelligence sources that were at issue in the estimate; a more influential source hovering over the 2005 NIE was the laptop documents that had been given to the CIA in 2004. The *Washington Post* would later report that those documents "formed the backbone" of the 2005 estimate's conclusions. Fingar confirmed that previously there had been "ambiguity about the purposes of the nuclear program," but that the laptop documents "did make it pretty clear."[59]

The fact that the source of those documents was affiliated with Mujahedeen-e-Khalq, the armed opposition group in Iran, and that German intelligence had determined that he was "unreliable" should have been explicitly discussed in the context of the NIE. One of the new standards governing intelligence assessment in light of the Iraq NIE disaster was aimed at ensuring that analysts were more informed on the identities and past records of human intelligence sources of key pieces of evidence. "More visibility on sources was a very important change," Fingar observed.[60]

Given the MEK's record of supplying false information, the revelation of a MEK role in providing the papers would have raised serious questions about their authenticity, whether they were attributed to Israel or not. Some—though not all—US intelligence analysts were extremely skeptical

56. *Iran: Nuclear Intentions and Capabilities*, National Intelligence Estimate, November 2007, 9, at http://www.dni.gov/files/documents/Newsroom/Reports%20and%20Pubs/20071203_release.pdf.

57. Interview with Pillar, January 27, 2009.

58. Interview with Pillar, October 25, 2012.

59. Peter Baker and Dafna Linzer, "Diving Deep, Unearthing a Surprise," *Washington Post*, December 8, 2007; interview with Fingar.

60. Interview with Fingar.

about relying on the MEK for such intelligence. "It's embarrassing to admit," said Pillar, "that Western analysts have to depend on such a group as the MEK."[61]

Apart from the question of the influence that the laptop documents had on the assumptions governing the estimate, the authors were not always scrupulous about making their claims of evidence for some of the conclusions reached. One former intelligence official who read the 2005 estimate noticed a discrepancy between a number of the conclusions in the text and the information in the supporting footnotes.[62]

The NIEs of 2001 and 2005 on the Iran nuclear program represented the accumulation of many years of institutional dynamics that distorted the intelligence assessments on that subject. At the lowest level was the narrow technical orientation of WINPAC, and on top of that was the incentive to find a nuclear weapons program in Iran that had been reinforced repeatedly by administration officials. Then there was the systematic empowerment of that center of analysis to dominate all WMD assessment. Past analyses on Iran legitimized continuing in the same vein, and finally, documentary evidence that appeared just in time to clinch the case was not seriously examined, as sound analytical tradecraft would have required.

## Warping Another Estimate: 2007

The 2007 National Intelligence Estimate on Iran has been reviled by those who believe that the threat of attack on Iran must be maintained, and praised by those who believe that it prevented a war against Iran. But a reconstruction of the process that led to the final estimate suggests that the truth is that it preserved more of the wrong-headed intelligence assessment of the past than it renounced.

The NIE came about because of worries among some key figures in Congress that the Bush administration's neoconservative core group might be planning to use force against Iran. Thomas Fingar, the deputy director of national intelligence for analysis at the time, revealed to me in an interview that Director of National Intelligence Mike McConnell had agreed to the estimate in 2006 in response to requests from those in Congress who wanted to prevent a war over Iran and wanted a more thorough analysis of Iran's real nuclear intentions.[63]

---

61. James Risen, "US Faces a Tricky Task in Assessment of Data on Iran," *New York Times*, March 17, 2012; interview with Pillar, January 27, 2009.

62. Author's interview with a former intelligence official who asked not to be identified, April 19, 2013.

63. Interview with Fingar.

One of the objectives of the estimate was supposed to be to go more deeply into that subject than previous estimates had done. The "Scope Note" attached to the published "Key Judgments" of the 2007 estimate shows that it was intended to examine both domestic and external factors affecting Iranian decision making and "the decisive factors that would lead Iran to choose one course of action over another." The note indicates specifically that the assessment would not begin with the assumption that Iran wanted nuclear weapons, but would reexamine that issue.[64]

But the draft completed in June 2007, after several months of work, broke no new ground on the subject. Instead, it simply reaffirmed the main conclusions of the 2005 estimate. "When I reviewed what we thought was the penultimate draft, we changed no key judgments," Fingar recalled.[65] In testimony in early July before the House Armed Services Committee, he said, "We assess that Tehran is determined to develop nuclear weapons, despite its international obligations and international pressure." Fingar was restating, word for word, the primary conclusion of the 2005 NIE.[66]

The readiness to embrace precisely the same conclusions as the most recent NIE, in spite of a mandate to reexamine its assumptions and the evidence on which it relied, was a reflection of what Fingar called "the deference that was paid to prior judgments." Previous NIEs "damn near came to be sacred texts," he said. "To go back and redo, relook at original information and judgment reached earlier—it simply wasn't done."[67]

Something else had bothered Fingar about the exercise, however, even as he prepared to essentially reaffirm the findings of the 2005 NIE. Walpole, who had managed the 2001 and 2005 estimates, called Fingar's attention to a "dog that didn't bark" in regard to the Iran nuclear program. "We haven't seen anything on weaponization," Walpole told him, and added, "We used to have a relatively large amount of stuff." That raised the obvious question: why not?[68] Nevertheless, the team was in the process of reaffirming the conclusions of previous estimates about Iranian nuclear intentions.

Then something quite unexpected happened that changed the direction of the assessment: US intelligence obtained new information, mainly, but not exclusively, from electronic intercepts, indicating that the Iranian government had halted all work on nuclear weapons in 2003. The new

---

64. "Scope Note," in *Iran: Nuclear Intentions and Capabilities*.

65. Interview with Fingar.

66. Global Security Assessment, July 11, 2007, before the House Armed Services Comm., 110th Cong., 1st sess., statement of Dr. Thomas S. Fingar, deputy director of national intelligence for analysis; comparison of key judgments of the 2005 and 2007 NIEs on Iran's nuclear program in *Iran: Nuclear Intentions and Capabilities*.

67. Interview with Fingar.

68. Ibid.

information was so compelling that it led to a critical review of the entire NIE. "Every bit of evidence had to be looked at again," Fingar recalled. "We had to go back to square one." In the end, the analysts determined that the information they had been citing as the basis for reaffirming the 2005 conclusion that Iran had been working on nuclear weapons didn't really support that conclusion.

Those who had argued strongly that the nuclear weapons program had continued to 2007 fought against the new conclusion.[69] But it was resolved by September, when the team rewrote the new estimate in light of the new discoveries. The new draft concluded that Iran's military had been "working under government direction to develop nuclear weapons" until 2003, but that Iran had "halted its nuclear weapons program" in 2003. It professed uncertainty about whether Iran "currently intends to develop nuclear weapons" but concluded that the 2003 halt suggested it was now "less determined to develop nuclear weapons than we have been judging since 2005."[70]

The next few weeks were spent thoroughly examining the possibility that they had been deliberately misled by a clever Iranian deception. "Red teams" were organized to challenge the new conclusion, and only after weeks of subjecting the evidence to the most strenuous arguments and tests, organized in part by CIA director Michael Hayden and his deputy Stephen Kappes, did the team finally conclude that such a deception was impossible.[71]

Meanwhile, the senators who had called for the estimate in the first place were upset by the delay in completing it. It was the third time in less than a year that significant delays in completing the estimate had occurred, according to Fingar, and they were convinced that the reason was political. "There wasn't any plan to go to war like Iraq," Fingar recalled. "But a lot of folks on the hill thought there was. That's what was driving it." McConnell gave those senators a commitment in September that the estimate would be issued by the end of November.[72]

The new information had obvious implications for the question of "how determined Iran was to continue the program," Fingar recalled. But by then, the analysts were facing time constraints. "Logically that would have required a real deep rethink of intentions. But we reached that judgment less than a week before the drop-dead date McConnell had promised

69. Greg Miller, "New Data Set Off a Series of Recalculations by the U.S. Intelligence Community," *Los Angeles Times*, December 5, 2007.

70. "Key Judgments," in *Iran: Nuclear Intentions and Capabilities.*

71. Interview with Fingar; Baker and Linzer, "Diving Deep."

72. Interview with Fingar.

the hill," he said. Fingar was afraid those working on the estimate would be seen as covering for an administration that was bent on war.

So the estimate did not do what McConnell had promised congressional leaders it would. The only thing about intentions that was addressed in the NIE was the assertion that when Iran shut down nuclear weapons work, it was in response to increased international pressure. But a long list of questions that Fingar had expected to be analyzed remained unanswered in the estimate. "Did they want to rejoin the community of nations? Was it related to Saddam? These are the questions we should and would have tackled," Fingar said.

Although the estimate failed to deliver a focused analysis of Iranian intentions and calculations, the authors nevertheless offered some very strong opinions on the subject. Convincing the Iranian leadership to "forgo the eventual development of nuclear weapons" would be "difficult," they suggested. They cited two reasons: first, "the linkage many within the leadership probably see between nuclear weapons development and Iran's key national security and foreign policy objectives," and second, "Iran's considerable effort from at least the late 1980s to 2003 to develop such weapons."[73]

Those conclusions reflected essentially the same analysis that had dominated the 2001 and 2005 NIEs. The authors assumed that everything that Iran did to obtain enrichment technology from the 1980s on was evidence of a nuclear weapons program. The analysts had refused to take into account the alternative analysis that had been advanced in previous assessments by the regional and country analysts that Iran was following a "hedging" strategy and was well aware of the costs and risks to Iranian security of actually becoming a nuclear weapons state.[74]

Although it departed from some conclusions in previous estimates, the 2007 NIE thus reaffirmed their overall thrust. "When we got the new information in 2007 that caused us to completely redo it, we didn't change most of the judgments," Fingar acknowledged.[75] The strong commitment of the authors of the 2007 estimate to the erroneous assumptions and methodologies of previous NIEs raises the question of whether they analyzed the new information objectively in judging that it showed a nuclear weapons program in 2003 or were simply engaged in more a priori reasoning.

Neither the published "Key Judgments" of the estimate nor the briefings for journalists after the public release gave any indication of what kind of nuclear weapons work was mentioned in the documentation, on

---

73. "Key Judgments," in *Iran: Nuclear Intentions and Capabilities*.

74. Fingar commented that the "hedging" issue had been dealt with in previous estimates, suggesting that it had been argued that it wasn't necessary to cover that terrain again. Interview with Fingar.

75. Ibid.

what scale, for what objective, and with what degree of coordination, if any. When asked by the author about the absence of any indication of what kind of nuclear weapons work had been going on, Fingar said such information was deliberately excluded from public release because the information was "too important to our continued ability to know what's going on. The last thing we wanted to do was lose access to it."[76]

But the briefings for journalists by intelligence officials involved in the NIE provided details about the means by which the intelligence was obtained that went well beyond the normal revelations about intelligence sources and methods. The *Washington Post* reported that the data included "intercepted calls between Iranian military commanders." And on December 8, the *Post* reported that "snippets of conversations" involved a military officer whose name appeared on the laptop." The *Los Angeles Times* reported that the conversations involved one Iranian officer "complaining in 2007 about the suspensions of the military program in 2003." The other key intelligence included information from the "journal or diary" of an Iranian "involved in the management of the military program."[77]

Thus intelligence officials who led the assessment went very far in revealing the sources of the information, presumably to lend credibility to the surprising conclusion in the estimate. Yet the briefings offered no clue about what kind and level of activities were involved: Were they basic science related to nuclear weapons? Laboratory research? Development and testing of components? And more important, what evidence, if any, did they find of a centrally controlled program, as opposed to individuals or offices pursuing their own pet projects?

When I pointed out the discrepancy in the "Key Judgments" between the details of the sources and methods and the lack of any characterization of the alleged nuclear weapons program, Fingar refused to go beyond the enigmatic published text.[78] But he did reveal one piece of information that provides a crucial clue to the question: Fingar himself had personally dissented from the NIE's "high confidence" that Iran had "halted its nuclear weapons program" in 2003. "The dissent," he explained to me, "was on the level of confidence that the halt had embraced all aspects of the program. I did not think we had enough specific information to have high confidence that it did."[79]

---

76. Ibid.

77. Baker and Linzer, "Diving Deep, Unearthing a Surprise"; Miller, "New Data."

78. Personal communication to the author from Thomas Fingar, February 14, 2013.

79. Personal communication to the author from Thomas Fingar, July 4, 2012. Fingar's dissent is found in the "Key Judgments" document in the top right cell of the comparison between the 2005 and 2007 NIEs, which states, "DOE and NIC [National Intelligence Council] have moderate confidence that the halt to those activities represent a

The logical implication of that expression of doubt about the judgment that "all aspects" of the alleged nuclear weapons program had been shut down, based on "insufficient information," is that the information obtained in 2007 referred to one or more activities rather than describing a coherent, centrally controlled program. Had there been evidence of a central decision to close down a well-defined and centrally coordinated program, a decision to end all nuclear weapons work could be presumed to be effective across the entire program, and there would have been no cause for concern about "insufficient information."

The conclusion of the NIE authors regarding that crucial issue were heavily biased by their long-standing convictions that a nuclear weapons program had been going on for many years and had continued beyond 2003. Even after new information entered the picture, moreover, some of those analysts involved in the NIE fought against the abandonment of that earlier assessment. The authors' judgment was also evidently distorted by the belief that the laptop documents were genuine. The "Key Judgments" document cites a "growing amount of intelligence" that "indicates Iran was engaged in covert uranium conversion" in 2003. The only information suggesting a plan for such covert uranium conversion that has ever surfaced, however, is in the laptop documents.[80] The estimate's authors were thus making inferences about an Iranian covert nuclear weapons program on the basis of the same assumptions that had repeatedly led them to false conclusions in the past.

Finally, the authors of the NIE were unaware of the considerable evidence showing that Iran's Supreme National Security Council had not approved projects on nuclear weapons and that Khamenei had issued a fatwa against nuclear weapons in order to compel individual researchers to cease any such work.

The 2007 NIE still had not come to grips with the central questions of the interests, intentions, and calculations underlying the program. And it was still shaped by a policy climate that rewarded conclusions that supported the aggressively anti-Iran policy of the Bush administration, just as it did in the case of WMD in Iraq. The pervasive intelligence failure on Iran was caused by a larger failure of US national security institutions to protect the national interest against narrow institutional and other parochial interests.

---

halt to Iran's entire nuclear weapons program." The 2007 estimate judged "with high confidence" that the halt had taken place.

80. GOV/2008/15, May 26, 2008, annex, 1. Neither the November 2011 IAEA annex nor any previous IAEA report contained any reference to alleged covert uranium conversion activity except for the "alleged studies" documents.

# 10

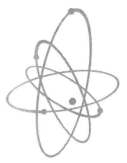

# The Phantom Bomb
# Test Chamber of Parchin

A few weeks after the November 2007 US National Intelligence Estimate concluded that Iran had halted work on nuclear weapons in 2003, an Israeli defense official complained to a journalist that it had "dropped quite a bomb" on Israel's long-term strategy toward Iran.[1] The well-informed defense analyst for *Haaretz*, Amos Harel, also wondered how this surprising development would affect the intersection between Israel's intelligence and propaganda policies. "Is Israel capable of presenting the Americans with any information that can prove to the Americans that their new evaluation is wrong?" Harel wondered.[2]

In fact, the head of Mossad, Meir Dagan, had begun in late 2006 to try his best to influence the US estimate, knowing that the outcome would either help or hinder Israel's strategy. Mossad had shared intelligence with the United States that purported to show that the Iranians were testing a neutron initiator for a nuclear weapon. The United States and Israel never share the actual intelligence report from an agent or an actual document with one another but only summaries of such evidence.[3] But the summary intelligence report from Mossad said that a "reliable agent" inside Iran had reported in 2006 that Iran had been "simulating zero-yield nuclear explosions without any weapons-grade materials." In other words, the report was saying that the Iranians were carrying out hydrodynamic testing of

---

1. Ron Ben-Yishai, "Exclusive: Annual Israeli Intelligence Estimate," Ynet News, December 16, 2007, http://www.ynetnews.com/articles/0,7340,L-3483116,00.html.

2. Amos Harel, "Nuclear Fallout: Who's Right Here?" *Haaretz* (Tel Aviv), December 5, 2007.

3. Author's interview with Flynt Leverett, former CIA analyst, May 2, 2006.

weapons designs.[4] That had been the premise of John Bolton's ploy involving satellite photos of Parchin and the demand for an IAEA inspection of those sites in 2004.

The problem was the Israeli agent had not produced any diagrams or specific details about where or when the testing had been carried out. In fact, the CIA had been unable to obtain any information about the purported Israeli agent. And as with previous Israeli intelligence in the case of Iraq, Dagan had sent the information directly to the White House. That kind of "stovepiping" of the information to high-level administration officials—especially in the office of the vice president—had became a familiar modus operandi for the Israelis in dealing with the Bush administration. But especially in the aftermath of the Iraq intelligence fiasco, that did not help the Israelis sell their claim at the CIA.

The worst thing about the NIE for Israel was that it weakened the Israeli strategy, in cooperation with the Bush administration, for using the laptop documents and the IAEA to build a media narrative of a continuing Iranian covert nuclear weapons program. Without warning, the NIE blunted the potential impact of that strategy by concluding that Iran had stopped its work on nuclear weapons in 2003. Israel now needed something that went beyond the laptop documents to advance its campaign to convince the world that Iran was running a covert nuclear weapons program.

But Mossad made a discovery that suggested one possible solution to that problem. One of Mossad's continuing preoccupations was to identify Russian scientists and engineers who had worked in Iran, and that process yielded a piece of information that must have excited senior Mossad officials: one of the experts who had worked in Iran for several years in the late 1990s, Vyacheslav Danilenko, had been employed in the main Soviet nuclear weapons complex at Chelyabinsk in the 1970s and 1980s.

Furthermore, Danilenko was a prominent researcher with an extensive publications record. By following that trail of publications, Mossad quickly learned that he was a specialist in the explosive formation of nanodiamonds and that he had also worked on measuring time intervals in explosions through an optical fiber system in the early 1990s. The research on his work also turned up the fact that he had designed a large explosives chamber for the production of nanodiamonds at around the same time he had worked in Iran. With their penchant for fitting every new piece of information into their master theory, Mossad officials may well have been convinced that Danilenko must have been doing something in Iran related to explosives tests for nuclear weapons. Why else, they may have asked, would the Iranians want to give someone with that background a contract to work in Iran from 1996 to 2002? Certainly not for his expertise on nano-diamonds, they may have concluded; that had to be a ruse to cover his real work in the country.

As was so often the case with Israeli intelligence on the Iranian nuclear program, the firm Israeli conviction that Iran must be actively working on the bomb inspired a propaganda strategy as well. And as was the case with the laptop documents, that strategy involved manufacturing documentary evidence to give the propaganda theme credibility.

The story would involve secret explosives tests of a system for initiating the detonation of a nuclear device. The Israelis linked Danilenko to a system for starting a high-explosive charge in a hemispheric shell, monitored with optical fiber cables like those mentioned in one of Danilenko's articles. And as a bonus, Danilenko would also be linked to a large explosives chamber similar to the one he had discussed in a Russian-language book the Israelis found, which they would suggest was to be used for carrying out hydrodynamic tests on nuclear weapons designs.

Mossad would provide enough details to the IAEA to create a presumption that Danilenko had done such things. Fashioning such a narrative would solve several Israeli problems simultaneously. Danilenko's work in a nuclear weapons complex, his stay in Iran for years, and his publications would be the confirmation of a broader story of Iranian tests on a nuclear bomb initiation system and hydrodynamic tests—the key point about which Mossad had been trying to convince the CIA during its work on the national intelligence estimate. It would show that Iran was much farther along by 2003 than anyone had ever guessed. And once the idea that Iran had been doing tests on nuclear weapons components and designs had been firmly established, other documents showing later experiments would be given new credibility.

The situation in the IAEA in 2008 was favorable for such an Israeli initiative. Olli Heinonen was ready to consider any evidence showing the Iranians working on a nuclear weapon to be credible. The Israelis had worked with him for more than four years, and Heinonen was now distancing himself from Mohamed ElBaradei's cautious attitude toward the laptop documents. There was no longer any need to filter the purported Iranian documents through a third party.

The "multi-point initiation system" using explosives in a hemispheric array was well known among nuclear weapons states. Crafting an account of experiments with the system that would sound authentic was not difficult for Mossad's staff. By April 2008, a new document was passed to Heinonen in Vienna: a long, Farsi-language account of the experiments with a technology involving a "shock generator system" that could only be used for testing a nuclear weapons initiator. Heinonen decided to include a five-page English-language summary of the longer Farsi document in the list of 13 documents to be shown to Iranian officials in meetings in late April and mid-May. The document was then listed and briefly described in the May 2008 IAEA report without distinguishing it from the rest of the laptop documents.[5]

Either at the same time or soon thereafter, the Israelis also gave Heinonen information on Danilenko's background and his time in Iran, explaining how he must have been involved in the experiments shown in the document they had given him earlier. The document referred to the use of "fiber optic cables" to monitor the shock waves. And the Israelis could point to Danilenko's 1992 paper on a system for measuring the intervals between shock waves with fiber-optic cables.[6] Later, they would claim to have found additional information on how Danilenko helped Iran build an explosives containment cylinder in which to carry out those hydrodynamic tests the Israelis had been alleging for years.

Heinonen didn't wait for the assessment of other intelligence agencies. The IAEA announced in its September 2008 report that it had information describing "experimentation in connection with symmetrical initiation of a hemispherical high explosive charge suitable for an implosion type nuclear device." And then it added that since the previous report, the agency had "obtained information indicating that the experimentation described in this document may have involved the assistance of foreign expertise."[7]

Heinonen concealed Israel's role in providing the document to the IAEA, even though hiding the provenance of such information represented yet another violation of what ElBaradei had called "due process" in regard to the accusations against Iran. When US and European officials decided in October 2008 to call the significance of the document to the attention of the *New York Times*, they also refused to reveal the origins of the document, citing the need to avoid exposing the source.[8]

5. *Excerpts from Internal IAEA Document on Alleged Iranian Nuclear Weaponization,* Institute for Science and International Security, October 2, 2009, 3; GOV/2008/15, May 26, 2008, annex, 1.

6. N. P. Kozeruk, V. V. Danilenko, B. V. Litvinov, P. P. Lysenko, I. V. Sanin, S. V. Samylov, V. I. Tarjanov, and I. V. Telichko, "Multichannel Optical Fiber System to Measure Time Intervals at Investigations of Explosive Phenomena," in *20th Congress on High Speed Photography and Photonics,* Proceedings of the Conference, September 21–25, 1992, Victoria, BC, Canada (International Society for Optical Engineering, 1993), 981–88.

7. GOV/2008/38, September 15, 2008, 4.

8. Elaine Sciolino, "Nuclear Aid by Russian to Iranians Suspected," *New York Times,* October 9, 2008.

That rationale for secrecy shouldn't apply, however, to the question of which member state of the IAEA is behind a given piece of intelligence. Transparency on the question of whose intelligence is being used would not have affected the confidentiality of intelligence "sources and methods." It would merely have allowed other states and the public to make a more informed evaluation of the reliability of the information. The IAEA was creating a precedent for allowing a state to anonymously provide evidence in the form of intelligence documents that was to become central to the IAEA case against Iran.

But Heinonen had said enough to lead David Albright at ISIS to conclude that the document had probably come from Israel. In an interview in September, just as the IAEA report highlighting the document was being circulated to IAEA delegations, Albright said, "One thing that changed Heinonen's mind [about the laptop documents] was a document from a state—probably Israel—that was confirming." Heinonen had told him it had been "important to him," Albright said.[9]

Theoretically, of course, Israel could have been lucky: a document from inside the Iranian nuclear program could have fallen into the hands of an Israeli spy in Iran. But apart from the highly unlikely coincidence in timing of the two discoveries just in time to solve Israel's political problems on Iran, getting such a document would have required an agent at the very heart of a secret nuclear weapons program. And that would have meant, in turn, that Israel should have been able to present a clear and relatively detailed picture of the structure of that program.

Despite official pronouncements by the Israeli government that Iran resumed its nuclear weapons program after 2003, however, Israeli intelligence had only the most fragmentary and impressionistic picture of such an Iranian program in 2008. Thomas Fingar, deputy director of intelligence and chairman of the National Intelligence Council until December 1, 2008, recalled in an interview that despite the public gnashing of teeth in Israel over the November 2007 NIE, Israeli military intelligence officers didn't challenge the 2007 estimate in private meetings with him. "I had my shouting matches with them in Israel," said Fingar. "I said we disagreed on two things: 'You think [the nuclear weapons program] has been moved to new locations, but you don't know where it is, and that it's run by a different person, but you don't know who it is.'"[10]

If Israeli intelligence had no real knowledge of the details of any Iranian nuclear weapons program, as Fingar's account of his exchange with Israeli intelligence officials suggests, it is highly unlikely that Israel could have

---

9. Author's interview with David Albright, September 15, 2008.

10. Author's interview with Thomas Fingar, Oxford, UK, February 7, 2013.

obtained intelligence on what would have been one of the most highly classified secrets in the country. Nevertheless, even more such intelligence documents, purporting to come from within the clandestine Iranian nuclear weapons program, were about to be provided by Israel to the IAEA. leading the agency to more dramatic conclusions.

## More Israeli Documents

In September 2008, Heinonen authorized his staff to begin drafting a paper that would assess all the intelligence that had been acquired by the agency on alleged Iranian nuclear weapons work. The idea of doing such a paper was evidently inspired by the Israeli document showing for the first time what was unambiguously a project to test the initiator of a nuclear weapon.

An early draft, written either in late 2008 or early 2009, showed how Heinonen sought to mimic the stance of an intelligence agency in relation to the laptop documents and new intelligence provided by Israel. In one paragraph after another, the draft used the phrase "the Agency assesses" or the "Agency further assesses" before offering far-reaching and alarming speculation about the possible implications of the information in question. "The Agency assesses," it said, "that it is possible that Iran has knowledge regarding the contents of a nuclear package, including fissile components that would be inserted inside the high explosive charge."[11]

The draft argued that the issue of the authenticity of the laptop papers should now be set aside. The papers were credible, it asserted, because "the information refers to known Iranian persons and institutions under both the military and civil apparatuses, as well as to some degree to their confirmed procurement activities."[12] A senior IAEA official whom I interviewed in 2009, however, pointed out that the names of people working in various organizations were well known. "It's not difficult to cook up," the official told me.[13]

The draft referred to "information received from a Member State" about a "shock generator system" that it "assessed" to be a system for "initiating hemispheric explosive charges." The draft concluded from that premise that "Iran may have developed an effective high explosive implosion system, which could be contained within a payload container believed to be small enough to fit into the re-entry body chamber of the Shahab-3 missile."[14]

---

11. Excerpts from Internal IAEA Document, 4.

12. Ibid., 3.

13. Author's interview with a senior IAEA official who insisted on not being identified, Vienna, September 7, 2009.

14. Excerpts from Internal IAEA Document, 3–4.

Heinonen obviously ordered the drafting of that paper with the intention that the agency would eventually publish it as an annex to one of its reports. But ElBaradei was dead set against any such publication. He regarded the information on which the analysis was based as still uncorroborated raw intelligence, so providing it to the board "would have gone against every principle of due process and would have lent an aura of credibility to unverified accusations," as he would later write.[15]

ElBaradei confirms in his memoirs that Israel provided the IAEA with intelligence documents that summer "purportedly showing that Iran had continued with nuclear weapon studies until at least 2007." Furthermore, ElBaradei claims that the agency's "technical experts" had "raised numerous questions about the documents' authenticity," which prompted a list of questions to be sent to the Israelis.[16]

It was not until the agency began to prepare its report in advance of an October 2009 board meeting that the United Kingdom, France, and Germany began to press ElBaradei to include the intelligence assessment as an annex to that report. It is no accident that the Western pressure on ElBaradei came after Israel turned over the new set of intelligence reports and documents to the IAEA with the obvious intention of having them be part of the expected annex. A remarkably candid Israeli press report in mid-August cited "officials and diplomats" as saying the IAEA had been refusing to publish evidence that had been obtained "over the past few months" that would show Iran was continuing to pursue "weaponization efforts."[17]

When it became clear that ElBaradei was actively posing obstacles to their documents being officially published by the agency, the Israelis decided it was time to call in their allies. In mid-August, the US, British, French, and German ambassadors to the IAEA, who had been briefed on the purported significance of the new documents, personally intervened with ElBaradei on the issue, insisting that he should publish the draft paper by Heinonen's Safeguards Department as an annex to the September report. German ambassador Ruediger Luedeking confirmed in an interview that he and other ambassadors "pressed for the Agency to produce an annex."[18]

Notably absent from the diplomatic pressures on ElBaradei was the Obama administration. The administration's reluctance was probably

---

15. ElBaradei, *Age of Deception*, 290.

16. Ibid., 292.

17. Barak Ravid, "Israelis Say IAEA Hiding Evidence on Iran," *Haaretz* (Tel Aviv), August 19, 2009.

18. Author's interview with Ambassador Ruediger Luedeking, Vienna, September 7, 2009.

because those pressures, reportedly coordinated by the Israeli Foreign Ministry and the director general of the Israeli Atomic Energy Commission, Dr. Shaul Horev, were aimed at proving that the US intelligence conclusion that Iran had halted its nuclear weaponization effort in 2003 was wrong. The ultimate aim, according to a leak to the Israeli press, was to ensure Russian and Chinese support for much tougher sanctions against Iran.[19]

ElBaradei was unmoved by the Western demand for publication of the intelligence annex, which he recognized as a political maneuver to promote an interpretation of the Iranian nuclear program that was not supported by authenticated evidence. His refusal to approve the publication was the signal for the next phase of the strategy, which was to leak to the news media the accusation that ElBaradei had deliberately suppressed intelligence showing that Iran had been doing experiments related to nuclear weapons. The warning shot to ElBaradei came in an article by George Jahn, Vienna correspondent of the Associated Press, which began, "For close to a year, diplomats say, a report on Iran's alleged nuclear experiments has been sitting in a drawer of a UN nuclear monitoring agency." It reported that three "senior Western diplomats" and an "international official" had confirmed the existence of the secret report on Iran's experiments. ElBaradei had balked even after being pushed by Western powers, according to the sources, "although even some of his senior aides favor publication."[20]

The leak of the accusation that ElBaradei was keeping important evidence from the rest of the world carefully avoided any specifics. It was an obvious warning to ElBaradei that his Israeli and Western adversaries were prepared to leak the details of the report to the press if he did not publish them. The timing of the story a little more than a week before the August report was designed to give ElBaradei an opportunity to reconsider his decision. But ElBaradei did not give in to the political pressure, even though he knew the probable consequences. The August 2009 report did not include the annex, titled "Possible Military Dimensions to Iran's Nuclear Program," that Israel and the Western powers were demanding he publish.

The response came in mid-September in a story from the same journalist who had been given the previous leak, the AP's George Jahn. This time Jahn was given a point-by-point briefing based on the "secret annex," which was explicitly identified as such by his diplomatic sources. His story summarized the most sensational items in the document about what agency analysts believed to be Iranian development, testing, and production of

19. Ravid, "Israelis Say IAEA Hiding Evidence"; Louis Charbonneau, "Western Powers Want ElBaradei Help on Russia, China," Reuters, August 20, 2009.

20. "Outgoing IAEA Chief Has Tough Choice on Iran," AP, Ynet News, August 20, 2009.

a nuclear weapon. He reported that the agency believed Iran had "sufficient information to be able to design and produce a workable implosion nuclear device" and that it had engaged in "probable testing" of explosives commonly used to detonate a nuclear warhead and worked on developing a system "for initiating a hemispherical high explosive charge" of the kind used to initiate a nuclear explosion.[21]

Two weeks after the AP story, the *New York Times* focused on the conclusion in the unpublished document that Iran had acquired "sufficient information to be able to design and produce" a nuclear weapon that would be "workable." Reporters William J. Broad and David E. Sanger also summarized the report as having concluded that "Iran has done much research and testing to perfect nuclear arms like making high-voltage detonators, firing test explosives and designing warheads."[22] The *Times* thus reduced the IAEA staff's highly speculative analysis, on the basis of "information" coming largely from a single source, to simple and alarming conclusions.

Predictably, the cable news networks picked up and magnified the two key sentences from the *Times* story that their audiences would immediately grasp. Fox News said Iran "has done extensive research and testing to perfect nuclear arms, such as firing test explosives and designing warheads." And CNN's John King declared, "Iran has cracked the code. It knows how to make a smaller warhead. It is closer to being able to build a bomb, a workable nuclear bomb."[23]

The press campaign had succeeded in creating a full-blown nuclear scare, portraying Iran as feverishly working on a secret nuclear weapons program and on the verge of building a nuclear weapon. But the Israelis wanted to achieve one more objective: to highlight the document they had provided to the IAEA in 2009 that appeared to show that Iran was pursuing nuclear weapons-related research well beyond 2003. This was a two-page, Farsi-language document purporting to outline a research plan on neutron sources that included work on what was evidently a neutron initiator.

This time the document was given to the *Times*, the Rupert Murdoch flagship London daily, which had followed a decidedly pro-Israel line in its coverage of the Middle East for more than two decades.[24] The *Times* reported in December 2009, "Confidential intelligence documents obtained by *The Times* show that Iran is working on testing a key final component of a nuclear bomb." It described one of the documents as a

---

21. George Jahn, "Nuke Agency Says Iran Can Make Bomb," AP, September 17, 2009.

22. William J. Broad and David E. Sanger, "Report Says Iran Has Data to Make a Nuclear Bomb," *New York Times*, October 4, 2009.

23. "Report: Iran Has Information to Make a Nuclear Bomb," transcript of *State of the Union with John King*, Fox News, October 4, 2009.

24. "Robert Fisk: Why I Had to Leave the Times," *Independent* (London), July 11, 2011.

"four-year plan" to "test a neutron initiator," or, as the headline called it, a "Nuclear Trigger." The story identified the source as "an Asian intelligence source," a phrase sometimes used in the context of stories on the Middle East to refer to Israeli intelligence. The source's unnamed government was said to believe the document was written in 2007, four years after Iran was "thought to have suspended its weapons programme."

The story suggested the "fallout" from the revelation of the document in Washington could be "explosive," given the US NIE's conclusion about Iran's halting weaponization work in 2003, and the British, French, and German intelligence agencies' disagreement with that American conclusion. The author of the story quoted the aggressively anti-Iran former State Department proliferation official Mark Fitzpatrick as saying the document "looks like a smoking gun. This is smoking uranium."[25]

But serious questions soon arose about the document's authenticity. Even David Sanger of the *New York Times*, who never missed an opportunity to hammer away at what he was convinced was a misguided 2007 NIE, reported two days later that US intelligence had not yet authenticated it, even though the document was said by one US official familiar with it to have been known to analysts "for well over a year." And even the European intelligence agencies that had openly disagreed with the US intelligence community's conclusion about a halt in nuclear weapons work in 2003 were unwilling to say that it was authentic.[26]

In fact, US intelligence analysts were not merely undecided about the "Nuclear Trigger" document but were quite suspicious of it. Former CIA official Philip Giraldi was told by intelligence sources that the analysts had dismissed the document as a fabrication.[27] Their distrust of the document was undoubtedly heightened by the fact that Israel had conveniently discovered it just when it was needed to discredit the 2007 estimate. The intelligence analysts also may have known that it was one of the documents the Israelis had pressed on the IAEA during summer 2009. ElBaradei recalled later that the new set of Israeli documents were aimed at showing that Iran had continued to work on nuclear weapons "until at least 2007"—the argument the Israelis were making about the "Nuclear Trigger" document.[28]

The Israelis knew that if the document were leaked to the *Times* while ElBaradei was still in office, he might dismiss it as of questionable

---

25. Catherine Philp, "Secret Document Exposes Iran's Nuclear Trigger," *Times* (London), December 14, 2009.

26. William J. Broad and David E. Sanger, "Nuclear Memo in Persian Puzzles Spy Agencies," *New York Times*, December 16, 2009.

27. Gareth Porter, "US Intel Found Iran Nuke Document Was Forged," Inter Press Service, December 28, 2009.

28. ElBaradei, *Age of Deception*, 291.

authenticity. It is no accident that the *Times* published the story on December 14, 2009, exactly two weeks after ElBaradei had been succeeded by Yukiya Amano of Japan.

With Amano in place as director general of the IAEA in December 2009, the United States at last had a team that it could rely on to follow its lead on Iran fully. The United States had worked for Amano's election as director general because he was known to have supported hard-line demands on Iran to abandon its nuclear program. Amano had been the Japanese ambassador to the IAEA and represented Japan as part of the "like-minded" group of states. At a meeting of that group in December 2008, when US ambassador Greg Schulte raised the possibility of demanding that Iran make a "confession" of its alleged past nuclear weapons work, Amano had said that an Iranian confession would not be enough. "What was needed," he was reported to have opined, "was a strategic decision from Iran"—presumably meaning a decision to stop enrichment completely.[29] After Amano's election, the US mission reported that he had displayed a "remarkable congruence of views with us on conducting the Agency mission in safeguards verification" and had explicitly assured the United States that he was "solidly in the U.S. court" on handling the Iran nuclear issue.[30]

## The Phantom Bomb Test Chamber

The annex to the November 2011 IAEA report was the final version of the document on which the Safeguards Department had started work in September 2008, based primarily on intelligence provided by Israel. It alleged Iranian activities involving nuclear components for an explosive device, experiments with a "multi-point initiation system," hydrodynamic experiments to test nuclear weapons designs, and work on a "neutron initiator."[31]

The information was packaged to convey to the news media and governments that its conclusions were not merely suspicions or speculation but were based on highly credible information. The IAEA devoted five long paragraphs to that theme in which it sought to lay the entire issue of authenticity of the "alleged studies" documents to rest, without raising it explicitly. It asserted that it had "received information from ten Member States" on the issue. But that figure was a red herring. The "information" from all those states included data on travel, financial records, health and safety arrangements, and manufacturing techniques

---

29. 07UNVIENNA742, US Embassy Vienna to State, December 7, 2007.

30. 09UNVIENNA478, US Embassy Vienna to State, October 16, 2009.

31. GOV/2011/65, November 8, 2011, 7–10.

for certain high-explosive components.[32] The agency did not get the intelligence on which the report's conclusions were based from 10 different governments. The *New York Times* reported the figure of 10 states contributing information, however, without pointing out that it did not pertain to allegations of nuclear weapons work. The *Times* suggested that detailing the number of sources of information was "an effort to anticipate the critique that the agency was recycling information from the CIA or Israel's Mossad."[33]

In fact, all of the major conclusions in the annex were based on information or documents that can be traced back to Israel. A story in the *Jerusalem Post* published on the day the IAEA annex was made public revealed, "Israel played a key role in helping IAEA compile the report, and over the years, its intelligence agencies provided critical information used in the report."[34]

The report itself referred to several of the crucial documents as having come from a single "Member State." One of them was the purported "four-year plan" to study a "neutron initiator" that had been leaked to one of Mossad's favorite news outlets for publication of its intelligence claims, the *Times* of London, but had been rejected by US and European intelligence agencies.[35]

The intelligence information in the report about a large cylinder for explosives containment allegedly installed at the Parchin military testing reservation in 2000 for hydrodynamic testing of nuclear weapons designs and about alleged testing of a "multipoint initiation concept" for a nuclear weapon came from the Israelis as well.

The IAEA reported that it had been told by a member state that the construction of a large explosives containment cylinder had been done with assistance of a foreign nuclear weapons specialist.[36] That was a reference to Danilenko, the foreign specialist the Israelis had identified in the information provided to Heinonen in 2008 to confirm the authenticity of the document on the "multipoint initiation" experiments.

But the central question surrounding the story of the Parchin bomb test cylinder is whether the IAEA ever had any real evidence to confirm the Israeli intelligence claim that Iran constructed such a cylinder for hydrodynamic experiments. The report implied that it had two kinds of evidence: satellite photography and information about the cylinder itself. A careful

---

32. GOV/2011/65, annex, 3.

33. David E. Sanger and William J. Broad, "US Hangs Back as Inspectors Prepare Report on Iran's Nuclear Program," *New York Times*, November 7, 2011, A4.

34. Yaakov Katz, "IAEA: Iran Designing Parts for Nuclear Weapons," *Jerusalem Post*, November 8, 2011.

35. GOV/2011/65, annex, 11, para. 56.

36. GOV/2011/65, 10, paras. 49–51.

reading of the paragraph devoted to that implied confirming evidence reveals, however, that the information identified by the authors does not confirm the central claim at all.

The report states, "A building was constructed at that time around a large cylindrical object at a location at the Parchin military complex. A large earth berm was subsequently constructed between the building containing the cylinder and a neighboring building, indicating the probable use of high explosives in the chamber." Then it goes on to refer to "commercial satellite images that are consistent with this information." Satellite images being "consistent with" those statements is quite different, however, from the images actually *confirming* the claim.[37]

Months later, "an official of a country tracking Iran's nuclear program" gave Jahn of the AP a computer-generated drawing of what the official said was the explosives containment chamber at Parchin and said it proved the structure exists.[38] But that drawing merely underlined the fact that there was no actual visual evidence of such a cylinder at Parchin. Jahn said a "senior diplomat familiar with the IAEA's investigation" said a satellite image had shown a cylinder similar to the drawing. But IAEA lawyers would never have used the much broader phrase "consistent with" if the agency actually had photos of such a cylinder at Parchin. And Albright's ISIS, which had long published satellite photography on Parchin that US or Israeli intelligence believed suspicious, going back to 2004, failed to publish any such image.

The IAEA report refers to "independent evidence, including a publication by the foreign expert" that the agency said enabled it to "confirm the date of construction of the cylinder and some of its design features." Among the specifics it claimed to have confirmed were its capacity to contain up to 70 kilograms (156 pounds) of explosives and that it would be "suitable" for carrying out a multipoint initiation system test.[39]

Former senior IAEA inspector Robert Kelley was immediately struck by the fact that what little information was provided in the report on the alleged bomb test chamber didn't seem technically plausible. The report stated clearly that Iran had "constructed a large explosives containment vessel in which to conduct hydrodynamic tests." In a video interview a few days after the report, however, Kelley explained that a hydrodynamic test

37. The *Financial Times*, failing to notice that distinction, reported mistakenly that the IAEA had satellite pictures of the explosives container at Parchin. James Blitz, "UN to Show Tehran's Intent to Test Nuclear Arms," *Financial Times* (London), November 7, 2011, 6.

38. George Jahn, AP exclusive, "Drawing of Structure Said to Shed Light on Iran's Secret Nuclear Work," *Washington Post*, May 13, 2012.

39. GOV/2011/65, annex, 10, para. 49.

of a nuclear weapon design would have involved "far more explosives" than the 156 pounds claimed as the capacity of the cylinder at Parchin.[40] Kelley would go on to pinpoint other technical reasons for doubting the authenticity of the reported siting of such a chamber at Parchin.

Kelley's credentials for challenging the IAEA on the issue were second to none. He had been project leader for nuclear intelligence at Los Alamos National Laboratory before becoming director of the IAEA's Action Team for Iraq in 1992–93. He was director of the US Department of Energy's Remote Sensing Laboratory from 1996 to 1998, where his job was to know everything about detecting foreign nuclear weapons programs. He rejoined the IAEA to head its Iraq Action Team again from 2001 to 2005. Kelley knew as much as anyone in the world about assessing claims of foreign nuclear weapons-related technology.

The IAEA report also suggested that the cylinder at Parchin "would be suitable" for carrying out experiments on a "multipoint initiation system." As Kelley pointed out, however, the chamber was "far too small to contain explosive proof tests of a full-size mockup [of a nuclear weapon] and far too big to contain smaller tests of research interest."[41] And in an interview with the author, Kelley pointed out that a "multipoint initiation" experiment such as the one cited in the report doesn't use uranium, so Iran would not have needed a bomb test chamber to do it.[42]

The report also said that Iran had carried out "at least one large-scale experiment in 2003" using multipoint initiation technology, but it did not allege that the experiment had been conducted at Parchin. Instead, it said it had been done in the region of Marivan, which is close to the Iranian border with Iraqi Kurdistan.[43] In any case, a multipoint initiation system can be used for either a nuclear weapon or conventional explosions. Moreover, when Iran offered to take an IAEA delegation to Marivan to check out that alleged site in January 2012, the IAEA declined, suggesting that it had been given no information specifying a site in the area and had found no satellite image to support the claim.[44]

In its August 2012 report, the IAEA revealed more information about the Parchin cylinder issue that further undermined the credibility of the

40. "Former IAEA Inspector: Misleading Report Proves Nothing," Real News Network, November 15, 2011, http://therealnews.com/t2/index.php?Itemid=74&id=31&jumival=7594&option=com_content&task=view.

41. Robert Kelley, "The IAEA and Parchin: Do the Claims Add Up?" Stockholm International Peace Research Institute, May 23, 2012.

42. Author's interview with Robert Kelley, January 15, 2012.

43. GOV/2011/65, annex, 9, para. 43.

44. Author's interview with Iranian permanent representative Ali Asghar Soltanieh, Vienna, March 14, 2012.

whole story. "The location of the site was only identified in March 2011," the report said, implying that the original Israeli claim about the installation of the cylinder at Parchin in 2000 had not included a specific site.

The report also revealed that the IAEA had only "notified Iran of that location in January 2012" when it sought permission to inspect the site. Even more significant was the revelation that it had reviewed the satellite imagery available for the entire period from February 2005 to January 2012 and that the imagery showed "virtually no activity at or near the building housing the containment vessel." That evidence from satellite imagery appears to prove definitively that Iran had no need to get rid of any evidence of tests at the site, contrary to the IAEA accusations in November 2011 and since then.[45]

Albright and an ISIS co-author later published an article citing two satellite images of the site at Parchin shown in the same article as evidence supporting the IAEA's claim that a building at the site had been constructed "around a large cylindrical object." They claimed that one satellite image of the site where the nuclear test vessel was allegedly located, dated March 14, 2000, "shows the foundation of the building that would contain the explosive test," but asserted that the alleged explosives chamber was "not yet placed on the foundation in this image."[46]

But Kelley and three former US intelligence officers with long experience in image interpretation all concluded from an examination of the image that it does not show a foundation for a building, as Albright and his co-author claimed. Kelley, who obtained the March 2000 image in January 2013, told the author, "You can see the roof is already on." Retired Army Col. Pat Lang, who had been the senior intelligence officer for the Middle East, South Asia, and counterterrorism at the Defense Intelligence Agency from 1985 to 1992, said in an e-mail, "The 'foundation' casts a large shadow in the direction of the top of the picture as do other structures," but "foundations do not normally cast shadows." Another former intelligence officer with extensive experience in photographic interpretation, who asked not to be named, told the author, "The object looks elevated, like a roof." A third former intelligence officer, who also has many years of experience in image interpretation and who requested anonymity, said the March 2000 image shows neither a foundation for an eventual building, nor a roof, but simply a concrete slab. He said he found "no evidence of trenching or refilling, which is necessary for a foundation footing." The same officer said

---

45. GOV/2012/37, August 30, 2012, 8.

46. David Albright and Paul Brannan, "Early Satellite Image Shows Foundation for High Explosives Test Chamber at Parchin Site in Iran: What Was the Chamber For?" Institute for Science and International Security, April 10, 2012.

the structure shown in images from 2004 and later years published by ISIS was "much larger than the slab imaged in 2000." The same officer also said it was "not a substantial structure, like others at Parchin," suggesting it was more like "a shed."

Although Kelley and the former intelligence analysts drew different conclusions about what the image showed, they were in agreement that it didn't prove Albright's claim. Even more significantly, Kelley and the three other experts on image interpretation said that the Parchin site shown in the images did not even display any of the characteristics that would be associated with a high-explosives testing site, let alone those associated with a nuclear weapons testing site. "The building in question is not a classical HE [high-explosives] building, that is for sure," Kelley said, despite the fact that Parchin has many other buildings that do have "classical high explosive signatures." He and two other former intelligence officers pointed out that the building is far too close to a major divided highway to be involved in such sensitive testing activity, and it lacked any special security features that would be expected of a top-secret facility.[47]

## Turning Danilenko into Iran's Nuclear Test Guru

Nothing published by the IAEA on Iran's nuclear program illustrates more dramatically the agency's transformation into a highly politicized organization with an agenda than its treatment of Vyacheslav Danilenko. He is the scientist who was portrayed in the November 2011 report as the foreign adviser behind Iran's alleged nuclear weapons testing at Parchin. The IAEA alleged that "the foreign expert" was "not only knowledgeable in these technologies" but spent "much of his career" in a nuclear weapons program working with a "high speed diagnostic configuration" to monitor what it called "related experiments."[48]

Although the report did not reveal his name, Albright, who appeared to be serving as the IAEA's de facto spokesman in Washington, revealed to the news media that the unnamed expert was Danilenko and that he had worked at the Soviet nuclear weapons complex at Chelyabinsk for decades.[49]

The IAEA report claimed to have based its firm conclusion about the bomb test cylinder at Parchin on "a publication by the foreign expert," thus

---

47. Gareth Porter, "How a Nonexistent Bomb Cylinder Distorts the Iran Nuclear Issue," *Truthout,* July 2, 2011.

48. GOV/2011/65, annex, 8–9.

49. David Albright, Paul Brannan, Mark Gorwitz, and Andrew Stricker, "Iran's Work and Foreign Assistance on a Multipoint Initiation System for a Nuclear Weapon," Institute for Science and International Security, November 13, 2011.

appearing to suggest that Danilenko's publication confirmed that he did indeed help build such an explosive cylinder at Parchin. What Danilenko actually wrote in a book published in 2003, however, is that in 1999–2000, he had "designed" a cylindrical chamber specifically for nanodiamond synthesis. The sketch accompanying his text shows unmistakably that the chamber was only for that purpose. It had air and water systems necessary for the cooling of the tank before and immediately after the explosion, as well as a system for automatically unloading the diamonds produced. The sketch includes none of the fiber-optic cables that would be needed to measure the shock waves in a nuclear weapons-related test.[50] The cylinder designed by Danilenko clearly was neither intended for use in carrying out nuclear weapons-related testing nor "suitable" for carrying out such tests. The brazenness of the IAEA in claiming that Danilenko's design enabled it to "confirm the date of construction" of the cylinder allegedly installed at Parchin is stunning.

Even before the IAEA report was released to the press, Albright leaked an account of Danilenko's background and role in Iran to the intelligence correspondent of the *Washington Post*, Joby Warrick, aimed at smearing him as an adviser to a covert nuclear weapons program. Citing two sources "with access to the IAEA's confidential files," Warrick reported that Danilenko had "acknowledged his role but said he thought his work was limited to assisting civilian engineering projects."[51] That made it sound like Danilenko had admitted he helped Iran build the cylinder at Parchin but didn't know it would be for a nuclear weapons program.

George Jahn, the AP correspondent in Vienna, reported that Danilenko himself had denied any involvement in the Iranian nuclear program or having worked on a bomb test chamber, but claimed that Danilenko's son-in-law Volodymir Padalko had told IAEA investigators that an explosives containment vessel was indeed built "under Danilenko's supervision." Jahn cited as his source the same diplomats who had informed him in advance of the IAEA report that it included evidence of the explosives containment chamber—that is, the Israelis.[52]

Albright immediately included the claim that Padalko had implicated Danilenko in the Parchin cylinder in his talking points in defense of the

50. "V. V. Danilenko's Expertise in Explosive Chambers: Translated Selections from the 2003 Book *Sintez i Sekanie Almaza Vzryvom,*" tr. by Robert Avagyan, Institute for Science and International Security, September 16, 2012, http://isis-online.org/uploads/isis-reports/documents/Danilenko_book_translation_17Sept2012.pdf.

51. Joby Warrick, "IAEA Says Foreign Expertise Has Brought Iran to Threshold of Nuclear Capability," *Washington Post*, November 5, 2011.

52. George Jahn, "IAEA Shows Iran Nuke Program Intel to 35 Nations," Reuters, *Guardian* (Manchester), November 11, 2011.

IAEA's position on Danilenko.[53] But on the same day that Jahn's story appeared, Padalko, who was director of ALIT, a Ukrainian company that produced industrial nanodiamonds, categorically denied the self-serving story being peddled by Jahn's sources. He told the Moscow journal *Kommersant* that Danilenko had been in Iran in the second half of the 1990s "working in nanodiamond technology and giving lectures." Padalko said he had tried to explain to IAEA and State Department officials that "nanodiamonds have nothing to do with nuclear weapons."[54]

And Danilenko flatly denied the role attributed to him by the IAEA report and by the *Post*. In a telephone interview with Radio Free Europe he said the Iranians "proposed that [I] write a series of lectures on the dynamic detonation synthesis of diamonds." He said he had spent the six years doing that and nothing more, and denounced the IAEA's description of him as "black PR."[55]

The *Post* reported that the confirming evidence of Danilenko's involvement in nuclear weapons research was that he had co-authored a paper in 1992 describing "a fiber-optic instrument that measures precisely when a shock wave arrives along thousands of different points along the surface of a sphere."[56] That certainly sounded suspiciously similar to the instruments used to monitor the experiment the IAEA had reported. But the fact that Mossad miraculously acquired the documentary evidence of an Iranian high-explosives experiment monitored with fiber-optic cables at about the same time it discovered the existence of a foreign scientist who had written an article on monitoring explosions with fiber-optic cables should have been regarded as far more suspicious.

Warrick portrayed Danilenko as someone who had been a nuclear weapons specialist throughout his career and who had some knowledge of nanodiamonds only because of his nuclear weapons expertise. It was a clever way of discrediting Danilenko. But virtually everything that Warrick wrote about him was untrue.

"When the Cold War abruptly ended in 1991," he wrote, "Vyacheslav Danilenko was a Soviet weapons scientist in need of a new line of work." Danilenko had "one marketable skill," according to Warrick: "the ability to make objects blow up with nanosecond precision. Warrick implied strongly that Danilenko had admitted working on nuclear weapon-related

53. Albright et al., "Iran's Work and Foreign Assistance."

54. Sergei Strokan and Elena Chernenko, "Exclusive: Is This Why Russia Is Backing Iran on Nuclear Weapons Report?" *Kommersant* (Moscow), November 11, 2011.

55. Heather Maher and Mykola Zakaluzhny, "Former Soviet Scientist Denies Helping Iran's Nuclear Program," Radio Free Europe/Radio Liberty, November 16, 2011.

56. Joby Warrick, "Russian Scientist Vyacheslav Danilenko's Aid to Iran Offers Peek at Nuclear Program," *Washington Post*, November 13, 2011.

research. He wrote that Danilenko had "publicly acknowledged the sensitive nature of his work at Chelyabinsk" by writing in a book chapter that "the experiments he conducted were 'highly classified.'" Warrick portrayed Danilenko's knowledge of nanodiamonds as a "fortuitous discovery" as a result of such highly classified weapons-related research.[57]

What Danilenko had actually written, however, was that "experiments aimed at developing methods of diamond synthesis were highly classified."[58] The difference was extremely significant because, contrary to the suggestion by Warrick and Albright's institute, Danilenko's diamond-synthesis work was not highly classified because it reflected knowledge related to nuclear weapons. As Danilenko pointed out in another publication, detonation nanodiamonds had been discovered separately by three different groups of researchers at different Soviet research institutes in the space of 19 years, and at two of them—the Institute of Hydrodynamics in Novosibirsk and the Institute of Problems Materials Science in Kiev—no nuclear weapons research had ever been done. Danilenko recalled, in fact, that all three groups of researchers had discovered nanodiamonds while working quite deliberately on diamond synthesis by shock compression.[59]

The experience of the first American to discover nanodiamond synthesis, N. Roy Greiner, parallels that of Danilenko and other Russian researchers. Greiner told me that none of the work he did on the subject was ever classified. Greiner also worked in a nuclear weapons complex, Los Alamos National Laboratory, but he never did research directly connected with nuclear weapons in his long career there. He discovered nanodiamonds while working on a project called "Fundamental Research on Explosives," during which he conducted experiments at the Fraunhofer Institute in West Germany on how gases reacted to explosives at different temperatures.[60]

Danilenko's bosses obviously recognized that the technique he had discovered for diamond synthesis had very significant economic value, which they could keep to themselves by classifying the information. Greiner said he is inclined to believe that the original classification of Danilenko's experiments by his bosses was "for some commercial reason."[61]

57. Joby Warrick, "Russian Scientist at Heart of Iran Riddle," *Washington Post*, November 14, 2011.

58. V. V. Danilenko, "On the Discovery of Detonation Nanodiamond," in Olga A. Shenderova and Dieter M. Gruen, eds., *Ultrananocrystalline Diamond: Synthesis, Properties and Applications* (Norwich, NY: William Andrew, 2006), 340.

59. V. V. Danilenko, "On the History of the Discovery of Nanodiamond Synthesis," *Physics of the Solid State* 46, no. 4 (2004): 595–99.

60. Author's interviews with N. Roy Greiner, April 17 and 18, 2013. On Greiner's role in nanodiamond synthesis, see N. Roy Greiner, D. S. Phillips, J. D. Johnson, and Fred Volk, "Diamonds in Detonation Soot," *Nature* 333 (June 2, 1988): 440–42.

61. Telephone interview with Greiner, April 18, 2013.

Significantly, Danilenko's studies were declassified in 1987, probably because of the realization that other Soviet research centers had discovered the same technique.[62]

Albright simply ignored the evidence that Danilenko had begun his career working on diamond synthesis, had switched to nanodiamond synthesis after 1963, and for four decades had remained one of the most preeminent specialists on the subject in the world.[63] Albright tried hard for many months to unearth some evidence that Danilenko had worked on nuclear weapons during this 30-year career at Chelyabinsk, but his researchers found none. The only thing his institute could say in the end was that the work of Danilenko's part of the complex on the effect of shock compression on various metals must have contributed indirectly to nuclear weapons research.[64]

Albright emphasized the fact that Danilenko contacted the Iranian embassy and offered his services in 1995 and was then contacted by Seyed Abbas Shahmoradi-Zavareh, the head of the Physics Research Center, the organization identified by the IAEA as the "command center" of Iran's covert nuclear weapons work. The fact that Danilenko signed a contract with Shahmoradi-Zavareh, he argued, indicated that the scientist was really being hired to work on a nuclear weapons project, not on nanodiamonds. "Synthetic diamond production is unlikely to have been a priority," Albright wrote, "although it has obvious value as a cover story."[65]

The idea that Shahmoradi-Zavareh was running a secret military nuclear program, which US, Israeli, and European intelligence all believed for many years, was based entirely on the infamous telexes involving procurement of dual-use equipment in the early 1990s. It should have been discarded when Iran provided documentary proof that the dual-use equipment that Shahmoradi-Zavareh procured or attempted to procure had been requested and used by Sharif University departments.[66]

Albright's remark dismissing the idea that Shahmoradi-Zavareh could have been interested in Danilenko because of his expertise in nanodiamonds also turned out to be yet another overreach by Albright as a

62. Danilenko, "On the History of the Discovery," 599.

63. On Danilenko's role in the history of nanodiamond synthesis, both before and after his work at Chelyabinsk, see Olga A. Shenderova and Dieter Gruen, *Ultrananocrystalline Diamond: Synthesis, Properties and Applications*, 2nd ed. (Oxford, UK: Elsevier, 2012), 135–40.

64. Mark Gorwitz, "Vyacheslav Danilenko—Background, Research and Proliferation Concerns," Institute for Science and International Security, November 29, 2011; Mark Gorwitz, "Revisiting Vyacheslav Danilenko: His Origins in the Soviet Nuclear Weapons Complex," Institute for Science and International Security, September 17, 2012.

65. Albright et al., "Iran's Work and Foreign Assistance."

66. GOV/2008/4, February 22, 2008, 3–4.

publicist. An Internet search revealed that Shahmoradi-Zavareh had a very strong professional interest in nanotechnology. In 1998, he established a company called Ara Research that specialized in providing equipment for nanotechnology research. Fourteen years later, the company was still going, and Shahmoradi-Zavareh was still its chief executive officer.[67]

It was hardly a stretch for Shahmoradi-Zavareh to want to bring the original discoverer of nanodiamond technology, who had sought to promote the technology in a business venture in Kiev, to Iran for an extended stay. Nanotechnology was already on its way to becoming a central focus of Iranian technological development. By 2012, Iran was ranked 12th in the world in nanotech development, and it was the first nation to have a public program in nanotech education for schoolchildren.[68]

## The Pink Shrouds of Parchin

Less than two weeks after the November 2011 IAEA report, an AP story from Vienna indicated that the sources behind the Parchin bomb chamber story were already at work trying to prepare public opinion for a possible IAEA visit to the site. AP correspondent George Jahn, who had been the conduit for earlier Israeli leaks related to the IAEA and Iran, reported that an official of an unidentified state had "cited intelligence from his home country, saying it appears that Iran is trying to cover its tracks by sanitizing the site and removing any evidence of nuclear research and development." Jahn quoted from an intelligence "summary" provided by the official. "Freight trucks, special haulage vehicles and cranes were seen entering and leaving," the summary said, adding, "Some equipment and dangerous materials were removed from the site." Officials from other IAEA member countries disagreed with Jahn's sources, however, telling him that there was no evidence of an attempted cover-up by the Iranians.[69]

The Israelis were obviously beginning to think about a possible IAEA visit to the Parchin site in which they expected the inspectors to find nothing. The explanation would have to be that Iran had cleaned up the site to remove all evidence of the alleged nuclear-related tests.

---

67. The founding date of Ara Research is given on its website, http://www.ara-research.com/en/aboutUs.html. Dr. Seyed Abbas Shahmoradi-Zavareh was listed as the head of Ara Research when it exhibited at the National Forum, Export of Knowledge-Based Goods and Services in January 2012, 45. See http://diplotech.isti.ir/en/download/DaneshBonyanEn.pdf.

68. Julian Taub, "Science and Sanctions: Nanotechnology in Iran," *Scientific American*, January 13, 2012.

69. George Jahn, AP exclusive, "Alleged Iran Nuke Site Being Watched," AP, November 21, 2011, http://cnsnews.com/node/458943.

What happened at the site subsequently is intertwined with negotiations that were about to begin between Iran and the IAEA. It was only on January 29, 2012, that the IAEA informed Iran about the location of the alleged bomb test cylinder in order to request an inspection visit to that site during the delegation's three-day stay in Iran. That request was made in the context of the first round of negotiations on an agreement to resolve the issue of possible military dimensions of the Iranian nuclear program. During the three-day meeting in Tehran, a first draft of an agreement was discussed, and an IAEA inspection of Parchin was one of the items that Iran agreed to include in its commitments.[70]

The negotiating text committed Iran to "facilitate a conclusive technical assessment of all issues of concern to the Agency." Iran pledged to cooperate on a series of IAEA demands, including "inspections by the Agency" as well as "access to relevant information, documentation and sites, material and personnel." But the IAEA was insisting on a provision in the text allowing it to "return" to issues even after they had been resolved, which Iran was resisting, in the belief that it would subject Iran to "an endless process," according to Iran's negotiator, Ambassador Ali Asghar Soltanieh. IAEA director general Amano later confirmed to reporters that Iran had sought to require that the agency "present a definitive list of questions," thus "denying us the right to revisit issues, or to deal with certain issues in parallel, to name just a few." Iran was also demanding that the IAEA "deliver" all the intelligence documents alleging that it had carried out covert weaponization activities to Iran before Iran was required to give definitive answers to the allegation, but the United States had refused in the past to allow the IAEA to provide copies to Iran.[71]

The information the IAEA had given Iran on the location of the site where Israel had alleged a bomb test cylinder was installed gave Iran a way of trying to influence those negotiations. Two weeks after the February round of negotiations, the AP reported satellite photographs of trucks and other moving equipment at the Parchin site, which diplomats from the usual unnamed countries suggested could mean the beginning of Iranian "sanitization" of the site.[72] In May, Albright began to claim that Iranians were trying to "clean up" the site at Parchin, publishing a satellite image dated April 9 that appeared to show a stream of water from one end of the

---

70. GOV/2012/9, February 24, 2012, 2–3; interview with Soltanieh, March 14, 2012.

71. Gareth Porter, "Details of Talks with IAEA Belie Charge Iran Refused Cooperation," Inter Press Service, March 20, 2012. The still unfinished three-page draft text of an agreement called "Clarification of Unresolved Issues," dated February 20, 2012, is at http://www.armscontrol.org/files/IAEA_Structured_ApproachFeb2012.pdf.

72. George Jahn, "Iran Cleaning Up Nuclear Site?" AP, *Dubuque Telegraph-Herald* (Dubuque, IA), March 8, 2012. See also GOV/2012/37, August 30, 2012, 8.

building along its side. Albright wrote that the image "raises concerns that Iran may have been washing inside the building or perhaps washing the items outside the building."[73]

The implication was that this could be an effort to wash away traces of radioactive material used in hydrodynamic tests. But as former IAEA inspector Robert Kelley explained, that claim made no sense in scientific terms. "Uranium signatures are very persistent in the environment," he wrote in an article for the Stockholm International Peace Research Institute in May. "If Iran is using hoses to wash contamination across a parking lot into a ditch, there will be enhanced opportunities for uranium collection if teams are allowed access."[74] Both the Iranian Foreign Ministry spokesman and former Iranian nuclear negotiator Seyed Hossein Mousavian said the same thing. "The Iranians know very well they couldn't eliminate traces of such activities even after 10 years," Mousavian said in an interview.[75]

Iran was acutely aware that Western intelligence satellites were photographing everything that happened at the Parchin site. And it was in Iran's interest to make its agreement to such a visit more valuable to the IAEA in the context of negotiating the new agreement with the agency. Greg Thielmann, former director of the Strategic, Proliferation and Military Affairs Office of the State Department's Bureau of Intelligence and Research, observed that whether Iran had consciously intended it or not, the movements of vehicles and the stream of water were bound to "increase the interest of the IAEA in an inspection at Parchin as soon as possible and to give Iran more leverage in the negotiations."[76]

But the anti-Iran coalition continued to construct a narrative of stubborn Iranian efforts to hide the evidence of nuclear testing at the site. Another satellite image from May 25 published by ISIS showed two small buildings demolished and the removal of some soil from not far away. In June, IAEA deputy director general Herman Nackaerts, head of the agency's Safeguards Department, displayed satellite images to member delegations showing the stream of water, the demolishing of the buildings, and removal of soil at the site. Robert Wood, the US permanent representative, professed to be alarmed by the images. "It was clear from some of the

---

73. David Albright and Paul Brannan, "New Satellite Image Shows Activity at Parchin," May 8, 2012, Institute for Science and International Security.

74. Kelley, "The IAEA and Parchin."

75. Rick Gladstone, "Iran May Not Open a Site to Inspections," *New York Times*, March 14, 2012, A14; Mousavian quote from Gareth Porter, "Changes at Parchin Suggest an Iranian Bargaining Ploy," Inter Press Service, June 8, 2012.

76. Porter, "Changes at Parchin."

images that were presented to us," he said, "that further sanitization efforts are ongoing at the site."[77]

In fact, the physical changes had no bearing on the possibility of verifying the presence of evidence of past testing. In a careful analysis of the changes that had been made by Iran at or near the site in Parchin, Kelley wrote that Iran had changed the landscape in the vicinity of the building that the IAEA said contained the bomb test cylinder, leveling dirt piles some 500 yards (457 meters) away to the north. Kelley noted, however, that the area to the immediate west of the building had been "largely untouched," which suggested that the earthmoving had been for construction and renovation, rather than to hide any traces of contamination. Kelley further noted that a small building, apparently a garage, had been demolished to make way for a new road, and two other smaller buildings had been renovated. But the building of interest to the IAEA had been left standing.[78]

In mid-August 2012, the propaganda politics of the Parchin site took an absurd new twist. Albright published a new satellite image that showed what he said "appears to be pink tent-like material" covering the building suspected of holding the mysterious cylinder and part of one other building. Albright suggested that the objective of the covering "could be to conceal further cleanup activity from overhead satellites or to contain the activity inside."[79] Ten days later, Jahn reported that Iran had "shrouded a building that the U.N. nuclear agency suspects was used for secret work on atomic weapons, meaning spy satellites can no longer monitor Tehran's alleged efforts to clean up the site, diplomats told The Associated Press."[80]

It was clear from the satellite image, however, that the pink covering was not hiding the building from the world at all. Kelley pointed out that the material was pink Styrofoam insulation, and that it appeared that the buildings were being reroofed as part of the renovation of the site.[81]

In its report in late August, two weeks before the regular quarterly Board of Governors meeting, the IAEA said in a report, "Iran has been conducting activities at [Parchin] that will significantly hamper the Agency's ability to conduct effective verification." At the board meeting, Wood dramatically accused Iran of "systematically demolishing" the Parchin site and claimed

77. Fredrick Dahl, "'Very Clear' Signs of Iran Sanitizing Military Site, Western Diplomats Say," Reuters, NBC News, May 31, 2012; Porter, "Changes at Parchin."

78. Robert E. Kelley, "The International Atomic Energy Agency and Parchin: Questions and Concerns," Stockholm International Peace Research Institute, January 18, 2013.

79. David Albright and Robert Avagyan, "New Phase of Suspect Activity at Parchin Site," Institute for Science and International Security, August 14, 2012.

80. George Jahn, "Iran Shrouds Suspected Nuclear Site," AP, *Salt Lake Tribune* (Salt Lake, UT), August 24, 2012.

81. Kelley, "International Atomic Energy Agency and Parchin."

to see no possible explanation but an Iranian effort to eliminate traces of past nuclear testing in Iran's refusal to allow the agency to carry out an inspection there. "If Iran has nothing to hide," he asked, "then why did it begin altering the site as soon as the IAEA asked to visit?"[82]

But the IAEA's Amano was not really interested in a visit to Parchin at all. While pointing indignantly at the supposed cover-up at Parchin, the IAEA and its great power patrons were playing an entirely different political-diplomatic game. The United States, Israel, and the European three did not want another agreement like ElBaradei's "work plan," which explains Amano's adamant refusal of any limit on the ability of the IAEA to return to an issue of its choice regardless of what information Iran might provide.

So Amano's role was to keep Iran under accusation while economic sanctions severe enough to bring Iran to its knees were being applied by the US-led coalition, spurred on by Israeli pressures. The function of the Parchin issue was thus to allow the manufactured crisis over Iran's nuclear program to continue indefinitely.

---

82. GOV/2012/37, August 30, 2012, 3; "US Says Iran 'Demolishing' Facility at Parchin Site," Reuters, September 13, 2012.

# 11

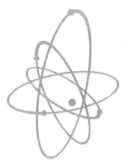

# Phony War Crises

In late May 2008, the Israeli air force carried out a two-week exercise called Glorious Spartan '08 that involved the entire force of 100 Israeli F-16 and F-15 fighters operating over the eastern Mediterranean and Greece. In the middle of the exercise, Deputy Prime Minister Shaul Mofaz issued the clearest and most belligerent threat of war with Iran that an Israeli official had ever delivered. "If Iran continues with its program for developing nuclear weapons," he declared, "we will attack."[1]

The week after the exercise was finished, the *New York Times* quoted Pentagon officials—not Israeli military officers, as might have been expected—as saying the Israelis were practicing the same maneuvers, including aerial refueling, that they would have to carry out in a strike against the Iranian nuclear program. The officials said one goal of the exercise was to "send a message" that Israel was prepared to carry out such a strike if all other efforts to stop Iran's nuclear program failed.[2] It appeared that the Pentagon was in on the Israeli planning for war against Iran.

That sequence of events triggered a widespread fear in the United States and Europe that Israel was indeed on the brink of war with Iran. The *Financial Times* regarded the threat and military exercise as sufficiently alarming to devote an entire page to two stories on it.[3]

But although Pentagon officials talked up the exercise as an indication of a serious threat of war, US intelligence officials who had studied the data

---

1. Reuters, "IAEA Slams Mofaz Remark That Attack on Iran Seems 'Unavoidable,'" *Haaretz* (Tel Aviv), June 6, 2008.

2. Michael Gordon and Eric Schmitt, "U.S. Says Israeli Exercise Seemed Directed at Iran," *New York Times*, June 20, 2008.

3. Roula Khalaf, Daniel Dombey, and Tobias Buck, "Israel's Threat to Strike Makes World Nervous," and "Olmert Weighs Cost of Any Attack," *Financial Times* (London), July 3, 2008.

from signals intercepts and radar tracking of Glorious Spartan were more skeptical. For one thing, they noticed that the Greek air force, which was supposed to have simulated Iran's defenses, had actually made little effort to intercept Israeli aircraft. One analyst concluded that the exercise was "essentially a sham," according to former US intelligence officer Matthew M. Aid, author of *Intel Wars*.[4]

In fact, the Israel Defense Forces (IDF) knew that it was not then capable of carrying out such a threat. Retired US Air Force Lt. Col. Rick Francona, who had visited Israel with two retired US Air Force generals in November 2006 and met with Israeli Air Force officials, told the author that the Israeli officers had acknowledged privately that the IDF lacked the capability to destroy Iranian nuclear sites. And Francona elaborated on the shortfall in a later interview. The Israeli officers "recognized they have a shortfall in aerial refueling," he said. The Israeli jets would have been "operating at about the limit of their range," which meant they could only carry two bombs per plane—not enough to ensure that they would destroy the targets.[5]

The Bush administration knew that as well. Earlier in 2008, Israeli prime minister Ehud Olmert had requested that the United States provide more powerful "bunker buster" bombs and refueling equipment, as well as permission to overfly US-controlled Iraqi airspace. That suggested that the Israelis knew they were unable to complete the mission successfully without the additional capabilities and full US support for the attack. The Bush administration never responded to the first two requests and gave a firm no to the third.[6]

After the 2008 Israeli exercise, four different studies by the Defense Intelligence Agency (DIA) and the CIA in 2008 and 2009 concluded that the IDF lacked the refueling tankers, bunker buster bombs, and electronic warfare capabilities necessary to carry out a strike on Iranian nuclear facilities. "The IDF had only a half dozen tankers capable of refueling their fighters," recalled Aid. "They would have needed five times that number to refuel all their 100 planes for such an operation." Francona confirmed that it had been the consensus view among intelligence analysts with whom he had spoken that the IDF had only five of the 24 tankers they would have needed.[7]

---

4. Matthew Aid, "Can Israel Attack Iran?" November 11, 2011, http://www.matthewaid.com/post/12692237199/can-israel-attack-iran.

5. Gareth Porter, "Israeli Realism on Iran Belies Threat Rhetoric," Inter Press Service, January 30, 2007; author's interview with Rick Francona, March 30, 2010.

6. David E. Sanger, "U.S. Rejected Aid for Israeli Raid on Iranian Nuclear Site," *New York Times*, January 11, 2009.

7. Author's interview with Matthew M. Aid, June 5, 2013; interview with Rick Francona, June 5, 2013.

The Olmert government's effort to sell the idea that it was planning to attack Iran was conceived by Defense Minister Ehud Barak. The reasoning behind Barak's 2008 war ruse was simple: the Bush administration, which was as friendly a US administration as Israel would ever get, would end in January 2009. So Barak was determined to take advantage of US help during the "favorable window of opportunity" of its remaining months in office to create the impression that Israel was preparing for an attack on Iran in order to increase the pressure on Iran.[8]

Secretary of Defense Robert Gates and the Joint Chiefs of Staff had already blocked a proposal by Vice President Cheney a year earlier to retaliate against Iran over some future incident in Iraq involving US casualties that could be blamed on Iran.[9] They were obviously in no mood to entertain any real possibility of any Israeli attack on Iran for the same reasons they had shot down the Cheney proposal: the fear of the unknown consequences of escalation. Nevertheless, Gates also believed it would be much more difficult to get Russian, Chinese, and European support for harsh economic sanctions against Iran unless they were afraid that a war was likely in the absence of effective sanctions. That was the reason Gates was upset by the National Intelligence Estimate of November 2007, which he believed took the military option off the table.[10]

The interests of Barak and Gates thus converged in summer 2008 on a scheme to simulate an Israeli preparation for war against Iran with the clear understanding that it was nothing more than a feint. And the Bush administration was happy to do its part to contribute to the impression of an Israeli attack threat to increase Iran's worries, although it couldn't say so openly.[11] The official position of the administration was the disingenuous claim that the United States had no control over Israel. Thus State Department spokesman Sean McCormick declared that the question of an Israeli strike is not "under our control."[12] But that claim is less than forthright, because Israeli decision making on the question of attacking Iran depended heavily on the United States.

8. On the "favorable window of opportunity" presented by the remaining months of the Bush administration, as seen by Israeli officials, see Ralf Beste, Cordula Meyer, and Christoph Schult, "Israel Ministers Mull Plans for Military Strike against Iran," *Der Spiegel*, June 16, 2008.

9. Gareth Porter, "Fearing Escalation, Pentagon Fought Cheney Plan," Inter Press Service, June 6, 2008.

10. Sanger, *Inheritance*, 4.

11. Peter Spiegel, "Risk to US Troops Seen If Israel Hits Iran," *Los Angeles Times*, July 3, 2008.

12. Dana Milbank, "Not So Quiet Third Front," *Washington Post*, July 3, 2008.

It was the beginning of a long campaign by Israel to create the impression that war against Iran was a serious possibility unless the United States and other powers were willing to force Iran to end its nuclear program. It was no accident that when Benjamin "Bibi" Netanyahu became prime minister again in 2009, he chose as his defense minister Ehud Barak, who had created the perception around the world in summer 2008 that Israel might be planning to bomb Iran's nuclear facilities within a matter of months. Together, Netanyahu and Barak plotted to keep the fear of an Israeli attack alive for nearly four years.

But it was all part of an elaborate deception aimed at manipulating the international politics of the Iran nuclear issue. The way the issue was covered by international news media, Netanyahu's war threat created tensions between Israel and the Obama administration. But in fact, Obama was from the beginning a witting participant in the phony Israeli threat of war.

## The Apocalyptic Netanyahu

The carefully constructed political myth of Netanyahu's fixation on the threat from Iran's nuclear program and on his role in saving Israel from the threat of extinction at the hands of the Iranian mullahs took shape even before he took over as prime minister. The pro-Israel American journalist Jeffrey Goldberg introduced that theme to the world in an April 2009 article reporting on an interview with Netanyahu shortly before he was sworn in as prime minister.[13]

Significantly, Netanyahu did not make any threat to attack Iran in the interview; instead he made it clear that he wanted the United States to "stop Iran from gaining nuclear weapons." But he portrayed Iran as "a country that glorifies blood and death, including its own self-immolation," adding, "You don't want a messianic apocalyptic cult controlling atomic bombs." Goldberg reported that Netanyahu's "principal military advisers" said Israeli timelines with regard to stopping the Iranian program "are now drawn in months, not years" and that Israel would not necessarily need US approval to launch an attack.

It was not only Goldberg who was getting such messages from Netanyahu's retinue. Aluf Benn, the editor in chief of the Israeli daily newspaper *Haaretz*, also wrote an article published on Netanyahu's first day in office that said "political circles" believed Netanyahu had "already made up his mind to destroy Iran's nuclear installations."[14]

---

13. Jeffrey Goldberg, "Netanyahu to Obama: Stop Iran—Or I Will," *Atlantic*, March 31, 2009, http://www.theatlantic.com/magazine/archive/2009/03/netanyahu-to-obama-stop-iran-or-i-will/307390/.
14. Aluf Benn, "Will Netanyahu Attack Iran?" *Haaretz* (Tel Aviv), April 1, 2009.

The Israeli military establishment generally supported Barak's strategy of seeking to convince the United States that the Iranian nuclear program was rapidly advancing to the point where it could no longer be stopped. US assistant secretary of defense Alexander Vershbow reported in mid-November 2009 that top IDF officials were arguing that the "window for stopping the program (by military means if necessary) is rapidly closing."[15] It was an unsubtle form of pressure on the Obama administration to take a more aggressive approach on Iran.

In a long article the following year, Goldberg further developed the theme of Netanyahu's commitment to the use of force if the Iran issue were not otherwise resolved. He wrote that he had interviewed 40 "current and past Israeli decision-makers about a military strike" and found a "consensus" that the chances were "better than 50/50 that Israel will launch a strike by next July." The evidence clinching the case that the Netanyahu threat was real, according to Goldberg, was the link between Netanyahu's view of the "existential threat" to Israel from Iran and his relationship with his then 100-year-old father, Ben-Zion Netanyahu. The elder Netanyahu had worked in his youth for the founder of the Revisionist Zionist movement, Ze'ev Jabotinsky, who promoted "Eretz Yisrael Ha-Shlema"—Greater Israel—a Zionist state that would include all territory west of the Jordan River to the sea. Ben-Zion Netanyahu famously considered all Arabs "an enemy by essence" with whom there could be no compromise. Goldberg cited the claim by a friend of Netanyahu's that the prime minister "worries that his father will think he's weak." Netanyahu is "different" from any previous Israeli leaders, Goldberg argued, because he sees himself in the messianic historical role of saving all Jews from another holocaust.[16] In fact, both Netanyahu and Barak had a set-piece presentation that each gave to visiting journalists and politicians emphasizing that they were personally responsible for "the existence of Israel."[17]

Neither Netanyahu's political history nor his actual performance as prime minister, however, supported the notion that he saw himself as a new messiah whose mission was to wage war against Iran regardless of the costs and risks to Israel. On the contrary, he had a well-established reputation in the Israeli political elite as an extremely risk-averse political figure whose public rhetoric was not necessarily matched by his eventual actions. Benn, the *Haaretz* editor, told me in a 2012 interview that Netanyahu was

---

15. WikiLeaks cable 09TELAVIV2482, US Embassy in Tel Aviv to State, November 16, 2009.

16. Jeffrey Goldberg, "The Point of No Return," *Atlantic*, September 2010, http://www.theatlantic.com/magazine/archive/2010/09/the-point-of-no-return/308186/.

17. Security journalist Ronen Bergman recounts Barak's recitation on that theme in "Will Israel Attack Iran?" *New York Times Magazine*, January 29, 2012.

perceived in Israeli politics as a "hesitant politician who would not dare to attack without American permission."[18] And a former Israeli official said that people who had worked under Netanyahu as well as under former prime ministers Ariel Sharon and Ehud Olmert had found Netanyahu "less decisive" on Iran than his predecessors.[19]

It was generally understood in Israeli political and security circles, moreover, that the IDF could not actually undertake an attack on Iranian nuclear sites without the active participation of the United States. Israel's security establishment, Benn noted, was arguing that "without a green light from Washington, Netanyahu and Barak will not be able to send in the air force."[20] *Haaretz* military analyst Amos Harel stated the Israeli dilemma starkly later in 2009. "It must be stated plainly," he wrote. "Israel does not have independent strike capability against Iran—not in the broad sense of the term." The Israeli Air Force, he said, could deliver "a certain amount of explosives to a given target and bring most of its aircraft back home intact," but it was "doubtful" that Israel could "act against the wishes of the United States" in regard to war against Iran. Nevertheless, the idea of an Israeli military option against Iran was vitally important, Harel concluded, to "prod the United States and Europe to exert more pressure on the Islamic Republic."[21]

That Israeli dilemma caused the security elite and the news media to remain generally silent about what they knew was an effort by Netanyahu to mislead the rest of the world. From time to time, however, prominent Israeli journalists alluded to the fact that Netanyahu's true policy toward war was not what he and Barak were suggesting. In a March 2010 article, Benn wrote that Netanyahu was "playing poker and hiding his most important card: the Israel Defense Forces' true capabilities to destroy Iran's nuclear installations." He credited Netanyahu with having "managed to convince the world that Israel is on the verge of preemptive war" and suggested that the prime minister could claim that his campaign was the reason Obama had adopted a much tougher line toward Iran.[22]

When Meir Dagan, the former chief of Mossad, broke publicly with Netanyahu's Iran policy in June 2011, a few months after retiring, it was the first crack in the security establishment's wall of silence on

18. Author's interview with Aluf Benn, Tel Aviv, March 20, 2012.

19. Author's interview with a former Israeli national security official who insisted on anonymity, Tel Aviv, March 21, 2012.

20. Benn, "Will Netanyahu Attack Iran?"

21. Amos Harel, "Israel Can't Launch Strike Against Iran on Its Own," *Haaretz* (Tel Aviv), December 30, 2009.

22. Aluf Benn, "Who Will Blink First in Iran's Nuclear Poker Game?" *Haaretz* (Tel Aviv), March 3, 2010.

Netanyahu's threat. Dagan criticized the policy of threatening to attack Iran because, he said, it "would mean regional war, and in that case you would have given Iran the best possible reason to continue the nuclear program."[23] He was saying publicly what virtually the entire security establishment knew was true but that most did not believe should be discussed publicly.

*Haaretz* senior correspondent Ari Shavit reflected that reluctance to criticize Netanyahu publicly when he took Dagan to task for having "eroded deterrence and brought up matters that are better left unspoken."[24] Yet later in 2011, Shavit revealed the Netanyahu subterfuge even as he defended it. He wrote that the threat to attack Iran "is crucial for scaring the Iranians and for goading on the Americans and the Europeans. It is also crucial for spurring on the Chinese and the Russians." And he concluded, "To ensure that Israel is not forced to bomb Iran, it must maintain the impression that it is about to bomb Iran."[25]

Yossi Alpher, a former senior official in Mossad and a former aide to Barak when he was prime minister, confirmed the reason the security elite remained quiet about the government's war threat. Netanyahu was "successfully bluffing and keeping the international community on edge, keeping the pressure on Iran," he told me in March 2012. Even though retired officials were overwhelmingly opposed to attacking Iran, Alpher said, "They don't want to spoil Bibi's successful bluster."[26]

## Obama and the Netanyahu War Ploy

President Obama appeared to be serious not only about negotiating directly with Iran on the nuclear issue and perhaps even on establishing a new relationship. He had made direct diplomatic engagement with Iran a major foreign policy issue during the 2008 US presidential campaign. And in the first weeks of his presidency, he even taped a video greeting to the Iranian people and "leaders" on the Persian New Year (*Nowruz*) that sought engagement that was "honest and grounded in mutual respect."[27]

23. Ethan Bronner, "A Former Spy Chief Questions the Judgment of Israeli Leaders," *New York Times*, June 3, 2011.

24. Ari Shavit, "Dagan Brought a Possible Attack on Iran Closer," *Haaretz* (Tel Aviv), January 20, 2011

25. Ari Shavit, "The Threat of Attack on Iran Is Needed to Deter It," *Haaretz* (Tel Aviv), June 16, 2011.

26. Author's interview with Yossi Alpher, Jerusalem, March 22, 2012.

27. "Transcript of Obama's Message in Celebration of Nowruz," *Wall Street Journal*, March 20, 2009.

But Obama's public stance was contradicted by what he actually decided during his first weeks in office. Only in 2012 was it revealed just how far Obama's real policy toward Iran had been from what the public had understood. That policy was closely linked to the aggressively anti-Iran policy of the newly elected Netanyahu government in three significant ways: First, Obama secretly authorized planning for a joint US-Israeli cyberattack on Iran's enrichment facility at Natanz. Second, he adopted a diplomatic posture toward Iran acceptable to Netanyahu in return for the latter's agreeing to a freeze on settlements in the West Bank. And third, he sought to exploit the Netanyahu threat to attack Iran to gain diplomatic leverage on Tehran.

Soon after his inauguration in 2009, Obama began meeting regularly with the cyberwarfare specialists from the National Security Agency (NSA) and CIA running the program called Olympic Games that had been initiated under the George W. Bush administration. And he soon approved the first specific cyberwarfare attack on Iran's enrichment facility at Natanz.[28] Obama was putting into action a program of cyberwarfare against Iran to which the US national security bureaucracy and Israel had both already become firmly committed. The program was the product of nearly three years of development by the NSA—the fastest growing national security bureaucracy in the still-expanding US national security universe—in collaboration with the CIA's Counter-Proliferation Division and Israel, which were jointly responsible for getting a computer virus into the Natanz plant.[29] It was the first national cyberattack to be aimed at the actual destruction of civilian infrastructure in another country.

Given Obama's public posture on Iran, one of the mysteries surrounding his policy was why he would have chosen Dennis Ross, well known in Washington as an aggressive advocate for Israeli interests, as co-director of the Iran policy review that Obama ordered soon after taking office.[30] Before joining the administration, Ross had openly advocated a policy of "engagement with pressure" not because he believed it would succeed in reaching an agreement with Iran, but because it would be a necessary step in preparing the ground for much more punishing sanctions. And Ross had

---

28. David E. Sanger, "Obama Order Sped Up Wave of Cyberattacks against Iran," *New York Times*, June 1, 2012.

29. James Bamford, "The Secret War," *Wired*, June 12, 2013; Ellen Nakashima and Joby Warrick, "Stuxnet Was Work of U.S. and Israeli Experts, Officials Say," *Washington Post*, June 1, 2012.

30. Trita Parsi, *A Single Roll of the Dice: Obama's Diplomacy with Iran* (New Haven, CT: Yale University Press, 2012), 54; author's interview with Reza Marashi, former State Department Iran desk officer, June 13, 2013.

told colleagues he believed the United States would have no choice in the end but to attack Iran's nuclear program.[31]

It turns out, as was later revealed by Peter Beinart, a senior writer for the *Daily Beast*, that Obama needed Ross because the president was primarily interested in getting Netanyahu to agree to an Israeli settlement freeze. Obama apparently calculated that he could get Netanyahu to agree to the settlement freeze as a quid pro quo for Obama's willingness to support a hard line on Iran. Obama had been led to believe that Netanyahu cared more about obtaining US support on Iran than about a settlement freeze. Having been told that Prime Minister Yitzhak Shamir had lost the 1992 election because of having alienated the United States, Obama thought Netanyahu would have to go along with such a deal.[32]

But Obama overestimated Netanyahu's willingness to give way on the settlements issue. The prime minister immediately pushed back, using his ability to manipulate Congress to support Israeli interests against a US president. In late May, just two weeks after Obama had insisted publicly that Israel had to freeze settlements in the occupied territories, the American Israel Public Affairs Committee (AIPAC) got 329 members of the House of Representatives—three-fourths of the total—to sign a letter to "strongly urge" Obama to "work closely and privately with our partner Israel, in a manner befitting strategic allies."[33] When he realized his miscalculation, Obama brought Ross over to the White House as a special adviser to help craft an approach on Israel and Palestine that would avoid a confrontation with Netanyahu.[34]

The idea of exploiting the threat of an Israeli attack for diplomatic leverage on Iran had been a fundamental element in the Obama administration's policy from the beginning. Obama's White House adviser on WMDs, Gary Samore, had advocated it quite explicitly before taking that job. At a symposium in September 2008, Samore had called the threat of an Israeli attack on Iranian nuclear sites "a good diplomatic instrument" for the United States. He concluded, moreover, that the next administration would not want to "act in a way that precludes the threat, because we're

---

31. Flynt Leverett and Hillary Mann Leverett, "Have We Already Lost Iran?", *New York Times*, May 24, 2009; Robert Dreyfuss, "Dennis Ross's Iran Plan," *Nation*, April 27, 2009.

32. Peter Beinart, "Obama Betrayed Ideals on Israel," *Newsweek*, May 11, 2012, http://mag.newsweek.com/2012/03/11/peter-beinart-obama-betrayed-ideals-on-israel.html

33. Parsi, *Single Roll of the Dice*, 167; Ben Smith, "Democrats Pressure Obama on Israel," *Politico*, June 1, 2009, http://www.politico.com/news/stories/0609/23207.html.

34. Beinart, "Obama Betrayed Ideals on Israel."

using the threat as a political instrument."[35] And Obama's choice for secretary of defense, Robert Gates, had supported the 2008 Israeli war threat.

On April 1, the very day Netanyahu was sworn in as prime minister, Gates, asked in an interview whether Israel would attack if Iran crossed an Israeli "red line," suggested that it could happen in "a year, two years, three years. It is somewhere in that window." And in congressional testimony the same day that appeared to have been coordinated with Gates, Gen. David Petraeus, head of the US Central Command, said, "The Israeli government may ultimately see itself as so threatened by the prospect of an Iranian nuclear weapon that it would take pre-emptive military action to derail or delay it."[36]

Obama's national security team was eager to promote the idea that Netanyahu was likely to take matters into his own hands, because they hoped to apply the Samore theory that the threat of war by Israel could be exploited to put pressure on Iran. Obama wrote to Supreme Leader Ali Khamenei in early May with a proposal to set up a separate bilateral channel to discuss a range of issues "without conditions," according to Samore.[37] But that didn't mean that he was ready to make a deal that would allow Iran to continue enriching uranium, or agree to relieve economic sanctions on Iran. Obama's March 20 *Nowruz* video message referred to Iran's "responsibilities."[38] That was an obvious reference to the existing US demand that Iran obey the 2006 UN Security Council resolution that called on Iran to carry out a "full and sustained suspension of all activities mentioned in this resolution"—referring to "enrichment-related and processing activities"—and demanded "compliance with all the steps required by the IAEA Board."[39] The requirement for compliance with IAEA board demands had already come to include Iran turning over classified information on missile programs and conventional weapons (see chapter 8).

Khamenei responded with a letter to Obama in late May or June, the gist of which has never been revealed by either government.[40] But

---

35. Transcript, "Iran and Policy Options for the Next Administration. Session I: The Nuclear Dimension and Iranian Foreign Policy," Council on Foreign Relations Symposium on Iran and Policy Options for the Next Administration, September 8, 2008.

36. Demetri Sevastopulo, "Israel Expected to Hold Back on Iran," *Financial Times* (London), April 1, 2009; Gareth Porter and Jim Lobe, "Obama Team Debates Stance on Israel Attack Threat," Inter Press Service, April 8, 2009.

37. Author's interview with Gary Samore, June 28, 2013. The timing of the proposal was reported as coming from an Iranian source. Barbara Slavin, "U.S. Contacted Iran's Ayatollah before the Election," *Washington Times*, June 24, 2009.

38. "Transcript of Obama's Message in Celebration of Nowruz."

39. See UN Security Resolution 1737 (2006), at http://www.un.org/News/Press/docs/2006/sc8928.doc.htm.

40. John Limbert, "The Obama Administration," *Iran Primer*, United States Institute of Peace, at http://iranprimer.usip.org/resource/obama-administration; Laura Rozen, "Ex Official: Obama Wrote Khamenei Twice, Ahmadinejad Wrote Obama Twice," *Politico*,

the primary point of Khamenei's response was that he rejected Obama's offer for unconditional talks, according to Samore.[41] Khamenei's public response to Obama's *Nowruz* message questioned whether Obama was free to make his own policy decisions on Iran, obviously referring to the overweening influence of Israel over US Iran policy, particularly through Congress. Khamenei rejected any effort to combine sanctions and diplomacy, insisting that the United States provide some indication that it had changed more than tactics in its policy toward Iran. The Iranian leader cited unfreezing Iranian assets and lifting sanctions as examples of such a change that Iran would regard as significant.[42] Khamenei's pessimistic reading of Obama's intentions turned out to be prescient. He could not have known that Obama had already approved the first major cyberattack on Iran, which was carried out in June, according to the evidence of the Stuxnet virus that could be gathered by outside monitoring.[43]

Furthermore, Obama was already preparing for much more serious economic sanctions against Iran if it did not accept the US proposal, a policy decision that clearly downgraded the role of diplomacy. In early March 2009, Daniel Glaser, acting assistant treasury secretary, was sent to Brussels to brief European Union officials on the Obama administration's "dual track" policy. Glaser's message was that "engagement" was most likely to succeed only if "pressure and incentives" were combined.[44] And in April, Secretary of State Hillary Clinton told the House Foreign Affairs Committee that the administration viewed "the diplomatic path" as a way to "gain credibility and influence with a number of nations who would have to participate in order to make the sanctions regime as tight and crippling as we want it to be."[45]

During summer 2009, Obama made a policy decision against serious diplomatic engagement with Iran. In response to a letter from Iran to the IAEA requesting help in obtaining a new source of fuel for its Tehran Research Reactor (TRR), which was well known to be producing isotopes

---

October 15, 2010, http://www.politico.com/blogs/laurarozen/1010/Exofficial_Obama_wrote_Khamenei_twice_Ahmadinejad_wrote_Obama_twice.html.

41. Interview with Samore.

42. For a translation of the Khamenei speech, see "OSC: Khamenei's Speech Replying to Obama," *Informed Comment* (blog), March 23, 2009, http://www.juancole.com/2009/03/osc-khameneis-speech-replying-to-obama.html.

43. Nicholas Falliere, Liam O. Murchu, and Eric Chien, "W32. Stuxnet Dossier," version 1.4, February 2011, *Symantec Security Response*, table 2, 8.

44. WikiLeaks cable, 09BRUSSELS536, US Mission EU to State, "AA/S Glaser Briers EU on Priority," April 8, 2009.

45. New Beginnings: Foreign Policy Priorities in the Obama Administration: Hearing on April 22, 2009, before the House Comm. on Foreign Affairs, 111th Cong., 2nd sess., testimony of Secretary of State Hillary Rodham Clinton, 19, 22.

for treatment of cancer patients, Obama adopted a proposal by Samore for what was called a "fuel swap." It called on Iran to ship out of the country nearly three-fourths of its stockpile of enriched uranium for a year or more in return for the promise of eventual supplies for the TRR. That proposal, which was unlikely to be acceptable to Iran, because it would deprive it of its key source of bargaining leverage, was self-evidently aimed at building support for sanctions after Iran refused it.[46] Two weeks before a meeting in Vienna of the United States, France, and Russia with Iran on the US proposal on October 20–21, 2009, a meeting of "Likeminded States on Iran"—the United States, its Western European allies, Canada, Australia, New Zealand, and Japan—was held without public announcement in Washington to discuss sanctions against Iran. The implicit premise of the meeting was that the Vienna talks probably would not succeed and the "engagement track" would be closed indefinitely in order to focus wholly on pressuring Iran by cutting off more and more of its international commerce.[47]

After the talks on the fuel swap failed because the Obama administration adopted a take-it-or-leave-it posture on its proposal, Obama immediately began working on a new round of international sanctions. The primary diplomatic concern was China, which had previously balked at such sanctions. The White House applied Samore's strategy of exploiting the Israeli attack threat to whip the Chinese into line on the sanctions issue.

Two weeks before Obama arrived in China on a state visit in mid-November 2009, he sent Dennis Ross and Jeffrey Bader of the NSC staff to Beijing to sell tougher sanctions on Iran to the Chinese. Their main message was that the United States would not be able to prevent Israel from attacking Iran's nuclear installations for much longer. After the Chinese agreed in late November to support a UN Security Council draft resolution that accused Iran of violating UN resolutions in constructing what the United States and the Europeans called a secret enrichment plant at Qom, the story of the Ross mission to China was leaked to the *Washington Post*.[48]

But the Obama administration had no reason to believe that Netanyahu would launch any such unilateral attack on Iran. During Netanyahu's first weeks in office, the Obama administration secretly sent CIA director Leon Panetta to Israel to obtain a pledge from Netanyahu and Barak not to

---

46. Leverett and Leverett, *Going to Tehran*, 359–61.

47. WikiLeaks cable 10ROME81, Embassy Rome to State, "STAFFDEL Kessler discusses Iran with MFA, ENI, PD," January 22, 2010.

48. Natasha Mozgovaya and Barak Ravid, "Obama Told China: I Can't Stop Israel Strike on Iran Indefinitely," *Haaretz* (Tel Aviv), December 17, 2009; John Pomfret and Joby Warrick, "China's Backing on Iran Followed Dire Predictions," *Washington Post*, November 26, 2009.

attack Iran without consulting Washington and had reportedly gotten such assurances, despite Netanyahu's rhetoric to the contrary.[49] And Obama's green light for cyberwar against Iran, his refusal to enter into far-reaching diplomatic talks with Iran, and his immediate shift to organizing the international coalition for sanctions against Iran had brought US policy toward Iran into fundamental alignment with Netanyahu's policy.

## Netanyahu and Barak at the Brink

Former Mossad chief Dagan was no dove. During his years as head of Israel's foreign intelligence organization, he had earned a reputation within the Israeli military and intelligence establishment as a hard-liner on both the Palestinian and Iran issues. It was Dagan who conceived and carried out a campaign of assassinations of Iranian nuclear scientists and engineers, ostensibly because they were involved in nuclear weapons work but actually to intimidate other Iranian scientists.[50]

A few days before stepping down as head of Mossad in January 2011, however, Dagan took the unprecedented step of arranging to take several journalists to a secret Mossad site for a three-hour, off-the-record briefing. He told them there was no need to contemplate the use of military force at that point, because Iran was still at least five years away from having a nuclear bomb—as it had been for two decades—that Israel lacked the capability to halt Iran's military program, and that an attack on Iran would be disastrous for Israel.[51]

In June 2011, Dagan publicly criticized Netanyahu's belligerent stance on Iran for the first time. As he explained it, when he was head of Mossad, he, the head of Internal Security Service Yuval Diskin, and IDF chief of staff Gabi Ashkenazi "could block any dangerous adventure. Now I am afraid that there is no one to stop Bibi and Barak."[52]

He did not explain that remark further. But in November 2012, the incident that had prompted Dagan to question Netanyahu's judgment was finally brought to light. The Israeli channel 2 program *Uvda* (Fact) broadcast a documentary reconstructing an episode sometime in 2010 in

---

49. "CIA Chief in Secret Israel Talks on Iran," Agence France-Presse, May 15, 2009; Aluf Benn, "Israel: U.S. Will Know Before Any Iran Strike," *Haaretz* (Tel Aviv), May 15, 2009.

50. Dan Raviv and Yossi Melman, *Spies Against Armageddon* (Cliff, NY: Levant Books, 2012), 11–14; Josef Federman, "Meir Dagan, Israel's Ex-Spymaster, Pans Netanyahu's Approach to Iran, Palestinians," *Huffington Post*, June 2, 2011, http://www.huffingtonpost.com/2011/06/02/meir-dagan-ex-israeli-spymaster-netanyahu-swipe_n_870638.html.

51. Ari Shavit, "Dagan Brought a Possible Attack on Iran Closer"; Bergman, "Will Israel Attack Iran?"

52. Bronner, "Former Spy Chief."

which Netanyahu had instructed Ashkenazi to put the IDF on the highest state of readiness for war, which is used only for an imminent attack. That was the account provided by "sources close to" Dagan and Ashkenazi—which appears to have meant the two former top security officials themselves. Netanyahu backed down only after Dagan and Ashkenazi opposed the order, according to the program. Dagan had called the move "illegal" because any move implying war required cabinet approval.[53]

The details of the episode revealed in the documentary make it clear, however, that it had been yet another effort by Netanyahu and Barak to convince the rest of the world of Israel's readiness to attack Iran and thus influence the United States and other powers on the issue of sanctions versus diplomacy. None of the sources suggested that those meeting in Netanyahu's security cabinet that day had discussed a reason for going to war. On the contrary, according to their account, after the meeting was over, as Dagan and Ashkenazi were leaving, Netanyahu "matter of factly" ordered the IDF chief of staff to put the military on the highest possible state of readiness for war.

Although military censors prevented the program from revealing the date on which the episode occurred, the evidence indicates that it was May 17, 2010, the day Turkish prime minister Recep Tayyip Erdoğan and Brazilian president Luiz Inacio Lula da Silva reached agreement with Iran on a fuel-swap deal identical to the one the Obama administration had proposed eight months earlier.[54] Netanyahu met with his "security cabinet"—also known as the "inner cabinet"—that same day to discuss how to respond to the development, which had clearly taken the Israeli government by surprise. There was no official response from Netanyahu or the Israeli Foreign Ministry, but the *Jerusalem Post* was told off the record that the ministers had concluded that the agreement was a maneuver by Iran to prevent the Security Council from agreeing on sanctions and that it would probably succeed.[55]

Netanyahu evidently believed there was a serious danger that the United States and the rest of the P5+1 group would go along with the fuel-swap deal. He and Barak were seeking to head off that possibility by raising the specter of an Israeli attack on Iran in the most convincing manner. Barak confirmed, in effect, that the state-of-war alert was intended to be a short-term bluff. He denied that "creating a situation in which the IDF are

---

53. "Security Chiefs Refused Order from PM in 2010 to Prepare Military to Strike Iran Within Hours If Necessary, TV Report Says," *Times of Israel* (Jerusalem), November 4, 2012. All quotes from the Israeli figures on the program are from this source.

54. For the background and details of the tripartite agreement, see Parsi, *Single Roll of the Dice*, 172–209.

55. "Gov't Rejects Iran Deal as a Ruse," *Jerusalem Post*, May 18, 2010.

on alert for a few hours or a few days to carry out certain operations forces Israel to go through with them."

Ashkenazi's statement on the program, moreover, seems to indicate that his problem with putting the IDF on a war-readiness status was not so much that he believed Netanyahu intended to attack but that it could easily provoke a military move by Iran. Ashkenazi was quoted as saying that such a move would create "facts on the ground that would lead to war."

Perhaps even more significant, however, Barak claimed on the same program that Ashkenazi had told him that the IDF did not have the ability to do what was being ordered. "Eventually, at the moment of truth, the answer that was given was that, in fact, the ability did not exist," Barak said, apparently referring to the ability to actually carry out an attack on Iran. It was entirely disingenuous for Barak to blame the IDF chief for the inability of Israel to actually carry out such an attack, because Barak himself had long known better than anyone else about the IDF's actual capabilities. Ashkenazi denied that charge, asserting that he had "prepared the option" and that "the army was ready for a strike," but that he had also said "a strike now would be a strategic mistake."

Dagan's later reference to a "dangerous adventure" by Netanyahu on Iran appeared to suggest that he believed Netanyahu actually intended to attack. But the danger of trying to use a state-of-war alert to spook the United States and other countries would have been enough in itself to justify his conclusion that Netanyahu was dangerously irresponsible. Dagan already held a grudge against Netanyahu for replacing him as head of Mossad in January 2011 because the January 2010 assassination of a senior Hamas official in Dubai had created serious diplomatic embarrassment for Israel.[56] Now Dagan had reason to argue that Netanyahu was unfit for leadership of the country and even a danger to it.

## Netanyahu's New War Crisis

The timing of both simulated Israeli war crises of 2008 and 2010 reflected specific external circumstances: the need to take advantage of the few remaining months of the George W. Bush administration in 2008 and the threat of the Iran-Turkey-Brazil fuel-swap agreement in 2010. And in late 2011, international developments again persuaded Netanyahu to intensify the threat of war.

This time it was the opportunity presented by the Obama administration's readiness to push for much heavier economic sanctions against Iran

---

56. Bergman, "Will Israel Attack Iran?"; Borzou Daraghi, "A Bumbling Mossad Hit Suspected in Dubai Assassination," *Los Angeles Times*, February 19, 2010.

only a few months after the last round had gone into effect. The IAEA was preparing a report consisting mainly of allegations of Iranian nuclear weapons work in early November that would serve as an instrument for pressuring Russia and China to support tougher sanctions, despite their public opposition to the idea. Netanyahu had long been pushing for "crippling sanctions" that would pressure European and Asian states importing Iranian oil to halt or dramatically reduce their purchases, thus dramatically weakening the Iranian economy. Now he was determined to make it happen.

But there was another factor that was equally or even more important to Netanyahu's plan. In summer and fall 2012, the US presidential election campaign would be under way, offering the single best opportunity for Netanyahu to manipulate US politics to pressure Obama to shift his Iran policy toward military confrontation with Iran.

That was the context in which the Israeli leaders made their first coordinated set of moves to heighten tension since 2010. In late October and early November 2011, they leaked to a number of Israeli newspapers that Netanyahu was seeking to persuade the cabinet to agree to an attack on Iran. The stories so obviously served the political interest of the Netanyahu government that some Israeli commentators warned that it could be disinformation aimed at supporting a new round of sanctions.[57]

In early November, *Haaretz* published a story taking up its entire front page that Netanyahu was seeking a majority in the inner cabinet for a strike against Iran's nuclear sites, citing a "senior Israeli official." The story also said there was still a slight majority in the cabinet against the proposal.[58] That carefully planted story came out on the same day as the test firing of a long-range Israeli missile, which Barak's office claimed had long been scheduled. The entire sequence was evidently part of carefully planned campaign to create what one Israeli analyst and former intelligence officer called "an atmosphere for the Security Council to impose harsher sanction against Iran."[59]

Later that month, Barak continued the campaign in an interview with CNN's Fareed Zakaria. He refused to say whether Israel was going to attack Iran but argued that Iran was entering what he called a "zone of immunity," in which a sufficient proportion of Iran's nuclear capabilities would be in sites protected from a potential Israeli attack, so that such an attack would

---

57. Dan Williams, "Israel Test Fires Missile as Iran Debate Rages," Reuters, November 2, 2011.

58. Barak Ravid, Amos Harel, Zvi Zraybiya, and Jonathan Lis, "Netanyahu Trying to Persuade Cabinet to Support Attack on Iran," *Haaretz* (Tel Aviv), November 2, 2011.

59. Williams, "Israel Test Fires Missile"; Samuel Segev, "Anti-Iran Strategem Bungled," *Winnipeg Free Press*, November 8, 2011.

be futile. Barak said he "couldn't predict" whether that point would be reached in "two quarters or three quarters or a year."[60]

Once the United States and the EU adopted sanctions against the Iranian oil-export sector and the Central Bank, however, the aim of the Netanyahu-Barak strategy shifted to persuading Obama to issue an ultimatum to Iran on its nuclear program. As Netanyahu prepared for a March 2012 meeting with Obama, a "senior Israeli official" told *Haaretz* that he would demand that Obama publicly state that he would use military force against Iran if it crossed Israel's "red lines." And he would accuse Obama of interfering in Israeli domestic affairs if US officials made statements suggesting opposition to an Israeli strike.[61]

A major element of the new phase of the campaign was to use Israeli and foreign news media to make the idea of an IDF attack on Iran appear perfectly rational. Barak had already set the tone for the campaign earlier by stating in late November that "less than" 500 Israelis would die if Israel were to attack Iran.[62] Then Barak persuaded Ethan Bronner of the *New York Times* to write a story in January 2012 citing "Israeli intelligence estimates, backed by academic studies" that "cast doubt" on the idea that attacking Iran would set off a "regional conflagration" and "sky-high oil prices." The purported intelligence assessments concluded that Iranian threats to retaliate were "overblown" and "partly bluff," according to the *Times*. But the story was clearly based on claims from top security officials working for Netanyahu and Barak. The *Times'* sources did not identify what entity had prepared the alleged assessments, nor did they offer any data from them on how many retaliatory missiles and rockets might land on Israeli cities. Indeed, the story provided no reason to believe that either Mossad or military intelligence had actually prepared any such intelligence estimates.[63]

In early April, Barak leaked to Israel's channel 10 an account of a briefing for the Israeli security cabinet on what was called a "worst case scenario" of war with Iran. The briefing predictably reassured the members of the cabinet that, after three weeks of "non-stop fighting," with "thousands" of missiles launched against Israel from Lebanon, Syria, and Gaza, less than 300 Israelis would have been killed, according to the report. The briefers

60. Transcript, interview with Ehud Barak, *Fareed Zakaria GPS*, CNN, November 20, 2011, http://transcripts.cnn.com/TRANSCRIPTS/1111/20/fzgps.01.html.

61. Barak Ravid, "Netanyahu Will Ask Obama to Threaten Iran Strike," *Haaretz* (Tel Aviv), February 29, 2012.

62. "Former Mossad Chief: Israeli Strike Will Lead to Regional War," *Haaretz* (Tel Aviv), November 29, 2011.

63. Ethan Bronner, "Israel Sees Bluffing in Iran's Threat of Retaliation," *New York Times*, January 28, 2012.

were also said to have referred to missiles that would be launched from Iran, but described Iranian missile capabilities as "limited."[64]

Normally such a briefing on a crucial national security issue would have been the responsibility of Mossad and IDF intelligence. But the briefers were identified only as "defense experts," meaning they were from Barak's own Ministry of Defense staff. That was a telltale sign that Barak could not get such assessments from Israel's intelligence services.

Iran's missile program had long been viewed by those who were not following it closely as being of little consequence in a war with Israel, as long as Iran had no nuclear weapons, because of its small numbers and lack of accuracy. But Uzi Rubin, who had been the head of Israel's missile defense program for nearly a decade before serving as the senior director for proliferation and technology on the Israeli National Security Council staff from 1999 to 2001, knew better. Rubin explained in a March 2012 interview that because of tremendous improvements in their precision in recent years, Iranian missiles now had the ability to hit key Israeli economic infrastructure and administrative targets and were near the point where they could even destroy Israel's relatively few airbases. "I'm asking my military friends how they feel about waging war without electricity," he said.[65]

Israel's Arrow anti-ballistic missile system, which Rubin had helped bring into existence, was often considered another reason not to worry about Iranian missiles. But Rubin acknowledged that although the Arrow system had an 80 percent interception rate in tests, it would not be that effective in an actual war. And in any case, the newest version of the system still had not been deployed.

It was hardly a secret by 2012 that Israel's military and intelligence leaders were in fundamental disagreement with Barak's effort to sell his happy-face view of war with Iran. Lt. Gen. Amnon Lipkin-Shahak, a former IDF intelligence chief and later chief of staff, noted that the Israeli security institutions had done little analysis of what would happen "the day after" retaliation by Iran and its allies, and that "almost the entire hierarchy of Israel's military and security establishment" was "apprehensive" about the "repercussions" of an attack on Iran.[66]

Gen. Shlomo Gazit, a former IDF intelligence chief, was even more outraged at Barak's hiding the reality of such a war. "An Israeli attack on Iran's nuclear reactors will lead to the liquidation of Israel," he declared. "We will cease to exist after such an attack." The main reason, he suggested, was its

---

64. "Report: Cabinet Hears 300 Would Die in Iran Strike," *Jerusalem Post*, April 3, 2012.
65. Author's interview with Uzi Rubin, Tel Aviv, March 21, 2012.
66. Kim Sengupta, "Israel's Military Leaders Warn against Iran Attack," *Independent* (London), February 2, 2012.

political impact more than its damage to Israeli society: Iran would use its power to disrupt the oil market to force the United Nations to pressure Israel on a Palestinian settlement returning to 1967 borders." Furthermore, Gazit predicted, such an attack would have precisely the opposite effect from what was intended, and Iran would "immediately become an explicit nuclear power."[67]

The Israeli intelligence community had never really been convinced, moreover, that Iran represented an existential threat to Israel. In a symposium at Tel Aviv University in 2009, yet another former head of military intelligence, Maj. Gen. Aharon Ze'evi Farkash, said Israel was not Iran's primary motive for seeking a nuclear weapons capability; it was to deter the United States from attacking to overthrow the regime. And Farkash maintained that Iran "had shown pragmatism and moderation whenever its survival was at stake" during its 30-year existence. Intelligence correspondent Ronen Bergman noted that Farkash's views were broadly representative of the intelligence and military elite.[68] The view of Iran and its nuclear program he articulated was so deeply imbedded in the country's security structure that even Barak publicly endorsed it. In a US television interview in November 2011, he said he would not "delude himself" into believing that Iranians are pursuing nuclear capability because of Israel.[69] Israeli intelligence had come around to the assessment of the US intelligence community on Iran's nuclear program. A prominent Israeli national security journalist, Ehud Yaari, wrote in late 2009, "The current assessment in Israel is that, although the Iranian regime long ago decided to get 'within reach' of a bomb and is doing its utmost to move toward that objective, no decision has been made to go for a 'breakout.'"[70] That was still the Israeli intelligence assessment in 2012.[71] And IDF chief of staff Benny Gantz even declared that he believed

67. Quoted in Sarah Leibowitz, "How the Day after an Israeli Attack on Iran Will Look," *Ma'ariv* (Tel Aviv) (in Hebrew), June 10, 2011, tr., by Richard Silverstein, *Tikun Olam* (blog), June 10, 2011, http://www.richardsilverstein.com/2011/06/10/an-attack-on-iran-will-end-israel-as-we-know-it/.

68. Ronen Bergman, "Letter from Tel Aviv: Netanyahu's Iranian Dilemma," *Foreign Affairs*, June 10, 2009.

69. Barak interviewed on the Charlie Rose show, November 17, 2011.

70. Ehud Yaari, *Iran's Nuclear Program: Deciphering Israel's Signals*, Policy Analysis no. 1597, Washington Institute for Near East Policy, November 15, 2009. The concept of "breakout" had no universally agreed definition, but it was generally understood to involve completion of the final stage of weapons enrichment of uranium in a relatively brief period.

71. Amos Harel, "Barak: Israel 'Very Far Off' from Decision on Iran Attack," *Haaretz* (Tel Aviv), January 18, 2012.

Iranian leaders were "very rational people" who he did not think would decide to build nuclear weapons.[72]

The military threat by the Netanyahu government was a very strange threat indeed. It did not reflect the view of Iran held by the leadership of Israel's national security establishment at all. But in that regard it was in line with the longer history of Israel's manipulation of a purported threat perception of Iran and its nuclear program that was vastly exaggerated for political-diplomatic purposes. And just as the Bush administration played along with the phony 2008 war crisis, the Obama administration sought to take advantage of the Netanyahu ploy to advance its own diplomatic strategy for Iran.

## A "Good Cop, Bad Cop" Routine

After Defense Secretary Leon Panetta's trip to Israel in October 2011, US officials leaked to the Israeli press that Netanyahu had failed to give Panetta an assurance that he would not order a strike against Iran without prior consultations with Washington.[73] That was the beginning of what the world's news media would cover for the next year as an intensified US-Israeli conflict over Netanyahu's readiness to go to war against Iran over its nuclear program. But in reality, the Obama and Netanyahu governments were playing out a "good cop, bad cop" routine over possible war on Iran.

Over the next three months, the Obama administration repeatedly sounded the alarm about the danger of an independent Israeli attack on Iran's nuclear facilities, as Obama and Netanyahu appeared to be engaged in intense maneuvering over that issue. On December 2, Panetta expressed concern that Iran would target US forces in the Middle East in retaliation for a war initiated by Israel. Three days later, Gen. Martin Dempsey, chairman of the Joint Chiefs of Staff, said in an interview with Reuters that he did not know whether Israel would give the United States prior notice if it decided to carry out military action against Iran.[74]

But Obama and Netanyahu were actually cooperating closely on a joint strategy aimed at a new round of much tougher sanctions against Iran and for building international support for it. The first step was to be an IAEA report that would accuse Iran, in effect, of running a covert nuclear

---

72. Amos Harel, "IDF Chief to Haaretz: I Do Not Believe Iran Will Decide to Develop Nuclear Weapons," *Haaretz* (Tel Aviv), April 25, 2012.

73. Barak Ravid, "U.S. Officials: Israel Refused to Commit to Withhold Surprise Attack on Iran," *Haaretz* (Tel Aviv), November 8, 2011.

74. Phil Stewart and Mark Hosenball, "Analysis—US Ramps Up Warnings on Iran Strike Risks," Reuters, December 5, 2011.

weapons program. The Israeli objective in providing "critical information" for the IAEA report was to "push through a new regime of sanctions" aimed at the Central Bank of Iran and Iran's oil export sector.[75] Barak said Israel had "not decided to embark on any operation," implicitly recognizing that the next phase of pressure on Iran would center on economic sanctions. And both Israeli and US responses to the IAEA report issued November 8, 2011, anticipated that it would help mobilize such support for new sanctions.[76]

The Obama administration was initially uncertain about whether to support the Israeli proposal to target Iran's Central Bank and Iran's oil exports, but the Israel lobby in the United States forced the issue. The Foundation for Defense of Democracies, a Washington, DC-based organization whose policy positions are closely aligned with the Likud Party, had drafted legislation mandating such sanctions, and AIPAC was already mobilizing support in Congress to pass it. Then, on December 2, the Senate passed legislation mandating sanctions against Iran's Central Bank and the export sector by a vote of 94 to 0.[77] The administration knew that Israel was committed to seeing how those sanctions would play out in Iranian policy.

The larger Obama administration political strategy, therefore, was to use the threat of an Israeli attack on Iran to increase the pressure on Russia and China to support these tougher sanctions. The good cop, bad cop routine over the long-running Netanyahu threat to Iran was part of an effort to hold together an extremely tenuous international coalition supporting economic sanctions against Iran as well as to increase the pressure on Iran to make concessions on enrichment at the negotiating table.

The leak by US officials to the Israeli press about Panetta's trip to Israel was not aimed at putting pressure on Netanyahu to set aside the idea of attacking Iran. It focused solely on the unwillingness of Israel to provide warning of any attack. A story that was circulating in US military circles in late 2011 about a meeting in early November between Obama and two top military officers—Joint Chiefs Chairman Dempsey and Gen. James N. Mattis, the new head of the Central Command—suggested that Obama was positioning the United States for the diplomatic campaign on Iran

---

75. Yaakov Katz and Reuters, "Some Intelligence in IAEA Report Came from Israel," *Jerusalem Post*, November 8, 2011. As discussed in chapter 10, Israel was the source of all the sensational information in the report suggesting a covert Iranian nuclear weapons program.

76. David E. Sanger and William J. Broad, "UN Agency Says Iran Data Points to A-Bomb Work," *New York Times*, November 8, 2011; Harriet Sherwood, "IAEA Report: Sanctions Likely as Fear Grows over Israeli Action," *Guardian* (Manchester), November 8, 2011.

77. Jim Lobe, "US Senate Passes New Sanctions on Iran," Inter Press Service, December 2, 2012.

sanctions and for negotiations with Iran. Dempsey and Mattis expressed their disappointment that the president had not been firm enough in opposing an Israeli attack on Iran, according to the story told by a military source to veteran journalist Richard Sale. But Obama responded that he "had no say over Israel" because "it is a sovereign country."[78] That was the same line that the Bush administration had taken in mid-2008 about the Israeli feint toward war. It was aimed at convincing Iran, Russia, and China—and perhaps some Europeans as well—that the United States couldn't restrain Israel from attacking Iran.

Obama administration officials were conveying the same line privately to their contacts in late 2011. One Washington insider said administration officials were saying that Obama couldn't tell Israel the United States would not come to Israel's aid if it launched on attack on Iran, because the administration would then lose its influence over Israeli policymaking. Trita Parsi, author of the definitive study of strategic interactions among the United States, Israel, and Iran, heard a similar account of Obama's policy toward the purported Israeli unilateral attacks threat from two knowledgeable sources that same month. "Obama has the view that he won't interfere," he told me, "and that he will convince the world that he has nothing to do with a possible Israeli attack."[79]

In taking that line, the Obama administration was deliberately denying the actual leverage that any US administration has on Israeli policy. By 2012, the CIA, the DIA, air force intelligence, and the director of national intelligence had prepared as many as a dozen intelligence assessments since mid-2008 on a possible Israeli strike on Iranian nuclear facilities, most of which had shown clearly that the IDF lacked the capability to carry out a significant strike against Iran without direct US involvement, according to former intelligence officer Matthew Aid.[80] And as Goldberg had reported based on his conversations with Israeli officials, if Obama were to learn about the strike in advance and demand that Israel desist from such a strike, several former Israeli officials believed the Israeli government would have to back down.[81]

The Obama administration's use of the Israeli war threat for political-diplomatic purposes surfaced again in mid-January 2012, when the

78. Richard Sale, "What Israel's War against Iran Would Look Like," *Truthout* (blog), December 8, 2012, http://www.truth-out.org/news/item/5483:what-israels-war-against-iran-would-look-like.

79. Interview with an arms-control specialist from a non-governmental organization who asked to remain anonymous, December 13, 2011; interview with Trita Parsi, National Iranian-American Council, December 14, 2011.

80. Matthew M. Aid, personal communication to the author, June 6, 2013.

81. Goldberg, "Point of No Return."

US-Israeli joint military exercise Austere Challenge '12, scheduled for sometime in the spring, was abruptly postponed. The initial official explanation from both sides for the postponement of an exercise to test the integration of US radar with the Israeli missile-defense system against a ballistic missile attack was that it was a joint decision.[82] But then Laura Rozen at Yahoo News reported that Barak had requested the postponement and US defense officials were "privately concerned that the Israeli request for a postponement of the exercise could be one potential warning sign that Israel is trying to leave its options open for conducting a strike on Iran's nuclear facilities in the spring."[83] The premise of that leak from the Pentagon was that Netanyahu and Barak would not want US troops in the country during such a strike against Iran. But the most plausible explanation for US officials expressing fear that the cancellation was part of a unilateral Israeli war plan is that it was an opportunity to increase Iranian—and perhaps Russian and Chinese—anxiety about a possible Israeli attack.

The credibility of that interpretation is strengthened by the way Panetta used *Washington Post* columnist David Ignatius in an even more obvious effort to exploit the Israeli threat just two weeks later. Ignatius reported February 1 that Panetta believed there was a "strong likelihood that Israel will strike Iran in April, May or June." Ostensibly, it was another expression of alarm at the Israeli government's readiness to act alone against Iran. Panetta suggested to Ignatius that Barak had identified this period when Iran would have entered the so-called zone of immunity, in which some unknown proportion of Iran's uranium enrichment assets would have been moved to sites deep underground that would be invulnerable to Israeli attack.[84]

But in fact, Barak had not singled out the April–June period in his November CNN interview. On the contrary, he had said he "couldn't predict" whether the point at which a decision on war would be reached would be in "two quarters or three quarters or a year."[85] Panetta's invocation of that period appears to have been an effort to take advantage of the July 1, 2012, date on which sanctions previously decided by the European Union

82. Yaakov Katz, "Joint U.S.-Israel Missile Drill Delayed," *Jerusalem Post*, January 15, 2012.

83. Laura Rozen, "Israel Requests Delay in U.S.-Israel Missile Defense Exercise," Yahoo News, January 15, 2012, http://news.yahoo.com/blogs/envoy/israel-requests-delay-us-israel-missile-defense-exercise-235400130.html.

84. David Ignatius, "Is Israel Preparing to Attack Iran?" *Washington Post*, February 2, 2012.

85. Zakaria interview with Barak. Two weeks earlier, Barak had said that the Israeli government had "no date for making decisions" on a possible attack on Iran, and that "the whole thing is very far off." Joel Greenberg, "Barak Says Israeli Decision on Iran Strike Remains 'Far Off,'" *Washington Post*, January 18 2012.

were scheduled to go into effect to increase the pressure on the Iranians to try to negotiate a deal in advance of that date.

"Israeli leaders are said to accept, and even welcome, the prospect of going it alone and demonstrating their resolve," Ignatius wrote. He quoted an unnamed Israeli official as saying, "You stand to the side and let us do it." That was patently false, because neither Netanyahu nor Barak wanted to "go it alone" on Iran; they schemed over the spring and summer to manipulate Obama to take responsibility for threatening Iran.

Then came an explicit giveaway of the real purpose of the leak: "U.S. officials see two possible ways to dissuade the Israelis from such an attack," Ignatius wrote. "Tehran could finally open up serious negotiations for a formula to verifiably guarantee that its nuclear program will remain a civilian one, or the United States could step up its covert actions to degrade the program so much that Israelis would decide that military action wasn't necessary."[86] That language left little room for doubt that Panetta was really trying to use the threat of an Israeli attack to get Iran back to the negotiating table and then to wrest bigger concessions from it. The P5+1 had agreed in October 2011 to a letter to Iran offering another series of negotiating sessions, but Iran had not yet responded.[87]

## Netanyahu's Maneuver Fails

Nearly two weeks after the Ignatius piece ran, however, Iran agreed to resume the nuclear talks with the P5+1.[88] The two sides quickly agreed to a series of meetings in various capitals, beginning with a round in Istanbul in April. At that point, the good cop, bad cop routine ended, and Israel began a new phase of pressuring Obama.

Netanyahu's maximum objective had always been to maneuver Obama into adopting Israel's red lines and agreeing to threaten Iran with US military action if it did not curb its enrichment program. Netanyahu could aspire to such an aggressively warlike objective only because Israel had enjoyed virtual control over congressional actions on Iran for so long through AIPAC. AIPAC could mobilize majorities in both houses of Congress for positions that would pressure Obama to accept Netanyahu's red lines as well.

Netanyahu's ability to use the power of the Israel lobby to manipulate the US political context of Iran policy was dramatically displayed in May

86. Ignatius, "Is Israel Preparing to Attack Iran?"

87. Fredrik Dahl, "Iran Nuclear Talks Could Resume Soon—EU's Ashton," Reuters, October 21, 2012.

88. Fredrik Dahl, "Iran Wants Early Resumption of Nuclear Talks: Letter," Reuters, February 16, 2012.

2012, when the House of Representatives passed by a vote of 401 to 11 an AIPAC-sponsored resolution affirming that it is US policy to prevent Iran from acquiring a "nuclear weapons capability."[89] The clear implication was that the United States should be prepared to use force if Iran moved beyond some ill-defined point of enrichment.

Just before the Moscow round of talks between the P5+1 and Iran on June 18 and 19, 2012, an AIPAC-drafted letter from 44 senators, evenly divided between Democrats and Republicans, urged Obama to "reconsider talks with Iran unless it agrees to immediate steps to curb its enrichment activity." That letter called for the United States to shift its policy from further negotiations to "significantly increasing the pressure on Iran through sanctions and making it clear that a credible military option exists." The letter went on to specify a set of demands on Iran in the talks that precisely paralleled those Israel had presented directly to the United States.[90] The knowledge that Congress could be used in that way had undoubtedly influenced the administration's acceptance of all those Israeli demands on US negotiators in late March in return for Israel's agreement to postpone the demand for a complete halt to all enrichment until a later stage of negotiations.[91]

For Netanyahu, the overwhelming congressional endorsement of his position on diplomacy and the military option was the anvil of his strategy for gaining control over Obama's policy. He hoped that the hammer would be an aggressive Republican challenge to Obama's policy toward Iran during the presidential election campaign. Barak had deliberately pointed in the November 2011 interview with CNN to summer and fall 2012 as the time when Israel would have to make a decision on Iran. When Mitt Romney clinched the Republican presidential nomination over the summer, Netanyahu hoped he would harshly criticize Obama for refusing to accept Israel's red line. The hope was based in large part on the fact that casino mogul Sheldon Adelson, an unabashed champion of Likud Party interests who had been Netanyahu's own primary financial backer for many years, was expected to plow as much as $100 million into Romney's campaign to defeat Obama.[92]

---

89. "Prevent Iranian Nuclear Weapons Capability," AIPAC website, http://www.aipac.org/learn/legislative-agenda/agenda-display?agendaid=%7B849C4482-D843-489E-B13C-4FDD77BB21D3%7D.

90. Jewish Telegraph Agency, "Senators: US Must Rethink Talks If Iran Doesn't Act," *Jerusalem Post*, June 16, 2012.

91. Gareth Porter, "U.S.-Israel Deal to Demand Qom Closure Threatens Nuclear Talks," Inter Press Service, April 12, 2012.

92. Clare O'Connor, "Sheldon Adelson Tops Romney Donor List That Now Includes 32 Billionaires," *Forbes*, June 13, 2012.

Netanyahu and Barak carefully choreographed the set-up for their ultimate aim—a deal with Obama to ratify his shift to Netanyahu's red line on Iran in return for dropping the prime minister's supposed plan for an attack on Iran. During the second week in August, they leaked stories to the Israeli press suggesting that Netanyahu had all but made the decision to attack Iran in the fall.[93] Then on August 10, two weeks before the Republican National Convention began, an official whom interviewer Ari Shavit identified as "a key figure in the security establishment"—obviously Barak—stated explicitly for the first time that the Netanyahu government's military option was primarily aimed at influencing US policy. "If Israel forgoes the chance to act and it becomes clear it no longer has the power to act," the anonymous official said, "the likelihood of an American action will decrease." The official suggested that Netanyahu was now prepared to offer a "compromise" to Obama, explaining that it was not realistic to expect the United States to "say clearly that, if by next spring, the Iranians still have a nuclear program, they will destroy it."[94]

The compromise formula came a few days later in an interview published by YNet News with an unnamed "senior official" who sounded very much like the same one interviewed by Shavit. The official said Obama would not have to threaten to go to war by a certain date if he would simply accept Netanyahu's red line that Iran must not be allowed to have the enrichment capability for a bomb. Israel would consider it as "a virtual commitment by the U.S. to act militarily if needed" and would "reconsider its unilateral measures and coordinate them" with Washington.[95] The same message was conveyed directly to the US ambassador to the United Nations Susan Rice, according to a story leaked to the conservative daily *Ma'ariv*, which often published leaks from Netanyahu government officials.[96]

But the next few weeks did not unfold at all the way Netanyahu had imagined. First, the Republican convention failed to make the Obama refusal to endorse Netanyahu's red line a central campaign issue. Presumably with an eye to polling data showing that the American voter was not going to support anything that smacked of yet another war, Romney and his advisers gave the main speech on foreign policy to former secretary of state

---

93. Jodi Rudoren, "Israeli Minister Asks Nations to Say Iran Talks Have Failed," *New York Times*, August 12, 2012.

94. Ari Shavit, "A Grave Warning on Iran from 'The Decisionmaker,'" *Haaretz* (Tel Aviv), August 11, 2012.

95. Ron Ben-Yishai, "Israeli Demands from Obama," YNet News, August 15, 2012, http://www.ynetnews.com/articles/0,7340,L-4268683,00.html.

96. Eli Bronstein, "Israel Demands Obama Declaration to Act Militarily against Iran," *Ma'ariv* (Tel Aviv) (in Hebrew), August 14, 2012.

Condoleezza Rice rather than to a hard-line neoconservative who would take a belligerent posture on Iran.[97]

After the GOP convention, Obama immediately sent a series of signals that he had no intention of accommodating Netanyahu—signals that he had chosen not to send in late 2011 and early 2012. On August 30, General Dempsey, talking to reporters in London, made the usual US point about a strike on Iran by Israel being ineffective, but then added, "I don't want to be complicit if they choose to do it."[98] It was the first time that a senior US official had made such an explicit statement indicating the Obama administration's refusal to be a party to a war provoked by a unilateral Israeli attack. Giora Eiland, who had been Ariel Sharon's national security adviser, viewed that statement as fundamentally altering the dynamics of the relationship, because Israeli leaders "cannot do anything in the face of a very explicit 'no' from the U.S. president." Netanyahu, he pointed out, had been arguing all year that the US "might not like" an Israeli attack but that it would "accept it the day after." Now all that had changed. "Such a public, bold statement," Eiland said, "meant the situation had to be reassessed."[99]

The Dempsey statement was apparently the opening move in a determined Obama counteroffensive against Netanyahu's strategy of pressure. In an interview with Bloomberg Radio on September 9, Secretary of State Clinton declared flatly, "We're not setting deadlines." That provoked an outburst by Netanyahu two days later. "Those in the international community who refuse to put red lines before Iran don't have a moral right to place a red light before Israel," he declared to the press.[100] That same night, Obama called Netanyahu to discuss the issue one on one for a full hour, according to a "senior administration official." During the conversation, Obama flatly rejected Netanyahu's two proposed red lines: a numerical limit on the amount of uranium enriched to the 20 percent level that Iran would be allowed and a limit on how long the United States would wait for Iran to comply with its negotiating demands.[101]

Meanwhile, the two sides had been maneuvering over the question of a meeting between Netanyahu and Obama during the prime minister's visit

97. Jim Lobe and Gareth Porter, "After Dempsey Warning, Israel May Curb War Threat," Inter Press Service, September 5, 2012.

98. Richard Norton-Taylor, "Israeli Attack on Iran Wouldn't Stop Nuclear Programme," Guardian (Manchester), August 30, 2012.

99. Crispian Balmer, "Analysis: Chastised Israel Seeks Way Forward with U.S. over Iran," Reuters, September 4, 2012.

100. Jeffrey Heller, "U.S. Has No Right to Block Israel on Iran: Netanyahu," Reuters, September 11, 2012.

101. Mark Landler and Helene Cooper, "Obama Rebuffs Netanyahu on Setting Limits on Iran's Nuclear Program," New York Times, September 13, 2012.

to the United States later that month. Netanyahu had been unable to get on Obama's schedule either during the meeting of the UN General Assembly or later in Washington. The White House cited "scheduling conflicts," and both sides initially denied Obama was snubbing Netanyahu. The day after the Obama telephone call to Netanyahu, an unnamed "senior official" in Jerusalem accused the White House of lying on the matter. But Netanyahu declined to make such an accusation on NBC's *Meet the Press* a few days later.[102]

In his speech to the UN General Assembly on September 27, Netanyahu gave no hint of any threat to take unilateral action against Iran if the United States refused to adopt his position. He drew a red line at an amount of uranium enriched to 20 percent that would be necessary for a nuclear bomb, which he said would be reached by summer 2013 at the latest. But he drew the line on a cartoon bomb that was inevitably likened to the Wile E Coyote ACME bomb of the Looney Tunes Road Runner series. Jeffrey Goldberg tweeted that Netanyahu had "turned a serious issue into a joke."[103]

Two weeks after Netanyahu's use of a bizarre prop in his UN speech came another sign that the long, phony war campaign was finally coming to an end. Israeli defense sources were quoted in a story in *Haaretz* as citing evidence that far from racing for a bomb, Iran appeared to be doing the opposite. "On a number of occasions in the recent past," the defense sources said, Iran had allocated uranium from its stockpile enriched to 20 percent to the manufacture of fuel rods for a research reactor in Tehran, which it said was manufacturing isotopes "for cancer treatment." That meant that the higher enriched uranium would not be available for further enrichment.

Netanyahu was no longer looking for a justification for attacking Iran. Instead, for the first time, Israel was taking note of an Iranian move to demonstrate restraint. Buried deep in the report by *Haaretz* on this unprecedented development was the real story: Netanyahu had backtracked from his threat because of the Obama administration's opposition and the

---

102. Yitzhak Benhorin, "White House Denies Obama Snubbed Netanyahu," Ynet News, September 11, 2012; "Jerusalem Official Accuses White House of Lying about Requested Netanyahu-Obama meeting," *Times of Israel* (Jerusalem), September 12, 2012; Office of the Prime Minister, Interview with David Gregory, *Meet the Press*, NBC, September 15, 2012.

103. Prime Minister Netanyahu's Remarks to the United Nations General Assembly, September 27, 2012, at http://www.cfr.org/israel/netanyahus-remarks-un-general-assembly-september-2012/p29167; Olga Khazan, "Netanyahu Draws An Actual Red Line . . . on a Bomb Cartoon," *Washington Post* WorldViews blog, September 27, 2012, http://www.washingtonpost.com/blogs/blogpost/post/netanyahu-draws-an-actual-red-line--on-a-bomb-cartoon/2012/09/27/0841941c-08d3-11e2-858a-5311df86ab04_blog.html.

objections of IDF and Mossad chiefs to threatening an attack that would not be coordinated with the United States.[104]

Without Obama's complicity, Netanyahu could no longer get any political-diplomatic leverage from a threat of war with Iran. In April 2013, Netanyahu returned to the theme that Israel was prepared to strike Iran alone if necessary, but this time neither Barak nor Israeli president Shimon Peres was supporting that line, and the Iranian chief of staff, Maj. Gen. Hassan Firoozabadi, reacted by commenting that the prime minister's threat should not be taken seriously.[105]

Netanyahu continued to maintain the pretense that he was prepared to attack Iran unless his demands were met as one of his two primary means of leverage on US policy toward Iran. But the utter failure to force Obama to adopt an explicit threat of war without actual evidence of an Iranian move toward weaponization had deprived the Israeli threat of war of its credibility. Still, the grip that AIPAC maintained over the US Congress in regard to Israel and Iran remained a potent means of leverage on US policy to ensure that the manufactured crisis would continue.

104. Amos Harel, "Iran Slowed Progress on Nuclear Weapons Program by Eight Months," *Haaretz* (Tel Aviv), October 9, 1012.

105. Isabel Kershner, "Officials in Israel Stress Readiness for a Lone Strike," *New York Times*, April 16, 2013.

# Epilogue

After the events described and analyzed in this book, the election of Hassan Rouhani as president of Iran in June 2013 introduced a major new element into the politics of Iran's nuclear program, with dramatic consequences.

Rouhani's election was a response by the Iranian political system to the economic decline that had accelerated greatly throughout 2012 as a result of the sanctions put into operation earlier that year. These sanctions cut Iran's oil revenues in half and prohibited Iran from accessing foreign exchange earnings held in all those countries that had signed on to the sanctions regime, under pressure from the United States. Iran could not access three-fourths of the $80 billion in its foreign exchange accounts except to pay for goods from the countries where these accounts were held. The impact of these sanctions on the Iranian economy was magnified, moreover, by the failure of the Ahmadinejad government to prepare for such an eventuality by reining in spending and maintaining an adequate level of foreign exchange reserves. By October 2012, the Iranian currency had lost 80 percent of the value it had held a year earlier.[1]

After his inauguration in August 2013, Rouhani moved quickly to signal his readiness to resolve Iran's conflict with the West through diplomacy. Rouhani and Obama exchanged letters, and Obama sent Deputy Secretary of State William Burns to meet secretly with Iranian counterparts in Oman before the UN General Assembly in September.[2] At those meetings Iranian officials communicated Rouhani's determination to achieve an agreement quickly.

Although Rouhani came to power in large part because of discontent fueled by the sanctions, his negotiating team's position on reaching a

---

1. Jeffrey Goldberg "America's Plan to Reward Iran, Without Lifting Sanctions," Bloomberg View, October 16, 2013, http://www.bloomberg.com/news/2013-10-16/america-s-plan-to-reward-iran-without-lifting-sanctions.html.; Roshanak Taghavi, "Iran's Currency: Why Did the Rial Tumble So Precipitously?" *Christian Science Monitor*, October 4, 2012.

2. Laura Rozen, "Exclusive: Burns Led Secret US Back Channel to Iran," *Al-Monitor*, November 24, 2013, http://backchannel.al-monitor.com/index.php/2013/11/7115/exclusive-burns-led-secret-us-back-channel-to-iran/.

nuclear deal was not prompted by the sanctions. It was reminiscent of the position put forward by Iranian negotiators eight years earlier, when Rouhani was in charge of Iran's nuclear policy. As recounted in chapter 3, when Rouhani and his team were confronted in March 2005 by the three EU foreign ministers who appeared determined to force Iran to give up its right to enrich, the Iranians had put together a far-reaching proposal providing for "immediate conversion of all enriched uranium to fuel rods to preclude even the technical possibility of further enrichment." Because Iran had no means of converting low-enriched uranium into fuel rods, the implication was that all the low-enriched uranium would be shipped to another country for that purpose. That in turn would mean that it would no longer be available for enrichment to higher levels without great difficulty and without being easily detected.

Rouhani's 2005 proposal had been aimed at reassuring the West of Iran's intention to remain a non-nuclear weapons state. In 2013, Rouhani directed his negotiators to come up with a similar approach to the talks with the United States and the other five powers for the same purpose. Significantly, the negotiating team was led by Foreign Minister Mohammad Javad Zarif, who had long been the most articulate advocate within the Iranian political elite of a policy of forgoing nuclear weapons.

At the first meeting with the P5+1 in Geneva in mid-October 2013, Zarif presented a detailed framework for resolving the conflict. He made it clear that Iran was prepared to stop enriching uranium to 20 percent and to draw down its existing stockpile of 20 percent enriched uranium to ease US concerns about the possibility that it could be used as feedstock for further enrichment up to weapons grade.

In his presentation in Geneva, Zarif offered to stop 20 percent enrichment, which was the primary US proliferation concern, to include guarantees in the final agreement that Iran's heavy water reactor at Arak, which US officials had insisted was a proliferation risk, could not be used to support a nuclear weapons program. He proposed including arrangements for all spent fuel to be removed from Iran immediately. He also offered to include in a future, comprehensive agreement a ban on the use of Iran's most efficient centrifuges, which would slow down the process, as well as limits on the total number of centrifuges. He made it clear that in return for giving up the option of keeping a capability to enrich uranium to weapons-grade levels, Iran would demand a clear statement of the "endgame," meaning an end to all economic sanctions against Iran as well as other forms of the abnormal state of hostility and pressure from Washington.[3]

---

3. Nathan Guttman, "Breaking Down What Iran Is Really Putting on the Table," *The Jewish Daily Forward* (New York), November 1, 2013 (published October 25, 2013).

In two days of intense negotiations with the Iranians in Geneva, November 7–8, the United States and Iran came close to agreeing on the complete draft text of an interim, "first step" agreement. But then Israeli prime minister Netanyahu used his special relationship with the government of French president François Hollande to disrupt the US-Iranian plan. On November 9, Hollande sent his foreign minister, Laurent Fabius, to Geneva, where he denounced the draft then being discussed and demanded revision of key elements of the deal.[4] The new demands, including language that denied Iran's right to enrichment, were unacceptable to Iran, and the three-day meeting ended without success.

But delaying an agreement too long was very risky for the Obama administration. It would give Netanyahu an opportunity to blow up the entire process, with the help of those in Congress responsive to Israeli interests. US senators who had worked closely with AIPAC on Iran were threatening to pass new sanctions against Iran without any flexibility for the president to use national security waivers to remove sanctions such as had been included in previous sanctions legislation.

In a marathon second round of negotiations, November 20–24, Iran and the six powers agreed to a "Joint Plan of Action" that specified the steps each side would take during a six-month interim period and the "elements" of a longer-term "comprehensive solution."[5]

Iran agreed to a long list of "voluntary" limits on its nuclear program for the six-month interim period, including halting enrichment of uranium to 20 percent, the dilution or fabrication into fuel rods of its existing stockpile of 20 percent enriched uranium, and no "further advances" of its activities at the Arak heavy water reactor. In addition, Iran agreed to much more intrusive IAEA inspections, including daily visits by inspectors to enrichment facilities. In return for these concessions, the United States and the other five powers agreed to allow a very limited easing of sanctions during the interim period, but no change in the most damaging sanctions of all—those that had cut Iranian foreign exchange earnings from oil exports in half.

Both sides promised that within a year they would "conclude negotiating and commence implementing" a longer-term comprehensive solution that would include a "mutually defined enrichment programme." The United States thus committed itself to allowing Iran to have an enrichment program—the primary red line of Iran in the negotiations. But that was

---

4. Gareth Porter, "Why the Iran Nuclear Talks Failed and Why They Will Get Tougher," *Truthout*, November 13, 2013, http://truth-out.org/news/item/19998-why-the-nuclear-talks-failed-and-why-they-will-get-tougher.

5. The full text of the "Joint Plan of Action" can be found at http://www.theguardian.com/world/interactive/2013/nov/24/iran-nuclear-deal-joint-plan-action.

also a red line for Israel, and whether such an agreement would actually be achieved would depend heavily on the willingness of the Obama administration to fight for a new relationship that could be politically costly. For years US officials had sent conflicting signals about whether Iran would be allowed to enrich uranium. Within hours of the signing of the "Joint Plan of Action," senior US officials repeatedly suggested in a background briefing for reporters that there was a real question about whether the negotiations would produce such a "comprehensive solution" involving Iranian enrichment.[6] Given the clear evidence in the talks of Iranian readiness to agree to limitations providing assurances against any effort to obtain a nuclear weapon, those statements appeared to reflect a belief that what Obama administration called the "architecture of sanctions" provided effective bargaining leverage over Iran on the nuclear issue. That suggested that US officials felt the United States could afford to lean hard on Iran in regard to enrichment and wait for Iran to give in on the issue.

Nevertheless, Netanyahu and his followers in the US Congress were certain to keep reminding the US public of the generally accepted narrative of Iranian duplicity and covert efforts to develop a nuclear weapon and to accuse Obama of cooperating with that alleged Iranian deception. Unfortunately, the Obama administration itself was unable to respond effectively, having perpetuated that very false narrative. For example, in a November 2011 speech at the Brookings Institution, Tom Donilon, then Obama's national security adviser, declared, "Iran has continued a record of deceit and deception. It's really spanned 30 years with regard to this [nuclear] program."[7] And before the preliminary P5+1 meeting with Iran in October 2013, the diplomat who was Obama's chief negotiator there, Wendy Sherman, told a Congressional committee that she did not trust the Iranians, because "we know that deception is part of the DNA."[8]

Given the natural desire of officials to avoid cognitive dissonance, it is doubtful that Obama administration policymakers and advisers or Obama himself were capable of distinguishing the false narrative about Iran's nuclear policy they had found so useful in the past from the reality. And even if they were capable of such a distinction, Obama could not disavow

---

6. Gareth Porter, "U.S. Officials Hint at Reservations on Final Nuclear Deal," Inter Press Service, November 26, 2013.

7. Tom Donilon, keynote remarks, "Iran and International Pressure: An Assessment of Multilateral Effort to Impede Iran's Nuclear Program," Brookings Institution, Washington, DC, November 22, 2011, 7, http://www.brookings.edu/~/media/events/2011/11/22%20iran%20nuclear%20program/20111122_iran_nuclear_program_keynote.

8. Paul Richter, "State Dept. Official Urges Congress to Delay New Sanctions," Los Angeles Times, October 3, 2013.

the premises on which his policy had been built for five years without severe political embarrassment.

Unable to respond directly to the false premises of the arguments, the administration was limited to pragmatic arguments about what could be realistically achieved by taking the more aggressive posture Netanyahu desired. Such arguments were bound to keep the administration on the defensive. One of the unanticipated consequences of the web of falsehood that had been spun around the Iranian nuclear program, therefore, was to make the fundamental strategic shift in US policy toward Iran that was so badly needed much more difficult.

# Dramatis Personae

*Note: The information below was current as of when the book went to print in December 2013.*

**Reza Aghazadeh:** Director of the AEOI from 1997 to 2009 and simultaneously served as Iran's vice-president for atomic energy.

**Mahmoud Ahmadinejad:** President of Iran from 2005 to 2013.

**Yossi Alpher:** Israeli intelligence analyst for the IDF and Mossad in the 1970s and 1980s; also a political figure in the 1990s under the Rabin and Barak governments.

**Yukiya Amano:** Director general of the IAEA since July 2009.

**Ehud Barak:** Prime minister of Israel from 1999 to 2001, served as deputy prime minister and minister of defense under Netanyahu from 2009 to 2013. Also the former head of Israel's Labor Party.

**Hans Blix:** Director general of the IAEA from 1981 to 1997.

**John Bolton:** US ambassador to the United Nations from August 2005 to December 2006; previously served in the State Department as under secretary of state for Arms Control and International Security (2001–5) and assistant secretary of state for International Organization Affairs (1989–93).

**Richard Brill:** US representative to the IAEA from 2001 to 2004.

**William Casey:** Director of the CIA from 1981 to 1987.

**Warren Christopher:** Secretary of state from 1993 to 1997.

**Vyacheslav Danilenko:** Ukrainian scientist specializing in nanodiamond synthesis whose work in Iran, 1996–2002, led some to speculate that he was involved in nuclear weapons research (see Chapter 10).

**Martin Dempsey:** Chairman of the Joint Chiefs of Staff from 2011 to the present.

**Mohamed ElBaradei:** Director general of the IAEA from 1997 to 2009.

**Thomas Fingar:** Chairman of the National Intelligence Council from 2005 to 2008 while concurrently the deputy director of national intelligence for analysis. Previously served in various positions in the State Department from 1986 to 2005.

**Robert Gates:** Secretary of defense from 2006 to 2011; previously served as the director of national intelligence (1991–93), deputy national security adviser (1989–91), and deputy director of national intelligence (1986–89).

**Amos Gilad:** Retired major general in the IDF and former director of the Political-Military Affairs Bureau of the Israeli Defense Ministry.

**Pierre Goldschmidt:** Deputy director general and head of the Department of Safeguards at the IAEA from 1999 to 2005.

**Porter Goss:** Director of the CIA from September 2004 to May 2005.

**Michael Hayden:** Director of the CIA from 2005 to 2009.

**Olli Heinonen:** Deputy director general and head of the Department of Safeguards at the IAEA from 2005 to 2010; previously served under Goldschmidt in that department (1999–2005).

**Martin Indyk:** US ambassador to Israel from 1995 to 1997 and 2000 to 2001; previously served as assistant secretary of state for Near East affairs (1997–2000), and on the National Security Council (1993–95). Also cofounded the Washington Institute for Near East Policy.

**Zalmay Khalilzad:** US ambassador to the United Nations from 2007 to 2009; previously served as US ambassador to Iraq (2005–7) and Afghanistan (2003–5).

**Ayatollah Ali Khamenei:** Supreme leader [highest political and religious authority] of Iran since 1989.

**Kamal Kharrazi:** Iranian minister of foreign affairs from 1997 to 2005; previously served as Iranian ambassador to the United Nations (1989–97).

**Mohammad Khatami:** President of Iran from 1997 to 2005.

**Ayatollah Ruhollah Khomeini:** First supreme leader of Iran from 1979 to 1989, a position established following the Islamic revolution.

**Ali Larijani:** Speaker of the Majlis (Iran's parliament) since 2008; previously served as secretary of the Supreme National Security Council from (2005–7), replacing Rouhani as Iran's chief nuclear negotiatior.

**Lewis "Scooter" Libby:** Chief of staff and national security adviser to Vice President Dick Cheney from 2001 to 2005.

**Seyed Hossein Mousavian:** Leader of the Iranian nuclear negotiations with Europe and the IAEA from 2003 to 2005 and head of the Foreign Relations Committee of Iran's National Security Council from 1997 to 2005; previously served as Iran's ambassador to Germany (1990–97).

**Masud Naraghi:** Iranian physicist specializing in centrifuge technology at the AEOI whose dealings with the A. Q. Khan network in the 1980s raised suspicions and led to IAEA investigations.

**Benjamin Netanyahu:** Prime minister of Israel since 2009 and previously from 1996 to 1999; leader of the Likud Party.

**Gordon Oehler:** Director of the Nonproliferation Center (NPC) at the CIA from 1992 to 1997; previously served as national intelligence officer for science, technology, and proliferation (1989–92).

**Ehud Olmert:** Prime minister of Israel from 2006 to 2009 and previously served on the cabinet (1988–92) and (2003–6) as a member of the Kadima Party.

**Reza Pahlavi:** oldest son of the late Shah of Iran who was ousted from power during the Islamic revolution in 1979; now living in the United States and outspoken on issues of Iranian politics.

**Leon Panetta:** Secretary of defense from 2011 to 2013 and director of the CIA from 2009 to 2011. Previously served as White House chief of staff (1994–97) and as a member of Congress (1977–93).

**James Pavitt:** Deputy director for operations at the CIA from 1999 to 2004.

**William Perry:** Secretary of defense from 1994 to 1997.

**Giandomenico Picco:** Assistant secretary-general of the United Nations for political affairs and veteran negotiator with Iran who helped secure the release of Western hostages in Lebanon in the 1980s.

**Yitzhak Rabin:** Prime minister of Israel from 1992 to 1995, until his assassination; member of the Labor Party.

**Itamar Rabinovich:** Adviser to Yitzhak Rabin and Israeli ambassador to the United States from 1993 to 1996.

**Ali Akbar Hashemi Rafsanjani:** President of Iran from 1989 to 1997; Previously served as speaker of the Majlis (1980–89).

**Bruce Riedel:** CIA analyst specializing in Middle East and North Africa issues; served on the National Intelligence Council and the National Security Council in various capacities from 1991 to 2002.

**Hassan Rouhani:** President of Iran since August 2013; previously served in multiple leadership positions including as deputy speaker of the Majlis and as secretary of the Supreme National Security Council (1989–2005). Also headed Iran's nuclear negotiation team (2003–5).

**Donald Rumsfeld:** Secretary of defense from 1975 to 1977 and again 2001 to 2006. Also served as White House chief of staff (1974–5).

**Ali Akbar Salehi:** Director of AEOI since August 2013 and also from 2009 to 2010. Previously served as Iranian foreign affairs minister (2010–13) and as the representative from Iran to the IAEA (1997–2005).

**Gary Samore:** White House coordinator for arms control and weapons of mass destruction from 2009 to 2013; previously served as senior director for non-proliferation on the National Security Council (1996 to 2000).

**Jackie Sanders:** US special envoy for nuclear non-proliferation to the IAEA from 2004 to 2005.

**Gregory L. Schulte:** US representative to the IAEA from 2005 to 2009.

**Brent Scowcroft:** National security adviser from 1989 to 1993, and previously from 1975 to 1977.

**Sayyed Abbas Shahmoradi-Zavareh:** Head of the Physics Research Center (PHRC) in Tehran and professor at Sharif University in the 1990s whose procurement activities were investigated by the IAEA (see chapter 7).

**Yitzhak Shamir:** Prime minister of Israel from the Likud party, serving two terms, from 1983 to 1984 and from 1986 to 1992.

**Ariel Sharon:** Prime minister of Israel from 2001 to 2006; previously served as a Likud Party member of the Knesset, holding ministerial posts from 1977 to 1992 and again 1996 to 1999.

**Shabtai Shavit:** Director general of Mossad from 1989 to 1996.

**Efraim Sneh:** Labor Party member of the Israeli Knesset from 1992 to 2008; served in several ministerial posts.

**Ali Asghar Soltanieh:** Representative of Iran to the IAEA from 2005 to 2013.

**Bukhary Sayed Abu Tahir:** Sri Lankan businessman involved in the A. Q. Khan network who was interviewed by the United States and the IAEA regarding Iran's connections to the network.

**George Tenet:** Director of central intelligence from 1996 to 2004.

**Ali Akbar Velayati:** Iranian foreign affairs minister from 1981 to 1997.

**Robert Walpole:** Principal deputy director of the National Counterproliferation Center since 2005; previously served on the National Intelligence Council (1998–2004), and as deputy director of the NPC (1992–97).

**Paul Wolfowitz:** Deputy secretary of defense from 2001 to 2005; previously served as under secretary of defense for policy (1989–93).

**Mohammad Javad Zarif:** Ambassador of Iran to the United Nations from 2002 to 2007.

# Acknowledgments

Authors' acknowledgments do not generally begin with the publisher. In the case of *Manufactured Crisis*, however, it is entirely appropriate. This book would certainly not have been published in a timely manner had it not been for Helena Cobban and Just World Books. Helena was enthusiastic about publishing it from the first, and her belief in the book was a crucial factor in bringing it to fruition. The author gratefully acknowledges her unflagging support and encouragement.

*Manufactured Crisis* is also the result of an innovative, crowdsourcing approach to financing the process of writing the book, which garnered support from some 150 people. The author is very grateful to all who gave, and especially to Michael Swanson, author of *The War State*; Harun Halim Rasip from Malaysia; H Reid Shaw; the Campaign Against Sanctions and Military Intervention in Iran; Anne H. Roberts from Washington, DC; and a number of other significant contributors who chose to remain anonymous.

The author is grateful to Jeremy Stone and his organization, Catalytic Diplomacy, for generously supporting the author's travel to Iran in December 2008, to Vienna in August 2009, and to Vienna and Israel in March 2012. That travel has contributed significantly to the author's ability to reconstruct the story told in this book.

The author also gratefully acknowledges the contribution of William Quandt of the University of Virginia, former National Security Council staff specialist on the Middle East, and a former president of the Middle East Studies Association, who read and made helpful comments and corrections on all the chapters in draft. A second reader, who has asked to remain anonymous, read and commented on selected chapters, which has also very helpful.

Ron Silverman did a masterful and efficient job of copyediting the manuscript while displaying great patience and Kimberly MacVaugh at Just World Books steered the book skillfully through production into its final form, all of which the author acknowledges with gratitude.

Scott Peterson of the *Christian Science Monitor*, who has long contributed well-informed and independent coverage of Iran, including on the nuclear issue, generously provided the author with his notes from an important interview with Olli Heinonen. Cyrus Safdari was kind enough to provide several articles from industry periodicals that are otherwise difficult—or expensive—to access.

A critical factor in being able to reconstruct the real history of the Iranian nuclear program is the fact that Seyed Hossein Mousavian, former Iranian ambassador and spokesman for Iran's nuclear negotiating team, has written an extraordinarily detailed and insightful book on the subject, and supplemented it with an interview focusing on the early period of the program's development.

Pierre Goldschmidt, the Deputy Director of Safeguards for the International Atomic Energy Agency from 1999 to 2005, agreed to answer the author's questions by e-mail on two key issues surrounding the IAEA's handling of the Iran file in 2004 and 2005.

The author was fortunate in having the opportunity to have very substantive interviews with Flynt Leverett and Hillary Mann Leverett about Bush administration policy and with former US intelligence officials whose experience and insights were extremely important in reconstructing the process of deriving US intelligence assessments on Iran's nuclear program. Paul Pillar agreed to speak with or respond to questions from the author on several occasions over the past four years. Thomas Fingar gave the author a long interview in Oxford, UK and answered follow-up questions by e-mail. Needless to say, the author does not consider the cooperation of these individuals as their endorsement of his analysis or his conclusions.

Two other former intelligence officials who declined to be identified have provided the author with important insights on U.S. intelligence matters over the years.

The author also acknowledges gratefully the contributions of a number of Iranian-Americans in covering specific stories on the "manufactured crisis" and the Iran nuclear scare over the years. They include Farideh Farhi, Trita Parsi, Muhammad Sahimi, Behrad Nakhai, Nader Bazargadeh, Sasan Fayezmanesh, and Reza Marashi. Nima Shirazi, a talented young blogger, helped in tracking down some references.

⟨𝒳⟩

CPSIA information can be obtained at www.ICGtesting.com
Printed in the USA
LVOW08s0629080815

449364LV00026B/793/P

**CURRENT AFFAIRS**

In *Manufactured Crisis,* Gareth Porter shows that the narrative that Western governments and media created over the course of two decades that Iran was pursuing a covert nuclear weapons program was based on falsehoods and fabricated "evidence." Based on eight years of covering the Iran nuclear issue and new resear and interviews with participants, Porter reconstructs the history of Iran's nuclear program and shows how the United States and Israel used the accusation about Iran's desire for nuclear weapons to try to pressure Tehran to give up its right to ha nuclear power for peaceful purposes.

Could unreliable or cooked intelligence one day lead to an attack on Iranian intentic that may not exist? I feel grateful to Gareth Porter for his intrusive and critical examination of intelligence material passed to the IAEA.

—**HANS BL**
Former Director General of the I/

[An] exceptionally timely, gripping account of the Iranian nuclear program and the diplomacy surrounding it.

—**Hon. CHAS W. FREEMAN,**
Former US Ambassador to Saudi Aral
Author, *America's Misadventures in the Middle E*

… extensive and meticulous research…

—**SHIREEN T. HUNT**
Visiting Professor, Georgetown Univers

… systematically and masterfully debunks three decades of US and allied lies and distortions about an Iranian nuclear weapons program that never really existed.

—**OLIVER STONE** and **PETER KUZNI**
Co-authors, *The Untold History of the United Sta*

**GARETH PORTER** is an investigative journalist and writer on US foreign and military policy. He has written four previous books, including *Perils of Dominance: Imbalance of Power and the Road to War in Vietnam* (University of California Press, 2005). His journalism has been published in *The Nation, Inter Press Service, Truthout*, and elsewhere. In 2012, he was awarded the Martha Gellhorn Prize for Investigative Journalism by the UK-based Gellhorn Trust.

**JUST WORLD BOOKS** is an imprint of
Just World Publishing, LLC
**WWW.JUSTWORLDBOOKS.COM**
Cover design by Jane Sickon
Front cover photo by Jason Szenes/epa/Corbis

ISBN 978-1-935982-3
90

9 781935 982333